Contemporary

Caribbean Cultures

and Societies in a

Global Context

Contemporary
Caribbean Cultures
and Societies in a
Global Context

EDITED BY

Franklin W. Knight and

Teresita Martínez-Vergne

The University of North Carolina Press

Chapel Hill

© 2005 The University of North Carolina Press

All rights reserved

Designed by Heidi Perov

Set in Scala

Manufactured in the United States of America

The paper in this book meets the guidelines for permanence and durability of the Committee on Production Guidelines for Book Longevity of the Council on Library Resources.

Library of Congress Cataloging-in-Publication Data

Contemporary Caribbean cultures and societies in a global context / edited by Franklin W. Knight and Teresita Martínez-Vergne.

    p. cm.

   Includes bibliographical references and index.

   ISBN 0-8078-2972-2 (cloth : alk. paper)

   ISBN 0-8078-5634-7 (pbk.: alk. paper)

  1. Antilles, Greater—Civilization—21st century. 2. Globalization.

  3. Caribbean Area. 1. Knight, Franklin W. 11. Martínez Vergne, Teresita.

   FI741.c66 2005

   972.905'3—dc22   2005010529

cloth 09 08 07 06 05 5 4 3 2 1

paper 09 08 07 06 05 5 4 3 2 1

THIS BOOK WAS DIGITALLY PRINTED

Contents

Acknowledgments

The extraordinary dynamism in Caribbean studies has been apparent for quite some time, and we had often thought about putting together a volume of original essays that reflect a few of the pertinent themes presently being pursued in this expanding field. The idea came together firmly in April 1999. The timing was impeccable—a meeting of the Association of Caribbean Historians in Havana, Cuba—and the location was most conducive to creative ideas especially at a time when the Cuban *paladar* culture was still in full swing. Yet in our case it was more than the fortuitous coincidence of time, place, and circumstances. Along with our fellow authors, we profoundly believe that the Caribbean offers a genuinely rewarding locale for examining some of the most important and provocative problems of our times.

The Caribbean, as unlikely as it seems to some, does provide a useful window on the wider world. Nor should this be too surprising. After all this was the area that first experienced the metamorphosing influences of colonialism and imperialism in the modern world. And today the Caribbean continues to reflect, often in an exaggerated manner, the profound effects of global integration. Scale, of course, is very important. Smallness sometimes presents a major disadvantage in global affairs but, as we illustrate here, size is not necessarily an insuperable handicap in the varied and ever-varying relationship between the Caribbean and the rest of the world. Caribbean people have proved themselves through the centuries to be resilient, creative, adaptive, and, above all, surprisingly strong. They have to be. Neither geography nor history has been kind to the Caribbean people so they manifest an admirably indomitable spirit, although sometimes one inevitably scarred by their collective experience.

The editors of this volume remain highly gratified at the enthusiastic response we got from our contributors when we first mentioned the possibility of doing this book. The essays sometimes forced these authors away from their familiar academic pursuits, but no one complained—even when we occasionally took editorial liberties with their presentations. Their spontaneous cooperation and promptness as we prepared the work has been for both of us a thoroughly delightful experience. Unfortunately we were deeply saddened that Antonio Benítez-Rojo, a monumental figure in the field of Caribbean and Latin America Studies, died unexpectedly shortly after sending us his final revisions. Benítez-Rojo was a warm, kind, and extremely friendly individual who will be forever missed. He leaves an enormous void in our hearts as well as our minds. Our profound grief is only slightly mitigated by the extremely rich contribution he made to our Caribbean literature and culture and by the measure of a man who magnanimously touched so many lives in so many indelible ways.

We thank all our contributors for their contagious generosity as well as exemplary collegiality; and also thank the outside readers from the press whose substantive contributions were accepted and treated respectfully. Each of us has family and friends who contributed directly and indirectly to the making of this book. For the sake of brevity we will refrain from listing them as has become the conventional practice but simply thank them en masse. During the process of assembling this volume, we had the good fortune of solidifying our long friendship and for that we pat each other on the back with mutual appreciation and respect. Elaine Maisner, Ron Maner, and David Hines of the University of North Carolina Press manifested exceptional kindness, patience, and understanding as they guided this project to completion and deserve our heartfelt gratitude. No single volume could capture the rich variety of intellectual ferment in the contemporary Caribbean, but we hope these essays provide a salutary introduction to an inherently interesting region of the world.

Contemporary
Caribbean Cultures
and Societies in a
Global Context

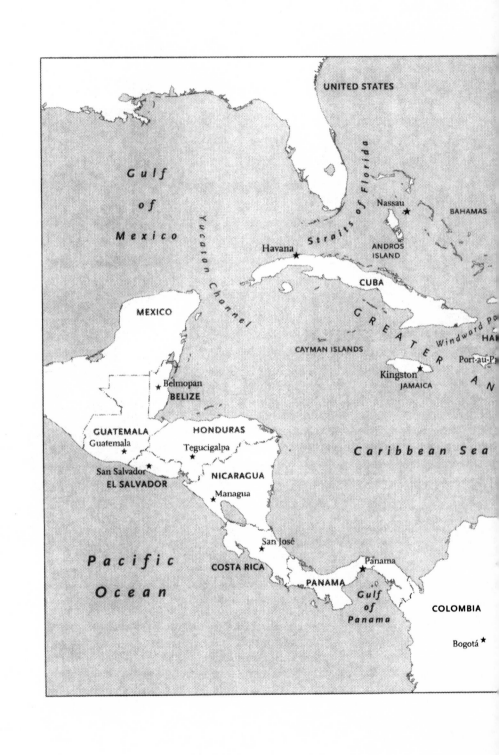

Atlantic

Ocean

TURKS & CAICOS ISLANDS

DOMINICAN
REPUBLIC

Canal de la Mona

LEEWARD ISLANDS

VIRGIN ISLANDS

ANGUILLA

San Juan

BARBUDA

Santo
Domingo

PUERTO
RICO

SAINT KITTS-NEVIS

ANTIGUA
St. Johns

MONTSERRAT

GUADELOUPE

LESSER ANTILLES

Basse-Terre

Roseau

DOMINICA

WINDWARD ISLANDS

Fort-de-France

MARTINIQUE

Castries

SAINT LUCIA

SAINT VINCENT

BARBADOS

Kingstown

Bridgetown

anjestad
ARUBA

CURAÇAO

BONAIRE

St. George's

GRENADA

Willemstad

Port of Spain

TRINIDAD & TOBAGO

Caracas

VENEZUELA

Georgetown

Paramaribo

GUYANA

SURINAME

ILLES

1

Introduction

TERESITA MARTÍNEZ-VERGNE AND FRANKLIN W. KNIGHT

The Caribbean is truly like no other place on the globe. This is not hyperbole. It is the historical reality. Before 1492 the Caribbean was marginal to the populous established landed empires of Aztec, Maya, and Inca that flourished on the American mainland. Then the arrival of Columbus changed everything everywhere in the Americas. The change was not immediate, of course, but inexorable and inevitable. For more than a century the Iberians dominated the region, moving outward from their newly created enclaves to subordinate the surrounding indigenous inhabitants wherever they could and eliminate them where they could not. For the scattered autochthonous peoples of the Caribbean islands, the post-Columbus changes constituted a veritable metamorphosis. Everything changed—their lives, their world, their physical environment, their relations to themselves and the outside world. By the time other non-Iberian Europeans arrived to establish their colonies in the seventeenth century, the societies of the indigenous people were totally shattered. Moreover, where the indigenous peoples survived, their numbers were considerably reduced by disease, warfare, and relentless exploitation by the European newcomers. The Europeans extensively repopulated the region and created a new Caribbean. Over time, concomitant with the fortunes of war, tropical staple production (especially sugar), and the slave trade, the region would move from periphery to center and back to the periphery of European affairs. That complex history, up to the end of the twentieth century, is rich and has been splendidly detailed in the recently published six-volume general history published under the auspices of the United Nations Educational, Scientific and Cultural Organization (UNESCO).[1] The volumes illustrate well the nuanced and ever-changing variety of the Caribbean social condition, and the pivotal roles played by slavery and the sugar plantation complex. The various European imperial powers abolished slavery over a long period of time, ending with the emancipation of the Cuban slaves in 1886. The sugar plantation culture continued until the latter half of the twentieth century.

During the twentieth century, the majority of the Caribbean societies stopped living under colonial political and economic systems and began constructing their own independent states. Most Caribbean states have adhered to a democratic political framework despite their diverse populations. The political changes reflected as well as stimulated the literary output across a number of fields. It gave voices to all sectors of the Caribbean peoples, and they were not reticent in expressing themselves. Political independence, however, has been like a double-edged sword.

The new societies of the Caribbean grew out of their European colonial and imperial past. Over time, Haiti created a distinctive language of its own—Haitian Creole, or Kreyol. But the principal languages of discourse for most territories remained largely the major European languages of the politically dominant groups that shaped the genesis of Caribbean history since 1492. The Caribbean peoples have dominated and enriched these languages. Almost every island and territory has had at least one distinguished writer, and the tradition goes back well into the nineteenth century with the great works of José Martí, Thomas Madiou, Eugenio María de Hostos, Ramón Emeterio Betances, and J. J. Thomas. During the twentieth century the literary scene flourished with an impressive list of creative writers including Alejo Carpentier, Nicolás Guillén, Luis Palés Matos, José Luis González, George Lamming, Cynthia Wilson, Aimé Césaire, C. L. R. James, Vidia Naipaul, Wilson Harris, John Hearne, Curdella Forbes, Derek Walcott, Jacques Roumain, Jamaica Kincaid, Julia Alvarez, Rosario Ferré, and Edwidge Danticat.

In common with the creative writers, the scientific writers have also been exploring the changing Caribbean condition and reevaluating its place in the broader scheme of things. The trajectory has not been surprising. Much of Caribbean social scientific and humanistic writing has been engaged in exploring the development of the Caribbean plantation society and the legacies of the transatlantic slave trade on the societies, economies, demography, and mentalities of the peoples of the region. Recently it has also had to examine and define its position vis-à-vis the inexorable, multifaceted influence of the United States of America. Articulating a Caribbean identity has been a major preoccupation in the twentieth century. Inescapably, given the emerging role of the United States of America on the region, North American–Caribbean relations have attracted considerable attention. But the world from the perspective of the Caribbean has become considerably more complex over the past fifty years.

With the arrival of the twenty-first century, scholars and policy makers felt the urgency of redefining the boundaries within which they would analyze currents of thought, implement development programs, examine movements of goods and population, measure ideological influences, and so on. Globalization (as the unprecedented back-and-forth transfer of products, people, and ideas evidenced in the latter third of the twentieth century has been called) left its particular mark on the Caribbean too. Looking back on the various islands' trajectories to assess the impact of technological advances and new attitudes, social scientists and humanists have assembled a number of seemingly contradictory impressions regarding these processes. By way of inventorying the panoply of observations around the changing global landscape, we explore some of these responses in this book. No single volume, however large and well constructed, can ever do full justice to the wide range of Caribbean realities. Our focus has, of necessity, to be selective. Although our examples reflect only the perspectives of the larger islands, we hope that they are sufficiently illustrative of the varied Caribbean responses across the region as a whole. More important, these essays should encourage further explorations of the phenomena of global impact, especially in the smaller island communities.

Globalization, some commentators have observed, is nothing new to the Caribbean region. Not only as ideology but also as material practice, its effects are similar to those brought about earlier by the ebb and flow of the regional experience under colonialism and imperialism. The political domination of one group of people over another, the exploitation of the oppressed for the material advantage of their "superiors," the elaborate philosophical framework that supported such a setup—these are the building blocks of the Euro-American nineteenth-century edifice, of U.S. expansion in the twentieth, and of the unfettered flow of goods and cultural practices in the twenty-first. Globalization, in short, has not so far resulted in a market relationship between the various participants that is more equitable and just. Rather it has accentuated hegemonies and manifestly reinforced global inequality.

Likewise, some would argue that the Caribbean was continuously defined and redefined to suit the purposes of its various "masters" under any one of these organized systems.[2] Both contemporaries and historians have treated the Commonwealth Caribbean more as the property of Great Britain than as specific islands with particular needs and development trajectories. For policy makers, strategic and geopolitical considerations have traditionally assumed

greater priority than humane considerations. To this day, history books charac-
terize the early twentieth century as the era of U.S. expansionism. And recent
events in the area point unequivocally to the generalized nature of change,
the facility of travel, as well as the boundless quality of the transformations
experienced locally.

As self-evident as these statements appear, their antitheses and other re-
finements to their postulates demand equal attention. Globalization, other
experts would assert, is indeed very new because the world is experiencing
unprecedented changes. The mind-boggling speed of travel—by ground, air, or
cyberspace—has reduced time and space so as to make almost instantaneous
the transfer of speech and nearly immediate the exchange of goods. The web
of players in any one transaction has become correspondingly complicated, as
modern technology makes it possible for communication to take place simultaneously on a global scale among infinite parties. The battery of responses to
economic, political, and social forces, internal or external, has become not only
more numerous but also more diverse, as experience and the flow of information facilitates visualizing various scenarios.[3]

The more optimistic students of the territories of the Caribbean, helpless
before global forces as they may seem to some, will argue that these processes
have historically resisted simplistic classification. Quite the contrary. Many
of these essays argue that Caribbean people are currently redefining the relationship between state and society in order to manipulate more effectively
the effects on their populations of the powerful avalanche of imported goods,
services, and ideologies. Caribbean societies are in fact reclaiming their space
in the global map and reassessing their priorities with the same rapidity, although with less visibility, that external forces alter the playing field. Simply
stated, if the modern Caribbean as a region was an invention of the twentieth
century that served the interests of the United States and, less so, of Western
Europe, a new conceptualization seems in order, with increased if not dominant input from the regional territories themselves.

One particular aspect of the globalization literature that has been challenged
consistently, as this volume makes evident, is the emphasis on economic
forces. Many studies detail the impact of so-called free trade, reduced fiscal
deficits, lower inflation rates, and other neoliberal reforms on the Caribbean.
Without exception, they call for a reexamination of the accompanying unemployment and underemployment, deterioration of health, environmental
degradation, deeper inequality, and financial instability. Less so, authors turn
their attention to the social and cultural effects of the transfer of commodities.
The world has also been shrinking for narco-traffickers, for example, and some

of the money these transactions generate enters and distorts the conventional political and social processes of Caribbean democracies. The dire conditions faced by the area's poorer people, encapsulated for some in the 1980s in the phrase "the feminization of poverty," have become so generalized as a result of the international movement of capital that the more farsighted and progressive commentators attach emergency status to a number of social and cultural manifestations of the absence of social and political controls: black urban plight, the "feminization of export processing zone industries, part-time work, domestic migrant workers, refugee camps, and the sex tourism industry."[4]

Another commonplace in the writings of globalization analysts is that homogeneity—and, worse, conformity—is the logical corollary to the indiscriminate exchange of articles that are vested with material and ideological value. As more and more people have access to information and to commodities in the market, they will inevitably desire to acquire the same products in an effort to improve their lives—or so the argument runs. In its most abominable incarnation, "glocalization" (global localization)—to employ the term used by Raquel Romberg in chapter 7—connects cities with strong corporate transnational interests with each other, thus networking centers of capital and influence and reinforcing their concentration to the exclusion of old configurations.[5] Either way, the ominous prediction is that there will be less room for diversity and, on the contrary, enormous pressure to adopt and an equally compelling eagerness to embrace uniformly Western First World tastes and values.

The Caribbean scholarly response to this argument has been twofold. In the first place, the assumption appears simplistic. Although there is evidence that U.S. influence in the Caribbean has resulted in precisely the erasure of cultural forms that were considered autochthonous, it is also true that other cultural forms have remained virtually untouched and that some of the newly introduced practices and items have obtained a highly localized reformulation and meaning. Second, many scholars have challenged the one-way quality that characterizes the process described. In other words, the Caribbean has not been a simple *tabula rasa* on which the powerful foreigners have consciously imported and inscribed variants of their cultures. The Caribbean people have not been merely passive recipients in the process of cultural transformation, in neither the past nor the present. Nor is agency easily attributable, given the way that culture develops. As this volume seeks to demonstrate, music, food, celebrations, and daily practices have moved with people and sometimes independently of population movement. The Caribbean diaspora communities in the United States, for example, retain organic links with the populations back home and recreate, with local variations, their cultural patterns with such compelling insistence that they have become an integral part of the community's dominant economy.

This is not to say that any one of the island-states of the Caribbean and the United States, to take the obvious "trading" partners, are equal participants in the exchange of commodities. Not only is the latter the most powerful country in the world because of its economic wherewithal; it is also true that the material and ideological flood that is the trademark of globalization has weakened local state controls to the point where resistance to the relentless flood of "superior" products and ideas becomes almost impossible, if not highly irrational.

It is not our purpose here to assess the (negative) impact of powerful economic and political forces worldwide and directly north of the Caribbean region. It is the underlying premise of this volume, instead, that realignments, political and economic, are both empirically and theoretically relevant insofar as they impact political, social, and cultural forms. Given the reduced importance of physical space to the men and women in government and in industry who are jointly, if not harmoniously, constructing a new world order, it is incumbent on the people who inhabit that narrowly defined physical space to reconfigure the edifice upon which social life and culture are molded. Perhaps a more secure sense of identity can be found in culture, race, language, ethnicity— notions that transcend and indeed fragment the old bonds imposed and cultivated by the nation-state. Understood in this way, the security of the region is assured not only by military and political forces, but also by environmental protection, responsible border controls, community-based decision making, supportive nongovernmental organization (NGO) collaboration, and other organized agencies with direct social impact.

At the heart of this understanding, and at the center of this volume, lies an attempt to redefine societies according to their felt needs and aspirations, and not to market forces beyond their control. This is not to say that any so-called nation-state in the region can reconstitute itself overnight according to newly fashioned parameters, such as racial mix, use of language, cultural practices— these kinds of loyalties take a relatively long time to form and reform, and it is unlikely that national allegiances, despite the alarmist cries of antiglobalization advocates, will weaken to the point of extinction in the immediate future. Geography will always continue to constitute a fundamental dimension of identity. What appears more probable, and may already be in evidence, is that notions of citizenship are changing from the bottom up—that talk of democracy in the Caribbean embraces much more than elections and now regularly includes "participation and policy choice on a continual basis and beyond parties, [and also] interest groups and other social movements."[6] When seen in such a way, globalization, although not exactly a mere ideological construct of the industrialized world that requires demystification, appears much more manageable and humanly amenable. It is in this spirit that the contributing authors of this volume approach their themes—in studying the impact of the forces of globalization in Caribbean geopolitics, they have found extraordinary richness, both theoretical and empirical, in the social and cultural manifestations of these phenomena.

Certainly the common implication of all these essays is that the Caribbean is a region of unusual resilience and remarkable creativity. Yet the fascinating variation across the region remains profound and the ways in which the Caribbean people confront the forces of globalization will vary according to the nature of the challenges presented as well as to the local conditions. In any case, the region remains an ideal location to examine and analyze not only the challenges of diversity but also the powerful imperatives to coalesce. Old issues of Caribbean life, history, and identity have not been obliterated by the challenges of globalization. But they have not remained static either. Economic dependence and political instability have, in the Caribbean as elsewhere, proved themselves compatible with cultural dynamism and creativity.

NOTES

1. UNESCO, *General History of the Caribbean.*
2. Not the least of these efforts has been delimiting the region for scholarly purposes, a task Sheller, *Consuming the Caribbean*, 5–8, and Hillman and D'Agostino, *Understanding the Contemporary Caribbean*, chap. 1, take up with verve.
3. Stiglitz, *Globalization and Its Discontents*; H. James, *The End of Globalization*; and Gwynne and Kay, *Latin America Transformed.*
4. Filomina C. Steady, "Introduction: Revisiting the Black Woman Cross-Culturally," in Steady, *Black Women*, 19.
5. Menno Vellinga, "The Dialectics of Globalization: Internationalization, Regionalization, and Subregional Response," in Vellinga, *The Dialectics of Globalization*, 8.
6. Ivelaw L. Griffith and Betty N. Sedoc-Dahlberg, "Introduction: Democracy and Human Rights in the Caribbean," in Griffith and Sedoc-Dahlberg, *Democracy and Human Rights in the Caribbean*, 3.

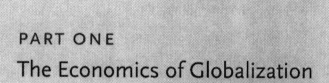

PART ONE

The Economics of Globalization

Historically, economic decision making has always played an extremely important role in shaping Caribbean societies. As the small Caribbean economies move away from the traditional agricultural exports and simple assembly manufacturing, they have become increasingly dependent on foreign economic aid, with the result that foreign economic actors play an ever-increasing role in the determination of domestic priorities, especially in the incessant efforts to establish sustained economic growth. As Helen McBain shows, the Anglophone Caribbean tried to anticipate the problems of small size by better organization of a regional community. For these primarily agricultural and service economies, there is an urgent need to construct new strategies for viable competitiveness under the arrangements of the emerging Free Trade Area of the Americas, and McBain analyzes the available regional human resources as well as some potential models for successful participation in the proposed new economic constellations.

Singularly or collectively, some Caribbean states do better than others. Nor can the general political problems be separated from the economic ones. In a thoughtful analysis of the general Haitian economic performance since the 1970s, Alex Dupuy persuasively demonstrates how the combination of political and economic factors and an inconsistent international agency savagely undermined the national economy. Despite its repeated assertions, the World Bank seemed less interested in the establishment of political democracy in Haiti than in assuring that that country became more market-friendly to international market penetration. For a decade or so, open markets became a sort of economic mantra for Latin America and the Caribbean. But open markets did not provide the panacea for Haitian economic and political ills. The Haitian experience with globalization over the past thirty years represents a clear and sobering warning of the political pitfalls of small economies and vulnerable governments. Nowhere was this clearer than in 2004 when external agents conspired to remove the democratically elected president of Haiti, Jean-Bertrand Aristide, despite the legitimacy of his government and the support of many of his neighboring Caribbean political leaders.

2

Challenges to Caribbean Economies in the Era of Globalization

HELEN MCBAIN

Caribbean countries have always had to face international challenges, given their long history of colonial relationships and their relatively open economies, among other factors. The challenges of the present period of globalization, however, are significantly different from those of previous periods of globalization.[1] For the purpose of this analysis, the three phases of globalization can be identified: 1870–1914, marked by trade, capital, and labor flows; 1945–73, marked by expansion of trade in manufactures among developed countries and restrictions on labor and capital mobility; and 1990 to the present, marked by the spread of free trade and movement of capital as well as a convergence in development approaches. The two markers of the end of the first two phases are the start of the First World War in 1914 and the end of the Bretton Woods system of fixed exchange rates in 1973.

CARIBBEAN ECONOMIES PRIOR TO THE 1970S

Caribbean countries coped with the changes that occurred after the Second World War through the preferential trading regime accorded to them because of their status as (former) colonies of metropolitan powers and through restrictions imposed on trade by both colonial and postcolonial governments. Import restrictions and exchange controls were instituted in the postwar period to monitor imports and to protect the balance of payments. Tariff and nontariff barriers were also used to promote the development of import-substitution manufacturing from the late 1940s.

Caribbean countries addressed the industrial gap between developed and developing countries by pursuing a strategy advocated by the Caribbean Nobel laureate in economics, Arthur Lewis, a strategy also followed in East Asia. However, unlike East Asian countries, they adopted a modified version of the Lewis model, which relied largely on foreign investment to develop capital-intensive final goods, such as soap, tires, processed food, and other consumer goods for domestic markets and intermediate goods geared toward export markets. East Asian economies exported labor-intensive final goods and developed and protected intermediate-goods industries, which provided inputs to the final-goods sector.

This approach to industrialization was ultimately unsustainable for Caribbean countries, given the small size and export dependence of their economies. However, the earnings from the export of primary products along with foreign grants and low-cost funds facilitated the development of an economic and social infrastructure that fostered the provision of electricity, water, housing, health care, and education.

Countries in the region also reduced their export dependence on sugar by diversifying into other areas such as bauxite mining and alumina refining (Jamaica, Guyana, and Suriname), petroleum and petroleum products (Trinidad and Tobago and the Netherlands Antilles), bananas (Jamaica and the Windward Islands), rice and gold (Guyana), and tourism (all countries). However, there was no free trade in the commodities exported by the region. The preferential Commonwealth trade arrangement governed most of the trade from the Caribbean region.

The main experiences of Caribbean economies during this period were significant growth of output and trade and diversification of products and trading partners (figures 1–6). Caribbean output growth, measured as gross domestic product, averaged about 5 percent per annum, whereas export growth averaged more than 8 percent between 1960 and 1973. Export growth therefore surpassed the growth of GDP during this phase of globalization. Export destinations during the 1960s were mainly the United States, the United Kingdom, and Canada in that order. During the 1970s the United States became the dominant export destination (as well as source of imports).

Whereas Caribbean countries exported agricultural commodities up to about the mid-twentieth century, nonagricultural raw materials and food gained significance from the 1950s. A major increase in exports to the United States in this period was due largely to petroleum and petroleum products from Trinidad and Tobago. On the other hand, the decline of these exports dur-

FIGURE 1. CARICOM Trade, 1960s–2002

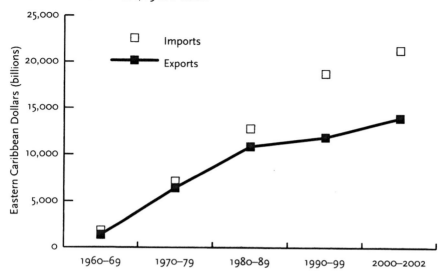

FIGURE 2. CARICOM Exports to Major Partners

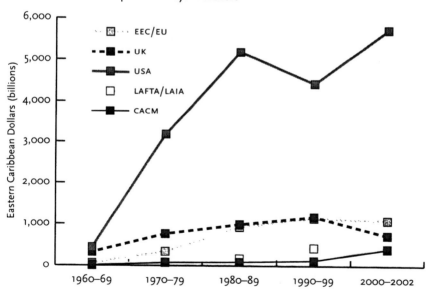

Note: EEC/EU = European Economic Community/European Union; LAFTA/LIAIA = Latin American Free Trade Area/Latin American Integration Association; CACM = Central American Common Market.

FIGURE 3. CARICOM Imports from Major Partners

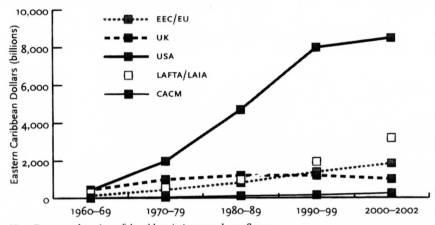

Note: For an explanation of the abbreviations used, see figure 2.

FIGURE 4. CARICOM Exports of Selected Product Groups

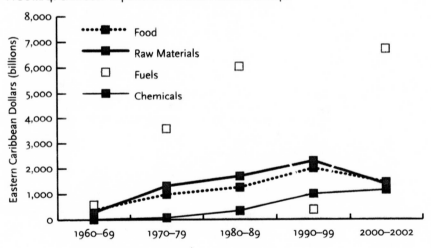

ing the 1990s could be attributed to the economic adjustment in Trinidad and Tobago during that period.

The economic structure of Caribbean countries also changed in terms of the contribution of the agricultural sector to output and employment. For example, Barbados, Guyana, and the Dominican Republic experienced significant declines in the proportion of their labor force in agriculture since the 1960s, although the latter two still have significant agricultural sectors. Jamaica and

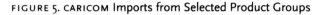

FIGURE 5. CARICOM Imports from Selected Product Groups

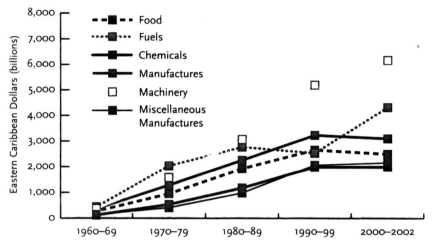

FIGURE 6. Caribbean GDP and Export Growth Rates (annual average)

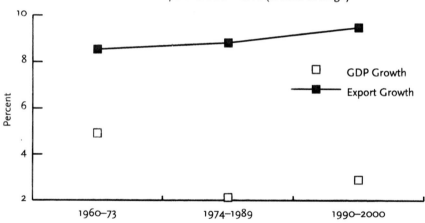

Trinidad and Tobago have experienced relatively small declines in their agricultural labor force, with the former having a more sizable agricultural sector than the latter (figure 7).

Almost all of these countries have developed significant service sectors, contributing between 50 and 80 percent of output, with tourism being the primary export of the sector. Antigua and Barbuda, the Bahamas, Barbados, and St. Kitts and Nevis are the main service producers in the region (figure 8).

FIGURE 7. Labor Force in Agriculture in Selected Caribbean Countries

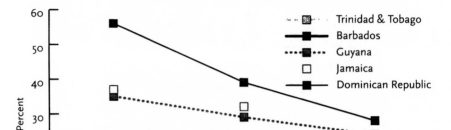

Although manufacturing's contribution to output surpassed that of agriculture beginning in the 1960s, manufacturing did not become the dominant sector. Instead, most countries made the leap from agriculture to mining and/or services. And their societies shifted from being agriculturally oriented societies to service-oriented societies, despite the pursuit of import-substitution industrialization. The latter resulted largely from the performance of a service, since most if not all of the inputs were imported.

Politically, one of the most significant changes since the end of the Second World War was the achievement of independence by most of the English-speaking countries in the Caribbean. Countries chose the route of a free-trade association in 1968 after the attempt by Britain to integrate them through a federal arrangement failed in 1962. The Caribbean Common Market established as part of the Caribbean Community (CARICOM) in 1973 became the catalyst to intraregional trade in manufactures. Although such trade was insignificant (less than 10 percent of total trade) compared with extraregional trade, it nevertheless contributed to the growth during the 1970s as well as to the development of a level of entrepreneurship in the region. However, the industries on which such trade was based did not contribute to employment creation on account of the capital-intensive nature of the operations. The creation of jobs therefore had to rely on the public sector and the service industries that were being developed.

Independence necessitated change in the economic relations between Caribbean countries and former colonial powers. Association agreements, in

FIGURE 8. Services Sector Contribution to GDP, 1986–2000 (percentage)

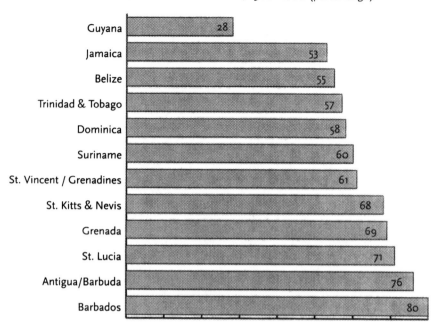

the form of the Yaoundé Convention (signed in 1963 and renewed in 1969) and the Lomé Convention (signed in 1975 and renewed at five-year intervals), between members of the European Community and their former colonies provided, among other things, preferential market access for commodities such as sugar, bananas, and rum. The Lomé Convention has since been replaced by the Cotonou Agreement, which is an interim arrangement that will be replaced by some form of reciprocal trade starting in 2007 between countries of the European Union and those in the African, Caribbean, and Pacific regions.

ADJUSTMENT DURING THE 1970S AND 1980S

The significant developments during the 1970s were the dismantling of the system of monetary regulation in 1973 and the oil price hikes of 1974 and 1979. Output growth slowed in the Caribbean region and in the world as a whole. Average growth in the region was 2 percent, or less than half of what it was between 1960 and 1973. This masks the situation in individual countries, in particular the negative real growth in Grenada and Jamaica. The deteriorating terms of trade of commodities relative to manufactures influenced not only the orientation toward the development of manufacturing industries but also the protectionism that was pursued in the region during the latter half of the 1970s. The significant balance-of-payments deficits that emerged during the early 1970s were exacerbated by the oil price hikes and provoked import restrictions by countries such as Guyana and Jamaica.

Internal Adjustment

One of the first challenges faced by Caribbean countries at the end of the second globalization phase was how to move from achieving economic growth toward achieving equitable distribution of income and greater self-reliance in producing essential goods, such as food and clothing. This was of particular importance for Jamaica, where income disparities were greater than in other Caribbean countries. The Jamaican government adopted a socialist ideology in its approach to addressing this challenge. Quantitative restrictions on trade and exchange control regulations were used to restrict imports and hence prevent deterioration in the balance of payments in the light of declining production and exports and a recurrent shortage of foreign exchange. An expanded role of government in the economy also resulted from the nationalization of enterprises, in particular those that were foreign-owned monopolies operating in strategic industries such as power and telecommunications.

The socialist experiments, in Guyana and Jamaica particularly, resulted in deteriorating macroeconomic imbalances from the latter half of the 1970s. Low or negative rates of economic growth, high inflation (more than 10 percent), unemployment, significant fiscal and current-account deficits, and increasing indebtedness were the main macroeconomic problems confronting the larger Caribbean countries in the 1980s. The smaller island members of the Organisation of Eastern Caribbean States (OECS) experienced relatively high growth during the 1980s. However, the threat of natural disasters widened the fiscal deficit and increased external indebtedness in a number of islands, in particular Antigua and Barbuda.

Most CARICOM countries had instituted protection of domestic industries. The system of protection was most extensive in Jamaica, Trinidad and Tobago, and Guyana. In Jamaica in 1972, the importation of most products required an import license. By the end of the 1970s almost all imports into Jamaica were restricted in one way or another. The tariff system was complex, with preferential tariffs (lower than general tariffs) applied to imports from Commonwealth countries. In addition, imported inputs to be used in production as well as some basic food items were all subject to zero or low rates of tariff.

With the establishment of CARICOM in 1973 a common external tariff (CET) was adopted. The CET rates represented the average of the individual national tariffs of Jamaica, Trinidad, Barbados, and Guyana.

The second challenge was liberalizing trade and exchange controls while pursuing macroeconomic stability. The globalization of ideology facilitated the adoption of policies that accelerated the process of liberalization. Developing countries pursued market-oriented policies under economic adjustment programs geared toward correcting imbalances in the economy. In the Caribbean region, countries undertook such programs at different points in time and to varying degrees within the last two decades of the twentieth century. The extent and pace of trade and financial liberalization and privatization of public enterprises were determined largely by initial conditions in the countries, the severity of imbalances, and the ability of governments to negotiate the adjustment process with the international financial institutions that were providing support. The impact of the policies therefore differed across countries.

Jamaica and Guyana, for example, began to experience economic imbalances in the 1970s but only embarked on economic adjustment programs after their economies had significantly deteriorated. They therefore had less bargaining power in the timing, content, and application of reforms. Policies to restore macroeconomic stability were therefore severe and adversely affected various groups, in particular those that were poor and marginalized. Three sets of policies and how they were implemented were critical in terms of their effects: currency devaluation, import liberalization, and price deregulation. Large devaluations of the local currency led to significant price inflation due to dependence on imports. In the case of Guyana, devaluations were large enough to counteract the effects of import liberalization. In Jamaica, the opposite tended to be the case, as the authorities were loath to use currency depreciation as a policy tool of adjustment.

Some of the negative effects of adjustment were due partly to the sequencing of reforms in Jamaica; liberalization of the capital and foreign-exchange markets preceded the liberalization of import policy. Equally important in both countries was the difficulty in cushioning the effects on the more-vulnerable groups in those countries and financing the restructuring that was needed to boost production and exports. The lack of international reserves and the heavy accumulation of debt limited the ability of the governments to upgrade economic and social infrastructure and provide fiscal and production incentives to private enterprise. In addition, the severity of the adjustment process was itself a disincentive to productive and investment activities.

The adjustment experiences of Trinidad and Tobago and Barbados were different from those of Guyana and Jamaica. Economic adjustment in Trinidad and Tobago was undertaken to address the consequences of management of the oil price boom of the 1970s and the fall in oil prices in the early 1980s. The economy experienced negative growth, balance-of-payments and fiscal deficits, and high inflation (more than 10 percent) and unemployment (more than 20 percent). Barbados undertook economic adjustment after the economy went into recession in the early 1990s on account of increasingly negative growth, high unemployment (more than 20 percent in 1992), growth in inflation, and fiscal deficits.

The imbalances in the former countries were not of the magnitude of those in the latter, and remedial actions were taken earlier. In addition, Trinidad and Tobago and Barbados pursued adjustment in the late 1980s and early 1990s, respectively, and hence were able to learn from Jamaica's experiences since the early 1980s. The former countries therefore had greater policy choice in their adjustment measures. Barbados, for example, eschewed the use of currency devaluation through a consensual approach to adjustment. Attention was also paid to timing and sequencing of liberalization. The impact of adjustment policies in these countries was therefore less harsh and of shorter duration than was the case in Jamaica and Guyana.

International Trade and Development Cooperation

The third challenge was securing preferential market access for nontraditional exports. The Lomé Convention of 1975, which was subsequently extended, provided access to both traditional and nontraditional export products. Caribbean countries found the rules of origin for duty-free access for manufactures difficult to meet. Led by Jamaica, they sought and were granted duty-free access to the United States market for a number of products with relatively liberal rules of origin under the 1984 Caribbean Basin Initiative (CBI). Items of importance to the region, such as textile and apparel products, footwear, leather goods, canned tuna, and petroleum and petroleum products were excluded. However, guaranteed access levels for textile and apparel products were subsequently secured. Unlike the Lomé Convention, the CBI was sponsored by the United States and was therefore subject to unilateral termination by the U.S. government. Moreover, it did not significantly increase the amount of products with duty-free access to the United States. The bulk of regional exports (80 percent) already had preferential access to the U.S. market under the Generalised System of Preferences (GSP) established during the 1960s.

The trade performance of most Caribbean countries relative to world trade declined during the decade of the 1980s. However, exports to the United States increased significantly relative to other markets (figure 2). Intraregional trade was affected by the economic problems that some of the larger countries faced, in particular Jamaica, which experienced depreciation of its currency during the first half of the 1980s.

Financial assistance from developed countries in the form of Overseas Development Assistance (ODA) grants, which were significant to the development of Caribbean countries in the 1960s and 1970s, declined from the 1980s. On the other hand, private financial flows grew as greater reliance was placed on the market by developed countries to deliver growth and development to less-developed countries.

By the end of the 1980s Caribbean countries were poised to liberalize their trade at a faster pace. Jamaica had already removed most of the nontariff restrictions on imports, which it had started to reduce in the early 1980s under its first adjustment program with the World Bank. Ideological convergence among Caribbean countries, which had embraced the neoliberal approach to growth and development, facilitated acceleration of further trade liberalization.

Caribbean countries also took the decision at the end of the 1980s to widen and deepen their economic integration. Haiti and Suriname subsequently became members of the integration grouping, while Dominican Republic obtained observer status. The Common Market arrangement was to be elevated to an Economic Union in the form of the CARICOM Single Market and Economy (CSME). The latter would involve not only free movement of goods but also free movement of services, capital, and labor.

Deeper economic integration, economic reforms to facilitate the functioning of markets and the flow of private investment, pursuit of preferential trading arrangements, and the adoption of a promarket philosophy were all responses to the international economic environment as well as to developments within Caribbean economies and societies resulting from the difficulties faced in the 1970s and 1980s.

DEVELOPMENTS DURING THE 1990S

The decade of the 1990s marked the beginning of a new and more extensive phase of globalization, including trade liberalization. The reduction of transport costs and the lifting of some trade barriers were significant stimuli. Other factors of equal importance were the globalization of production through the separation and segmentation of the production process, the end of the ideological divide between East and West, and the revolution in information and communications technology, notably mobile telephony and the internet.

Transport costs leveled off during this phase, and the cost of communication—telecommunications and computers—continued to decline. The reduction in transport costs made trade cheaper between countries that were geographically far apart. However, this was less so in the case of bulk trade, since ocean freight charges had not fallen significantly since the 1960s (table 1). Hence Caribbean countries that were still trading heavily in primary commodities would not have gained significant benefits.

Developments in the area of information and communications technology (ICT) have significantly influenced the pace of globalization during this current phase. The cost of a telephone call has been falling quite dramatically since the 1970s. The same is true of the cost of personal computers (PCs) and other related devices. Fax machines, cellular telephones, and internet connections have all reduced the cost of doing business and increased personal contacts.

Access to fixed telephony in the region is most significant in the smaller countries in the eastern Caribbean as well as in the Bahamas in the northern Caribbean (table 2). Cellular mobile telephony has grown rapidly since the start of liberalization of the telecommunications industry. This growth is particularly the case in countries with low coverage of fixed telephony, such as Guyana, Jamaica, and Suriname. Although internet and PC penetration is relatively low, internet usage is relatively high, especially in Guyana where there are five internet hosts serving the entire population and only about two personal computers for every 100 inhabitants. This suggests a high level of shared access.

The real time in which information and images can be transmitted has facilitated globalization of production and network linkages among small and medium-sized businesses. It has also facilitated the development of non-traditional service exports, such as information processing and electronic commerce. However, tourism service exports remain the dominant exports for several Caribbean countries in the current globalization phase. Nevertheless, ICT is also facilitating the development of the tourism industry through related services, such as online reservations and payments.

Caribbean countries have gained increased access to the new information technologies but they have not on the whole been able to develop competitive exports significantly in these areas. One of the constraints has been the provision of telecommunications services by monopolies in these countries. Although the new communication technologies facilitate bypass of the network of monopoly telecommunication suppliers, bypass is restricted in Caribbean

TABLE 1. Declining Cost of Transport and Communications (1990 U.S.$)

YEAR	SEA FREIGHT (average ocean freight and port charges per ton)	AIR TRANSPORT (average revenue per passenger mile)	TELEPHONE CALL (3 minutes, New York– London)	COMPUTERS (1990 = 100)
1920	95	—	—	—
1930	60	0.68	245	—
1940	63	0.46	189	—
1950	34	0.30	53	—
1960	27	0.24	46	12,500
1970	27	0.16	32	1,947
1980	24	0.10	5	362
1990	29	0.11	3	100

Source: *UNDP, Human Development Report*, 1999.

countries for varying periods of time. In Barbados, Jamaica, and Trinidad and Tobago, for example, bypass will not be permitted until 2012, 2013, and 2010, respectively. In Antigua and Bermuda, Belize, and Grenada, bypass will not be permitted until 2012, 2007, and 2006 respectively.

Liberalization of Trade in Goods and Services
The decade of the 1990s marked significant trade liberalization at both regional and multilateral levels. Caribbean countries embarked on import tariff reduction with the amendment of the CARICOM CET in 1991. The minimum tariff was to remain at the original level of 5 percent but the maximum level was to be reduced from 45 to 20 percent by the end of the decade (table 3). The CET did make allowance for the phasing-in of reform so that a zero percent tariff would still apply to agricultural inputs and some basic goods and a maximum of 40 percent would still be levied on agricultural products until the reduction in tariffs at the multilateral level was finally agreed on.

At the regional level, CARICOM countries approved in 2002 a number of protocols that revised the 1973 Treaty of Chaguaramas and established the CSME. The latter would allow for the free movement of goods, labor, and capital; the removal of all barriers to intraregional trade; the right of establishing companies anywhere in the region; harmonization of fiscal, monetary, and industrial policies; a single currency for the region; and coordination of relations with non-CARICOM countries.

TABLE 2. ICT Indicators for Selected Caribbean Countries, 2001

	Main Telephone Lines per 100 Inhabitants	Cellular Mobile Subscribers per 100 Inhabitants	Cellular Mobile Subscribers as % Total Telephone Subscribers
Antigua & Barbuda	47.3	31.7	40.2
Bahamas	40.0	19.6	32.9
Barbados	46.3[a]	10.6[a]	18.7[a]
Belize	14.4	11.5	44.4
Dominica	29.0	1.5[a]	5.0[a]
Grenada	32.7	6.4	16.4
Guyana	9.2	8.6	48.5
Jamaica	19.7	26.9	57.7
St. Kitts & Nevis	56.8[a]	3.1[a]	5.2[a]
St. Vincent & Grenadines	21.9[a]	2.1[a]	8.7[a]
Suriname	17.6	19.1	52.1
Trinidad & Tobago	24.0	17.3	42.0

Source: International Telecommunication Union and Caribbean Association of National
Telecommunication Organizations, various years.
[a] Data for 2000.
[b] Data for 1999.

Most of the barriers to intraregional trade in goods have been removed. However, intraregional trade in services is constrained by the limited movement of labor; only graduates of tertiary institutions are currently permitted free movement. On the other hand, greater liberalization of the foreign-exchange and capital markets in the region has facilitated trade in financial services as well as in goods.

The multilateral level the Uruguay Round of Trade negotiations were concluded with the signing of the Marrakech Agreements and the establishment of the World Trade Organization (WTO) in 1994. The Uruguay Round focused on liberalizing nontariff barriers to trade. Liberalization of industrial tariffs was not as significant as liberalization of barriers to trade in agricultural products. Tariff rates on industrial products were relatively low prior to the Uruguay Round. The highest tariffs were those on textiles and apparel. However, the major barriers to trade in these products have been quota restrictions under the Multi-Fibre Agreement. These are to be phased out and the products fully integrated into the WTO agreements by 2005. Caribbean countries may not

Internet Hosts per 10,000 Inhabitants	Internet Users per 10,000 Inhabitants	Estimated PCs per100 Inhabitants
99.8	652.0[a]	—
0.9	549.4	—
4.8	373.8[a]	9.3
13.6	737.7	13.5
27.8	777.7[a]	7.5
1.2	520.0	13.0
0.2	1,091.9	2.6
5.5	384.9	5.0
0.7	516.1[b]	19.0
0.3	308.5[a]	11.6
1.3	330.0	—
52.8	923.1	6.9

benefit from trade liberalization in textiles and apparel on account of their inability to compete with low-cost producers in Asia, in particular China.

The Uruguay Round began the process of agricultural trade liberalization. It involved establishment of tariff equivalents of the nontariff barriers, binding of the tariffs, and reduction in average tariffs over time. Tariffs on agricultural products increased significantly, as most countries bound their tariffs at relatively high levels. The high tariffs along with quotas on specific commodities such as bananas and sugar constrained the growth of trade in agriculture. However, Caribbean countries may not benefit from the abolition of quotas because of their inability to compete with Latin American banana producers, for example.

Liberalization of services began with the negotiations during the Uruguay Round and culminated in the General Agreement on Trade in Services (GATS) in 1994. The GATS covers all internationally traded services, except public services supplied on a noncommercial basis, as well as their mode of delivery. Mode of delivery is defined in terms of the following categories: cross-border

TABLE 3. CARICOM Common External Tariff Rates

	1991	1993–94	1995–96	1997	1998
CARICOM CET	5–45	5–30/35	5–25/30	5–20/25	5–50

Source: CARICOM, *Common External Tariff of the Common Market.*

supply (from one country to another country, e.g., telephone call); consumption abroad (consumer moving to country of supplier, e.g., tourism); commercial presence (supplier establishing in consumer country, e.g., branches of foreign companies); and movement of "natural persons" (supplier moving to country of consumer, e.g., consultants).

Barriers to trade in services consist of regulations imposed by governments that discriminate against foreign suppliers. Liberalization therefore would involve the removal or modification of those restrictions through commitments to provide market access and national treatment, which refers to equal treatment of local and foreign suppliers of services. It has been argued that developing countries could benefit from receipts of more than $150 billion per year from temporary access (of labor) to developed-country markets.[2] This finding would tend to support a Caribbean negotiation strategy to secure service liberalization through the movement of medium- and low-skilled labor.

Trade Performance
Caribbean trade has changed significantly since the 1980s. Imports into the region have continued on a growth trajectory, especially in light of the significant reduction in trade barriers between the latter half of the 1980s and the early 1990s. However, exports have been growing more slowly and in some cases have even declined. The result has been a significant divergence in the growth paths of imports and exports since the 1980s (figure 1). This has led to an increasing deficit on the merchandise trade account. A notable development has been the diversification of trade partners, with increasing exports to the Central American Common Market and increasing imports from the wider Latin American region. Of note also is the significant increase in the export of chemicals and imports of fuel and machinery (figures 4 and 5). Nevertheless, the Caribbean is still dependent on raw material exports despite the fact that commodity prices have been falling significantly since the early twentieth century.

The leading exports of the region are fresh food, processed food, and clothing. The exports of Guyana, Jamaica, Belize, Dominica, Grenada, St. Lucia, and St. Vincent are concentrated in primary products. Barbados and Trinidad and

Tobago have more-diversified export structures. Only Barbados, Trinidad and Tobago, and Dominica have significant human-capital-intensive exports. Most of the oecs countries have significant technology-intensive exports on account of their assembly operations in electronic components and nonelectrical machinery and transport equipment.

Trade in services has grown significantly during the 1990s. Almost all countries in the region saw significant increase in services exports. The largest exporters were the Bahamas, Dominican Republic, and Jamaica. The most significant exporters in the oecs region were Antigua and Barbuda and St. Lucia. Exports were highly dependent on the tourism industry in the region. Financial service exports became significant for the smaller islands of the eastern and northern Caribbean such as Antigua and Barbuda, Barbados, and the Bahamas. Destination of exports and source of imports were mainly North America and the United Kingdom.[3]

Despite a dependence on tourism exports, CARICOM countries lost market share to other Caribbean countries, especially Cuba and the Dominican Republic during the 1990s. The CARICOM region's share of visitor arrivals declined from about 38 percent in 1990 to 34 percent at the end of the decade. As a consequence, visitor expenditure as a proportion of gross income also declined. This decline had the most significant impact on the economies of Antigua and Barbuda and Jamaica where the expenditure-GDP ratio moved from 21 and 25 percent respectively in 1992 to 16 and 18 percent respectively in 1999. The decline continued to 14 and 17 percent respectively in 2001. The main source for tourists is the United States except for Antigua and Barbuda and Barbados, which rely mainly on the European market for their supply of tourists.[4]

Caribbean countries, in particular the larger services exporters, have increased their share of world service exports. The Dominican Republic increased its share from 1.4 percent in 1992 to 2.2 percent in 2000. Jamaica's share in global service exports grew from 1.1 to 1.4 percent over the same period, while Barbados's share grew modestly from 0.63 to 0.73 percent. The share of the Bahamas remained stagnant at 1.4 percent, whereas Trinidad and Tobago's share declined from 0.46 percent in 1992 to 0.38 percent in 1998. The shares of Caribbean countries in global service imports, however, have remained relatively small compared with their shares in world service exports.

The Caribbean as a whole is more dependent on services than on goods for its earnings of foreign exchange (table 4). The deficit on the balance-of-trade account widened during the decade of the 1990s due largely to the acceleration of trade liberalization in some of the more-developed countries such as Jamaica and Trinidad and Tobago. On the other hand, the surplus on the bal-

TABLE 4. Level of Export Specialization in Services for Selected Caribbean Countries (ratio of services/goods exports)

	1980	1985	1990	1995	1999	2000
Antigua & Barbuda	150	750	616	870	1,075	4,060
Barbados	144	120	285	351	383	390
Belize	—	24	75	83	83	80
Dominica	60	33	55	122	190	172
Grenada	105	155	210	490	360	362
Guyana	4	22	—	29	—	—
Jamaica	39	99	84	109	157	153
St. Kitts & Nevis	40	115	180	400	323	310
St. Lucia	68	116	114	220	533	767
St. Vincent & Grenadines	90	31	51	180	248	248
Suriname	32	20	6	21	21	21
Trinidad & Tobago	9	11	15	13	21	—

Source: Based on WTO data.
Note: Data excludes services supplied through foreign affiliates and by the movement of
    natural persons.

ance of trade in the services account increased significantly between 1993 and 1998 due in large part to the earnings of the more-developed countries in the region, namely Barbados, Jamaica, and Trinidad and Tobago (figure 9).

Foreign Investment and Export Specialization

Ideological convergence during the current phase of globalization resulted in a shift from commitment to the provision of aid or ODA grants to greater reliance on private flows to finance development projects in developing countries. Official net financial flows including grants declined from 59 percent of total flows in 1990 to 6 percent in 2000. On the other hand, private capital flows to the Caribbean grew from 26 percent of total flows in 1990 to 93 percent in 2000. Most of the less-developed countries in the OECS regions relied on concessionary official flows for their infrastructure development over the years and found themselves unable to attract sizable private flows largely on account of small size and limited resources.

During the decade of the 1990s, net foreign direct investment (FDI) flows to the region grew from U.S.$378 million in 1990 to U.S.$1,671 million in 1999 and further to U.S.$1,923 million in 2001. The bulk of flows (more than 80

FIGURE 9. Caribbean Trade Balance in Goods and Services, 1992–2000

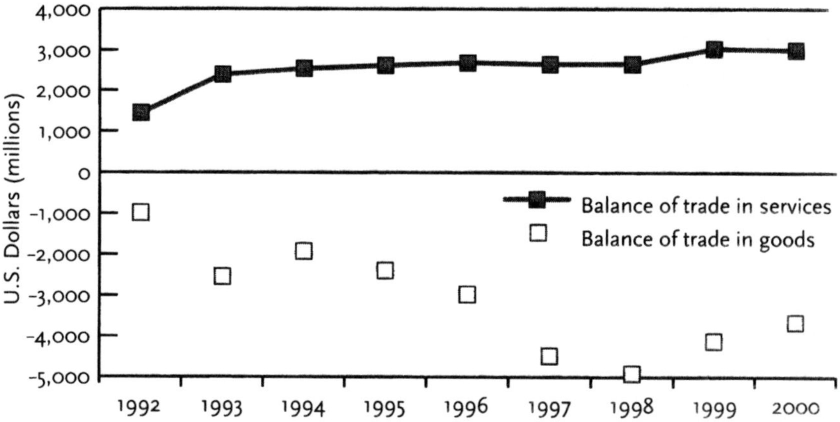

percent in 2001) went to Trinidad and Tobago and Jamaica. Most of the flows to Trinidad and Tobago went into the petroleum industry. Most of the flows into Jamaica were directed into textiles and apparel and the tourism industry. FDI flows, however, have been shifting in terms of sector allocation. Flows into services have grown eightfold from the late 1990s to the early 2000, whereas flows into the primary and manufacturing sectors have grown fivefold and fourfold, respectively, during the same period. This shift has been influencing the pattern of export specialization toward such areas as tourism and information and communications technology.

New Trade Initiatives
Initiatives in pursuit of further trade liberalization that have had or will have a significant impact on the economies of Caribbean countries were undertaken from about the mid-1990s. The first of these was the 1994 North American Free Trade Agreement (NAFTA) among the United States, Canada, and Mexico. This agreement was the precursor to subsequent free-trade agreements negotiated with the United States. The second initiative was the launch of the process to create a Free Trade Area of the Americas (FTAA) in 1996 at the Summit of the Americas. The third event was the signing of the Cotonou Framework Agreement in 2000 between the European Union and a group of African, Caribbean, and Pacific countries to begin a process of negotiations toward a new trade partnership. The fourth was the Doha declaration in 2001 that launched the Doha Round of multilateral trade negotiations.

NAFTA is the only initiative concluded and implemented during the decade of the 1990s. Its effect on Caribbean countries would have been largely through the free access it provided to Mexico for textile and apparel exports to the U.S. market. Caribbean countries had been given specific access levels for their exports of those products, which had been excluded from duty-free treatment under the CBI. Jamaica's exports of apparel products to the United States declined from 1997 but not mainly on account of NAFTA. Exports from the Dominican Republic, which also benefited from special access for textile and apparel products increased significantly during the same period despite the advantage Mexico had in terms of duty-free access. NAFTA did benefit its members in terms of a major increase in intra-NAFTA trade, from 41 percent in 1990 to 56 percent in 2002. By the start of the twenty-first century (2000), the United States had signed the Caribbean Basin Trade Partnership Act (CBTPA), which provided duty-free treatment to those products that had been excluded from the CBI.

Negotiations for an Economic Partnership Agreement (EPA) between the European Union and Caribbean countries were launched in 2004 and should be completed in 2007. The EPA would replace the preferential arrangement of the Lomé Convention with a more reciprocal relationship.

The Doha Round of the WTO provided the mandate for negotiations in several areas including agriculture and services, which began in 2000. The deadline for completion of the negotiations is 2005. The process stalled in 2003 due to the failure to reach consensus on any of the items on the negotiating agenda at the Cancun Ministerial Conference in Mexico. However, a new consensus was reached in August 2004 to relaunch the round with an agreement in principle to eliminate export subsidies and trade-distorting domestic support to agriculture.

The process for the establishment of a free-trade area of the Americas (FTAA) excluding Cuba was launched at the Summit of the Americas in Miami in 1994, which gave support for the pursuit of economic integration and free trade in the Americas. Measures were taken following the Second Summit of the Americas in Santiago, Chile, in 1998 to initiate negotiations for the FTAA. Nine negotiating groups were set up to address issues in specific areas such as agriculture and services.[5] In addition, a Consultative Group on Smaller Economies was created to address issues of concern to the smaller economies in the hemisphere. A Trade Negotiations Committee (TNC) was established to guide the work of the negotiating groups as well as to ensure that the concerns of smaller economies were dealt with in each negotiating group.

In keeping with the objectives of ensuring full participation of smaller economies in the FTAA and facilitating an increase in their level of development, the ministers of trade meeting in Quito, Ecuador, in 2002 approved a Hemispheric Cooperation Program (HCP) developed by the Consultative Group on Smaller Economies. The HCP is intended to strengthen the capacity of countries to participate fully in the FTAA and to facilitate increased hemispheric cooperation and provision of technical assistance through, among other things, coordination among donor agencies and beneficiary countries. A dialogue was initiated between countries needing assistance and potential donors in Washington in October 2003, in order for countries to present their national strategies for capacity building and for donors to indicate their interest in future cooperation.

The United States had envisaged a comprehensive trade agreement along the lines of NAFTA. However, the short time frame within which to conclude an agreement and the divergence of views between the United States and some countries in the hemisphere, especially Brazil and the Southern Integration Movement (MERCOSUR), led to the recognition that "countries may assume different levels of commitments" within the FTAA and may choose to agree to "additional obligations and benefits."[6] Like the Doha Round, the FTAA process stalled in 2004 due to failure to agree on guidelines for the different levels of negotiations. Progress on restarting negotiations is not envisaged until after the U.S. presidential elections in November 2004.

MEETING THE CHALLENGES OF GLOBALIZATION

A number of significant changes over the past decades set the parameters within which Caribbean countries will have to operate to meet the challenges of new international trade configurations. One is the erosion leading to eventual cessation of preferential market access for Caribbean exports to developed countries. Another is the reduction in policy space, within the context of the WTO agreements, to pursue measures to protect domestic producers. The challenges to be met include not only the quest for economic development but maintenance of existing standards of living. The strategies that Caribbean countries will have to pursue in meeting these challenges include developing more-resilient economic structures while forging partnerships to leverage optimal international trade arrangements. A critical requirement is reducing dependence on the export of primary products and natural-resource-based manufactures and developing knowledge-based export products.

The need to shift from dependence on export of primary products is urgent for most Caribbean countries, given their small size and the declining significance of primary products in world exports. More than two-thirds of CARICOM member countries account for a major share (between 50 and 90 percent) of primary products in their merchandise exports. Medium-technology manufactures account for the largest share of world exports (more than 30 percent), whereas high-technology manufactures have been the fastest-growing category of exports (10–25 percent) over the period 1998–2000.[7] On the other hand, exports of primary products as a percentage of world exports have been declining significantly.

The development of medium- and high-technology exports can be facilitated by, among other things, encouragement of innovation and technological development. One of the ways to develop such exports is through outsourcing arrangements with foreign companies. India and, more recently, Brazil and China have been taking advantage of outsourcing of computer and telemarketing operations by large American firms, which seek to reduce their operating expenses.

The main requirement for developing the capability to take advantage of the fast-growing information technology (IT) industry, which is estimated to be worth about $1 trillion globally and which provides substantial employment, is greater access to education and training and to internet resources. Despite the progress made in a number of Caribbean countries, internet connectivity is still relatively low in the region. Reduction in cost is a necessary condition for improving access.

Deficits in education are still significant in the Caribbean region. Although gross primary school enrollment rates are relatively high, reaching 100 percent in many cases, they remain relatively low for some countries at the secondary level—59 percent in Dominican Republic and 63 percent in Grenada, for example—as well as at the tertiary level, for example, less than 20 percent for countries such as Jamaica.[8] Adult illiteracy is less than 10 percent for most countries in the region except Antigua and Barbuda (14 percent), Jamaica (13 percent), St. Vincent and the Grenadines (11 percent), the Dominican Republic (16 percent), and Haiti (49 percent). In addition, public expenditure on education has not been increasing in the region and has even declined in some countries largely on account of fiscal constraints and the economic reforms of the past couple of decades. Greater private-sector contribution to funding basic education has also been constrained by the diversion of resources into restructuring enterprises and industries to enhance competitiveness.

Caribbean countries have benefited from being members of the CARICOM integration grouping. Trade liberalization during the 1990s resulted in increased intraregional exports, from 8 percent of total exports in 1990 to 13 percent in 2002. In order to benefit further from deeper economic integration, there needs to be greater political commitment to liberalize fully the free movement of the factors of production within the region. An important benefit of the integration arrangement has been the strengthening of the bargaining position of Caribbean countries in international trade negotiations. That position can be further enhanced by widening integration to include Caribbean communities in foreign countries.

The size of the Caribbean diaspora is estimated at about 2.8 million people in the United States, 0.3 million in Canada, and 0.6 million in the United Kingdom. About one-third of the people of the English-speaking Caribbean live in either the United States or Canada. These estimates could be higher if undocumented workers are taken into account. Caribbean populations abroad constitute significant markets for Caribbean products.

The diaspora has been having a substantial impact on Caribbean economies through increased tourism exports. It can be harnessed to provide investment in tourism and other ventures. Remittances have been the focus of government policy toward the Caribbean diaspora, as such flows have grown in significance with the liberalization of financial services (see table 5). It is estimated that about 10 percent of remittances may be contributing to pension funds and the development of small businesses in the Caribbean.[9] Integrating the diaspora with the region could facilitate not only the development of industries and regions but also effective lobbying in the host countries to ensure that Caribbean countries get the best deals possible in new trade agreements.

The small size and openness of Caribbean economies as well as their geographic location limit their ability to pursue independent policies. Political integration is a rational option for pooling and hence maximizing economic resources for development purposes. However, this seems unlikely in the foreseeable future, given the competitive political system in the region that militates against political union. Nevertheless, Caribbean countries will have to pool their negotiating resources to secure advantages at the international level. The CARICOM Regional Negotiating Machinery was established to serve that purpose by articulating the regional position in international trade negotiations. Strategic alliance, in particular with larger countries, is another option for securing advantage in international trade negotiations.[10]

The relatively weak capacity of Caribbean countries to take advantage of further trade liberalization at regional and global levels dictates consideration of special measures to facilitate their participation in and benefit from free-trade arrangements. Despite acceptance of the principle of "special and differential

TABLE 5. Remittances to Caribbean Countries, 2002

COUNTRY	REMITTANCE ($millions)
Barbados[a]	84
Dominican Republic	1,935
Guyana	120
Haiti	800
Jamaica	1,200
Trinidad & Tobago	50

Source: Orozco, "The Impact of Migration in the Caribbean and Central American Region."

[a] Figure at 2000.

treatment" for smaller economies within the WTO and its extension to the negotiations for the FTAA, where it is conceived largely in terms of longer grace periods for compliance with liberalization commitments and the provision of technical assistance to build trade capacity, Caribbean countries may have to be prepared to offer at least some level of reciprocity in order to gain favorable market access.

Smaller economies in the hemisphere favor a regional financing mechanism to facilitate their integration into the proposed FTAA.[11] This type of mechanism has precedence in the Structural Funds set up by the European Economic Community to facilitate the development of backward regions and countries that lagged behind in terms of the European Community's average per capita income. Funds to support integration were also established in Central America and the Andean Community to facilitate regional integration.

The challenge for Caribbean countries is to propose a financing model that would address simultaneously the needs in relation to both the proposed FTAA and the European Union–CARICOM Economic Partnership Agreement (EPA). A financing mechanism to foster development within liberalized trade arrangements would provide additional resources for investment in development projects without unduly putting pressure on inadequate budgetary resources of governments.

The issue of inadequate budgetary resources is related to the fiscal performance of Caribbean economies. The pursuit of an expansionary fiscal policy—that is, increasing government expenditure that cannot be financed by tax revenue—has resulted in significant increase in debt accumulation to finance the fiscal deficit. For example, the public debt–GDP ratio increased from

62 to 85 percent from 1997 to 2003, making the Caribbean one of the most indebted regions in the world.[12]

Increased export earnings and net capital inflows are critical to the economic growth and development of Caribbean countries. However, Caribbean economies are vulnerable to external shocks from changes in international trade regimes as well as to natural disasters. As a result of the former shock, Dominica experienced severe economic crisis in 2002. In terms of the latter shock, a number of Caribbean countries, in particular Grenada, experienced severe dislocations to their economies from the passage of Hurricane Ivan. Grenada's economic growth will significantly decline and the fiscal and current-account deficits will deteriorate as a result. A financing mechanism is therefore critical for addressing both of these types of shocks, as well as the adjustment required for participation in free-trade arrangements.

CONCLUSION

Caribbean countries have had different experiences in developing their economies over the past four decades or so. Smaller countries, in particular those with limited natural resources, made an early shift from commodity exports to services exports. Those countries such as Barbados, Cayman Islands, and most of the countries of the OECS region achieved relatively high per capita incomes. Larger countries, notably Guyana, Jamaica, and Trinidad and Tobago, continued to rely on commodity exports and, with the exception of Trinidad and Tobago, experienced lower per capita incomes. Increasing or even maintaining existing income levels poses a major challenge to Caribbean countries as they pursue strategies to increase exports and financial inflows during the present period of globalization.

Policy choices, economic management, and political stability played significant roles in facilitating the economic outcome in individual countries. The range of policy choice has narrowed with the increase in globalization since the 1990s, leaving countries more vulnerable to adverse effects of global change. Small size has become a handicap in the current period of globalization. It is therefore imperative that Caribbean countries fully liberalize trade and factor movements within the region and pursue strategic alliances at the international level to ensure that they get the best possible deals in trade negotiations. A challenge not discussed is the globalization of crime to which all countries are now vulnerable and the measures instituted by the United States to counter the threat of bioterrorism. Those measures are likely to become effective non-tariff barriers to trade on account of the cost of compliance that must be borne by exporting countries and the discretion allowed to U.S. officials. Improved access to U.S. markets could therefore be negated by antiterrorism measures.

NOTES

The views expressed do not necessarily represent those of the Economic Commission for Latin America and the Caribbean (ECLAC).

1. The concept of globalization is multidimensional and hence defies a single definition of the term. However, globalization can be referred to as "the growing influence exerted at the local, national and regional levels by financial, economic, environmental, political, social and cultural processes that are global in scope." See ECLAC, *Globalization and Development*.

2. See *Negotiating* by Alan Winters and others who make the case for liberalization of mode 4 delivery of services.

3. International Monetary Fund, *Balance of Payments and CARICOM Trade in Services*.

4. An assessment of tourism in the CARICOM region points to the lack of dynamism in the sector due largely to the structural characteristics of the tourism industry such as weak linkages to other sectors and high leakage from the industry itself. This is contained in ECLAC, *Caribbean Tourism, Trends, Policies and Impact, 1985–2002*.

5. Details of these can be found at <www.ftaa-alca.org>, accessed November 2004.

6. See the Ministerial Declaration of the "Free Trade of the Americas Eighth Ministerial Meeting," Miami, November 20, 2003, <www.ftaa-alca.org>, and "Free Trade of Americas May Be Limited," <www.washingtonpost.com>, both accessed November 2004.

7. See Bacchetta and Bora, "Industrial Tariffs Liberalization and the Doha Development Agenda."

8. Data obtained from UNESCO at <www.unesco.org>, accessed November 2004.

9. See "The Impact of Migration in the Caribbean and the Central American Region," <www.focal.ca>, accessed November 2004.

10. This type of strategy was pursued by the Group of Twenty developing countries led by Brazil at the WTO meeting in Cancun, Mexico, September 2003.

11. The idea of a Regional Integration Fund came from the Guyana government in 1996.

12. See ECLAC, *Economic Survey of the Caribbean, 2003–2004*.

3

Globalization, the World Bank, and the Haitian Economy

ALEX DUPUY

In 1996, 1998, and 2002 the World Bank issued reports that marked a turning point in its analysis of the causes of underdevelopment and poverty in Haiti. For the first time since the bank began to formulate development policy for that Caribbean nation in the 1970s, it argued that poverty remained pervasive and even deepened because of the long history of political instability, poor governance, corruption, and the misuse of public funds. The bank's criticism went even further. Borrowing the language of the Left, the bank indicted the entire political system and the dominant wealthy Haitian elite. As the bank put it, "Haiti has never had a tradition of governance aimed at providing services to the population or creating an environment conducive to sustainable growth. Instead, a small elite has supported a 'predatory state' that makes only negligible investments in human resources and basic infrastructure. At the same time, pervasive repression through army, police, and paramilitary groups has created deep-seated distrust between civil society and the state."[1] Even after the restoration of civilian rule in 1994, the bank argued, conditions have not improved. There continues to be an absence of leadership; charges of corruption, abuse of power, and human rights violations abound; and the issues of justice, insecurity, economic hardship, and budgetary crisis remain unresolved and exacerbate the situation.

When parliamentary elections in 1997 and 2000 resulted in victory for Jean-Bertrand Aristide's political party, and when Aristide himself was reelected president in 2000 for another five-year term, the United States, the European Union (EU), the World Bank, and other international financial institutions

(IFIS) suspended the disbursement of foreign aid to Haiti. Also in 2000, the World Bank transferred its Haitian representative to the Dominican Republic. Those organizations and governments now insist that for them to reengage in Haiti there must be critical governmental reforms. In particular, the World Bank demands measures to increase transparency and accountability in public spending. Institutional reforms must also be undertaken, with particular attention paid to the factors that prevent the full implementation of the bank's and International Monetary Fund's (IMF) structural adjustment program. This includes above all the privatization of public enterprises and the provision of social services. Lastly, a vigorous civil society must be allowed to flourish so that citizens can "challenge public authorities to enhance their performance and responsiveness to the citizenry."

The World Bank's critical attitude toward the democratically elected governments and its indictment of the predatory state are radically different from its attitude toward the Duvalier dictatorship from 1971 to 1986, as well as the military governments that succeeded Jean-Claude Duvalier between 1986 and 1990. Though the Duvalier regime and the successive military governments were ideal-typical cases of repressive predatory states, the bank looked for reasons to continue to support them. When it criticized the practices of those regimes, the bank refrained from calling them predatory states that engaged in widespread repression; and it never called on them to be transparent and to create the political conditions for the existence of a vibrant civil society that could challenge their authority and hold them accountable. Moreover, the bank never insisted before that the continued flow of foreign aid and loans to those regimes would be contingent on their implementing the requisite reforms and eliminate corruption.

What, then, explains the bank's suspension of aid to elected governments (following the parliamentary elections of 1997 and 2000 and the presidential election of 2000) after supporting dictatorships for two decades between 1971 and 1990? Even if one argued that the bank did not "discover" the concept of "good governance" and democracy as necessary conditions for sustainable economic development until 1989–90, it was fully aware of the corruption, brutality, and unaccountability of the dictatorships with which it collaborated. Moreover, it is well known that throughout the 1960s and 1970s the bank supported murderous military dictatorships in different parts of the world, even after they had overthrown democratically elected governments it had refused to fund, such as in Brazil, Argentina, Chile, Uruguay, Indonesia, and the Philippines. The Cold War was then at its height, and the United States opposed those democratic governments because of their socialist, nationalist, or anti-

American ideologies; and if it was not itself directly involved in the respective coups d'état, the United States moved quickly to support the military juntas that carried them out. In that period, the bank's decision to provide or withhold aid to a government had little to do with whether a government practiced "good governance," as the bank now defines it, but with whether the United States supported or opposed that government, be it a dictatorship or a democracy.

As I will show here, this policy continues to be the case. The World Bank's support of the dictatorships in Haiti between 1971 and 1990, and its decision to withhold loans from the democratically elected governments in Haiti in 1995, 1997, and 2000 have more to do with U.S. policy toward those respective governments than with whether they complied with bank recommendations and expectations. Whereas under the administration of President René Préval (1996–2001) parliament was the immediate problem, in 2000 the problem became the control of both parliament and the executive branch by Aristide and his Fanmi Lavalas (FL) party after the elections of May and November, respectively. The bank's current use of "governance" to compel implementa- tion of its (and other IFIS') "conditionalities," and its disregard of that issue in earlier times, I argue, is to be understood in the context of the changes in the dynamics associated with the current phase of globalization and the post–Cold War era. The politicization of economic reforms occurred in the late 1980s under the aegis of what came to be known as the "Washington Consensus."

The Washington Consensus, also known as the "neoliberal" or "structural adjustment" reforms, became the new mantra of the international financial institutions, especially after 1989–90. The Washington Consensus sought to weaken the interventionist powers of the state and open the Third World economies to the markets and capital of the advanced or core capitalist coun- tries. Thus, what changed was not so much the subservience of the World Bank to U.S. policies, but the reasons for denying aid. If during the Cold War the main reasons were a government's socialist or anti-imperialist tendencies, in the post–Cold War era they are ostensibly about a government's opposition or lack of commitment to the neoliberal policies of the Washington Consen- sus, or U.S. animosity toward that government, or both.

In the case of Haiti, the transition to democracy in 1991 and especially after 1994 offered the World Bank the opportunity to push for the fuller implemen- tation of the structural adjustment and institutional reforms. The fact that the post-1990 governments had been elected to office (except for the three years of military rule between 1991 and 1994) made them more vulnerable to external pressure than the dictatorships who retained power, or intended to do so, indefinitely. Consequently, the bank and the other IFIS could exert greater economic leverage against them by threatening to withhold the delivery of foreign-aid money if they refused to comply with the structural adjustment policies (SAPS). Unlike dictatorships, democratic governments generally depend on their performance to retain the support of voters. In poor peripheral societies like Haiti, where the government depends on foreign aid to finance public programs and services, the cutoff of such aid could undermine the ability of the government to deliver on its promises and hence alienate it from voters. Moreover, since the collapse of the Soviet Union and the Soviet bloc in 1989, the unchallenged supremacy of capitalism, and the discrediting of socialist and state-centered models of development, governments that would defy the IFIS or the United States would have nowhere to turn for possible alternative trade partners and sources of support.

While the World Bank's criticism of the predatory state's antidevelopmental policies is correct, the bank's own policies—and, by extension, those of the other IFIS—were equally antidevelopmental. Those policies led to the steady deterioration of the Haitian economy since the 1970s and its transformation into an essentially labor-exporting economy increasingly dependent on remittances from Haitian migrants, foreign aid, and drug trafficking.[2] In short, though ostensibly designed to alleviate poverty by stimulating sustainable economic growth, the policies of the bank and the other IFIS in fact maintained Haiti's position in the international division of labor as a supplier of cheap labor to foreign capital.

GLOBALIZATION AND THE WORLD BANK'S POLITICAL CONDITIONALITIES

The term "globalization" began to enter popular and academic discourses in the early 1970s. It refers to a process of integration of the economies of the world in the international division of labor of the capitalist world system and a concomitant shift of power from nation-states to multinational corporations and other organizations controlled by the core capitalist countries. Globalization may be seen as an unfolding of the internal logic of the capitalist system characterized by dramatic new developments in the international financial system; the concentration of capital, knowledge, information, and technology in the core countries; the internationalization of production; and the intensification of competition among the core capitalist economies. Competition among the core states has led to a new division of the world economy into three distinct zones or blocs over which different core states exercise greater or lesser influence: the United

States over the North and South American bloc, the European Economic Community where Germany and France vie for dominance over the (West and East) European bloc, and Japan over the East Asian bloc. From this, it follows that nation-states are integrated in the world economy through trade, investment, and production relations in proportion to their position in the international division of labor, such that the core economies tend to trade and invest mostly among themselves; Latin America and the Caribbean trade mostly with the United States; the Asian countries trade mostly among themselves and with Japan; and sub-Saharan Africa trades mostly with the European Union.

The reconfiguration of the international division of labor associated with the globalization process has not altered the hierarchical structure of the world economy and the division of labor between the core, semiperipheral, and peripheral countries. The new international division of labor is characterized by a shift from capital-intensive to technology- or information-based production and services in the core economies, and capital- and labor-intensive industries in the lower-wage semiperipheral and peripheral countries. Thus, the position of countries in the international division of labor is still determined by the types of goods and services they produce: whether high-value goods and services based on highly skilled and informational labor (predominantly in core countries); high-volume goods and services with lower-cost labor (predominantly in semiperipheral countries such as Brazil, Mexico, Chile, South Korea, and Taiwan, and some sectors in core countries); or raw materials based on natural endowments; or whether their labor is redundant, devalued, and marginalized (characteristic of peripheral countries in sub-Saharan Africa, parts of Asia, Latin America, and the Caribbean).

Even the World Bank recognizes that the current phase of globalization has not benefited all countries equally. Some of the countries it calls the "new globalizers," twenty-four in all, have experienced high levels of growth by opening their economies and improving their climates for foreign capital investment to make the shift from primary commodity exports to the production of manufactured goods and services for the world market. The rest of the developing world, incorporating some 2 billion people (excluding China and India), however, has not made the transition. Those countries not only remain poor, but they are trading even less than they did twenty years ago. The bank simply calls them "losers." Globalization, then, produces "winners" and "losers," both within and between countries; and the "losers," with declining incomes and rising poverty, are becoming increasingly redundant and marginalized in the world economy. For many of those countries, the bank concludes, it may be too late to reverse their situation, even if they pursued the bank's policies of "openness." This is because world demand for manufactures and services is limited. Moreover, agglomeration economies lead firms from the advanced countries to locate in clusters, and while there may be room for many clusters, countries that offer the advantage of low-cost labor may find it difficult to attract firms that are already located in other labor-abundant countries. Despite this conclusion, the bank and the other IFIS have not reconsidered their argument that adopting the "right policies" is the best way for the "losers" to participate in and benefit from globalization.

Even sympathetic analysts who evaluated the performance of the developing countries that followed World Bank policies during the 1980s and 1990s concluded that their response "has not been what could have been expected. . . . Zero per capita growth on average after major reforms is a disappointing outcome whatever the cause. . . . Many, even stationary, country characteristics widely thought to be favorable for growth (or at least favorable for level of income) have improved, yet developing countries on average have stagnated. This in itself is a blow to the optimism surrounding the 'Washington Consensus' prior to the experience of the last two decades."[3] Moreover, as William Easterly, Michael Kremer, Lant Pritchett, and Lawrence Summers found, there is no correlation between country characteristics and growth rates over time. "With a few famous exceptions, the same countries do not do well period after period; countries are 'success stories' one period and disappointments the next."[4]

At this juncture one can best understand the convergence between the dynamics of globalization and the ideological propositions clustered under the Washington Consensus. Formulated in the 1980s by the U.S. Treasury Department, the World Bank, and the IMF, the Washington Consensus reflected the ideology and political objectives of the state actors and policy makers of the Reagan administration.[5] It corresponded with the collapse of the Soviet system and the discrediting of central planning and state-centered development models of the 1950s to the 1970s in the Third World. As Easterly put it, the "new consensus" emphasized "market-friendly economic policies by developing country governments. The development consensus shifted away from state planning towards markets, away from import substitution towards outward orientation, away from state controls of prices and interest rates towards 'getting the prices right.'"[6] The advocates of the consensus exploited the huge debts accumulated by Third World countries—largely at the urgings of the World Bank itself—to demand that they restructure their economies, open them more to the operation of the market, and facilitate the takeover of their assets by foreign capital.

Basically, the consensus view held that to achieve macrostability, the debtor countries of Latin America, Asia, and Africa needed to "liberalize" their economies—that is, lower or eliminate tariff barriers, deregulate their markets, and end subsidies to and privatize their public-sector enterprises. Many of these ideas were incorporated in World Bank analyses and recommendations before the late 1980s, but since the end of the Cold War the Bank and the IMF began to insist even more on making loans conditional on carrying out the mandated reforms. This insistence was based on the belief that the borrowing countries could undergo economic expansion and growth only if they removed all restrictions on imports and exports, allowed foreign-currency transactions, and opened their economies to outside investments. As Moises Naim points out, however, what the IFIS and the governments that were called upon to implement the core requirements of the consensus understood by that term changed throughout the 1990s. "Reforming governments everywhere saw how the policy goals that just a few years, or even months, earlier had been specified as the final frontier of the reform process became just a mere precondition for success. New, more complex, and more difficult goals were constantly added to the list of requirements for an acceptable performance."[7] As I show here, the case of Haiti fits that pattern well.

THE BANK AND THE DICTATORSHIPS IN HAITI, 1971–1990

By all measures, Haiti would have to be considered one of those "loser" states that didn't live up to the expectations of the Washington Consensus even though the World Bank classified it among the "more globalized" countries that followed bank policies, opened up to foreign capital and the world market, and had increased trade to GDP from the 1970s to the 1990s. Haiti, as is repeatedly stated in official and public reports and the media, is the poorest country in the Western Hemisphere, and one of the poorest in the world. In 2000 its per capita income was $480, and two-thirds of its nearly 8 million people lived below the poverty level. Half of its adult population was illiterate; less than one-quarter of rural children received a primary education. Half the population lacked access to health services, and less than 40 percent had access to safe drinking water. The economy has stagnated or declined during the past sixteen years.

The World Bank blames Haiti's internal factors, and not the combination of those factors and the policies it and the other IFIS encouraged Haiti to adopt since 1971, as being primarily responsible for its failure to develop. Poor insti-

tutions and poor governance now top the bank's list as the "greatest impediment to effective development assistance. . . . Without fundamental reforms to
the political and institutional obstacles to progress, no other reforms, however
important in their own right, will work."[8] In particular, the bank identified the
following factors as the primary causes of the country's poor economic performance: the "low intensity conflict" that has caused political and economic
paralysis since 1991;[9] the lack of public-sector capacity for aid absorption; the
disappearance of many of the institutions that existed under the Duvalier regime; the brain drain that has depleted the ranks of professionals and techni-
cians; the failure to decentralize and offer financial support to public institutions and to secure political support from the center; and the absence of public
financial accountability and oversight of public spending by parliament, which
has encouraged corruption, and the misuse and misallocation of government
expenditures and external funding for public-sector projects.

But the World Bank did not always explain Haiti's poor economic performance in these terms. Indeed, the bank believed that the Duvalier and post-
Duvalier military dictatorships could and did achieve rapid economic growth
when they followed the "right" policies considered essential at the time, without their having implemented political reforms, having been transparent or
accountable to the elected representatives of the people in parliament, or having tolerated the existence of a vibrant civil society that participated in public
affairs and challenged public authorities.

The following summary of the performance of the Haitian economy from
the 1970s to 1990, drawn largely from bank reports, tells the story. When "Baby
Doc" Jean-Claude Duvalier inherited the "presidency-for-life" from his father in 1971, the United States, the World Bank, the IMF, and the IDB (Inter-
American Development Bank) committed themselves to supporting the regime. The young dictator was determined to preserve the corrupt practices and
repressive apparatuses of the predatory state system his father had instituted.[10]
Although it never broached the subject of political reforms, that is, democratization, and human rights violations, that is, social justice, the World Bank
repeatedly admonished the government to undertake budgetary reforms to
curb "waste and expenditure that would not stand scrutiny," and "unidentified
recurrent expenditure, especially 'Special Obligations' and 'sans justification'
budget lines," and to use the misused and misappropriated funds for development.

But the regime was committed to the free-market system and was pro–
United States. Haiti was seen as an "open" economy with a fully convertible
currency and no controls on foreign-capital flows and foreign-exchange move-

ments. Moreover, the regime was receptive to the development strategy recommended by the United States and the bank, and willing to offer all the
necessary advantages to foreign, mainly U.S., investors. In short, the regime
created a climate the bank thought favored economic growth. In 1981 Ernest
Preeg, U.S. ambassador to Haiti from 1981 to 1983, boasted "the stage was set
for what was to be the most active period of collaboration between [the] two
governments in at least twenty-five years."[11]

The advantages that especially attracted foreign investors to Haiti consisted
primarily of an abundant supply of unskilled and cheap but "dexterous, and
relatively non-militant" labor; close proximity to the U.S. market; no foreign-
exchange controls and free circulation of the U.S. dollar; absence of government interference; tax incentives with exemptions on income and profit taxes;
and tariff exemptions on imported raw materials, machinery, or other assets
used in the operation of the assembly industries, as well as on the export of
the assembled products. Even though the gap between the wages of Haitians
and workers in other countries in the region was high enough to offset transportation, tariff, and other costs, "[it] may not be able to offset the bureaucratic
and political risks in Haiti which [were] still perceived as formidable. Thus
assembly industry may be lost if wages [rose] to higher levels, [even if they re-
mained] below those of relevant international competitors."[12] In other words,
unless workers' demands for higher wages, better working conditions, and
the right to form independent unions to engage in collective bargaining were
suppressed, foreign investors would simply move their operations elsewhere.
As the World Bank recognized implicitly in its analysis of the current phase
of globalization, with an abundant and untapped supply of cheap labor in the
"loser" countries of the Third World, foreign capital from the core countries
has a great deal of leverage on its side to compel governments desperate for
foreign investments to offer the maximum advantage to the latter.

With significant infusion of foreign financial and technical assistance for
public-sector and infrastructure expenditures and foreign investments in the
subcontracting export assembly industries, the Haitian economy experienced
rapid economic growth between 1970 and 1977. Real GDP grew at an annual
rate of 4.1 percent during that period, in contrast to the 1960s when the economy stagnated; and the assembly industry, construction, and public utilities
emerged as the most dynamic sectors. Substantial increases in coffee prices
during that time also benefited Haitian coffee exports and contributed to the
GDP growth as well. Overall, however, the agricultural sector, which employed
about 74 percent of the labor force during that period, remained weak. Even
though domestic crop production increased at an annual average rate of 2.2

percent during the period, this was not enough to meet the growing demand for food and to increase exports. Consequently food imports rose significantly during that period and worsened Haiti's foreign-trade balance. Haiti's total exports paid for only 75 percent of imports. Industrial growth averaged 7 percent per year during that period—compared with an average of 0.6 percent per year during the 1960s—and contributed about 13 percent to GDP in 1977. By the end of the 1970s, assembly exports accounted for about 25 percent of all the income generated in the manufacturing sector and about the same proportion of Haiti's export earnings; and it employed 80 percent of the industrial work force. That 80 percent of the work force, however, represented only about 6 to 7 percent of the total labor force; thus it had a limited impact on the underestimated 38 percent rate of unemployment of the active labor force during that time period.

Despite the optimistic predictions of the proponents of the export assembly strategy, it had a short-lived "golden age" of expansion between 1970 and the early 1980s, and began to decline after 1984. The World Bank gave most of the reasons why. In addition to not solving the unemployment crisis, the assembly industry had at best a neutral effect on income distribution, and also a negative effect on the balance of goods and services, because it encouraged more imports of consumer goods. The industry also contributed little to government revenues because of the tax exemptions on profits and other fiscal incentives, which, along with the subsidized costs of public services and utilities, represented a transfer to the foreign investors and the Haitian entrepreneurs who subcontracted with them for the operation of the assembly industries. Other than construction and services (transportation and catering services), the assembly industry did not contribute to the expansion of other industrial sectors because it imported its raw materials and other industrial inputs rather than relying on domestic supplies; and its products were not used by other Haitian industries but exported to the United States.

The processing industry was entirely dependent on the U.S. market for its products because it relied on contracts from U.S. firms. Thus, when the limits on U.S. import quotas were met, or if demand decreased, the industry could not expand its production. Because the assembly industry relied almost exclusively on unskilled and cheap labor, it neither stimulated the growth of a skilled industrial labor force nor attracted more advanced capital-intensive industries, thereby discouraging the transfer of technologies and the development of new industrial sectors. Lastly, the assembly industry drained more foreign exchange than it brought in. It did this in two ways. First, most of the profits of the foreign investors were not reinvested in that sector, and the absence of expanded investment opportunities led Haitian entrepreneurs—involved in the assembly industries and other sectors of the economy—to invest their savings outside of Haiti, most often in U.S. real estate. Second, the import of consumer and producer goods (intermediate and capital goods) surpassed the total exports of the modern industrial sector, thereby draining foreign exchange from the economy.

In light of its own analysis, then, the World Bank could not but conclude that the "impact that industry [both the foreign assembly industry and the smaller domestic industrial sector] has had on the development of the economy as a whole has remained limited. Even [in the years when the expansion of the assembly industry] was particularly marked, little of this dynamism trickled down to other sectors."[13] The bank reached that conclusion before the assembly industry went into decline after 1984; since then, it has not reached the level of employment or percentage of GDP of the 1970s. Whereas in 1977 the assembly industry contributed 13 percent of GDP, in 2000 it represented only 7.1 percent.

This fact and the bank's own assessment of the negative effects of the processing industry on the overall economy notwithstanding, it continued to advocate the export assembly strategy until such time that Haiti could develop its agriculture, expand its infrastructure, educate its labor force, and diversify its industrial structure. But the experience of the period under consideration and the bank's own data contradicted this optimistic expectation. Despite the importance of agriculture to the economy, it received an average of 9.7 percent of public investments between 1972 and 1976; education received 5.2 percent; and health received 6.7 percent. In other words, the bank was well aware even then that the dictatorship and the tiny wealthy Haitian elite—that is, the predatory state system—it was fully supporting had a long tradition of enriching themselves by appropriating all they could from the population while providing few essential services or creating the conditions for sustainable human development in return. By 1976 the bank recognized that Haiti's income distribution had become extremely skewed. Seventy-five percent of the population lived in conditions of absolute poverty. Average per capita national income was about $190, but more than 60 percent of the population received an annual income of around $60. At the upper end of the income distribution curve, however, about 5 percent of the population appropriated more than 50 percent of the national income, and the average per capita income of the highest income bracket comprising less than 1 percent of the population was 176 times as high as the lowest bracket comprising about 61 percent of the population. By 2002 the polarization between the dominant class and the rest of the population was even larger. There was even a growing disparity among the wealthier sectors of the population: whereas 4 percent of the population possessed 66 percent of all assets in the country, 1 percent appropriated more than 50 percent of the national income in contrast to the situation in the 1970s. At the other end of the class structure, 70 percent of the population possessed about 20 percent of revenues.

The industrial sector was not the only sector of the economy that failed to generate sustainable development in response to the bank's export-oriented strategy. Its liberalization policies had equally devastating effects on Haitian agriculture. In 1985 the agricultural sector employed about 65 percent of the active population and accounted for about 35 percent of the GDP. Between 1986 and 1988, the governments (three military and one quasi-civilian) that succeeded the thirty-year-old Duvalier dictatorship implemented a series of reforms that dealt with fiscal management and taxes, import and export tariffs, public spending, the public enterprises, price fixing and price controls, free-market competition, and inducements to investments. At the same time that government spending was reduced, taxes on basic consumer goods were lowered, as were their prices. Income taxes were modified; import taxes were replaced with ad valorem taxes; quantitative restrictions on most imports were eliminated; and subsidies to and protection of domestic import-substitution industries were limited to encourage free-market prices and competition. Taxes on the export of coffee and other agricultural products were gradually lowered or completely eliminated. And two unprofitable industrial public enterprises were closed and others were streamlined.

As a result of these measures, the economy showed signs of modest growth in real GDP; internal and external imbalances were reduced, as was inflation, and employment rates grew at 1.6 percent per year. But by mid-1987 the economy experienced a downturn and continued to deteriorate until 1990. Despite evidence to the contrary, the World Bank believed that the reforms being pursued by the military dictatorships would have led to higher GDP growth rates in all sectors, including agriculture, had it not been for the negative effects of the political unrest and contraband imports on domestic agricultural prices.

The "political unrest" the bank alluded to but did not specify was the popular democratic movement the military tried to suppress unsuccessfully between 1986 and 1990 and that culminated in the election of Jean-Bertrand Aristide to the presidency in November 1990 despite strong U.S. opposition. By blaming these "historical events" for aborting the beneficial effects of the reforms of 1986–87, the bank seemed to suggest that the democracy movement interfered with the military governments' efforts to provide "a reasonable framework for economic development." Thus, even though the bank had developed the concept of "good governance" in 1989, and linked it to its concerns with institutional reforms and public-sector management in the 1980s, it was not yet ready to argue in 1991 that the post-Duvalier military dictatorships in Haiti and their predatory characteristics were incompatible with sound economic policies.

If the World Bank avoided equating "good governance" and democracy with sound economic policies in the late 1980s in Haiti, it also disregarded other evidence that the trade and other reforms adopted by the military regimes had devastating effects on Haitian agriculture and did not lead to a rebounding of the export processing industry. There is no doubt that the illicit trade in consumer goods in which government and military officials participated hurt domestic food production. But the lowering or removal of the protective tariffs that accompanied the first set of structural adjustment reforms implemented in 1986 were also detrimental. Haitian rice farmers, for example, were especially hard hit by the trade liberalization measures. The Haitian market soon became flooded with subsidized "Miami rice" that sold for less than the rice produced in Haiti. As a result, household rice consumption doubled and domestic rice production fell steadily to the point that by 1995 Haitian farmers produced only about 50 percent of domestic needs. Rice imported from the United States made up the difference. In 1984 Haiti imported 5,000 metric tons (MT) of rice from the United States, but by 1995 the level reached nearly 200,000 MT, thereby making Haiti the highest per capita consumer of rice in the Western Hemisphere. Equally as significant was the fact that a single U.S. rice corporation, in partnership with a Haitian subsidiary, had a monopoly on rice imports.[14]

Other domestic food crops suffered the same fate as rice. As other imports became known in the market, and sold for less than crops produced locally, such as corn and other cereals, tubers, and vegetables, they altered the tastes and consumption patterns of Haitian consumers to the detriment of domestic producers of those crops. At the same time, a policy urged by the U.S. Agency for International Development (AID) and adopted by the Duvalier regime in the early 1980s in response to the African swine fever that entered Haiti from the Dominican Republic virtually wiped out the domestic pig population. With funds from U.S. agricultural interest groups, the Haitian government slaughtered more than 1 million Haitian pigs valued at $600 million, thereby dealing a deadly blow to Haitian farmers who historically relied on pigs as a form of savings. The attempt to substitute U.S.-imported pigs to replace the Haitian pig population failed because the former were not suited for conditions in Haiti. Subsequently hundreds of thousands of small Haitian farmers lost their source of income and were uprooted. The consequence of those policies, combined with the erosion of the soil,[15] gradually transformed Haiti into a net importer of foodstuffs. Whereas Haiti imported about 10 percent of its food needs in the 1970s, in 1981 it imported 23 percent of its needs and 42 percent in 1993. Haiti today is the third largest importer of foodstuffs from the United States in the Caribbean.

Until 1990, and disregarding evidence to the contrary, the World Bank believed the Duvalier and post-Duvalier military dictatorships were capable of pursuing the "right" policies and reforms that opened the Haitian economy to foreign investments and markets, stimulated the private sector, and led to real GDP growth, all without having to democratize. According to the bank, it was, in fact, the unfortunate "series of political crises" caused by the democracy movement in the late 1980s that interrupted the path to recovery being pursued by the military dictatorships. As such, it is fair to conclude, as Gerard Schmitz does, that at least until 1990, the "key thing [for the bank] to ask of developing countries was not whether they were democracies or autocracies, but whether they had the governing will and wherewithal to create the 'appropriate policy framework' required to achieve efficient markets and the successful implementation of donor and creditor-mandated economic liberalization programs."[16]

THE WORLD BANK AND THE TRANSITION TO DEMOCRACY

The World Bank initially welcomed the election of Aristide to the presidency in November 1990, seeing it as a "window of opportunity" that could allow the country to "move toward sustained social and economic progress."[17] But that would be the case, the bank argued, only if the government pursued the "right" policies, which by 1991 the bank called the "market-friendly approach to development" in keeping with the prescriptions of the Washington Consensus. For low-income developing countries like Haiti, the bank argued, the state must play a complementary role for the private sector by providing a "stable macroeconomic environment"[18] and be open to trade and market competition, both domestically and internationally. Because the domestic market is too small, the economy must be export-oriented and opened to foreign investments. This argument was simply a rehash of previous bank recommendations, with the only difference being that now the target was the state itself. The objective was to reduce as much as possible the interventionist, regulatory, and protectionist role of the state in the economy and maximize that of the private sector by adopting the standard structural adjustment program. Henceforth, the issue of what to do with the public-sector enterprises became a central focus of the recommended reforms. The bank recommended that some of the nine main public-sector enterprises could be privatized or opened to private participation by selling stocks or shares,[19] whereas others could be streamlined and provided with a better regulatory framework to maintain their efficiency.

Aristide had been elected on a populist and left-of-center platform, however. To maintain the support of his mass base, he espoused an anticapitalist rhetoric and promised to eradicate past injustices, dismantle the predatory and repressive apparatuses of the Duvalierist state, and prioritize the interests of the impoverished masses. At the same time, in order not to alienate the business class whose investments he needed to encourage, Aristide promised to safeguard their property and enter into a partnership with them. Aristide's dual and contradictory discourse succeeded only in alienating the Haitian bourgeoisie, the Duvalierists who had vowed to overthrow him, and the United States, which labeled him a "radical firebrand." Once he assumed power in February 1991, however, other than trying unsuccessfully to raise the daily minimum wage of urban workers in the assembly industries, Aristide pursued an economic program in line with much of the World Bank's and the IMF's structural adjustment policies and reached agreement with them shortly before he was overthrown in September 1991.

It was not until the U.S.-led multinational force returned Aristide to office in October 1994 that the World Bank and the other IFIs began to adopt a tougher attitude toward him.[20] As one of the conditions of his return, Aristide was compelled to accept the Emergency Economic Recovery Program (EERP) devised in Washington by a multinational task force of the IDB, the World Bank, the IMF, and the U.S. AID. The stipulations of the EERP, which became incorporated in the Haitian government's Strategy of Social and Economic Reconstruction (SSER), contained all the elements of the structural adjustment program. But the SSER went further than the bank's recommendations to the Haitian government in 1991 by emphasizing the immediate or partial sale of several public enterprises. Rather than referring to this policy as the privatization of the public enterprises, the government preferred to call it their "democratization" to placate the opponents of the policy. The problem, however, was that Aristide's popular supporters opposed these policies. He blamed his prime minister, Smarck Michel, for the neoliberal policies and forced him to resign in November 1995.

Aristide then replaced Michel with Claudette Werleigh, who was in Michel's cabinet and belonged to the faction in parliament opposed to the neoliberal reforms. Werleigh immediately suspended further implementation of the reforms, especially those concerning the sale of the major public enterprises. Once again Aristide fell out of favor with Washington, and the IFIS responded by halting the delivery of aid money to the government until it resumed the reforms.

Here, then, was the new paradox that confronted the democratically elected governments of Aristide in 1990, René Préval in 1995, and Aristide again in 2000. At the same time that Haiti was embarking on a precarious transition to democracy, its governments were being made more responsive and accountable to international institutions rather than to the people through their elected representatives. Tying the release of foreign aid to the implementation of World Bank and IMF policies, then, not only represented a radical break with the bank's dealings with the dictatorships, but contradicted the bank's equation of democracy with a government that is accountable to the people through their elected representatives. Indeed, the bank was well aware that democracy could be an obstacle to the adoption of its policies if an elected government was more responsive to the needs and interests of the people than to the bank.

The World Bank, then, faced a serious dilemma as it tried to link good governance and liberal democracy with the pursuit of the free-market ideology of the Washington Consensus. As Schmitz argued, if, as a result of widespread popular opposition and antigovernment protests against the adjustment policies in the Third World, governments with domestic democratic legitimacy were to begin to repudiate, rather than enforce, the bank's development model, the unintended consequences of the "crisis of governance" would indeed hit home! The contrast between democracy's appeal and its unreliability (for elite-approved purposes) spells looming trouble for the notion that "good governance"—on terms decided by governing elites in the North for their counterparts in the South—is just the rescue operation that is needed to sustain the dominant economic development model and the "orderly" integration of developing economies into the global capitalist political economy.[21]

This is exactly the situation the World Bank and the IMF faced in Haiti. The bank conceded that in Haiti a "broad spectrum of grassroots organizations and members of parliament" and other factions were "ideologically opposed to structural adjustment," and that sectors of the "economic elite who [benefit] from the lack of appropriate government structures and control (e.g., through large scale tax evasion)" remained "skeptical of the role of donors in the reform process." Consequently, these groups needed "to be convinced of the benefits

of economic reform and a revised role of the state."[22] To convince their opponents, however, the bank and the IMF would blackmail Haiti's lawmakers by
threatening to withhold foreign aid unless they implemented the mandated
reforms.

In 1996 the Haitian parliament was scheduled to debate the government's
economic program for ratification. Uncertain of the outcome of that debate,
the then managing director of the IMF, Michael Camdessus, traveled to Haiti
to sign the agreement reached between the government and the IMF and to
remind the parliamentarians of their responsibility: "President Préval made
[the program] his responsibility," Camdessus declared, and "I have no doubt
that the Haitian people as well as the parliament will do the same. . . . Should
the Haitian people through their representatives reject this program . . . it
will have to accept responsibility for that [decision] . . . [because this would
represent] not only a rejection of the assistance it desperately needs, but also,
of the entire policy of the international community and of President Préval for
Haiti." To reinforce his point, Camdessus warned that, while the $1.2 billion
in foreign aid that the IFIS already promised to Haiti was guaranteed, this aid
stream would not last forever because there were many other demands, and
"there [was] a crisis in international assistance."[23] The members of parliament
got the message and voted for the government's privatization and administrative reform program in September 1996, despite mounting popular opposition. The IMF subsequently released $226 million in foreign aid. That these
practices undermined the democratic legitimacy the World Bank equated with
"good governance" eluded its critical reports on the post-1994 period.

The political climate worsened in 1996 when a major split occurred within
the broad Lavalas Political Platform coalition in power since Aristide's return
in 1994. Tensions between the Organisation Politique Lavalas (OPL) and Aristide's faction increased and reached the point of rupture in November 1996.
The dispute had more to do with the creation of a democratically structured
political party, which Aristide opposed, than with serious ideological differences around the structural adjustment policies. Aristide left the coalition and
formed his own Fanmi Lavalas political party. It became immediately apparent
that the OPL would have difficulty maintaining its majority in parliament. The
April 1997 legislative elections bore this out. The OPL claimed that the Conseil
Électoral Provisoire (CEP; Provisional Electoral Council) rigged the elections
in favor of Aristide's FL candidates, demanded the creation of a new CEP, and
boycotted the second round, which President Préval ultimately canceled.[24] The
Clinton administration, which initially considered the elections "free and fair,"
changed its mind when it realized that the FL had fared well in the first round

and was poised to win enough seats in the second round to have veto power in parliament. In that event it was feared that the FL could bloc the further implementation of the structural adjustment reforms supported by the OPL and Prime Minister Rosny Smarth. The issue for the United States, it must be noted, has never been whether a government was elected in free and fair elections but rather whether that government was willing to defend its policies.

Prime Minister Smarth resigned in June 1997 over the election results and the stalled privatization reforms. Because President Préval had canceled the second round, the OPL, which by then had changed its name to Organisation du Peuple en Lutte (Organization of the People in Struggle) though not its acronym, retained a slight majority in parliament and blocked several attempts to replace Prime Minister Smarth. In January 1999 President Préval refused to renew parliament's term that had expired and ruled by decree until the end of his five-year term in February 2001. The IFIs had suspended the further release of the money earmarked for Haiti pending the resolution of this crisis with the election of a new parliament and president in 2000.

The parliamentary and presidential elections of 2000, however, not only failed to resolve the political crisis; they deepened it. With Aristide assured of winning the presidential election in November, the candidates for his FL party swept the May parliamentary elections as well. As a result, the OPL became a minority party. Soon after the elections, however, the OPL and other non-Lavalas parties formed a new coalition called the Convergence Démocratique (CD) to oppose Aristide and immediately won the support of the United States.[25] The CD declared the entire elections to have been fraudulent, but if its exaggerated and unsubstantiated allegations lacked credibility, it was not so easy to dismiss the charges of irregularities and other malpractices in the electoral process, primarily in the elections for the senate, made by the Organization of American States (OAS). The OAS challenged the illegal method the CEP used to calculate the returns in the senatorial polling that granted a first-round victory to eight FL candidates, who in fact had not received the majority necessary to avoid a second round (50 percent plus one). The OAS insisted on a recount and a second-round vote for the eight seats awarded to FL in the Senate, but the CEP refused. The OAS in turn refused to monitor the second-round elections in July (excluding the contested senate seats) as well as the presidential election in November. Subsequently the United States and the IFIs suspended nearly $600 million in foreign aid and debt relief to Haiti.

The primary reason why the United States and the OAS did not allow the CEP to get away with the malpractices in the 2000 elections was because Aristide's party won them and would have had overwhelming control of both houses of parliament, and also because there was by then an opposition the United States supported.[26] The important point, then, is this. As a result of elections they did not like, both in 1997 and in 2000, the United States, the EU, and the IFIS suspended loans and foreign aid to Haiti. Thus, the suspension of aid was political in the strict sense of the term, based as it was on those entities' disapproval of the political party and president who came to power after these elections. The aid embargo had nothing to do with the Aristide government's rejection of the structural adjustment reforms or "poor governance," since it was denied aid before it became the official government in February 2001. Moreover, even if Aristide and his party in parliament opposed the reforms, it does not follow that they lacked democratic legitimacy as a result. After Aristide assumed power for his second term in 2001, however, his government faced a serious "crisis of governance." But this crisis was due more to the government's abuse of power and repressive practices against its opponents than its opposition to the neoliberal policies.[27] In any case, the post-2000 crisis of the Aristide government occurred after it had already been denied aid. Therefore for the World Bank to use the government's "poor governance" as a justification for denying aid amounts to a post hoc, ergo propter hoc argument.

To make the point differently, consider the attitude of the United States and the IFIS in 1997 when Préval was in power and the parliament was dominated by the OPL. As I already mentioned, the OPL gained a majority in parliament through fraudulent elections in 1995, but the United States and the United Nations still accepted the results because the OPL supported the structural adjustment reforms. The United States and the IFIS offered financial aid to the Préval government until the parliamentary elections of 1997 changed the balance of power in favor of Aristide's Lavalas party. Moreover, even though the United States and the IFIS considered the Préval government legitimate, charges of corruption, abuse of power, and human rights violations abounded, as the World Bank noted in its 1998 report. The real issue, then, is whether a government supports, or can be trusted to implement, the reforms of the Washington Consensus, not how it wins elections or governs.

Despite the charges of "poor governance" and the aid embargo against his government, Aristide had not reversed the "liberalization" of the economy initiated in 1986 by the illegitimate Namphy government and continued after 1994 by him and his successor. As former minister of planning and external cooperation, Marc Bazin, pointed out in his reply to the World Bank in 2001, Haiti has one of the more open and liberal economies in Latin America. The average basic tariff is 5 percent, with no tariff for more than half of the 1,600 tariff positions. The exchange rate system remains flexible and the rate of exchange between the national currency (the gourde) and the U.S. dollar fluctuates freely according to market conditions; and the foreign debt in relation to the GDP is relatively low. Under Préval in 1997 and 1999, respectively, the national flour milling and cement companies were privatized. A joint U.S.-Haitian consortium bought the flour mill, and a Swiss, Colombian, and Haitian consortium obtained a controlling share of the cement company. Other public enterprises that were not fully privatized were opened to foreign participation. Since 1994, under Aristide, the national telephone company signed contracts with U.S. companies like MCI, AT&T, and Sprint to provide services and technology and to share in the lucrative market between Haiti and the United States. As Bazin concluded, "the liberalization effort has taken place virtually without a decent level of external aid and Haiti has paid a very high price for its foray into globalization, given, in particular, the inadequacy of human and physical resources, as reflected in particular in higher unemployment, reduced purchasing power, greater inequalities, and low per capita food production."[28]

Indeed, since the "liberalization" of the economy over the past seventeen years, Haiti has experienced a generalized devaluation of its labor force and marginalization of its economy. Both agriculture and industry have declined, and Haiti's annual average GNP growth rate has been stagnant or negative during the past twenty years. The labor force is largely uneducated and unskilled, and infrastructural development and technical skill in the methods of production remain low. Even though the wages of the mostly women workers in the assembly industries have been kept deliberately low to maintain Haiti's "comparative advantage," the assembly industry has not recovered since it started to decline in 1984. In 1998 that sector employed an estimated 30,000 people (about 70 percent of the peak level in 1986) in the production of textiles, leather goods, electronics, and handicrafts for the U.S. market.

Decreasing agricultural productivity has led to a long-term decline of the cash crops, such as coffee, and a fall in real prices to agricultural producers. Haitian farmers have a low level of savings, and their assets have been devalued. The public sector is anemic. Corruption is widespread. The government has no agricultural or industrial policies. And the basic needs of its citizens in terms of health care, nutrition, education, housing, employment, and income remain unmet. The decline of agriculture and manufacturing production has also led to a shift in the composition of the labor force and of the primary sources of employment in favor of the informal sector. The majority of people who are working now find employment in the informal sector rather than in agriculture, the formal private or manufacturing sector, or the public sector. In

1999, whereas 44.5 percent of the working population, or around 1.2 million people, were engaged in agriculture, 2.8 percent, or 78,000 people were in the formal private sector, 1.3 percent or 36,000 people were in the public sector, and 51.4 percent, or nearly 1.5 million people were in the informal sector. The informal sector, then, now employs around 93 percent of the nonagricultural working population. But because of its low wages and precarious employment conditions, the informal sector is primarily a means of survival rather than an alternative engine of growth for the Haitian economy.

In addition to the decline of agriculture, manufacturing, and public-sector employment and the growth of the informal sector, Haiti has also become a labor-exporting economy increasingly reliant on remittances from Haitian migrants. Haiti has been exporting its labor force since the late 1970s at the same time that it became dependent on the export assembly industries. The stagnation of agriculture and the growth of export industries in Port-au-Prince compelled rural inhabitants to migrate first toward that metropolitan center, which has grown from a city of more than half a million people in 1971 to 720,000 in 1982 and approximately 2 million in 1995. Unable to sustain their lives in the rural or urban areas, increasing numbers of Haitians emigrated, legally or illegally. Emigration has now become a necessary and permanent alternative for increasing numbers of Haitians. It is estimated that more than 1.6 million Haitians (or about 19 percent of the population) now live abroad, with about 800,000 in the United States and Canada, 70,000 in the French overseas territories of the Caribbean, 60,000 in the Bahamas, and about 700,000 in the Dominican Republic.

Migration is not only a safety valve or an alternative to unemployment and poverty. It is also becoming an increasingly important lifeline to the economy itself. The remittances of Haitian emigrants are estimated at between $300 and $600 million per year. Haiti's total exports were valued at $349 million in 1999 and $327 million in 2000, while its imports were valued at just over $1.01 billion and $1.08 billion, respectively. The remittances become even more important if one adds to them other noncash or in-kind transfers such as food, clothing, furniture, appliances, and even cars. As the World Bank notes, however, estimates of remittances may be unreliable because those who receive them may underreport them to avoid paying taxes or becoming targets of theft or to protect the identity of the emigrants who may be living abroad illegally. Whatever the exact amount of remittances, there is little doubt that they are vital to the survival of large numbers of families, as well as sustaining certain economic activities, such as construction and the import and retail sectors.

Insofar as emigration is a self-selective process (except in the case of those who are fleeing persecution), the tendency is not for the very poor to emigrate, but rather those who are marginally better off socially, are experiencing some degree of upward mobility, and whose education and skills are at or above the national average. To the extent that such emigration becomes permanent, it constitutes a drain of skills and important human resources from the country. This explains in part why Haiti is becoming more reliant on the use of foreign personnel and know-how, as seen, for example, in the proliferation of foreign NGOS, to provide essential health, technical, and other social services to the population. Migration also has a gender dimension, which in turn affects households and families. Insofar as men are most likely to emigrate abroad, this has given rise to a higher percentage of female-headed households in the urban areas. Such households now constitute about 36 percent of all households.

The remarkable fact about the current dismal economic picture in Haiti is that neither the Aristide government nor the World Bank and the other IFIs had proposed any solution other than to pursue the same failed policies of the past. Still believing that Haiti's cheap labor was its best asset, the Aristide government and the bank collaborated to expand the export manufacturing industry by linking it with its counterpart in the neighboring Dominican Republic. The World Bank's International Finance Corporation (IFC) approved a $20 million loan to help finance the first of fourteen projected free-trade zones for assembly industries along the border between Haiti and the Dominican Republic, which began operation in August 2003. In addition, with the consent of the U.S. government, the debts of the Dominican Republic to the United States, and those of Haiti to the IDB, would be transferred to the Hispaniola Fund, which was also financing the project.

The World Bank and Dominican manufacturers saw the free-trade zones in Haiti as a very attractive proposition, which allowed them to tap into the much cheaper pool of Haitian workers, who receive a mere $1.25 a day in contrast to the $13 a day paid to Dominican workers. And because the Dominican producers have exceeded their import quotas into the United States, while Haitian textile manufacturers have not, locating the free-trade zones on the Haitian side of the border allowed them to continue to export their products to the United States.

While clearly advantageous to the investors who will benefit from cheap infrastructure, tax exemptions, no restrictions on the repatriation of profits, and the cheapest labor costs in the Caribbean, the free-trade zones will be disastrous for the peasant farmers in the border region of the Maribahoux Plain in the northeast of Haiti, one of the most fertile agricultural regions of the country. The farmers who own or lease the land in the area are being evicted, and neither the compensation the government is offering them nor the prospects of working in the assembly industries will enable them to earn as much as they do now from their farms. It is estimated that the loss of some 1,200 acres to the free-trade zone will cost farmers between $1 million and $2.4 million; and production and earning levels could be even higher if the government provided farmers with better irrigation and access to credit and other agricultural support. Moreover, as with the free-trade zones in the Port-au-Prince area, far from creating enough jobs for the population of the affected area, the new free-trade zones will fuel rural-to-urban migration, and the migration of more Haitians to the Dominican Republic and elsewhere.

The World Bank's participation in the financing of the free-trade zone, then, makes it clear that it had no qualms about working with the Aristide government when it was willing to evict farmers from their land to clear the way for a free-trade zone and guarantee the supply of a cheap labor force and other incentives to foreign and Haitian investors. But it would not authorize loans to that government directly because of its "poor governance." Still, Aristide was determined to win the bank's confidence and was willing to do whatever it took to do so. In June 2003 he signed an agreement with the IMF that obligated Haiti to cut deficit spending, reduce inflation, clear external payment arrears, and monitor spending in public-sector enterprises. This agreement was a precondition for an approximately $200 million loan from the IDB, which the government concluded in July 2003 after nearly depleting its foreign reserves to pay U.S.$35 million in arrears to that bank.

This recent IDB loan, however, did not mean an end to the aid embargo against Aristide. According to IDB president Enrique Iglesias, the resumption of cooperation with the government was linked to concrete political reforms and was "an integral part of the strategy of the international community."[29] And the strategy of the international community has been clear from the start: either to weaken Aristide politically and force him to comply fully with the dictates of the Washington Consensus, or to continue to support the opposition coalition against Aristide whose goal was to remove Aristide from office and replace him with a government more responsive to the interests of the international community.

The second solution is exactly what happened on February 29, 2004, when Aristide was forced from office by an armed insurgency of former members of the Haitian Armed Forces and sent into exile, first to the Central African Republic and now to South Africa. France and the United States supported the insurgents by endorsing the opposition coalition's rejection of a plan proposed by the leaders of the Caribbean Community (CARICOM) that might have resolved the crisis peacefully. The plan, initially approved by the OAS, France, and the United States and immediately accepted by Aristide, called for the appointment of a prime minister from the opposition, the holding of new parliamentary elections, and support for Aristide to serve out the remainder of his term through February 2006. When, as expected, the opposition coalition rejected the plan, France and the United States changed their position, called on Aristide to resign, and refused to deploy peace-keeping forces until a political settlement was reached. As the insurgents advanced toward Port-au-Prince, the United States gave Aristide the choice of either staying and being killed or resigning and leaving the country.

Shortly after Aristide's departure, an interim "government of national unity" was appointed, with Gérard Latortue, a former UN official, as prime minister, and a cabinet of "technocrats" drawn from members of the traditional elite. Prime Minister Latortue showed his debt to and affinity with the rebel forces, several of whom have criminal records, by publicly embracing them as "freedom fighters," and the new interior minister, ex-army general Hérard Abraham, made clear his plans to integrate the rebels who ousted Aristide into the police force and reinstate the army that Aristide disbanded in 1995.[30] And since their victory, the still-armed rebel soldiers have engaged in a systematic persecution and killing of Aristide supporters with impunity from the Latortue government.[31]

Despite having been appointed and not elected to office, its disregard for the rule of law, and its alarming human rights record, the Latortue government received a pledge of $1.08 billion from the United States, Canada, France, and the donor community. The United States offered $230 million over two years, the European Commission $325 million in grants, Canada $112 million, the IDB $260 million in soft loans, and the World Bank $155 million in grants and interest-free loans.[32] CARICOM, thus far, is the only bloc of countries that refuses to recognize the Latortue government on the principle that it lacks democratic legitimacy.

Though not surprising, these developments are yet another indicator that, for institutions like the World Bank, what really matters is not whether a government is democratic, upholds the rule of law, and protects the rights of its citizens, but whether it is acceptable to the United States and willing to abide by the dictates of the Washington Consensus, as is the Latortue government. That, as I have shown, is the real meaning of "good governance," and the political dilemma of most small peripheral states in the contemporary era of globalization.

NOTES

1. World Bank, *Haiti: Country Assistance Strategy*, 1.
2. The U.S. State Department estimates that currently about 8 percent of all cocaine entering the United States from South America passes through Haiti. See Taft-Morales, "Haiti: Issues for Congress," 11–12. Domestic usage of cocaine is very low, but the effects of the clandestine trafficking are evident in increasing violent crimes and killings by armed gangs involved in the drug trade, the corruption of police and government officials, money laundering, and the luxurious life-style of traffickers. See Arthur, "Raising the States," 42–43.
3. Easterly, "The Lost Decade," 138.
4. Easterly et al., "Good Policy or Good Luck?," 460.
5. The actual term "Washington Consensus" was coined by John Williamson in 1989 to refer to the set of "liberalizing policy reforms" that the Washington-based institutions—the World Bank, the IMF, and the IDB—were "addressing" to the countries of Latin America. See Williamson, "What Washington Means by Policy Reform," 7–19.
6. Easterly "The Lost Decade," 135.
7. Naim, "Fads and Fashion in Economic Reforms," 508.
8. World Bank, *Globalization*, 3–4.
9. That is, since the transition to democracy in Haiti: the election and overthrow of Aristide in 1991, the three years of military rule from 1991 to 1994, the return of Aristide in 1994, the conflicts surrounding the parliamentary elections of 1997 and 2000, and the reelection of Aristide in 2000.
10. Dupuy, *Haiti in the World Economy*, 155–85.
11. Preeg, *Haiti and the CBI*, 22.
12. Grunwald, Delatour, and Voltaire, "Offshore Assembly in Haiti," 237–38. See also Dupuy, *Haiti in the World Economy*, 177.
13. World Bank, *Current Economic Position* (1978), 3.
14. Richardson, "Feeding Dependency, Starving Democracy," 5–6; McGowan, "Democracy Undermined, Economic Justice Denied," 24–25.
15. Soil erosion is due in large part to deforestation; a predatory state that invests little in agricultural development; and limited access to credit and other productive inputs by Haiti's small farmers.

16. Schmitz, "Democratization and Demystification," 69.

17. World Bank, *Haiti: Restoration*, 1.

18. World Bank, *World Development Report*, 11–15, 20–23.

19. These include the Ciment d'Haiti (a cement company), the Minoterie d'Haiti (a flour mill), the Telecommunications d'Haiti (telephone company), the Centrale Autonome d'Eau Potable and Société Nationale d'Eau Potable (water companies), the Électricité d'Haiti (electricity company), the Authorité Portuaire Nationale (port authority), the Banque Nationale de Crédit (BNC, National Bank of Credit), and the Banque Populaire Haitienne (BPH, Haitian Popular Bank).

20. The reasons for this are the following. In 1990 Aristide came to office with massive popular support. The United States could not deny the legitimacy of his victory and hence recognized that to undermine or antagonize him overtly could have led to severe social unrest, as was shown by the swift popular reaction to an attempted coup d'état against him in January 1991. By 1994, however, conditions had changed dramatically. Three years of repression under the military junta had decimated the popular organizations that supported Aristide and resisted the military, and Aristide was now beholden to the United States for returning him to office. He was therefore weaker politically and hence could be pressured more to abide by U.S. directives. See Dupuy, *Haiti in the New World Order*, 137–66.

21. Schmitz, "Democratization and Demystification," 70, 72.

22. World Bank, *Haiti: Country Assistance Strategy*, 5–6.

23. Haiti en Marche, "Visite houleuse," 1, 7.

24. It is interesting to note, however, that in 1995 the parties opposed to the broad Lavalas coalition, of which the OPL was then a dominant faction, charged that the then CEP had rigged the elections in favor of the OPL, which gained a majority in parliament. The opposition also boycotted the second round as well.

25. Democratic Convergence is a coalition of twenty-two or so parties and groups of diverse and seemingly incompatible ideologies, ranging from neo-Duvalierist, centrist, religious, and social democratic, to former members of the Lavalas coalition and close allies of Aristide.

26. To underline the double standard, consider the example of Peru, which also held presidential elections in May 2000. The OAS also observed and detected widespread fraud in that election, which denied an outright victory to opposition candidate Alejandro Toledo against incumbent President Alberto Fujimori. As in Haiti, the OAS refused to monitor the second round in Peru. But unlike in Haiti, the United States and the OAS accepted the results and approved Fujimori as the winner. The difference between Peru and Haiti is that in Peru there was a president with autocratic tendencies who supported the free-trade policies and war on drugs of the United States, whereas in Haiti there was a president with autocratic tendencies whom the United States disliked and distrusted. The former could get away with fraud; the latter didn't have a chance. The political paralysis caused by the dis-

pute over the May 2000 senatorial elections remains unresolved, and so does the suspension of foreign aid.

27. Since his overthrow in 1991, Aristide's aim was to win and maintain power by weakening his opponents as much as possible. Also fearing a return of the Haitian military he disbanded in 1994, or an independent police force that could act against him, Aristide sought to monopolize the means of violence as well. To that end, he decided to politicize and control the police force and to maintain a popular base of support he could call on when necessary to intimidate his opponents. As such, he failed to take an unconditional stance against acts of violence carried out in his name by his popular supporters and armed gangs against his opponents. His government interfered with judicial authorities and the police to investigate, arrest, and prosecute the perpetrators of acts of violence and human rights violations. Aristide, in other words, feared a genuine democracy and independent branches of government that exercised checks and balances on his authority. Governing without an effective opposition and checks and balances, however, opened the door to abuses of power and widespread corruption by government officials, and facilitated the emergence of rival factions and power struggles within the governing party itself. Under such conditions, responsible, accountable, and effective government became impossible. Thus, despite his promise to "democratize democracy," and to bring transparency, honesty, and an end to impunity, his government continued the predatory practices of his predecessors. See Dupuy, "Haiti: Social Crisis and Population Displacement."

28. Bazin, "Government Comments (B): English Version," 70–71. It is worth noting that Bazin, a former bank official, was a presidential candidate supported by the United States in the election of 1990 that Aristide won. He also served as de facto prime minister from June 1992 to June 1993 under the military junta that had overthrown Aristide.

29. AlterPresse, "BID/Haiti: Reprise de la cooperation."

30. Among those with criminal convictions are Louis Jodel Chamblain, a former leader of the paramilitary organization Front for the Advancement and Progress of Haiti (FRAPH) that was responsible for many human rights violations and the death of thousands of Aristide supporters during the three-year exile of Aristide between 1991 and 1994. In 1995, Chamblain and thirteen others were convicted in absentia in 1993 for the murder of Antoine Izméry, a well-known Aristide supporter, and for his implication of a massacre of Aristide supporters in Raboteau in 1994. Another rebel fighter, Jackson Joanis, was also convicted in absentia for the Izméry murder. Recently both Chamblain and Joanis, who had voluntarily turned themselves in to the police, were acquitted in a hasty trial held in the middle of the night that many human rights organizations, including Amnesty International, called a sham and a travesty of justice. Moreover, Justice Minister Bernard Gousse indicated that the government might pardon Chamblain for any other convictions because of "his

great service to the nation." See Villelabeitia and Delva, "Haiti to Integrate Rebels"; Amnesty International, "Haiti: Chamblain and Joanis Overnight Trials"; Council on Hemispheric Affairs, "Travesty of Justice in Haiti."

31. Institute for Justice and Democracy in Haiti, "Human Rights Violations"; "Human Rights Update."

32. Marquis, "$1 Billion Is Pledged."

PART TWO

Diasporas in a Global World

One consequence of migration has been the establishment of diaspora communities with organic reciprocal ties between the host countries and the sending societies. Influences flow back and forth between the two societies but they often get catalyzed in transit obscuring the precise sources of innovation.

According to Antonio Benítez-Rojo, Havana has been a site of globalizing tendencies for centuries. As the locale where imported cultures as well as local music, literature, and art fuse to form uniquely Cuban and Caribbean forms, over the years the port city has shown a remarkable resilience to predictable con-formity that, according to him, has subverted foreign and domestic attempts to impose any new order. Even the revolutionary Cuban government of Fidel Castro has been forced to compromise with the unusual qualities that make Havana a singular Caribbean case of combining innovation with tradition.

Puerto Rico constitutes an interesting crossroads where the global and the local clash with intriguingly unpredictable results. "Showing Face" by Frances Negrón-Muntaner discusses the complex ways in which sports may delimit national loyalties, even as those terms are being actively defined and articulated by people simultaneously constructing national pride and political cohesion. The complexity is further exacerbated by the twin passions of colonialism and race in Puerto Rico and highlighted most clearly in perhaps that most passionate of island sports, boxing.

Juan Flores puts forward two related arguments about contemporary Caribbean culture and identity within the cauldron of globalization. The first is that the most active site for contemporary Caribbean creolization and intercultural entanglements can be found, not so much within the region but rather among the large transnational diasporic communities dwelling in the large global cities abroad. The second argument is that many of the creolized cultural forms and values adopted through social interactions in the diaspora travel back to the home territories through return migration or the media. Issues of race, gender, and class relations, in particular, resurface in new ways within the local national population as a sort of "cultural remittance," with profound effect on the conceptualization as well as commodification of national cultures and traditions.

This reconceptualization and commodification is sharply and richly detailed in Raquel Romberg's "Glocal Spirituality." Within the long tradition of globalization in the Caribbean, and especially in Puerto Rico, varied and eclectic adaptations have been the norm among folk religions. Nevertheless, with the end of the hegemony of Catholic beliefs, folk religions have entered a new transnational arena of ritual experimentation and eclecticism conditioned by widening market forces. The production of essential ethnic identities for local as well as global consumption has resulted in the revitalization of vernacular religious practices in a strikingly subtle process that the author describes as "glocalization." Using the practices of brujos (witch-healers) in Puerto Rico, her ethnographic account deftly explores the relations between practitioners, clients, and suppliers of ritual goods. It meticulously details the interesting ways in which the entrepreneurial aspect of this spirituality leads to a strategic integration of transnational deities; healing and magic rituals are constantly valorized and revalorized consistent with, rather than in opposition to, mainstream consumer and multicultural ideologies. In these cases, the local and the global proceed in perfect harmony and reciprocal well-being.

Creolization in Havana:
The Oldest Form of Globalization

ANTONIO BENÍTEZ-ROJO, translated by JAMES MARANISS

The mayor of Havana, with a letter dated January 30, 1937, wrote to the ethnographer Fernando Ortiz, president of the Society of Afro-Cuban Studies, asking what he thought about the possible reappearance of Afro-Cuban *comparsas* (floats) at carnival time. Although these music and dance groups had been banned from processions for more than twenty years, the Municipal Department of Tourism's Advisory Commission had recommended their return. In light of the widespread poverty that the world depression had brought to Cuba, and which the deflated price for sugar had exacerbated, the commission's members were recalling the dollars spent by tourists in past carnivals, where *comparsas* had figured among the chief attractions.

In 1912, when the Florida train reached Key West and Henry Flagler decked Miami out with luxury hotels, orchestras, golf courses, polo grounds, and tennis courts, Havana's destiny as one of the North-South tourist system's preferred venues, with the winter as its peak season, began to be realized. The Panama Canal, opened in 1914, turned Havana into a port of call for interoceanic shipping. The First World War (1914–18) also contributed to the city's development; fear of German submarines and Europe's war climate provoked a shift in North American transatlantic tourism away from Europe and toward Florida, the Caribbean, and Latin America. In addition, the high prices that sugar was then bringing allowed the Cuban government to modernize the island's infrastructure, particularly Havana's. In the 1920s, as a group of international entrepreneurs was constructing all kinds of tourist attractions in Havana and its environs, including beaches and night clubs, the city was linked to the United States by no fewer than twenty steamships per week, by the "flying boats" of Aeromarine Airways, and by the ferry from Key West, which would unload dozens of cars on the docks after a crossing of only a few hours.[1] By that time, the tourist guides and brochures painted Havana as a place of palm trees, music, and rum cocktails (particularly attractive during Prohibition in the United States). Still, there was a need to offer tourists a cultural destination, something spectacular and exotic, and nothing was to meet this need better than a revival of the Afro-Cuban *comparsas* with their street processions.

In his response, Ortiz endorsed the *comparsas'* return for more than just the purposes of tourism: "The *comparsas* do not belong to the blacks, nor to the whites, nor to the *mestizos*. They bring together all the colors and traditions accumulated in our people. If there were one ethnic category that I might put them in, it could only be mulatto, not because they are composed precisely of people of color, but rather because of the profuse heterogeneity of the ethnic contributions that make them up."[2] The parade of Afro-Cuban *comparsas* in the 1937 Havana carnival helped to make those festivities a huge tourist attraction. Seven cruise ships docked at Havana, carrying more than 16,000 visitors from the United States and Europe.[3] The celebration lasted twenty-two days and gave a meaningful economic boost to the city. Of course, this case is just one example among many of Havana's culture and its long-standing relation to tourism.

HAVANA DURING ITS FIRST TWO CENTURIES

The first report we have of dancing in the streets of Cuba dates from the year 1570, when the municipal government of the town of Havana—not to be called a city until 1592—made a deal with one Pedro Castillo to organize, for the feast of Corpus Christi, "a dance, and to help with the expenses His Grace the Governor will give . . . a half dozen ducados."[4] The modest spectacle must have pleased the town authorities, because three years later they ordered the free blacks to meet with Castillo and to work with him in his "inventions." The Corpus Christi celebrations grew more complex in the years that followed: in 1597 the town council asked for "dances and interludes," while in the churches there were black women who sang accompanied by percussion instruments. Thanks to this report, we know today that in the last quarter of the sixteenth century there began to develop in Havana a creolized culture that included elements originating in both Europe and Africa, negotiated within the relations of power and resistance present in that early society.

These manifestations, on being exported from Havana to Seville, would inform dances that were quite popular, called *zarabanda, retambo, yeyé, para-cumbé, zambapalo, gurrumbé, cachumba,* and, above all, the *chacona,* which is mentioned in the works of Cervantes, Quevedo, and Lope de Vega. The variety of these names can be explained by the ethnic differences present in both Havana and Seville in the sixteenth century, which made for the coexistence of different creolized rhythms and dances. A document from 1552 naming a total of 271 men in Havana capable of taking up arms listed 159 Spaniards, 25 blacks, 39 Indians, 4 mulattoes, 23 mestizos, 19 Portuguese, a Flem, and a Frenchman. Given the list's military purpose, it did not include the names of African slaves or Canary Islander immigrants; nor did it include the names of women and children, among whom there were many people of color. For example, during the last quarter of the sixteenth century, 6 of the 18 women to receive land for housing construction were black.[5] This land was given by the municipal government with the proviso that it would contribute, with the rental of one or more rooms in the house, to the lodging of the many travelers who, since the decade of the 1560s, were stopping in the city because of the colonial trade regulations.

Havana, situated a few miles from the Gulf Stream and on the Florida Strait, was the ideal port for the Spanish convoys (*flotas*) to resupply ships with water, food, and firewood, as well as to make repairs and to board crew and last-minute passengers before making the trip to Seville. And its bay, wide and deep, whose entrance had the shape of a bottleneck, was relatively easy to defend and offered protection from the corsairs and pirates who marauded along the route of the Spanish galleons. In light of these considerations, it was commanded, in 1543, that ships trading in the Indies were to come together in Havana to return in a single convoy. Following other complementary regulations, the definitive system of *flotas* and *armadas* (warships to defend the convoys and patrol the waters of the Caribbean) was in operation by 1561, with recognition of Havana's strategic importance and confirming it as the place of assembly for the *flotas*. If Santiago de Cuba would indeed continue to be the island's capital until 1607, the requirement made in 1553 that all governors should reside in Havana identified this bustling port town as the de facto capital.

The *flotas* had a tremendous impact on the local economy. Given that the first convoy had to await the arrival of the second before it could sail home, the city enjoyed a true tourist bonanza every year. This could extend from a period of one month (preferably May or June) to several months, since it was forbidden to sail during the hurricane season and also when there was known presence of privateers in the waters of the Atlantic. For example, in the period

1591–95 the Mexican convoy stayed in the port for an average of 130 days, and the one from Cartagena for 111 days. In 1594 the people of Havana had to provide lodging, food, drink, and entertainment with song and dance for seven months to the 5,000 people who visited in the two *flotas*, many of whom had sufficient means for the enjoyment of the pleasures that the city then offered. Thanks to this early tourism, the surrounding lands began to be developed, being used for the production of cattle, hogs, and chickens and the cultivation of fruits and vegetables, among them the native *yuca* (or cassava) for the making of cassava bread.[6]

Nevertheless, the stay of thousands of idle travelers fostered robbery and speculation, as well as the growth of social vices such as gambling, prostitution, and drunkenness. Soon the city was to be characterized as a site of licentious customs. As it was the final port on the Spanish main, soldiers deserted there, and delinquents and people sentenced to exile, including priests, sought refuge.[7] Furthermore, considering that passengers and crew were not subject to the local law but rather to that of the captain general of the fleet, they committed all kinds of misdemeanors that generally went unpunished. The oldest gravestone to have been conserved in Havana indicates that it was not rare for blood to flow. Its inscription, translated from the Latin, reads: "Here died Doña María Cepero, shot accidentally by harquebus the year 1557."

Given that the regulations stipulated that in the cases of long stays the ships should transfer their most valuable cargoes to secure places, the fortification of Havana became an imperative, above all if one takes into account that the port had been sacked by pirates more than once.[8] It was decided then to build the La Fuerza fortress (1558–77), the first stone military edifice in America; later, to protect the entrance to the bay, the fortresses of El Morro (1589–1610) and La Punta (1589–1600) were constructed, along with some lookout towers along the coast. The shipbuilding industry was developed, too, because the defensive system included armed fleets capable of patrolling and attacking enemy ships. The completion in 1592 of an important aqueduct taking water from the Chorrera (now the Almendares) River, benefited not only the people of Havana but also the ships of the *flotas*, who could take on fresh water at a fountain in the city. It was the first public work of its kind and magnitude to be built by Europeans in America. With the end of the sixteenth century there were concentrated in Havana and its environs between 7,000 and 10,000 inhabitants, approximately half of the total population of Cuba. In this epoch the sugar industry began to develop in the city's outskirts, which was called on to become the island's principal source of enrichment. If Havana then was indeed a slovenly urban nucleus with a few stone buildings, some of the dynamics of its transformation into a big city were coming into play.

HAVANA IN THE EIGHTEENTH CENTURY

The Havana of the 1770s, with more than 40,000 inhabitants and more in its hinterland, was the largest port city in the Spanish American colonies, and, barely surpassed by Philadelphia, the second largest in the hemisphere. Its diversified economy had its foundation in the exporting of tobacco, sugar, and hides; in the building of warships (it had the best shipyard in the Spanish empire); in the maintenance of fortifications, fleets, and military garrisons; and in cattle raising and farming of the adjacent lands, which served the city's inhabitants as well as the crews of the many merchant ships and men of war that anchored in the harbor. Further, Havana's economy was generously subsidized by the so-called *situados* (or subsidies) of Mexico, which in times of war would raise several million pesos. The English occupation of Havana (1762–63) during the Seven Years' War accelerated the already established tendency toward the growth of the slave plantation. Beginning in 1791, as a consequence of the great slave rebellion in Saint Domingue and the destruction of its plantations, the price of sugar went up extraordinarily. The Havana plantation owners took advantage of this situation to get the Crown to grant them a series of privileges that would favor development of the sugar industry, including the free importation of slaves—hence the tripling of sugar exports between 1792 and 1799.

All during the eighteenth century the local culture grew more cosmopolitan as the population came into close contact with thousands of French, English, and U.S. visitors. By virtue of the Bourbon alliance between France and Spain, Havana lived in a period of economic growth in which French commerce played an essential role; furthermore, ever since the War of Spanish Succession, French warships had been visiting the city, sometimes for several months. Keep in mind also that the people of Havana lodged and fed the English occupying troops for almost a year, a time in which the moneyed class danced the reel, the minuet, and the country dance for the first time. As for the U.S. visitors, in the century's last decade an active commerce began between Havana and cities in the United States. For example, in the period 1797–99 more than 150 ships from Philadelphia visited Havana.[9]

However, as the city opened itself up to Western culture, it was penetrated also by African cultures thanks to a continual growth of the slave trade. It is enough to say that the total population of color almost equaled the white. In 1792 the slaves of the region (city and hinterland) added up to more that 40,000 and the population of free blacks and mulattoes to more than 16,000. Cultural negotiation was effected on several levels of society. For example, there had existed ever since the preceding century a militia of blacks and mulattoes formed into two battalions, who made up the nucleus of a petite bourgeoisie of color. On a lower social level there were the so-called *cabildos de negros* (Negro guilds), religious and mutual aid associations that were organized according to their members' African nation of origin. The *cabildos* bore names representative of their different nations, such as Congo Real, Apapá, Mandinga, Arará, Lucumí, Carabalí, Mina Popó, and others. Almost all of them owned the houses where their meetings, dances, and songs, in which women participated, were held. The fact that there were saints' altars in them indicates already a religious syncretism that, with time, would be known as *santería*. The *cabildos* kept musical instruments and costumes that, to the degree possible, resembled those used in Africa; both were taken out into the streets on festive days on which processions were authorized. This is the origin of the Afro-Cuban *comparsas*.

Considering that the *cabildo* members had to contribute money to the associations' coffers, we may suppose that they must have been made up primarily of freedmen—that is, people who earned their living as masons, stevedores, carpenters, shoemakers, tailors, seamstresses, cooks, or washerwomen. Nevertheless, there was one day of the year on which slaves were allowed to participate in the associations' *comparsas*; that day was January 6, the date of the Epiphany or the Adoration of the Three Kings, which in the Hispanic world is known as Día de Reyes. And so, on this magical day, the slave would go in the morning to a *cabildo* that represented his nation. The procession would begin in front of the governor's palace, where money was given out. Afterward, each *comparsa*, playing its drums and instruments, singing its own songs and dancing its own dances, went along in a noisy celebration that had as its setting the streets of Havana and ceased only at nightfall. This great Afro-Cuban festival won the admiration of painters and engravers, local and foreign writers, musicians and poets.

There can be no doubt that Havana in the eighteenth century was already a city of rhythms and dances that had been substantially creolized. This was aided by the existence of so many feast days (Sundays and other civic and religious festivals) having the participation of the Negro guilds, particularly on the dates of Corpus Christi, Saint Christopher (the city's patron saint), and Saint John, Saint Peter, Saint Dominic, and Saint James. Further, it was the custom in the Spanish Empire to celebrate a famous military victory, the signing of a peace treaty, the advent of a new king, a local wedding, or the birth of a prince with a holiday. Other popular centers of cultural interchange among whites, blacks, and foreigners were the gambling houses and those that offered cock-fights. The number of each of these was so great that in 1742 the chief of police was charged with inspecting even the suburban farms for "swindlers, thieves and anyone who might commit crimes such as illegal commerce with foreigners."[10]

Still, above and beyond gambling and other vices, music and dance were the principal entertainments that Havana offered the traveler. In 1798 the chronicler Buenaventura Ferrer estimated that the city had some fifty balls per day. Many of them were advertised in the *Papel Periódico* (Havana's daily newspaper) and their variety reflected the cosmopolitan nature of the city. With the inauguration of the Teatro Principal hall (1776), where the opera *Dido Abandonada* was sung, there began to develop, in the social elite, a taste for theatrical activities, among them comedies, tragedies, operas, operettas, dance performances, and concerts.[11] At the same time, in the *cabildos* blacks danced and sang, to the rhythm of drumbeats, the *Piqui piquimbín* or *Engó teraneme* or *Cángala lagontó*, and in the gambling houses and brothels they danced the *chuchumbé*, a creolized dance that can be taken as an antecedent of the *rumba*. Also, on the Día de Reyes slaves danced the famous pantomime called *matar la culebra* (to kill the snake). This dance and its different songs, in addition to awakening the interest of many visitors, would influence the works of Nicolás Guillén, Alejo Carpentier, and José Lezama Lima. However, the big musical development would occur at the end of the century. With the arrival of tens of thousands of Frenchmen and creoles fleeing the revolution in Saint Domingue, popular music would be influenced by that of the neighboring island. Thus, with the arrival of the *contredance*, already creolized by African rhythms, there would come the *contradanza*, danced by blacks and whites, now a part of the national culture of Cuba.

SLAVE SOCIETY, MODERNITY, AND ENLIGHTENED VISITORS

A century can shorten or lengthen itself in several ways, all of them arbitrary. From the sociological point of view, I think that the nineteenth century in Cuba ended in 1886, the year in which the slave system was abolished.[12] In addition, the date marks the beginning of a new kind of campaign, the Negro's fight for social and cultural equality.

Until then the island's society—and particularly Havana's—had lived with a great contradiction: on the social level, the obsolete nature of slavery; on the scientific and technological level, the rapid utilization of the advances that, with the Industrial Revolution well established, the modern world was offering. And so slavery in Havana coexisted with these advances: the MacAdam road paving system, 1818; the steamship line between Havana and Matanzas, 1819; the steamship line linking Havana to New Orleans, circa 1820; the great urban reforms begun under the government of general Tacón, 1834–38; the rail service between Havana and Bejucal, 1837; ferry service between Havana and Regla, 1837; the Almendares, the first Cuban steamship, circa 1840; the public gaslight system, 1848; the inauguration of telegraph service, 1851; public bus service using animal power, 1862; construction of the modern aqueduct at Albear, 1874–93; telephone service, 1881. Outside the city, toward the south, the west, and above all the east, the sugar industry had extended as it modernized. In 1864, of the 1,318 sugar mills in Cuba, 889 operated with steam energy and 64 were mechanized and incorporated the latest advances in the technique of sugar manufacture. Notwithstanding this technical progress, in 1862 Cuba's population was distributed in the following manner: whites, 53.7 percent; slaves, 27.1 percent; free people of color, 16.3 percent; others, 2.9 percent.

Considering that on the plantations the slaves lived as isolated from civil society as if they were prisoners in a concentration camp, the urban statistics in particular are the ones that speak of the relations between blacks and whites. In this respect, the 1857 census gave, for the city of Havana, a total of 29,420 slaves, almost all of them domestics, who belonged to 9,421 persons—that is, an average of 3.1 slaves per person. Another indicator is the number of free blacks and mulattoes, who in the Havana of 1862 represented some 20 percent of the city's total population. According to estimates made at the time, the growing increase in sugar production occasioned an annual 10 percent deficit in this industry's work force. That situation was such that, to complement the importation of slaves, the plantation oligarchy would undertake to bring in Chinese workers, shipped principally from the ports of Canton, Amoy, Macao, Swatow, and Hong Kong. In spite of the extraordinarily high mortality during the long crossing of the Pacific, Indian, and Atlantic oceans, some 125,000 Chinese disembarked in Havana between 1848 and 1874. They came contracted for ten years and almost all of them were men destined for the plantations. Nonetheless, in 1872 there were some 5,000 Chinese in Havana, of whom 2,254 were already free. At this time the Barrio Chino (Chinatown) was organized in the city; its population made the existing culture richer, above all in music, religion, cuisine, pharmacopoeia, and gambling. Social discrimination also came to the Chinese; they married black and mulatto women, creating a new type of mestizo. When the Ten Years' War (first war of independence) began in 1868, they participated actively in it alongside black and white Cubans. Given that the war was fought only in the eastern and central regions of the island, it did not have major consequences for the sugar industry, which was concentrated to the west of the affected zones. It is worth noting that in 1873, when Major General Ignacio Agramonte's death was being mourned in Camagüey, the Havana oligarchy celebrated at the time of the Carnival a record production of almost 400,000 tons of sugar.

In contrast to the city in the eighteenth century, pictured with the coldness characteristic of neoclassic engravings, the Havana of the nineteenth century shows its ethnic complexity in the lithographs, engravings, and paintings of Federico Mialhe and Victor Patricio Landaluze.[13] The sugar mill, always an unavoidable reality, is represented as the myth of Havana's wealth and power in a deluxe portfolio of twenty-eight lithographs published in 1857 by Eduardo Laplante. The commercial impulse that underwrote the printing of engravings and lithographs can be seen today in the expensive collections of *marquillas* (cigar bands or rings) that we see in museums. In the decade of the 1850s, as photography was starting to be popular, Havana would be one of the first cities of the Americas to be have its portrait taken.[14]

The Negro, or rather the white made up as one, appeared on the stages of popular theaters during the first years of the century. The writer and actor Francisco Covarrubias created the character of the *negrito*, anticipating the minstrel shows. Bartolomé Crespo Borbón, known as Creto Gangá, continued this tradition. In his works there appeared the characters of the *negrito* and the *mulata*.[15] If it is true that, as in the case of the minstrels, the attitude toward the Negro shown by this type of theater was paternalistic and humiliating, many of the rhythms performed on the stage (*cantos de cabildo, tangos, danzas, danzones,* and possibly *rumbas*) had their roots in Africa and represented an indirect acknowledgment of African influence in popular culture. Moreover, Havana's blackface theater was a step toward the emergence, in later years, of a musical theater that staged the socioeconomic problems of the people of color.

The musical genres and subgenres that became popular in the Havana of the nineteenth century are too numerous to be named here; the musicologist Natalio Galán lists about thirty that could be considered Cuban. Spanish and Canary Island folklore contributed to the *punto habanero* and the *zapateo;* the Viennese waltz became slower and more stately in the *vals tropical;* the *canción cubana* took something from the lied, the French *romanza,* and the Neapolitan song. But the most popular genre, by far, was the creolized *danza.*

It was danced by everybody and everywhere, from high society balls to the *cuna* dances, organized in houses of ill repute and attended by women of color and young whites. During the late 1870s the *danzón*, a creolized genre derived from the *danza*, was created. Popularized by Miguel Failde, it was to be the most important Cuban dance until the *son* craze of the 1930s.

The first encounters between Cuban and U.S. music occurred in the second half of the century. The first U.S. composer to absorb and utilize Cuban music was Louis Moreau Gottschalk. Born in New Orleans in 1829, Gottschalk spoke Spanish and traveled to Havana several times, where he made friends with the principal musicians. Among his many compositions influenced by Afro-Cuban rhythms, one can find the symphony *Nuit de Tropiques*, whose premiere took place in 1861 in Havana's Teatro Tacón. Its debut was a big event; Gottschalk conducted a huge orchestra of 900 players, with 80 trumpeters, a 100-voice chorus, 15 soloists, and an ensemble of 50 Afro-Cuban drums played by blacks; two months later he gave, in the same theater, a concert with 49 pianos. The fact that Gottschalk could bring together several hundred musicians in a great choir of voices who could read their respective parts gives an idea not only of music's importance in the Havana of the 1860s but also that of the musical profession, which was traditionally dominated by people of color.

The impact in New Orleans of the music that was being played in Havana started to be noticed in the 1880s, when the music of the *danzas* and *danzones* was published there at the same time that the *tango* rhythm of the *habanera* was becoming popular. This syncopated music was to contribute to the creation of the first ragtimes and protoblues of Scott Joplin, Jelly Roll Morton, and later the "St. Louis Blues" of W. C. Handy. Nonetheless, the abolition of slavery brought people of color and their culture under greater governmental control. In accordance with an 1881 law, the *cabildos de negros* started to be supervised by the local authorities; in 1884 a decree issued by Havana's civil government prohibited the gatherings of Afro-Cuban groups, as well as *comparsas* and processions during the Día de Reyes and other religious festivals. A few years later, the *cabildos* would be replaced by pan-African associations with little or no religious meaning.

If it is quite certain that Cuba's national music and dance took off in the nineteenth century, its literature did too. Here what interests us particularly is the literary circle of Domingo Delmonte, a group of intellectuals with reformist ideas who were active between 1834 and 1844. Their nationalist program included first the suppression of the slave trade, a measure that they hoped would halt the growth of the black population and would bring about the gradual abolition of slavery. We're dealing here with a racist project, since it proposed that Cuba could be "whitened" through European immigration. The project also meant to reorganize and modernize the growing of sugar cane, to renovate the means of transportation and communication, to promote scientific studies, to reform the educational system, and, particularly in Havana, to wipe out vagrancy and vice. To spread its message, the group decided to make use of Havana's many printing presses and those of neighboring Matanzas. Soon new magazines began to appear in both cities, with articles dealing with Cuba's geography, natural sciences, economics, social sciences, education, lexicography, literature, and literary criticism.

As to literature, the group's members wrote a significant body of works that included drama, poetry, articles, stories, novellas, and novels. In general, the slave in these works was looked upon with compassion; some of them, the ones that are most interesting today, had an abolitionist message: the stories of Félix Tanco y Bosmeniel, the novel *Francisco* by Anselmo Suárez y Romero, and the autobiography of the slave poet Juan Francisco Manzano. None of these was published in colonial Cuba owing to censorship. Manzano's autobiography, as well as some of his poems and other authors' materials, was published in London in 1840 by the abolitionist Richard Madden.[16] At any rate, Delmonte's group was able to keep its literary reformism going only until 1844. That was the year of the so-called Conspiración de la Escalera (Conspiracy of the Ladder), which the colonial authorities said was a plot to organize a great slave rebellion. As a consequence of the ensuing repression, the mulatto poet Gabriel de la Concepción Valdés (Plácido) was shot, Manzano was tortured, and Delmonte exiled. Literary activity declined substantially during the next few decades. In the 1850s, political stability was ruptured by an intense climate of conspiracy against Spanish rule, and between 1868 and 1878 the Ten Years' War divided the island. After that came the prolific political and literary work of José Martí, but it would be the work of an exile.

The cultural boom that Havana enjoyed during the nineteenth century was propelled, to a great extent, by the local development of the sugar industry. Thanks to the free importation of slaves granted by the Spanish Crown, Havana sugar barons were able to meet the growing demand for sugar in the world market, particularly in the United States. During the century Cuba became the world's greatest sugar producer and exporter. Havana, the island's administrative and commercial center, was not only one of the busiest port cities of the Americas but also one of the richest.

The fact that Spain did not build a true plantation economy in Cuba until the end of the eighteenth century had consequences of such importance as to differentiate historically the Hispanic from the non-Hispanic colonies in the

Caribbean. During most of the 1700s, Cuba was more a colony of settlement than of exploitation. While Havana grew like a city similar to those in Spain, other Caribbean cities grew like plantation enclaves. When the Creoles of Havana decided to expand the sugar industry, it was a matter of people who had lived there for years in relation to civic institutions like the church, the school, the university, the press, book publishing, the theater, the opera, the concert, the botanical garden, and the learned society. When the plantation economy started to materialize, it had to adapt itself to the model of settlement that already existed. Nevertheless, because the growth of sugar production and exports were based on the growth of the slave population, Havana was not only a city of deep social contrasts, but also a cultural site characterized by a degree of creolization that was unparalleled in the Caribbean.

Among the many thousands of foreigners who visited Havana during the century, more than a hundred published their impressions of the city. These were writings that, in spite of their limitations, proffered interesting opinions that may aid in the understanding of the city's daily life. Their commentaries note Havana's busy commercial activity, the many ships anchored in the bay, and the bothersome vehicular traffic in the narrow streets; or the coexistence of palaces and miserable houses, the contrast between the squalor of poverty and slavery against the elegant carriages and clothes of the people of quality. They also pay attention to the love of the people of Havana for music and dance and speak of the *cabildo's comparsas* as well as the high society balls in the Teatro Tacón.

RACISM, AFRO-CUBANISM, AND TOURISM

During the first quarter of the twentieth century racial discrimination in Cuba reached extreme levels. Promises of equality given to the masses of soldiers of color who fought in the Ten Years' War and the War of Independence (1895–98) were not kept. During the U.S. military occupation that the island underwent between 1898 and 1902, the democratic program of José Martí was forgotten and racism was institutionalized, in spite of the fact that people of color constituted one-third of the total population. The governments that followed, aided by the most influential sectors of society, did nothing to solve the problem of the Afro-Cuban, whose participation in politics, the armed forces, the judicial system, the civil service, and education was extremely scant. Gradually, out of the frustration of blacks and mulattoes grew a situation that in 1908 underlay the founding of the Independent Party of Color. When this was declared to be illegal, the army and paramilitary bands unleashed, in 1912, a ferocious repression against groups of leaders and sympathizers who had organized an armed protest in Oriente province.

Discrimination, more than ever, extended into the realm of culture. In 1900, under the U.S. government of occupation, the mayoralty of Havana prohibited the use of drums of African origin in all types of gatherings, whether held on public streets or within buildings; in 1903 the Abakuá Society was prohibited, its members accused of kidnapping and murdering children for the purpose of witchcraft; in 1913 the black *comparsas* were suppressed, and in 1922 a resolution of the secretary of interior prohibited ceremonial festivals and dances pertaining to Afro-Cuban beliefs throughout the island. Nevertheless, by the middle of the 1920s the music of the *son*, born in the previous century in the mountains of Oriente province and much more influenced by African percussion than the *danzón*, started to become popular in Havana. If it was indeed soon the object of discrimination—a 1924 piano piece was called "Mama Doesn't Want Me to Dance the Son"—in the end, the white population accepted it. Its polyrhythm and its structure transformed other genres (*danzón, bolero, guajira, guaracha*); it was the predecessor of the *mambo* and the *chachachá*, the substance of salsa, and one of the ingredients of Latin Jazz. Known in the United States as rhumba, it was launched into the world by Hollywood films and the many recordings of the Trío Matamoros, the Sexteto Habanero, and the Septeto Nacional. Further, it opened a way for strongly Africanized genres like the *conga*, the *rumba*, as well as commercialized forms of *santería* ritual dances.

Quickly the young intelligentsia that defined itself as white began to look at the blacks in a new way. In addition to the positive consequences that the popularization of the *son* had, a number of things helped form this new attitude: the search for a more democratic form of nationalism, anthropological curiosity, the coming of African art to Europe, the literary and artistic achievements of the Harlem Renaissance, and even the winds of political utopianism inspired by revolutions in China, Mexico, and Russia. It was this unrest, both artistic and social, that moved Ortiz to make his first studies of the folklore of the Cuban blacks, while at the same time composers such as Amadeo Roldán and Alejandro García Caturla brought the rhythms of the *música de color* to the symphony orchestras. In 1927 Cuba's musical theater began with the operetta *La niña Rita o La Habana de 1830*, by Ernesto Lecuona and Eliseo Grenet, which popularized the piece "Ay mamá Inés." One year later, the singer Rita Montaner recorded, in New York, a *son* of the composer Moisés Simons, "El manicero" (The Peanut Vendor), which was to be one of the greatest triumphs of Cuban music. These successes were aided by the new technological advances in the radio and phonograph; now the compositions, voices, instruments, and rhythms of the *música de color* could be listened and danced to in white people's homes without the presence of blacks. Nevertheless, the blacks would gradually find in music a space for coexistence with whites, certainly not without racial tension, but yet a space where they would be recognized and applauded as performers and would be sought after and paid to play at private parties, theaters, dancehalls, and cabarets. Blacks were even put under contract as artists to work in radio programs or to make recordings in New York or Paris.

Impelled by the *son*, Afro-Cubanism overflowed the course of music and invaded the realms of literature and art. In 1928 the first *negrista* poems were published; this was a literary current that would reach its greatest significance in the 1930s with the poetry of Nicolás Guillén (*Motivos de son, Sóngoro cosongo, West Indies, Ltd.*). In his work, Guillén did not just poetize the Havana black colloquial language, but he also revealed the libido of the Negro, transgressing the mechanisms of sexual censorship that the plantation had applied to the race. In a parallel fashion, the new national art began to represent, although in a manner imbued with exoticism, the figure of the black and mulatto woman in the works of Victor Manuel (*Gitana tropical, La negrita*) and Eduardo Abela (*El triunfo de la rumba, El gallo místico*). The black sculptor Teodoro Ramos Blanco received a gold medal at the Seville Exposition (1929); his wood statues and busts were characterized by their accentuation of his models' African features.

During the decade of the 1940s, the Afro-Cuban theme ceased to be the fashion in literature and symphonic music, but the contrary occurred in the plastic arts and in popular music. In spite of the democratic inclinations of the new constitution (1940), black people continued to be victims of racial segregation, although not in the open and generalized way of the preceding years. With the *comparsas* now allowed at carnival, the paintings of Wifredo Lam began to fill the world's artistic capitals with surrealist Afro-Cubanism. Speaking of his art, Lam said: "I wanted to paint the drama of the Negro spirit, the beauty of the plastic art of the blacks. In this way I could act as a Trojan horse that would spew forth hallucinating figures with the power to surprise, to disturb the dreams of the exploiters."[17] Also in the 1940s, popular music entered a period of renovation thanks to ensembles and orchestras such as Arsenio Rodríguez's, the Conjunto Casino, Arcaño y sus Maravillas, the Riverside, and the Sonora Matancera, from whence would come the unforgettable voice of Celia Cruz; Joseíto Fernández made "La Guantanamera" popular and the brothers Orestes and Israel López (Cachao) transformed the *danzón*, adding a new part to it which someone would call *mambo*. Soon thereafter, Dámaso Pérez Prado used the same term to denominate a series of syncopated rhythms, with recurring themes, conceived for big bands with powerful Cuban percussion sections. One of his first singers was Benny Moré, who would become one of the stars of the 1950s. Pérez Prado's triumph was instantaneous and the *mambo* became an international genre. In New York, Miguelito Valdés (Mr. Babalú) sang with Xavier Cugat's band and Francisco Grillo (Machito) started his successful band Machito and His Afro-Cubans while the percussionist Chano Pozo, hired by Dizzy Gillespie, introduced Afro-Cubanism to jazz with numbers such as "Manteca" and *"Tin Tin Deo."*

Havana in the 1950s was beyond doubt the cultural capital of the Caribbean. It had a ballet company with an international reputation, an excellent symphony orchestra, botanical and zoological gardens, a new museum of fine art, a sales center for arts and crafts, and impressive sports centers. Old nightclubs like the Tropicana, Sans Souci, and Montmartre were renovated and presented shows where the names of the best Cuban and Latin American artists alternated with those of Nat King Cole, Liberace, Tony Martin, Cab Calloway, Tony Bennett, Jimmy Durante, June Christy, Dorothy Dandridge, Eartha Kitt, Maurice Chevalier, Edith Piaf, Carmen Amaya, Sarita Montiel and Lola Flores, or they might present entire companies such as the Folies Bergäre, the Lido, and José Greco's flamenco troupe. New hotels and casinos were built; some of them run by the mafia (Meyer Lansky, Santo Trafficante, and Joe Silesis). To the old tourist bars like El Floridita and La Bodeguita del Medio—the ones that Hemingway preferred—and Sloppy Joe's were added up to several dozen more offering music for all tastes, even including tastes for certain musicians and singers, as one reads in Guillermo Cabrera Infante's *Three Trapped Tigers*. Furthermore, excellent restaurants appeared where, in addition to the traditional cuisine, diners could eat the food of the entire world. The city, more than ever, was portrayed by the travel agencies and the air and sea transport lines as the ideal place for enjoying pleasures ranging from innocent romance to perversion made possible by some 10,000 prostitutes. Something similar occurred in Hollywood: the film version of *Guys and Dolls* (1955) showed Marlon Brando courting Jean Simmons in a romantic colonial plaza and in a dive filled with whores and toughs; in *Our Man in Havana* (1957), a trio of indefatigable *soneros* followed Noel Coward's steps along Havana's streets; in *Affair in Havana* (1957), Raymond Burr and John Cassavetes share the screen with Celia Cruz, and in 1958 Lucy remembered her first trip to Havana, where she met Ricky Ricardo.

As the *mambos* of Pérez Prado sold millions of records, Enrique Jorrín created a new rhythm, the *chachachá*, which immediately became popular. In certain bars of the city, a new type of *bolero*, called "feeling," mixed jazz guitar chords with creole rhythms and spoke of love. Its principal composers were José Antonio Méndez, César Portillo de la Luz, and Frank Domínguez. The Afro-Cuban religions, particularly *santería*, now had a great number of whites among their believers; the *orishas* of Yoruba origin and the *íremes* of the *abakuá* were trivialized on television programs and cabaret presentations. At the close of the decade it could be said that the cultural mainstream had "nationalized" Afro-Cubanism. Nonetheless, there were certain forms of *rumba*, certain *abakuá* rituals and elements of *congo* wizardry, certain secrets of *santería* that remained in the sociocultural substructure of the black population.

The impact of tourism on Havana's culture has hardly been studied. The industry began taking on importance during the 1920s, when Prohibition criminalized the sale of alcoholic beverages in the United States. During those thirteen years, waves of tourists traveled to Havana to partake of cocktails such as the *daiquirí*, the *Cuba libre*, and the *mojito*, whose base was Bacardí white rum. But there were many further attractions.

The island possessed the potential to compete favorably with Europe for the luxury tourist trade, with California for adventurers, with Florida for golfers, with Saratoga for horsemen, and with New York for entertainment. Lush tropical foliage, climate, and location were fortunate accidents of nature, but human inventiveness, imagination, and perseverance turned Havana into a naughty Paris of the Western Hemisphere and a luxurious Riviera of the Americas for tourists. Businessmen baited the hook for a consumerist, hedonistic market, and tourists leaped at the temptation.

In 1933 publicity for the film *Havana Widows* with Joan Blondell said: "This gold-digging farce plays upon Havana as the current recreation area for millionaires, as attractive women use their charms as bait in fishing for riches." And in *Weekend in Havana* (1941), with a stellar cast (Alice Faye, John Payne, Carmen Miranda, and César Romero), the synopsis said: "A woman's trip to Cuba leads to romance, laughter and sizzling songs." This type of publicity, sent out endlessly to innumerable potential tourists, contributed to visitors from the United States spending $50 million in Cuba, almost all in Havana. How much of this money went toward creating new employment for musicians, singers, chorus girls, dancers, choreographers, artists, artisans, photographers, playwrights, journalists, writers, theater people, film makers, set designers, lighting technicians, masters of ceremonies, stage producers, and costume designers? And how many young people began to study in conservatories and art schools, dance and theater academies, attracted by the great possibilities for employment that the tourist industry, including radio and television, offered? Nobody knows. But there is another unknown as well: To what extent was Afro-Cubanism influenced by the millions of tourists who traveled in search of exotic cultural manifestations like the Afro-Cuban *comparsas* at carnival or the elaborate Afro-Cuban shows at the Tropicana or the *rumbas* of the Chori, so pleasing to Marlon Brando and Frank Sinatra? And yet more important questions: To what degree did tourism affect the people's personality or their social conduct or ideological profile? What role has it played in the increase in prostitution, and the consumption of drugs and alcoholic beverages? Has it made for a lessening of local racism?

We may never have exact answers to these questions, although in my opinion tourism in general is a strong incentive both toward preserving old cultural traditions and transforming the cultural forms that exist. For example, the creole rhythm which we call *conga* comes from Africa, from the Bantu culture. Transplanted to Cuba, it was danced by the Congo *cabildos* for the Día de Reyes and other festivities. Toward the beginning of the twentieth century it entered the Afro-Cuban *comparsas*, and after 1917, without having lost its street character, it was taken up by political parties in their campaigns. When the *comparsas* were resuscitated in 1937, the *conga* was established choreographically, eventually adapting to the tourist taste and ceasing to be a dance exclusive to people of color. Also for reasons of tourism, the dance was brought to the cabaret shows, where it lost its street character. From there it went on to be what is known as the *conga de salón*, in which the dancers, grabbing each other at the waist, snake happily among the tables. This variant moved quickly into Hollywood movies where it was called "conga line," and from there it gained universal popularity. In short, if indeed a long process of change brought on by global influences intervened between the turbulent *conga* of the Día de Reyes and the regimented conga line, the old one-two-three-hop! rhythm has managed not just to last but has been internationalized as well and has contributed to the creolization of other cultural forms.

REVOLUTION AND CULTURE

During the first thirty years of Castro's government the island lost almost all of its touristic value. There are multiple reasons for this. In the first place, the average tourist was repelled by dangerous situations like the missile crisis of 1962, whose impact lingered in the world's memory. Likewise, he or she didn't tend to travel to countries in revolution, where political imprisonment, public executions, and violations of human rights were daily events. Further, Cuba's alignment with the Soviet Union, proclaimed the number one enemy of the "free world," as well as the American embargo, which still bars trips to Cuba, eliminated the island as the preferred site for grand tourism. There were also reasons imposed by the Cuban government, for example, the impossibility of moving freely through the country or meeting with politically suspect persons, or even taking photos of unauthorized places. This being so, Cuba suffered a double isolation, from without and from within, which also extended into the cultural domain.

To start with, as the state took ownership of almost all of the productive economy and private services and as the government required the populace to change its ideology, more than a million Cubans preferred to live in exile, among them thousands of intellectuals and artists, as well as people connected to cultural activities. This flight of talent has caused a substantial number of the greatest exponents of Cuban culture to continue their artistic or intellectual work abroad.[18] If it is true that the government created institutions that at the beginning contributed to the development of arts and letters, between 1968 and 1978 the cultural policy hardened considerably, above all in the matter of official censorship.[19] Some of the world's artists and intellectuals, on learning of the incarceration, for political reasons, of the poet Heberto Padilla, severed their ties to Cuba, accusing Castro's government of having a Stalinist cultural policy. The persecution of homosexuality, made official at the First Congress of Education and Culture (1971), provoked harsh criticism outside Cuba and paralyzed the artistic activity of hundreds of people. These years were also characterized by official repression of all religious activity, including Afro-Cuban celebrations, from educational programs to the traditional *comparsas*. If it is true that the world kept dancing *sones*, *mambos*, and *chachachás*, the production of new rhythms was stultified, while the émigré musicians contributed to the creation of the salsa in New York. During the 1980s, the cultural policy became less inflexible, but the adverse impact of the previous decade was not wholly erased.

The disintegration of the Soviet Union brought as its result not just an end to the economic aid that it gave to Cuba but also some serious problems affecting agricultural and industrial production, the import and export trades, and investments in both the productive and service sectors. This critical situation forced the government in 1990 to follow a policy of austerity that greatly restricted imports. Facing this hard reality, the government found itself forced to adopt a series of survival measures, such as the introduction of foreign investments, the legalization of the dollar (a prohibited currency to Cubans until then), the accelerated development of tourism, self-employment, new forms of land use, free markets, and the reorganization of the entire state administration, including the sugar industry. In short, the old economy based on the development of a socialist consciousness and a renunciation of material interests started to be replaced by a mixed economy.

Tourism very soon became the principal source of income, a fact that had real historical significance, as Cuba had been the quintessential "sugar island." With no time lost, making use of huge sums in foreign investments, old hotels, bars, nightclubs, and restaurants were renovated, while many others were built. In addition to the traditional resorts (the beach at Varadero), new ones were developed (the complex at Cayo Romano), and the publicity of tourism was activated worldwide. Cuba began to appear in the best travel guides; magazines as dissimilar as *Playboy* and the *National Geographic* praised the beauty of the mixed-race women and the natural beauty of the island. There was also a revival of Afro-Cubanism, to the extent that the ritual dances of the Afro-Cuban religions and the ethnographic museums started to form a part of the picturesque attractions that the city now offered. But among the Western, white, heterosexual men, perhaps the main attraction was sex. The legalization of the dollar made prostitution an important source of hard-currency income, and, consequently, the number of prostitutes increased to a record level. On the assumption—published by sex guides—that Cuban women are not really prostitutes but nice girls who like to have a good time, a continuous flow of male tourism crowds hotels and bars. In 1994 the new waves of tourists left $850 million in the country. According to official figures, this became $1.7 billion eight years later. Estimates for 2003 suggest 1.9 million people will have visited Cuba that year—some 80,000 U.S. visitors and the rest mostly Europeans, among them 75,000 travelers of Cuban origin coming to see their families.

Recognizing a custom of nineteenth-century travelers, the libraries and bookstores exhibit today dozens of works on Cuba written by foreigners. Although they see the ruinous nature of Havana, they all are impressed at its beauty as well as the halo of nostalgia that seems to envelop the city. Beyond that, opinions vary. Some praise the state systems of public education and health, others criticize the abundance of prostitutes and lament that the general public is forbidden to enter the tourist hotels. They all speak of the Cubans' taste for music and dance, celebrate their good humor in spite of their poverty, and marvel that Chevys and Fords from the 1950s are still running and in the streets. As far as culture is concerned, many find the shows and chorus lines at the Tropicana to be outdated, although they recognize that the young people are interested in other types of music such as the *songo* and the *timba*, which they dance with a defiant and assured sensuality. There is also a Cuban underground form of hip hop. Orishas, the only rap group to transcend the island's boundaries, traveled to Paris in 1998 and made a hit record adding *son*, *rumba*, and *santería* beats to their music—that is, creolizing further an already creolized genre.

Although Havana—both the urban settlement and its sociocultural characteristics—shares with other Caribbean cities a common pattern shaped by the slaveholding plantation as well as the historical impact of colonialism and other global forces, it represents a unique case within the area. To my way of thinking, differences with other Caribbean port cities can be explained by the interaction of three principal factors: geographic conditions, late development of a full plantation system, and economic dependence on the United States. We have already seen that Havana's position at the exit of the Gulf of Mexico had determined its commercial and military importance since the middle of the sixteenth century. Its nearness to the United States made it possible that, from 1795, the greater part of its sugar exports would go to that country's ports, to establish an active commercial to-and-fro of North American shipping. The expansionist interests of the United States fostered the war with Spain of 1898, the results of which were the military occupation of the island; enormous U.S. investments in the sugar industry and other enterprises, including the development and modernization of Havana for tourist purposes; the introduction of the habit of consuming U.S. products (automobiles, radios, refrigerators, electric fans and irons, kitchen appliances, record players, television sets, air conditioners, and even clothing, food products, and the adoption of baseball as a national sport); and a political and economic dependency that was to last until 1959.

Also, the late development of the plantation system, as we have seen, contributed to Havana's having grown with numerous institutions. With the slave plantation set in motion by Havana's patricians, the profits earned through sugar exports and the slave traffic, instead of going to the mother country, would underwrite the construction of palaces, public squares, modern docks and warehouses, avenues, theaters, cafés, markets, hospitals, and public buildings, and one of the world's first railroads. At the same time, the late development of the plantation had demographic consequences that were very different from those of the English, French, and Dutch colonies in the Caribbean. Given that most of the latter, since the seventeenth century, grew as plantation enclaves with slave labor, the great majority of the population consisted of slaves. The situation in Cuba—particularly in Havana—was much more balanced.

For example, in 1827 the island's population was distributed in the following manner: whites, 44 percent; slaves, 41 percent; free people of color, 15 percent. These proportions favored, more so than in other colonies, the processes of creolization among the cultures from Africa and Europe, in syncretic forms that ranged from the religious to the culinary.

Nothing like the Afro-Cuban movement (not even *négritude*), with its notable manifestations in popular music, symphonic music, dance, theater, art, literature, film, and folkloric and anthropological investigations, existed in any other Caribbean nation. Moreover, thanks to commercial contacts and economic dependence on the United States, Afro-Cubanism was transmitted in the 1920s to the island's entire population via the first radios, victrolas, and disk recordings; later the vehicles would be the movies and television. Meanwhile, the proximity of the United States contributed (through tourism, the recording industry, and the interchange of music and performers) to the development of both local creolization and its influence abroad. At present, thanks to the post-Soviet crisis, Havana has started to resemble what it was: a cosmopolitan port city with a complex, creolized culture whose population looks toward the sea with hope.

NOTES

1. Schwartz, *Pleasure Island*, 3–15.
2. Ortiz, "Informe del doctor Fernando Ortiz, Presidente de la Sociedad de Estudios Afrocubanos," 17.
3. Moore, *Nationalizing Blackness*, 84.
4. Marrero, *Cuba: Economía y sociedad*, 2:384.
5. Ibid., 82–84.
6. To put a brake on speculation while the flotas were in port, the town government fixed the prices of certain foods. It also ordered the suppliers to make available 150 head of cattle and 40,000 pounds of casabe in anticipation of the flota's arrival. The information is for the years 1554–56. See ibid., 158–59.
7. Ibid., 152–54.
8. In the summer of 1555 Havana was taken, sacked, and burned by the French corsair Jacque de Sores. A month later, it was again overrun by another pirate.
9. Salvucci, "Supply, Demand, and the Making of a Market," particularly table 2.1 on pp. 42–43.
10. Marrero, *Cuba: Economía y sociedad*, 8:230.
11. Carpentier, *La música en Cuba*, 93.
12. The process of abolishing slavery in Cuba extended from 1870, the date of the

Moret Law, which, among other things, conferred liberty on the children born of slave parents; to 1880, the date of the law that freed the slaves but obliged them to stay in service for eight years under the patronage system; to 1886, the date of the decree that dissolved the patronage system and recognized the de facto freedom of the former slave. See Knight, *Slave Society in Cuba*, 172–78.

13. Both Mialhe and Landaluze represented, in their works, the street dances of the Día de Reyes. Among Mialhe's most estimable works, one finds the thirteen lithographs that illustrated, in color, the *Viaje pintoresco alrededor de la isla de Cuba*, one of the jewels of Cuban graphic arts. Of Landaluze there are his droll watercolors and his illustrations to *Tipos y costumbres de la isla de Cuba*.

14. Photographs of Havana in the 1850s appear in Dorronsoro, *Pal Rosti: Una visión de América Latina*; and in Levine, *Cuba in the 1850s*.

15. Castellanos, *Cultura afrocubana*, 4:210–22.

16. See Edward J. Mullen's facsimile edition, *The Life and Poems of a Cuban Slave: Juan Francisco Manzano, 1797–1854*. Gertrudis Gómez de Avellaneda, a noted Cuban author, published the abolitionist novel *Sab* (1841) in Spain. In addition to founding Cuba's national literature, the writers of the Delmonte circle established Cuban literature's great theme: racial and ethnic differences within the social fabric. This theme runs up and down Cuba's literary production, to the extent that no important author has failed to play it. Examples include the works of Gertrudis Gómez de Avellaneda, Cirilio Villaverde, Nicolás Guillén, Alejo Carpentier, José Lezama Lima, Severo Sarduy, and Guillermo Cabrera Infante, among others. This is not to mention the works of Fernando Ortiz and Lydia Cabrera.

17. Sims, "Myth and Primitivism," 77.

18. For example, Agustín Acosta, Néstor Almendros, Alberto Alonso, Armando Alvarez Bravo, Reinaldo Arenas, Gastón Baquero, José Bedia, Cundo Bermúdez, Lydia Cabrera, Guillermo Cabrera Infante, Servando Cabrera Moreno, Mario Carreño, Antonio Conte, Celia Cruz, María Elena Cruz Varela, Arturo Cuenca, Paquito D'Rivera, Jesús Díaz, Frank Domínguez, Antonia Eiriz, Agustín Fernández, Norberto Fuentes, Natalio Galán, Lorenzo García Vega, Olga Guillot, Enrique Labrador Ruiz, César Leante, Ernesto Lecuona, Tania León, Rolando López Dirube, Jorge Mañach, Leví Marrero, Ana Mendieta, Carlos Montenegro, Matías Montes Huidobro, Manuel Moreno Fraginals, Lino Novás Calvo, Heberto Padilla, Justo Rodríguez Santos, Tomás Sánchez, Arturo Sandoval, Mongo Santamaría, Severo Sarduy, Leandro Soto, José Triana, Bebo Valdés, Aurelio de la Vega, Carlos Victoria, among many others. Also, there are new international stars such as Albita, Gloria Estefan, Andy García, Gonzalo Rubalcaba, and Zoé Valdés.

19. Among the institutions created by the revolutionary government are the Casa de las Américas, the Instituto Cubano de Arte e Industria Cinematográficos (ICAIC), the Unión de Escritores y Artistas de Cuba (UNEAC), the Instituto Cubano del Libro (ICL), and the Consejo Nacional de Cultura (CNC), later converted to the Ministerio de Cultura, whose operations relate to all forms of cultural expression.

5

¡Hay que dar la cara
y darla con valor!
(You must show face
and show it honorably!)
—RUBÉN BLADES, "Tiburón"

Showing Face: Boxing and Nation Building in Contemporary Puerto Rico

FRANCES NEGRÓN-MUNTANER

For the past half century, Puerto Ricans have contested colonial domination and racist humiliation in multiple ways. At the same time, the cultural arena has become increasingly significant. This is the case in part because of two simultaneous phenomena: the Puerto Rican majority's desire to maintain economic and political ties to the United States, either as an autonomous territory or as the fifty-first state; and their critical stance regarding the subordination implicit in those ties. Given this ambiguity, *boricuas*, as Puerto Ricans are sometimes called, on the island and the U.S. mainland are constantly called upon or feel compelled to affirm the value of the collective identity through ethnonational performances that underscore the group's worth. Rather than mount conventional nationalist political resistance, many Puerto Ricans counter everyday colonial and racist shame by *dando cara* or "showing face" through cultural practices.

In this symbolic transaction, the global marketplace plays a fundamental and complex role. Putting the best face on the nation for the largest possible audience requires publicity and symbolic capital, so performances by Puerto Rican pop stars, athletes, and celebrities are especially valued. Although not the only site of cultural negotiation, the significant investment in star power by many Puerto Rican consumers appears to recognize that, by becoming a commodity, a person "transcend[s] particularity, embodiment, and domesticity, the spaces where the disfranchised have historically been made to dwell."[1] Puerto Rican stars show the group's most public face often in an explicit attempt to counter the low symbolic capital attributed to this ethnonational body, a "humble people of this small 110-by-35 mile island" and its diaspora.[2] Ironically, the faces of Puerto Rican star commodities are circulated largely through the U.S.-dominated mass media that plays a significant role in shaping how colonial subjects show face and obtain value in relation to other national groups.

Due to the global success of several Puerto Rican movie and recording stars, most recent scholarly and media attention has focused on U.S. pop culture over other cultural spaces. This attention is understandable as pop stars are sites at which shamed subjects negotiate the ambivalent effects of national visibility and transnational desire.[3] Yet sport is an equally important foundational stage for *boricua* ethnonational performances, offering a matching space to perform for the nation. As Toby Miller argues, "Sport is a crucible of the nation, cognate to the rites of passage of war or revolution."[4] Whereas Puerto Rican pop stars tend to negotiate with the politics of beauty and desirability, sports heroes put the nation to work, flexing the collective muscle to display the vitality and endurance of a community that constantly feels belittled.

Because dominant representations of Puerto Ricans emphasize the group's "weaknesses" such as the island's small size, limited economic resources, subordinated political incorporation into the U.S. body politic, and unwillingness to fight for the founding of an independent nation-state, the sport of boxing takes on a special value in the fight for the nation's worth and offers both popular and elite sectors a way to narrate, enjoy, and perform nationhood. As James C. Scott suggests, "An individual who is affronted may develop a personal fantasy of revenge and confrontation, but when the insult is but a variant of affronts suffered systematically by a whole race, class, or strata, then the fantasy can become a collective cultural product."[5] Although boxers worldwide compete as individuals, boxers in Puerto Rico are often "deified"[6] and viewed as national treasures or heroes, embodying the desires and tribulations of fellow nationals. Even when battered, boxers are often perceived to show the most dignified national "face" when confronting a "foreign" threat.

AND BOXING FOR ALL: SPORTS, THE STATE, AND
NATIONAL PERFORMANCES

In Puerto Rico, boxing and baseball have largely coexisted as the two most popular sports for the past 100 years. Similar to other Caribbean countries such as Cuba and the Dominican Republic, baseball was initially associated with modernity and the democratic values of the United States, particularly versus the former metropolis of Spain. After Puerto Rico became an unincorporated territory of the United States, baseball became not only a local pastime but also a credible path to social valorization and international fame. The dream to play for the U.S. baseball major leagues intensified after World War II for a variety of reasons, including the breaking down of the color line in U.S. sports, a recognition of Puerto Rican talent for the game, and a renewed faith in the possibility of upward mobility within the existing order.

Yet, if baseball makes Puerto Ricans proud as it showcases their worth on the northern diamond, mostly in boxing have *boricuas* achieved fame as Puerto Rican nationals and not part of anyone else's team or nation. This is evident in the fact that Puerto Rico's first major sports star was Sixto Escobar, the world's bantamweight champion during the late 1930s, and that all of Puerto Rico's six Olympic medals have been earned by boxers. Most recently, island government authorities allotted thousands of dollars of state funds so the island's inmate population could watch the fight when welterweight Félix (Tito) Trinidad became world champion in 2001 and later gave employees the day off to celebrate the local hero's victory. A letter to the editor from a Puerto Rican at Fort Bragg sums up the significance of boxing to discourses of national worth and dignity: "We Puerto Ricans, the poorest group among twenty million Hispanics who live under the American flag, can tell the world that we have the best fighters in the world."[7]

Arguably, the "moods" of a country can be gauged by the sport currently in vogue. In Puerto Rico, the shifts in popularity and symbolic centrality of baseball, boxing, and basketball at certain junctures coincide with the intensification of cultural nationalist ideologies among the island's population, the quality of a given athletic pool, and the dominance of popular over elite forms of articulating notions of national culture. Baseball was once seen as an excellent vehicle for upward mobility, acceptance into American society, and respectability for young, mostly black youth. Yet Puerto Rico seems to have lost interest in what Adrián Burgos has called "America's game." The situation has become so critical for some that, to rekindle interest and increase the numbers of Puerto Ricans in Major League Baseball, former baseball player Edwin Correa founded a "baseball school" in Carolina with the assistance of Roberto Clemente's widow. Significantly, baseball's appeal has waned at the precise moment in which a few Puerto Ricans are the most integrated into the Major Leagues and others are the most skeptical about its notions of progress, democracy, and modernity.

In contrast to baseball, boxing offers a more pristine space to show that, despite the island's political ambiguity and economic precariousness, Puerto Ricans have not given up the fight to signify on their own terms, increasingly in Latino and/or black worlds, as these groups amply dominate the lower divisions. Whereas each member of a Major League team must wear the same uniform representing a U.S. or Canadian city, virtually every major Puerto Rican boxer since the 1970s has worn the Puerto Rican flag on his body or brought out the Puerto Rican flag at the time of victory. This trend is not confined to male boxers from Puerto Rico. U.S.-born Puerto Rican female boxers such as the International Women's Boxing Federation junior-lightweight champ Melissa Salamone, also wears the flag in her trunks, "a sequined echo of her native Puerto Rican flag."[8] Yet the current appeal to boxing as a nation-building space may exceed the labored conflation of body and nation on the ring. Because boxing continues to be a rogue, unregulated activity, where fighters can even meet their deaths, and influential people can rig fights, the sport offers an alternative view about the nature of power and politics than baseball, with its perfectly manicured lawn and clearly established rules. As Jack Newfield sums up, "In boxing, nothing is clear; victory and defeat are matters of interpretation by judge"[9]—like Puerto Rican identity politics.

Because Puerto Rico is not a nation-state but a culturally defined national community, Puerto Rican athletes represent the nation on a global scale, establish an alternative way of measuring "nationhood" as sports sovereignty, and affirm cultural citizenship. Sport provides what is denied elsewhere: Puerto Rican political agency and dignity. Puerto Rico's third boxing champ, the light heavyweight José "Chegüí" Torres, for example, embraces his role as a specifically Puerto Rican athlete in the diaspora: "I wanted to be a good example for Puerto Ricans here to do good. To fight for the human rights of Puerto Ricans in the United States."[10] Sports provided an arena where Puerto Ricans could compete as national subjects and be counted.

Not coincidentally, with the Western-style nation-state established as a global norm after World War II, local Puerto Rican elites were eager to simulate the rituals of nationhood by fielding an Olympic team. In 1948, the same year Congress passed an amendment to the Jones Act that granted islanders the right to elect their own governor, Puerto Rico joined the International Olympic Committee.[11] The mainstream press, largely pro-autonomist, applauded the move: "Puerto Rico marched yesterday . . . as a sovereign nation, in the Fourteenth Olympic Games." Observers differed on which flag the team flew with some claiming the flagless delegation carried the Olympic emblem and others that the Puerto Rican delegation carried a U.S. flag. "The United States protested," comments Gabrielle Paese, "claiming that two countries could not use the same flag at the same time."[12] Four years later, a series of negotiations led to the founding of the Commonwealth of Puerto Rico, a colonial arrangement that did not fundamentally alter the power dynamics between the metropolis and the island, but did expand the local elites' power over its subalterns and granted the community the remaining symbolic accessories of nationhood: a flag, an anthem, and official languages.

Although largely unremarked by the international press, the "national" status of the Puerto Rican delegation changed dramatically fourteen days into the Helsinki Olympics Games when the referendum on commonwealth status passed on July 25, 1952. The delegation first appeared in the Opening Ceremonies carrying two flags, one representing the International Olympic Committee and a second bearing the coat of arms of the city of San Juan; the delegation left with the newly inaugurated official flag of the commonwealth.[13] Sports commentator Elliott Castro observed: "The creation of the Commonwealth had a direct effect on sports. . . . Olympic officials went to the center of the Olympic Village, where the flags of each nation are flown, and took down the IOC flag and hoisted the new Puerto Rican flag. It was the first time the new flag was flown internationally and the only time in history a country changed flags in the middle of the Olympics."[14] Recognition by the international community helped cleanse the Puerto Rican flag of the pariah status it attained as a separatist symbol during the preceding years of U.S. rule.

Gaining Olympic membership can then be seen as one of the first "foreign policy" decisions made on the island by Puerto Ricans.[15] This reminds us of Toby Miller's observation that "we can think of sport as a kind of prepolitical activity, an arena where needs, demands, and desires can take shape and receive sustenance before they are institutionally articulated as politics."[16] Yet, true to *boricua* political form, the first athlete to carry a Puerto Rican flag was a statehooder, Roberto Santana, in the Mexican-hosted Pan American Games of 1954.[17] Becoming part of the Olympic team, like the ceremony founding the Estado Libre Asociado (ELA) or Commonwealth, was a space in which to project the nation without contesting metropolitan power over the island nor even compromising one's local ideological positions.[18] This sets a precedent that holds to this day: the state often encourages the channeling of Puerto Rican political and cultural energy into spectacles of nationality rather than in structurally transforming U.S.–Puerto Rico relations.

Significantly, by competing in the family of nations, Puerto Rico wins a political victory at the Olympics regardless of how Puerto Rican athletes perform for at least two reasons. First, given Puerto Rico's ambiguous status, the most important political victory is to have sports sovereignty at all, particularly as a colonial possession of the world's major sports power. Second, because the state does not invest in producing world-quality athletes as in neighboring

Cuba and often the best Puerto Rican athletes can also compete on behalf of the United States, the island's Olympic Team is a show of faith in the nation's ability to perform and endure against all odds. Because most athletes are not exactly going for the gold, Puerto Rican spectators tend to be more invested in commodified performances by individuals in the professional arena where victory is more likely. Here, Olympic participation is fiercely defended.

The Puerto Rican plebiscite consultation of 1993 serves as a clear example of how sports sovereignty serves as a fetishized site for political hopes and fears. In this consultation, the option for remaining a commonwealth beat out the statehood option by 2 percent. Political analyst Juan Manuel García Passalacqua attributes the commonwealth edge to an ad showing a Puerto Rican athlete being stripped of his medals. This ad suggests that it is commonwealth status that allows Puerto Ricans symbolically to stay in the game of nationhood. At the same time, given that the Puerto Rican referendum was not binding, the vote indicated a clear desire to maintain a symbol of specificity and self-worth in which Puerto Rico has already invested. In this fetishization of sport, an athlete resolves the contradictions of national life by symbolically standing up for the nation rather than against colonial economic or political structures.

The fact that Puerto Ricans do not dwell on their Olympic performance but in their ability to perform as Olympians should not be confused with a lower standard of national expectations. The extent to which Puerto Ricans expect all athletes to represent Puerto Rico in Olympic or sponsored competitions and consider a deviation from this norm a major offense is evident in the case of tennis player Gigi Fernández. In 1992 Fernández opted to represent the United States in the Barcelona Olympics in order to have a chance to win a medal since with the American delegation her doubles partner would be a ranked player. Although Fernández went on to become the first Puerto Rican woman to win an Olympic gold medal, she was vilified for her "treason" and she eventually stayed in the United States to play professionally.

Fernández, however, is not the only Puerto Rican athlete to have represented the United States; others include swimmer Cheyenne Vasallo, boxer Chegüí Torres, and basketball player María "Cucusa" Rivera. In a less common move, U.S. nationals have also crossed the boundary to compete as Puerto Ricans, as in the case of basketball player Jerome Mincy,[19] due to the relative ease with which a "foreign" player can establish residency in only three years. Sports, like the Commonwealth, provides Puerto Ricans with several options of self-representation as national, ethnic, or ethnonational subjects. Yet, as the "treason" of so many athletes reveals, sports sovereignty is a national symbol that can expose the very contradictions it seeks to obscure.

BLACK AND BLUE: THE NATIONAL CAREER OF TITO TRINIDAD

Despite the fact that in Puerto Rico most boxers have historically emerged from racial and class backgrounds associated with low symbolic capital, these axes of identity are generally downplayed in contemporary nationalist narratives. Even at a local level where the audience is Puerto Rican, boxers are represented as essentially national subjects, taking punches on behalf of the nation and not for their class and/or race. In a marked shift from earlier decades when the state tried to "whiten" Puerto Rican sports representatives for public consumption and black athletes decried those attempts, any public discourse that exposes divisions within the national body—including tensions between the diaspora and the islanders—is virtually suppressed.

Whereas in 1969 former world medium-weight champion José "Chegüi" Torres complained that black Puerto Rican boxers were assumed to lack intellect ("the boxer has no brain, but yes, he has a pair of good fists, a strong and muscular body and a flat nose"),[20] today race is not acknowledged in public discourse on boxing at all. As Ben Carrington has observed in the British context, "Blacks, and Black athletes in particular, will be rewarded if they subscribe to the view that racism is non-existent . . . or at least that it is a minor aberration."[21] Even for organic intellectuals of the statehood movement such as columnist Luis Dávila Colón—one of the few who acknowledges boxing champ Félix "Tito" Trinidad's class if not his racial location—the boxer's triumphs are not only, or even primarily, for him, his family, his "race," or his barrio. He boxes for the national collectivity: "Tito's championship is everyone's triumph. . . . At a time when the country's self-esteem was so low . . . Tito's Victory was a gift."[22]

According to Dávila Colón, the setbacks that Trinidad helped the country overcome included the island voters' confounding "none of the above" vote in the 1998 status consultation, the controversy over the release of several pro-independence political prisoners, and the growing debate over the presence of the U.S. Navy in Vieques. In this sense, "national" performances that show Puerto Ricans in a "positive" light are deemed more important to collective well-being than "nationalist" political action, which is almost always divisive. The cultural sphere is the privileged site for articulating Puerto Rican solidarity beyond the partisan politics that divides the community along the axis of pro- or anti-annexation to the United States. In the words of pro-statehood Representative Kenneth McClintock, "These two victories gave us all the opportunity to go in caravans, because here everyone caravaned together and this does not happen during election time."[23] Concerning how this expression of cultural nationalism would affect the statehood project, McClintock responded, "A society that produces [artists and athletes] has a lot to offer the American nation."[24]

If boxing articulates a politics of difference in the cultural realm, like all mass spectacles staged for profit the sport also affirms the values associated with capitalism: hard work, upward mobility, individualism: "Trinidad's triumph is the story of how one can escape poverty chasing a dream."[25] At the same time, Dávila Colón's pride in Trinidad was partly due to the latter's style of unaffected perseverance, which greatly contrasted to challenger Oscar De la Hoya's tendency to punch and duck. Highlighting the conjunction of nationalist and capitalist values with masculinity, Dávila Colón compared De la Hoya's style to that of a *picaflor* (hummingbird), an allusion that in Puerto Rico connotes effeminacy. Not coincidentally, De la Hoya was also described by the local press as *el estadounidense*[26] and not a Latino or Mexican American, suggesting that Puerto Ricans, particularly black men, were more "macho" than U.S. Latinos. Trinidad's fighting style is simultaneously an index of superior masculinity, Puerto Ricanness, and the safe inclusion of black men in the imagined nation. Underscoring that he is a good black and a better Puerto Rican, Trinidad accepts his place as a national hero, when all he asks is to be remembered as "the humble young man who has never had problems with anyone."[27]

Whereas the De la Hoya–Trinidad match underscored the relationship between black Puerto Ricanness and masculinity, Trinidad's next matches against two African American boxers were staged strictly in international terms. During the first fight against William Joppy, Trinidad's performance included the wearing of an island-shaped Puerto Rican flag on his neck, in contrast to the U.S. flag emblazoned in Joppy's robe. Speaking in Spanish, the announcer described Trinidad as *el gran campeón puertorriqueño*, the great Puerto Rican champ. The pro-Trinidad crowd—estimated at 18,235[28]—responded by chanting "Trinidad," frantically waving Puerto Rican flags, holding up signs that read "Viva Puerto Rico #1," and booing the U.S. anthem.

The Puerto Rican ethnonation—including islanders and U.S. Puerto Ricans—symbolically occupied Madison Square Garden in a national spectacle tied to but not identical with the show on center stage. Trinidad's victory, however, articulated both stages, producing a joint nationalist performance between sports star and fans. As a reward for raising the cultural value of Puerto Rican bodies, massive crowds welcomed Trinidad after he beat Joppy. The headline of *El Nuevo Día*, the largest newspaper in Puerto Rico, said it all: "¡Somos grandes!" (We Are Big!).[29] The feeling that Puerto Ricans were superior to Americans at least in the boxing ring gave Trinidad's victory "the dramatic intensity such as is reached in few theatres."[30]

To add to the euphoria of Trinidad's victory, Denise Quiñones won the Miss Universe crown that same weekend. A barrage of advertising celebrated the coronation of two Puerto Rican–born "monarchs" and promoted a wide range of services and commodities, including cars, newspapers, and mortgages. As witnessed with the rise of Ricky Martin as a globalized megastar, private business sold itself through the largely uncontested idiom of national pride. These commercial pitches all delivered the same message, exposing the collusion of economic, political, and cultural elites in mobilizing nationalism to combat the symbolic humiliation of colonialism while maintaining the colonial status. Examples of the "we're big; spend big" pitch abound. From "Bella" Honda: "Today the whole world cannot shake its amazement. A small country has demonstrated that there is no greater wealth than the quality of its people."[31] Doral Financial Corporation, a mortgage and financing service provider, displayed a retouched photo of Tito Trinidad wearing Denise Quiñones' crown and she wearing his belt under the headline of "Puerto Rico is number 1 . . . and its flag waves high for the pride of those of us who inhabit this beautiful land."[32]

Symptomatically, reference to the island's status, colonialism, and political subordination were as rare in these ads as any mention of Trinidad's race or class. The issue was instead articulated in terms of stature, suggesting that Puerto Rican "inferiority" stems not from social relations but from the island's size: "We tend to fall into the temptation of wanting to achieve as to distinguish ourselves, perhaps seeking to overcome the smallness of our soil."[33] A variation on this theme was Banco Popular's one-page ad in a collector's edition simply titled "Denise y Tito: Orgullo Nuestro" (Denise and Tito: Our Pride), in which a map shows the island of Puerto Rico larger than any other land mass, including North and South America. The caption reads: "Thank you for showing how big we really are."[34]

In a handmade sign addressed to Trinidad and held by several men of varied ages, one could read: "Thank you, thank you, for raising Puerto Rico to the highest place."[35] If the elite feels "small" due to political and economic constraints, the majority suggests that Puerto Ricans are considered "low" due not only to the class and racial associations with *boricua* nationality. Popular discourse hence rejects both constitutional definitions and economic statistics that measure Puerto Rican value unfavorably. Puerto Rico may be a colony and the island's per capita income may be half of Mississippi's, but the victories of the "monarchs" suggest that *boricuas* are as worthy and valuable as any other people. In the words of one *El Nuevo Dia* reader, "Boxing demonstrates to many Puerto Ricans that pride and dignity are not the product of political status or ideologies; it comes out of the person herself or himself."[36] Objective markers of inferiority are hence canceled by the high quality of the island's only "native" resource: its people. Yet, as their place in advertising suggests, Denise and Tito have value not as sovereign rulers but also as global *boricua* commodities.

ABOVE THE BELT: COMMODIFYING
NATIONALIST EMOTION IN THE GLOBAL MARKETPLACE

Trinidad's next fight with Bernard Hopkins, a tough "ex-con" from Philadel-phia, coalesced the specific ways that nationalism, capitalism, and a carni-valesque desire to affirm that social hierarchies can be upset and won over by the lowliest of nationals. Unlike the subdued Joppy, Hopkins resented the lack of recognition afforded to him as a champion and had no qualms in raising the economic and symbolic stakes of the match by disparaging Puerto Ricans as a national group.[37] Revealingly, the Trinidad-Hopkins match also suggested that assumptions regarding national value could not be taken for granted in the global economy. Although Hopkins was born and raised in the United States—the most "powerful" nation in the world—it was Trinidad's market value and dedicated fan-consumer base that raised the financial stakes of the match and finally made Hopkins a rich man. In a textbook case, Hopkins be-came the "ugly (low) American" to Trinidad's (high) class act.

Apparently appalled at the booing of the U.S. anthem during the Trinidad-Joppy title fight and Trinidad's taunts using a Puerto Rican flag, Hopkins took the defense of American pride (and purse) in his hands. During two press conferences, one in New York and one in Puerto Rico, Hopkins threw a *boricua* flag to the ground and stomped on it. When he did that the first time in New York, no one became violent. In Puerto Rico, however, a near riot occurred on July 11, 2001: "Within seconds of the act, hundreds of irate Trinidad fans stormed Hopkins, knocking over the main podium and forcing 'The Execu-tioner' to make a hasty retreat to one of the dressing rooms at the west end of the Coliseum."[38] The manipulation of nationalist emotion recalls the common "instructions" given to broadcasters before and during boxing matches: "Cre-ate a feeling that the competitors don't like each other. . . . Studies have shown that fans react better, and are more emotionally involved, if aggressive hostility is present." The nation was incensed, meaning more people than ever would see the fight. At pharmacies and cafeterias and on street corners, portable television sets popped up to show the native son beat the American.

After the riot calmed down, the Trinidad-Hopkins fight was presented as a struggle to safeguard Puerto Rico's honor, and Tito's responsibility was to defend "national dignity." Trinidad promised to teach Hopkins that, "a nation's flag should be respected"[39] and to "chop his head off and throw it to the public so they can eat it like piranhas."[40] Given the nationally inflected competition, Hopkins's management of the Puerto Rican flag immediately raised the question of whether Trinidad should display the U.S. flag as well as the Puerto Rican flag when he traveled to Madison Square Garden on September 29, bringing the island's liminal political location to the fore. As recorded in the press, most readers appeared to support the display of both flags but for different reasons. Among the reasons cited were to express solidarity with the United States after the 9/11 attacks; to demonstrate that countries can live under two flags without "insulting" anyone; to signify that Puerto Ricans are American citizens; and to show that Puerto Ricans are respectful.[41] Trinidad's camp ultimately took the high ground and decided to display both flags in solidarity with the United States, suggesting that nationalist symbols are displayed strategically to convey a wide range of messages.

But the national pressure on Trinidad probably did not help him in the ring. Despite the great national investment and his trunks bearing the Puerto Rican flag, Hopkins defeated Trinidad. Although Hopkins's first words of victory—"USA"—followed the nationalist script, he later declared that he won the fight for his "family" and to prove his masculinity. "I am the macho," the boxer affirmed.[42] For Hopkins, nationalism as publicity ploy had little bearing on his performance against Trinidad; he later apologized to Puerto Ricans, saying that "we are all equal." If there was little national impact to Hopkins's victory, Trinidad's first career loss was summed up as having a "painful national impact."[43] In this sense, whereas the match was a commodified event that clearly intended to manipulate nationalist emotion for profit, Trinidad's loss was publicly articulated not in economic but symbolic terms.

Having little to gain after winning three titles and multimillion-dollar purses, Trinidad decided to retire from boxing. A major *fiesta del pueblo* was organized for Tito to say goodbye and for the fans to thank him for all that he had done for Puerto Rico, namely, to provide the people with joy and *intensas emociones* (intense emotions). Not coincidentally, Trinidad was afraid that he would become *too* emotional in conveying his decision to the people and planned to counter any frustration by *entregarse' a su pueblo* (giving himself to the people).[44] At the Hiram Bithorn stadium, what animated Trinidad's career—to be thought of as a nice (black) boy and be loved—met commerce and nationalism in signs such as "Tito #1" put out by Budweiser. To the extent, however, that Puerto Rican sports spectators are never passive but engaged in reproducing or disrupting the spectacle of nation, sports remains a critical site for playing with the national self, defining its borders, and struggling over who speaks (for) it. In addition, demonstrating once again that the performing *boricua* body is never far from politics, Trinidad announced that he was not discarding an entry into local party politics.

THE DIASPORA KNOCKS: THE CASE OF JOHN "QUIET MAN" RUIZ

With Trinidad, boxing offered a way of engendering Puerto Rican lower-class and racialized masculinity as national but left the question of the diaspora out of the ring—until the Massachusetts-born and -raised boxer John Ruiz became the first U.S. Latino to win the World Boxing Association heavyweight title on March 4, 2001. Although Ruiz was not considered, pound per pound, the best boxer in the world, as was Trinidad, Puerto Ricans celebrated his victory to a significant extent because Americans have largely dominated the heavyweight division for more than five decades. Latino and Caribbean boxers have tended to excel in the lower weight divisions, which command less spectatorship, prestige, and purses. In the words of columnist Sandra Rodríguez, Ruiz's "victory destroyed the myth that Latin Americans, and specially Puerto Ricans, could not win in this category destined for only gringo glories."[45] At 6'1" and weighing 230 pounds, Ruiz made the Puerto Rican concern with "smallness" history.

Yet, although the initial Puerto Rican reaction to Ruiz's victory was of jubilation, this joy was soon to be interrupted by Tito Trinidad's trainer and father, Félix Trinidad Rodríguez Sr. The Puerto Rico Boxing Federation awarded Ruiz the "Boxer of the Year" award on February 21, 2002, and Governor Sila María Calderón provided funds for Ruiz's hometown of Sabana Grande to stage a "national hero's welcome" for the returning son. On a radio show called Super Kadena's Knockout, however, "Papa Trinidad" called in to say that Ruiz should not receive the award or the recognition because he was "not Puerto Rican." Furthermore, "To be a national hero is not easy and even though John is the son of Puerto Rican parents, he was not raised in Puerto Rico. I think we need to save our celebration for when we have a champion of our own. I don't think it's fair that we are bestowing a title on John that doesn't belong to him since he was born and raised in the Boston area."[46] The fact that Ruiz had never represented Puerto Rico or identified as a Puerto Rican prior to the fight was also noted: "Why didn't they sing Puerto Rico's national anthem before the fight and only the U.S. anthem? It's because he considers himself North American."[47]

Trinidad Sr. went on to file a lawsuit, specifically "seeking an injunction to stop the awards ceremonies until the Commission reveals its selection criteria."[48] At the heart of the dispute seemed to be Trinidad's ambitions for one of his boxers, Fres Oquendo, whom he hoped would become the first Puerto Rican heavyweight champion. True to his nickname of "quiet man," Ruiz had little to say about the critique, except that he was hurt and believed that Trinidad Sr. was "more of a man than that."[49] But Congressman José Serrano from New York, a veteran of such skirmishes, took on the fight on his behalf. Alluding to the importance of the U.S. Puerto Rican leadership in resolving the impasse over the U.S. Navy's presence in Vieques, Serrano declared: "If we are Puerto Ricans to help bring peace to Vieques, we should also be when we obtain a world boxing championship."[50]

As Gregory Rodríguez has observed in the Chicana/o context, "boxing offers one form of serious fun where we see people at work constructing or deconstructing ways of being this or that kind of 'man,' or that kind of 'American,' or this or that kind of 'Latino.'"[51] Equally important, if sport is one of the ways that communities "publicly display their community identity and in some cases their political aspirations,"[52] the debate generated by Trinidad's attacks on Ruiz connotes a shift in the ways that U.S. Puerto Rican celebrities circulate on the island now as compared with the past three decades. In other instances where the "Puerto Ricanness" of U.S. Puerto Rican celebrities and public figures, such as *salsero* Willie Colón and Congressman Serrano himself, was questioned, island Puerto Ricans clearly perceived their U.S. counterparts as inferior, as they considered them to be culturally polluted, ignorant, and "low class."

The raging debate around what constitutes Puerto Ricanness offered an opportunity to negotiate the parameters of nationhood and articulate the relation between the local and the global. While stereotypes remain regarding "Nuyoricans" and U.S.-raised Puerto Ricans in general, these are no longer as widely used or acceptable in public discourse as they once were. For most commentators in the print media, Puerto Ricanness was not defined by place of birth or residence but by "feelings" of affinity and ancestry. Ruiz was Puerto

Rican because "his veins boil of braveness with his boricua blood."[53] This repositioning bears the profound mark that for the first time in history more Puerto Ricans live in the United States than on the island.

Unlike earlier decades, there is no longer any Puerto Rican unaffected by the diaspora experience—regardless of class or race. Whereas the largest wave of migrants to the mainland was poor and often racialized as "black," the migratory experience is no longer that of the "exportation" of a single class. At the same time, if Puerto Ricans in the United States, particularly in cities like New York, Chicago, and Hartford, were considered the poorest and least desirable of immigrants by the white power structure, the identification of Puerto Ricans as Latinos, the largest aggregate ethnic group in the United States, has resignified Puerto Rican status. The days in which Puerto Rican boxers fought in the ring for "human rights" have now been eclipsed for a struggle over the market worth of Puerto Ricans as the ultimate measure in value.

The courting of Latinos as a major market, a block of votes, and power brokers in the nation's largest cities has been also accompanied by the rise in visibility and social value of Puerto Ricans in the United States. In the words of one fan from Santurce: "Mr. Félix Trinidad missed the boat with those comments, with a son who is going to fight in New York in May, and 90% of those fans are New York–born boricuas."[54] In addition, most world-class Puerto Rican celebrities are U.S. born and/or raised, including Jennifer López, Marc Anthony, and Benicio del Toro. For the same mix of national affirmation and commerce, U.S. Puerto Rican stars and politicians have incorporated *boricua* identity as part of their public personas, bringing unprecedented visibility and prestige to Puerto Ricans as a group. As former sports coach and commentator Fufi Santori observed, "it was convenient for Ruiz's promoters that he was Hispanic because his victory over Holyfield would set a world record. . . . How many times hasn't Don King brought out his little Puerto Rican flag in press conferences? Is that solidarity with our nationhood and our causes or is that solidarity with the sale of boxing tickets?"[55]

Ruiz shrugged off any attempt to question his national loyalties by admitting that although he was English-speaking and hence "American only in language" (*norteamericano de boca*), he was really "a Puerto Rican from Sabana Grande."[56] His mother Gladys, who lives in Sabana Grande, spoke for him on more than one occasion: "My son is a true *boricua*, he is Puerto Rican and not an American."[57] Ruiz's Puerto Ricanness also was coded by his "humility," which was deemed to be comparable with that of Trinidad, if not his father. "Everybody identified with John. Those who know him and those who don't. He is such a humble person that he says that the strikes to the head, the elbowing and everything else that Holyfield, who fought a very dirty fight, did, is normal."[58] Puerto Ricans from both sides of the puddle saw Ruiz's victory as "the biggest gift that you gave us, the first heavyweight crown for Latin America, and specially, for Puerto Rico,"[59] and this made him part of *la gran familia boricua*.

The largely negative response to Trinidad Sr.'s comments implied the increased acceptance of the "Puerto Ricanness" of U.S. *boricuas* but also underscored the nonalignment between avowed political ideology concerning the status debate and practices of exclusion toward other Puerto Ricans. Some pro-independence commentators, for instance, criticized Trinidad Sr. for failing to recognize that Puerto Rican culture has indeed survived in the United States while the noted trainer—who is a staunch pro-statehooder—proposed an even more territorial articulation of nation than political nationalists. "I have said and I repeat it now that John Ruiz should bring his Puerto Ricannes out from his heart where he says that he has it. It's not enough to feel proud in your heart. You have to bring your pride out to raise the name of Puerto Rico and the boricua nation very high. . . . My recommendation to John Ruiz is that he demands from his manager and promoter that they play the Puerto Rican anthem and that you can see Puerto Rico's flags on the ring before his fights begin."[60] The simultaneous claims that Puerto Ricans in the United States are still equally *boricua* due to a common culture, and that they are not if it conflicts with local interests, inadvertently weakens the culturalist argument against statehood and reveals the largely symbolic use of culture as a political ruse.

While Trinidad Sr. criticized the opportunism of the state—the "all-powerful" government that uses public funding to manufacture nationalist pride[61]—for his own business-opportunistic reasons, thousands of people in the hometown of the Ruiz family "did not sleep" celebrating the victory. "Thousands of people threw themselves into the street in this western Puerto Rican city at dawn yesterday to celebrate with dancing, screams, hugs, and parties."[62] The fact that *la gente no durmió en Sabana Grande* (the people did not sleep) underscores that the feelings evoked by the fight were so intense and pleasurable that people did not want to let go of them. In the neighborhood of Gladys Ruiz, the boxer's mother, accounts suggest that all "5,000 inhabitants . . . were partying because of the boxer's feat."[63] The Sabana Grande response was repeated a few weeks later when more than 1,500 people greeted John Ruiz at the Luis Muñoz Marín Airport "waving Puerto Rican flags and carrying signs that read 'welcome home' as well as dancing to a *plena* beat."[64]

Among the greeters was Governor Sila María Calderón, members of the legislature, and fellow boxers, each there for a different reason. Calderón went the furthest in equating Ruiz with Puerto Rico itself: "John embodies what Puerto Rico is: a peaceful country, *apacible*, but strong, firm, brave like this boxer is."[65] Given the high rates of crime and the violence in Puerto Rico, the governor's comments could only be read politically, in the context of the Vieques struggle. Probably removed from it all, Ruiz reciprocated by displaying his World Boxing Association title belt and telling the crowd, "this championship is for all of you."[66] Ruiz then traveled by car to meet the people of Sabana Grande, who first celebrated until dawn the day of Ruiz's victory and then assembled at the heart of the town to give their absent son a national hero's welcome.

Sabana Grande's mayor, Miguel Ortiz, believed the celebrations to be not only local but also "national": "Ruiz's arrival will be a great national event."[67] The title of "national hero" was in fact the most seriously contested aspect of Ruiz's reception in Puerto Rico by Trinidad Sr. and even others sympathetic to Ruiz. Regardless of Trinidad's intentions, the awarding of the title to a boxer who before his title fight had never said he was Puerto Rican and had never labored on behalf of any "national" cause or under any national discourse does raise the question of what the title of a "national hero" means in the context of (post) modern Puerto Rico. If in the past, a national hero or patriot was someone who did something substantial to improve the quality of life of Puerto Ricans, today just beating an opponent in a ring and bringing out a flag is more than enough. This suggests not only that politics has moved to "culture" for many but that "culture" is a simulacrum to be enjoyed instantaneously and then discarded until the next thrill.

HANGING UP THE GLOVES, OR BY WAY OF CONCLUSION

Although Puerto Rican cultural nationalism remains essentially performative, this should not obscure the fact that nationalist ideologies appear to be largely uncontested in public culture and are used for a wide range of purposes, from mobilizing voters to selling beer. If even a substantial minority of Puerto Ricans did not conceive of themselves as national subjects, opposition to the idea of a separate Olympic identity or critique to the expectation that all Puerto Rican athletes represent a common nation and not, for instance, the United States would likely surface. As Mike Cronin has observed in the context of the multiple Irelands, sport can be theorized as an important vehicle in nation building, but only if it promotes "nationalist values that are uncontested,"[68] which is the case in Puerto Rico.

Whereas Puerto Ricans and other interlocutors generally perceive *boricuas* as deeply divided between "different" political projects such as supporting statehood, independence, and commonwealth, these distinctions only offer a difference in style of elite rule and subaltern modes of symbolic defiance. This leaves us with an ambiguous—can we expect anything else of Puerto Rico?—conclusion. Boxing and other sports offer spaces for Puerto Ricans to perform as independent nationals, a practice that can be read as a desire for national recognition and political independence. In the words of Mayor Willie Miranda Marín of Caguas, the victories of Denise and Tito, for instance, signified "that the island is capable of self-government."[69] Yet, these desires are largely played out through activities that athletes and spectators know will not alter the political status, which clearly links Puerto Ricans to the metropolis. As C. L. R. James observes in his classic study of cricket and politics in the British Caribbean, "I am equally certain that in these years, social and political passions, denied normal outlets, expressed themselves so fiercely in cricket (and other games) precisely because they were games."[70] Sports, then, allows Puerto Ricans to reject not the metropolitan citizenship and any benefits that may accrue from it but values that measure the worth of people in capitalist and normative national terms.

Even further—and perhaps the most important aspect of sports as a national simulacrum—is its affirmation of the present. Whereas the projects of change embodied in statehood and independence discourses articulate a future in which things will be better, discourse around boxing and beauty queen victories suggest a different articulation of change, one that understands life as the perpetual crowning and uncrowning of kings with specific joys and pains, not as linear progress toward a specific, utopian, goal. The emphasis on individual self-improvement and self-esteem, while supportive of the capitalist status quo that devalues Puerto Ricans as an ethnonational group, also indicates that the future status of plenty can be accessed now. "From them we learned to believe in ourselves, there are no impossible dreams, nor unattainable goals."[71]

While Martin and Miller argue that once the nation "can no longer be taken as a stable receptacle of society, the belief in natural attachment of the self to the body is no more secure,"[72] the Puerto Rican case suggests that a national formation at its most insecure can find an even greater attachment to sports as a legitimizing arena. Not coincidentally, the day that Trinidad lost, he was also knocked out of public view. If a boxer cannot put the nation's best, star-studded face forward, there is no room for him in the public sphere for his defeat reminds everyone of the nation's embattled status. Letting the people down and falling out of the limelight seems to have triggered a bout of melancholia for Trinidad, who in 2003, with Arnold Schwarzenegger charm and in the same place and at the same time as John Ruiz was fighting in Atlantic City, announced, "I'll be back." "Puerto Rico," asserts sports columnist Gabrielle Paese, "has been reeling in the aftershock ever since."[73] Ready for the next, ephemeral fight for another crown.

NOTES

I would like to thank Celeste Fraser Delgado, for her indispensable editorial guidance, and my research assistants Katerina Seligmann and Kairos Lloberas.

1. Flatley, "Warhol Gives Good Face: Publicity and the Politics of Prosopopoeia," 104.
2. "Quietly Deservedly Proud," *Sun Sentinel*, June 14, 2001.
3. Negrón-Muntaner, *Boricua Pop*.
4. T. Miller, "Competing Allegories," 21.
5. J. Scott, *Domination and the Arts of Resistance*, 9.
6. Masters, "Breeding Cuba's Champs."
7. Torres Rivera, "Aplausos para John Ruiz," 166.
8. Balmaseda, "Grace, Talent, Heart: Female Boxer Represents Sports' Ideal," 1B.
9. Newfield, "The Shame of Boxing," 2.
10. Interview, *Nuyoricans*, video directed by Alan Glazen (Puerto Rico, 2002).
11. Morris, *Puerto Rico*.
12. Paese, "Commonwealth Gives Puerto Rico a Sports Identity."
13. Ibid.
14. Elliott Castro, quoted in ibid.
15. Merret, "Sport and Nationalism," 33–59.
16. R. Martin and Miller, "Fielding Sport: A Preface to Politics," 12.
17. Paese, "Commonwealth Gives Puerto Rico a Sports Identity."
18. Zenón Cruz, *Narciso Descubre su trasero*, 1:181.
19. López Nieves, "Debate Olímpico," 79.
20. Quoted in Zenón Cruz, *Narciso Descubre su trasero*, 1:200.
21. Carrington, "Double Consciousness and the Black British Athlete," 134.
22. Dávila Colón, "Irma y su milagroso caldo de gallina," 124–25.
23. P. García, "Tranquilo el liderato estadista," 30.
24. Ibid.
25. Dávila Colón, "Irma y su milagroso caldo de gallina," 123.
26. "No habrá una revancha Trinidad–De la Hoya," Associated Press, May 6, 2001, 1C.
27. Vega Curry, "Latente en la mente de Tito la posibilidad del retiro," 156.
28. Paese, "Trinidad Wins WBA Middleweight Title," 110.
29. "¡Somos grandes!," *El Nuevo Día*, May 13, 2001, 1.
30. C. L. R. James, *Beyond a Boundary*, 196.
31. Honda Ad, *San Juan Star*, May 17, 2001, 94.

32. Doral Financial Corporation Ad, *San Juan Star*, May 15, 2001, 71.

33. Arrieta Vilá, "De todo un poco," 93.

34. "Denise y Tito: Orgullo Nuestro," Banco Popular Ad, *El Nuevo Día*, July 2001, 8.

35. *El Nuevo Día*, May 15, 1001, 30.

36. Torres Rivera, "Aplausos para John Ruiz," 166.

37. T. Miller, "Competing Allegories," 27.

38. Edwards, "Rumble at Clemente: Hopkins Runs Gauntlet of Angry Fans," 94.

39. Ibid., 95.

40. Pérez, "'Explican' a Bernard Hopkins," 143.

41. "Con una o dos banderas?," *El Nuevo Día*, September 26, 2001, 153.

42. Ribas, "Soy un boxeador más completo," 123.

43. Vega Curry, "Vuelve a salir el sol," 124.

44. Santiago Arce, "Siempre seré la misma persona," 126.

45. S. Rodriguez, "Boricua, aquí o allá.

46. Roman, "Another False Choice," 222.

47. Fonseca, "Trinidad Sr.: Commission Should Not Honor Ruiz," 81.

48. Paese, "Cast Your Vote."

49. Correa Velázquez, "John Ruiz."

50. "Mensaje era para Comisión de Boxeo," *El Vocero*, March 9, 2001, 61.

51. G. Rodríguez, "Boxing and Masculinity," 253.

52. J. Harvie and A. Bairner, *Sport and Community Relations in Northern Ireland* (Leicester: Leicester University Press, 1995), 119. Quoted in Cronin, "Which Nation, Which Flag?," 143.

53. C. García, "Una victoria a pulso de coragón," 6c.

54. Quoted in "Respuesta pública a las expresiones," *El Nuevo Día*, March 11, 2001, 169.

55. Santori, "De aquí . . . ¿o de allá?," 129.

56. Moreno, "Ruiz se suelta a hablar: Le lanza reto a Lewis."

57. "Enorme fiesta boricua," *El Nuevo Herald*, March 5, 2001, 1c.

58. Santiago Arce, "Abrazo sabaneño para el campeón," 128.

59. Torres Rivera, "Aplausos para John Ruiz," 166.

60. "Carta abierta al pueblo de Puerto Rico de don Félix Trinidad," *El Vocero*, March 23, 2001.

61. Cruz, "Trinidad Sr. vs. Ruiz Controversy Endless," 67.

62. "Enorme fiesta boricua," *El Nuevo Herald*, March 5, 2001, 1c.

63. Ibid.

64. Colón Díaz, "Puerto Rico Welcomes John Ruiz as a National Hero."

65. "Puerto Rico recibe como héroe a Ruiz," *Miami Herald*, March 23, 2001, 1D.

66. Colón Díaz, "Puerto Rico Welcomes John Ruiz as a National Hero."

67. Santiago Arce, "Abrazo sabaneño para el campeón," 128.

68. Cronin, "Which Nation, Which Flag?," 135.

69. Dávila Colón, "Entre las sogas y las pasarelas," 37.

70. C. L. R. James, *Beyond a Boundary*, 376.

71. "Denise y Tito: Orgullo Nuestro."

72. R. Martin and Toby Miller, "Fielding Sport: A Preface to Politics," 2.

73. Paese, "Trinidad Coming out of Retirement? Volleyball, Gold Notes."

6

Creolité in the Hood:
Diaspora as Source and Challenge

JUAN FLORES

The flight attendant let out an icy scream of terror when she noticed a pair of hefty *jueyes*, native Puerto Rican land crabs, strutting down the center aisle of the plane. It was one of those infamous red-eye flights from San Juan to New York, filled to the last seat with Puerto Ricans from all walks of life. The panicky flight attendant is a stereotypical white-bread *gringa*, "angelical and innocent, a frigid blond like Kim Novak in her days as a frigid blond." What is this, a prank, or a hijacking? Who are these terrorist *jueyes*? The hysteria spread to the crew, and to the passengers, though among the *boricuas* there is an underlying but pervasive giggle, that familiar jocularity laced with irony that Puerto Ricans call *jaibería*, or *el arte de bregar*, "the art of dealing with the situation."[1] The stage for a dramatic cultural collision is set.

Students of contemporary Caribbean culture may well recognize this memorable scene from the opening sentences of the fanciful essay by Puerto Rican author Luis Rafael Sánchez entitled "La guagua aérea," or the "air bus."[2] This highly entertaining and suggestive story set aboard the air shuttle known to the majority of his countrymen has become nothing less than canonical since its publication in 1983, capturing as it does the existential feel of a people caught up in a relentless process of circular migration and carrying their indelible cultural trappings back and forth between the beloved but troubled homeland and the cold and inimical but somehow also very familiar setting in the urban United States. The story struck such a chord among its reading public that it has been republished countless times in a range of languages; is required reading in many schools and colleges on the island, in the United States, and in Latin America and the Caribbean; became the basis of a widely publicized movie; and serves as the guiding metaphor for two books about modern-day Puerto Rico, significantly titled *The Commuter Nation* and *Puerto Rican Nation on the Move*.[3] Its irresistible title alone, *La guagua aérea*, has assured its place as perhaps the best-known work of contemporary Puerto Rican literature.

Present-day migration, no longer the momentous, once-in-a-lifetime trauma of earlier times, is now a commute, an everyday kind of excursion, like jumping on a bus or subway and arriving at an equally familiar destination. In the story, the feeling aboard that hilariously nervous flight is so matter-of-course that passengers even comment how they lose track which way they're headed—whether they'll be arriving in New York or San Juan. The two end points become interchangeable, so much so that the *jueyes* caught and cleaned in Bayamón are sure to find their place in a stewpot in the Bronx, no questions asked. No serious danger of losing the culture by being away from the island, either, for the cultural practices and sensibilities typical of the home culture are just as at home in New York, New Jersey, Chicago, or Florida. How resilient, how immutable, *el arte de bregar*, how ineradicable that famous *mancha de plátano*! The fears of a national schizophrenia, or cultural genocide, are assuaged by the comforting sense of translocal equilibrium.

Yet, when looked at more closely, *la guagua aérea* in the well-known story only moves in one direction; the migratory voyage, presented as a commute, is still basically one-way. That is, the cultural baggage aboard the flight is entirely that of the island, the readily familiar, almost stereotypical trappings of the national traditions, emblematized by the shocking land crabs but omnipresent in the gestures, humor, and gregarious, gossipy ways of the passengers. As for the other final stop of the commute, the New York City environment and its cultural life, mention is made of the Bronx and El Barrio and other familiar scenes, but only as sites for the playing out and preservation of traditional island lifeways, not as a setting that is in fact home and the primary cultural base of half of those binational commuters. The rich liminal space between home culture and diaspora becomes nothing but a zone of cultural authentication, while the cultural and human salience of that "other" home is reduced to the anxieties of an uptight gringa airline stewardess plagued by nightmares of King Kong atop the Empire State Building.

Thus the story begs a key question: what about the cultural baggage that goes the other way, the experience and expressions learned and forged in the diaspora that make their way back to the homeland, there to have their impact on those rapidly changing traditions and lifeways? With all the vast and burgeoning studies devoted to the cultural changes brought by modern migrations, transnational flows, and diaspora communities, and with the widespread understanding that these movements are most commonly circular and multidirectional, it is indeed striking how little attention has gone to the cultural experience and consequences of the massive population of return migrants and their children who grew up in the diaspora. For too long, and too uncritically, I would suggest, it has been assumed that the main cultural flow, and especially the main line of cultural resistance, has been from the colonial or postcolonial point of presumed "origin" to the diaspora enclave in the metropolis, and that the flow in the other direction, from the metropolis to the colony/postcolony, is strictly "from above," hegemonic, and reinforcing of the prevailing structure of cultural imposition and domination.

These abiding assumptions, I would further suggest in line with the theme of our conference, have been amply present in the discussion of Caribbean music and may go to perpetuate a sometimes misleading sense of the dynamic of Caribbean musical innovation and change, and therefore of the place and function of the music in contemporary Caribbean communities. In some recent writings there has been a beginning discussion of what is called "transnationalism from below" and "social remittances," which I have extended in referring to "cultural remittances." Some of these lines of thinking might have interesting bearings on our understanding of Caribbean music, historically and especially in our own times. I invite you to join me, then, on the *guagua aérea* and head in the other direction, from the diaspora to the islands, and thereby glimpse some of the history of Caribbean music from a different aerial view than is more commonly the case.

One of the most frequent passengers on the cultural airbus is Willie Colón. His life and music commute back and forth between his home turf in the Bronx and his ancestral Puerto Rico, with more than casual stop-offs in other musical zones of the Caribbean. His first albums, produced in the later 1960s at the threshold of the salsa era, attest to his programmatically and defiantly eclectic stylistic agenda; while comprising mainly Cuban-based *sones* and *guaguancós*, the titles and cover images of *El Malo* (Bad Boy), *The Hustler, Cosa Nuestra*, and *The Big Break/La Gran Fuga* proudly present the persona of the Latin superfly, the borderline criminal street thug. The music, too, veers off from its Afro-Cuban base by references to and samplings from styles from Puerto Rico, Colombia, Panama, and that "other" ancestral homeland, Africa, while also demonstrating the young Nuyorican's native familiarity with jazz, soul, and rock. Along with his partner in crime, vocalist Hector Lavoe, Colón projects from the beginning of his pioneering salsa career the new musical mixes resounding in his beloved Nueva York barrios, a singularly diasporic "creolité in the hood."

But it is in *Asalto Navideño*, his immensely and enduringly popular Christmas album released in 1971, that Colón transports us on the airbus and makes the relation between diaspora and Caribbean homeland the central theme of his work. An undisputed classic of the salsa canon, this compilation puts the lie to the widespread notion that salsa is no more than an imitation of purely Cuban sources by mostly Puerto Rican exponents, and that Puerto Rican music has little or no presence. Rather, the educated listener recognizes immediately that the strongly accented *son, guaracha*, and *guaguancó* weave of the musical fabric is laced with vocal, instrumental, and rhythmic qualities typical of Puerto Rican *seis, aguinaldo, bomba*, and *plena*. Most notably, aside from the decidedly *jíbaro* quality of Lavoe's vocals, Colón brings in the famed Yomo Toro on the *cuatro*, the emblematic instrument of traditional Puerto Rican music. This *popurrí navideño* (Christmas medley), as one of the cuts is titled, is clearly intended as a dialogue with Puerto Rican culture. Even the album title, in its use of the word *asalto*, makes reference to the age-old tradition of Christmastide musical "invasions" of the houses of close friends and neighbors for the sake of partying and sharing in the holiday spirit, much in line with the primarily adoring, nostalgic tenor of that diaspora-island dialogue. But in light of the sequence of previous album titles, there is a thinly veiled double-entendre here, with the even more common meaning of *asalto* as "attack" or "mugging" lurking ominously close to the surface.

Two selections from that compilation, "Traigo la salsa" (I bring you salsa) and "Esta Navidad" (This Christmas), are of special interest to our discussion, since both lyrically and musically they enact the diaspora addressing the island culture in a complex, loving, but, at the same time, mildly challenging way. At one level, "Traigo la salsa" is about "bringing" Latin music to the immediate New York or North American audience and, along with it, holiday cheer from the warm tropics. Yet even here, it is not the usual salsa fare that is being offered; at one point the lyrics state, "Yo les traigo una rareza," "a rarity," and the singer goes on to explain that on this occasion he is adding in the *cuatro*, an instrument atypical of salsa, "por motivo de Navidad." At this level, though, salsa plus *cuatro* is clearly a sign of the island cultures being "brought" to the New York scene as a delicious Christmas offering, or as an *asalto* on North American culture much like the land crabs aboard the airbus. However, another dimension to this act of "bearing" or "bringing" the music is at play here, and it refers to bringing New York salsa to the island. Indeed, the opening words

and body of the lyrics, beginning with "Oígame señor, préstame atención . . . ,"
would seem to be addressing the personified island itself, and to be saying that
the singer is bringing salsa for him ("para tí"). The closing lines of the stanza,
which say "como allá en la isla" (like there on the island), make this geographical differentiation evident. That is, in addition to being a marker of Puerto Rican or Latino authenticity in the New York setting, salsa is at the same time, in
Puerto Rico itself, a marker of diasporic Nuyorican authenticity, distinct from
and originating externally to island musical traditions. In other words, as Juan
Otero Garabís has argued in a recent paper which I have found extremely helpful in preparing the present reflections, on the return trip aboard "la guagua
aérea" "traigo la salsa" (on the air bus I carry salsa).[4] Salsa is the musical baggage, the stylistic remittance of the diaspora on its return to the island.

This ambivalence, or bidirectional meaning, is conveyed in the musical
texture of the song as well, and in the album as a whole. Yomo Toro's *cuatro*,
for example, with all its symbolic weight as an authentication of Puerto Rican
culture, is deployed for both Christmas airs of *la música típica* and, as is most
obvious in the opening cut, "Introducción," for virtuoso riffs more resonant
of jazz and rock than of the familiar cadences of *seis décimas* or *aguinaldos*.
Another diaspora-based departure from the traditional Caribbean sources of
the salsa instrumentation is, of course, Colón's trombone, a stylistic device introduced into the New York Latin sound by Barry Rogers, José Rodríguez, and
other masters of Eddie Palmieri's pathbreaking "trombanga" band, La Perfecta,
in the early 1960s. It is the improvisational trombone lines that are perhaps
the sharpest marker of the urban diaspora in Afro-Caribbean music, the herald
of the friendly yet defiant musical *asalto* on territorially and nationally circum-
scribed tradition. Let's not forget that as late as 1978 salsa was still referred to
by some on the island as "an offensive, strident, stupefying, intoxicating and
frenetic music openly associated with the effects of sex, alcohol and drugs." As
Otero Garabís notes, people of that mind-set uphold the idea that to claim salsa
as "typical Puerto Rican music" "would be to plant a bomb in the foundation of
the national culture."

It should be mentioned in this regard that ironically, though fully consonant
with the logic of the music industry and a commoditized cultural nationalism,
by the early 1990s salsa had been domesticated and comfortably repatriated to
the island, to the point that it came to be equated with Puerto Rican identity
as such. As signs of this reversal, the Puerto Rico pavilion at the 1992 Columbus Quincentenary celebrations in Madrid was emblazoned with the slogan
"Puerto Rico Es Salsa," and the independent documentary of those same years,
Roqueros y Cocolos, showed salsa fans on the island justifying their preference

for salsa over the advertently foreign, imposed rock music with the claim that "salsa es de aquí" (salsa is from here). The prevalent interpretation is actually a Pan-Latino or Latin Americanist version of this nationalist appropriation, salsa being commonly identified as "tropical music" or, in the most influential book on the subject, *El libro de la salsa*, as "música del Caribe urbano."[5]

In any case, the Christmas celebrated in *Asalto Navideño* is obviously not the usual holiday occasion but a very special one that is somehow askew of the expected and accepted customs; it is, in short, one that, rather than enforcing the comfort of a known and familiar identity, is rather riddled by contrasting and, to some degree, clashing and contending identity claims. It is, emphatically, "*esta* navidad" (*this* Christmas). This complex, contradictory relation between diaspora and island cultures is addressed even more directly in the tune of that title, "Esta Navidad." There, the multiplicity of claims is dramatized in the frequent and varied naming of the symbol of Puerto Rican identity, "el jíbaro." Striking up a contagious *aguinaldo* air at the beginning, the typical *cuatro* parts play in continual counterpoint with the mischievously playful trombone line, as though setting up a counterpoint that will run through the entire piece. The lyrics tell of the attitude of the "jíbaros" who arrive from the United States only to look down on their island friends with "un aire de superioridad" (an air of superiority) and of great wisdom. This theme of the song is most remembered by the public and is generally assumed to be its main message: that those from the diaspora have been corrupted by their experience away from the homeland and authentic home culture, and try to overcome it, or fake it, as captured in the word *guillar*. But then, in an interesting twist, the lyrics continue with the speaker identifying himself as one of those "jíbaros guillados," a kind of bogus *jíbaro*, who is nonetheless, in a bold assertion, "pero un jíbaro de verdad" (but a *jíbaro* for real): "Hay jíbaros que saben más / y aquí queda demonstrado / soy un jíbaro guillado / pero un jíbaro de verdad" (roughly: There are *jíbaros* that know more / and here it's clearly shown / I am a would-be *jíbaro* / but a *jíbaro* for real). What entitles this returning diaspora Puerto Rican to feel confident about his knowledge and to claim "realness" after all? Evidently it is the song itself, as suggested in the phrase "aquí queda demonstrado" (here it is shown). Indeed, the song proceeds to the chorus, "Esta navidad, vamos a gozar," and then ends in vocal and instrumental improvisations very much in the *guaguancó*-based salsa style, the *tumbaito*, which by the end explicitly replaces the trappings and cadences of *típica*, the *lei-lo-lai*, with which it had begun. Or actually, in tune with that diasporic wisdom suggested in the lyrics, the lead voice draws the traditional holiday music into the eclectic, inclusive jam of this special Christmas celebration, making sure to add, "tambien invitaré a mi amigo, mi amigo Yomo Toro" (I'll also invite my friend, my dear friend Yomo Toro).

The music known as salsa, then, which has become the prototypical marker of Spanish Caribbean expressive identity, is in its inception the stylistic voice and practice of the Puerto Rican diaspora concentrated in New York City. Rather than the direct extension or imitation of Cuban or native Puerto Rican styles, it is rather the source of a newly hybridized and creolized adaptation of those styles in their interaction and admixture with other forms of music making at play in the diasporic environment. Even prior to the official advent of salsa by that name, and in even more dramatic ways, Nuyorican and Cuban musicians and music publics had fused *son* and *mambo* sounds with vernacular African American styles such as rhythm and blues and soul music, as evidenced in the short-lived but wildly popular experiments of Latin *boogaloo*. And more famously, in the 1940s New York Latin music had witnessed the momentous innovations of Cubop and Latin jazz, which, along with the *mambo*, were more strongly rooted in the urban diaspora than in the Caribbean, the original home of those traditions.

But it is in times closer to our own, with the dramatic growth and increased diversity of the Caribbean diaspora, and with decades of ongoing interaction with Afro-American culture, that we witness the full force of diaspora as source and challenge in Caribbean music history. In the post-salsa period, it is hip hop that has emerged as the most influential and innovative field of musical expression in most parts of the Caribbean. In this case there can of course be no doubt as to the music's urban diasporic origins, though it is still less than accepted knowledge that Puerto Ricans, Jamaicans, Dominicans, and other Caribbean diaspora peoples and their music played a formative role in its story since the beginning in the 1970s and 1980s. Purists and traditionalists from those background cultures are still bent on denying or minimizing the Caribbean-ness or Latinismo of hip hop in its many manifestations and on regarding it as strictly African American; at times, as in the call to ban hip hop floats from the Puerto Rican Day Parade, this demarcation takes on blatantly racist overtones. But in all cases it indicates a failure to understand the dynamic of contemporary diasporic cultural realities, particularly among the kind of diasporic youth who have taken part in the founding of hip hop; this dynamic is well described by Robin Cohen: "Aesthetic styles, identifications and affinities, dispositions and behaviors, musical genres, linguistic patterns, moralities, religious practices and other cultural phenomena are more globalized, cosmopolitan and creolized or 'hybrid' than ever before. This is especially the case among youth of transnational communities, whose initial socialization has taken place within the cross-currents of more than one cultural field, and whose ongoing forms of cultural expression and identity are often self-consciously selected, syncretized and elaborated from more than one cultural heritage."[6] Fortunately, a book like Raquel Rivera's recent *New York Ricans from the Hip Hop Zone* is guided by just such an understanding and helps identify the role and importance of diaspora youth in forging new stylistic possibilities without abandoning or turning away from their inherited cultural background.[7]

While it remains important thus to document and analyze the diasporic origins and social roots of emerging Caribbean music making, close attention should also be given to the diffusion of new styles and themes in the Caribbean home countries and the challenges they bring to traditional assumptions about national and regional musical traditions. Before undertaking her pioneering work on Puerto Ricans in the New York hip hop scene, Rivera was studying the arrival of rap in her native Puerto Rico and found herself confronting the avid resistance of cultural gatekeepers of all political stripes. She ascertained that it was return Nuyoricans who initiated hip hop styles and practices on the island in the late 1970s and early 1980s. As she put it, "Rap, being a form of expression shared by Caribbeans and African Americans in the mainland ghettos, forms part of the cultural baggage of the young people who return or arrive on the Island. Being an integral part of the cultural life of the young [return] migrants, it therefore cannot be considered a mere foreign import."[8] Even Vico C., the first rapper to gain wide recognition, was born in Brooklyn, and teamed up with his partner Glenn from California to write his early rhymes, which gave voice to life in the working-class neighborhood of Puerto de Tierra in San Juan where he grew up. The style migrated from the "hood" in the United States to the island, and even though it was quickly commercialized and domesticated in Puerto Rico by the mid-1980s, the underground scene continued to serve as a venue for the articulation of life in the marginalized and impoverished *calles* and *caseríos*, which had been out of bounds for all other forms of artistic expression.

While the introduction of rap in Puerto Rico was first dismissed as a fad and then more ominously regarded as still another instance of American cultural imperialism, history has it that hip hop went on to take firm root in its new location and in fact articulated important shifts already afoot in the national imaginary. The diasporic content provoked new sensibilities on issues of sex, gender, and race, while rap's social moorings among the urban poor raised uncomfortable problems of class and social inequality typically ignored by the cultured elite. Interestingly, there was also a notable reverse in the direction of social desire for the geographical other: while traditionally the translocal Puerto

Rican sensibility was characterized by the emigrant longing for the beauties of the long-lost island, in some rap texts and among street youth it was the urban diaspora settings of the Bronx and El Barrio that became places of fascination and nostalgia. Nuyoricans, commonly the object of public disdain and discrimination on the island, became sources of admiration and solidarity among many Puerto Rican young people who had never left the national territory. Such radical challenges to traditional cultural values and assumptions, largely associated with the hip hop invasion, have retained their appeal in subsequent decades, such that important young verbal artists like Tego Calderón and José Raúl González ("Gallego") continue to voice a fresh sense of what it means to be Puerto Rican in our changing times, in both cases with positive reference to the example set by their counterparts in the diaspora.

From being an isolated, subcultural phenomenon on the island's cultural scene, rap has over the years established its place as a ubiquitous component of everyday life, vibrantly present in town festivals and religious events, at activities on street corners, and in schoolyards and neighborhood parks. It has also found its place in the country's musical soundscape and has been fused with more familiar styles like salsa, *bomba*, and *plena*. Hip hop's presence in Puerto Rico also has its Caribbean dimensions, its introduction coinciding in significant ways with the inroads of reggae and *merengue*, with meren-rap and reggaeton being but the best known of the varied fusions and crossovers present in the contemporary repertoire.

Nor is Puerto Rico unique, of course, in its importation of rap via its return diaspora aboard *la guagua aérea*. The influence of its huge diasporas in New York and San Juan has been of dramatic note in the Dominican Republic, and again hip hop has been a crucial conduit. One Dominican cultural critic has gone so far as to title his book *El retorno de las yolas* (The Return of the Rafts),[9] while a prominent historian has commented on the full-scale transformation of Dominican national identity resulting from the urban diaspora experience and makes direct reference to the new musical sensibility:

> Social and racial discrimination as experienced by thousands of Dominicans in the urban ghettos of New York made them aware of their actual racial constitution, and taught them that they are not too different from the West Indian neighbors. ... Many returned to Santo Domingo and their home towns transformed both outwardly and inwardly in their thoughts, their clothes, their feelings, their language, and their music. ... Afro-Caribbean music and dance were incorporated into Dominican folk dances and songs, particularly in the national merengue, while music

groups expanded their repertoires . . . , showing, not always consciously, how much Afro-American culture had pervaded Dominican popular culture. The discovery of Dominican négritude was not the result of an intellectual campaign as had been the case in Haiti and Martinique, after Jean Price-Mars and Aimé Césaire. The real discovery of the Dominican black roots was a result of the behavior of the returning migrants. . . . Racial and cultural denial worked for many years, but migration to the United States finally cracked down the ideological block of the traditional definition of Dominican national identity.[10]

All over the Caribbean, and in growing numbers of countries in the postcolonial era, "The diaspora strikes back!"

Throughout their history Caribbean cultures have been traveling cultures, transformative departures and arrivals to and from, between and among and en route, and Caribbean musics are traveling musics best understood in their full range and complexity from the privileged vantage of *la guagua aérea*. In our times of mass and multidirectional migrations of people, styles, and practices, many new islands have been added to the archipelago, new sites of creolization and transculturation, unimagined in earlier periods of cultural definition and self-definition and catalyzing unimagined changes in both lands of origin and places of arrival and settlement.

Paris, London, Toronto, Amsterdam, New York, and a range of other far-flung urban centers are now Caribbean islands, of sorts, or actually new poles of interaction and intersection among diverse Caribbean and non-Caribbean cultural experiences and traditions. The magnitude and structural implications of these contemporary diasporic formations is well captured in these terms by Orlando Patterson:

> In structural terms, the mass migration of peoples from the periphery in this new context of cheap transportation and communication has produced a wholly different kind of social system. . . . What has emerged is, from the viewpoint of the peripheral states, distinctive societies in which there is no longer any meaningful identification of political and social boundaries. Thus, more than half of the adult working populations of many of the smaller eastern Caribbean states now live outside of these societies, mainly in the immigrant enclaves of the United States. About 40 per cent of all Jamaicans, and perhaps half of all Puerto Ricans, live outside of the political boundaries of these societies, mainly in America.

> The interesting thing about these communities is that their members
> feel as at home in the mainland segment as in the original politically
> bounded areas. . . . The former colonies now become the mother country;
> the imperial metropolis becomes the frontier of infinite resources.

Patterson concludes by observing, "Jamaican, Puerto Rican, Dominican, and Barbadian societies are no longer principally defined by the political-geographical units of Jamaica, Puerto Rico, the Dominican Republic and Barbados, but by *both* the populations and cultures of these units *and* their postnational colonies in the cosmopolis."[11]

Caribbean societies, cultures, and musics cannot be understood today in isolation from the diasporic pole of their translocal realities, or strictly from the vantage point of the diaspora alone. Rather, it is the relation between and among the poles of national and regional history and diasporic re-creation—what has been referred to, in a discussion of Haitian *konpas*, for example, as negotiation across the "insular-diasporic barrier"[12]—that provides the key to present-day analysis of Caribbean expressive possibilities. Thus the long march of Caribbean creolization proceeds apace in our time, but under radically altered geographic circumstances, with the diasporic settings located well outside of national and regional territories, making for the most intense "points of entanglement," to use Edouard Glissant's felicitous phrase. It is this "creolité in the hood," the infinitely inventive mingling and mixing of Caribbean experience and expressive ways in the urban centers of the metropolis, that is most radically refashioning what being Caribbean is about, and what Caribbean music sounds like, a process that becomes most clearly visible when we are attentive to the impact of this new mix as it reaches back to the historical region itself.

Of course, this kind of reverse flow, if you will, from the metropolis to the colonial or postcolonial societies is not new in Caribbean cultural and musical history, nor should it be separated from the ongoing and forceful movement in the other direction which has wrought so much change, most of it unacknowledged, to the imperial societies themselves. Perhaps the key thing about this cultural migration is that it is and has been circular, as the age-old back-and-forth between jazz and Cuban music, or reggae and rhythm and blues, or the zigzag stories of *merengue*, calypso, or *konpas*, illustrates so well in the archive of Caribbean sounds and rhythms.[13] Throughout that history, creative innovations have resulted from the travels and sojourns of musicians themselves, and for over a century recordings, radio broadcasts, movies, television, and the whole range of media have exposed musical practitioners and audiences to music making from elsewhere, in great preponderance from the disproportionately endowed metropolitan centers, and very often as part of the imperial project.

But today's musical remittances are different; there has been a shift, as one study of the history of *merengue* in New York puts it, "from transplant to transnational circuit."[14] That is, these musical remittances are not just contemporary instances of traveling musics or of media-induced exoticist fascination, whether that fascination is based on healthy curiosity or on ideological or commercial persuasion. Rather, the return "home" of Caribbean music that has been recycled through the urban diaspora experience is a mass collective and historically structured process corresponding directly to patterns of circular migration and the formation of transnational communities. The musical baggage borne by return diasporas, while rooted in the traditions and practices of the Caribbean cultures of origin, are forged in social locations having their own historical trajectories and stylistic environments, and are thus simultaneously internal and external to the presumed parameters of national and regional musical cultures. This ambivalence explains the mix of consternation and adulation with which they are received on their entry, or reentry, into the home societies: they can neither be repelled out of hand for being imposed by foreigners, nor do they square neatly with the musical and cultural dynamic at work in the societies from which they originally sprang.

Much of this work of transnational diffusion, of course, is done by the corporate media and aligns directly with the taste-making and trend-setting projects and hierarchies of imperial power. No doubt "transnationalism from above" remains a prominent if not the predominant driving power behind this uprooting and rerouting of styles and practices and their reintroduction into the societies of origin in diluted and bastardized form. But since prevailing regimes of accumulation and the coercive management of flexible labor forces impel patterns of circulatory migration and manage the shifting locations of transnational communities, the formation and the relocation of diaspora musics and cultures may also exemplify the process of what is called "transnationalism from below," that is, nonhegemonic and to some degree counterhegemonic transnationalism, or, as one commentator capsulized it, "labor's analog to the multinational corporation."[15] Despite and in the face of corporate and state power, Caribbean music today, and its movement to and from its massive diasporas, remains *popular* music in the deepest and persistent sense: whether in the region or in its diaspora settings, and in its migration back and forth between them, it lives on as the vernacular expression of people and communities seeking, and finding, their own voice and rhythm.

All of this, and more, are lessons to be learned aboard the *guagua aérea*, but only if we take the time and effort to travel round-trip.

NOTES

1. See Díaz Quiñones, *El arte de bregar*. On *jaibería*, see Negrón-Muntaner and Grosfoguel, *Puerto Rican Jam*.
2. Sánchez, *La guagua aérea*.
3. See Torres, *The Commuter Nation*, and Duany, *The Puerto Rican Nation on the Move*.
4. See Otero Garabís, "Terroristas culturales." See also Otero Garabís, *Nación y ritmo*.
5. Rondón, *El libro de la salsa*. See also Quintero Rivera, *Salsa, sabor y control*, and Padilla, "Salsa Music," 28–45.
6. Cohen, *Global Diasporas*, 128.
7. Rivera, *New York Ricans from the Hip Hop Zone*.
8. Rivera, "Para rapear en puertorriqueño."
9. Torres-Saillant, *El retorno de las yolas*.
10. Moya Pons, "Dominican National Identity in Historical Perspective," 23–25.
11. Patterson, "Ecumenical America," 468.
12. See Averill, "Moving the Big Apple," 152.
13. For helpful and informative discussions of some of these interactions, see Allen and Wilcken, *Island Sounds in the Global City*.
14. Austerlitz, "From Transplant to Transnational Circuit," 44–60.
15. Portes, "Global Villagers," 74–77.

7

Glocal Spirituality: Consumerism and Heritage in a Puerto Rican Afro-Latin Folk Religion

RAQUEL ROMBERG

Over the span of five centuries, various layered histories originating in distant places have shaped the practices of Puerto Rican *brujería* (witch-healing).[1] In this tortuous history, *brujería* has incorporated at different periods the gestures of popular Spanish Catholicism, French Spiritism (encoded by Allan Kardec [1804–69] as Scientific Spiritism, or Espiritismo Científico), folk U.S. Protestantism, and Cuban *santería*. These religious practices came together as a result of the political, economic and social conditions brought by colonialism, slavery, nation building, and migration—all of which were shaped by global forces of various kinds. After centuries of gradual change, the practices of *brujería* have recently changed again as a result of colonial relations that tie the U.S. mainland with the island under the commonwealth status, and which have inserted Puerto Rico into economic and cultural global markets. These ties, which began with the U.S. invasion of 1898, are economic as well as ideological; they have transformed Puerto Rican modes of production and consumption under free trade and consumerism and have established a stronger dependency on the U.S. federal government through the system of welfare capitalism. Further, the indeterminate political status of the island under the commonwealth forged a particular variety of nationalism (defined by some as cultural nationalism) construed almost solely around the centrality of the "ethno" nation, or primordial cultural relations and less around the "sovereign" nation, or contractual political associations.[2]

Puerto Rico under the Estado Libre Asociado (ELA, or Commonwealth) occupies an ambiguous position between total independence from and total annexation to the United States. Rather than the result of positive political action, the commonwealth seems to be the result of an irresolute electorate, or, as Doris Sommer says, "an electorate very decided on not deciding."[3] After decades of deferred controversies, visible in the enactment of endless plebiscites, the future of Puerto Rico's status is still entangled in irreconcilable options between state sovereignty and annexation. Much like the French and Dutch colonies in the postwar Caribbean, Puerto Rico's status could be defined today as a "modern colony," following Ramón Grosfoguel,[4] or, as Duany has suggested half ironically, a "postcolonial colony."[5] What characterizes modern (as opposed to neocolonial) colonies is that they enjoy the economic benefits of receiving "annual transfers of billions of dollars of social capital from the metropolitan state" in the form of food stamps, health, education, and unemployment benefits and of participating in metropolitan standards of mass consumption. It also means extending to colonial people political rights that include the "constitutional recognition of metropolitan citizenship and democratic/civil rights, [and] the possibility of migration without the risks of illegality."[6]

Under the effects of welfare capitalism and cultural nationalism, two seemingly opposed global processes of change—expansion and essentialism—have reshaped the practices of *brujería*, adding new layers of meaning to its rituals and icons. In a nutshell, *brujería* practices have undergone a process of overall commodification and expansion. This process has increased the visibility and recognition of *brujos* (witch-healers) and their activities in the public sphere. There is a more inclusive and open attitude toward indigenous and African-derived forms of worship, as well as toward an increasing transnational pool of ritual experts and commodities. Finally, *brujos* have extended their field of expertise in accordance with local U.S. federal government agencies and U.S.-based businesses.

In fact, with the recent intensification of the circulation of ritual experts and commodities, folk religions such as Puerto Rican *brujería* have entered a *transnational* arena of ritual experimentation and eclecticism. Simultaneously, however, as a result of cultural nationalism, the production of an authentic Puerto Rican ethnic identity (encouraged also by the U.S. ideology of multiculturalism) has lead to processes of revitalization of *local* vernacular religious practices—processes that conveniently also cater to global desires for the consumption of heritage or local authenticities. This essay explores the effects of both these trends—increasing *global* interconnectedness and revived *local* particularity—on the practices of *brujos* in Puerto Rico, hence the "glocal" in the title. Due to similar colonial and neocolonial trajectories, these vernacular religious processes have their similar if not exact counterparts in other

Caribbean societies. Through an intimate ethnographic account that traces the encounters between practitioners, clients, and suppliers of ritual goods, I ask how *commodification* and the production of *heritage*—the outcome of two seemingly opposed global processes—shape folk religions, leading in the case of Puerto Rico to the unprecedented expansion of *brujería* practices, the professionalization of *brujos*, and the revalorization of their expertise in the public realm in line with, not in opposition to, mainstream consumer and multicultural ideologies.

WHY "GLOCAL SPIRITUALITY"?

Since roughly the 1980s a vast number of scholars in various fields—sociology, anthropology, economics, political science, art, and literary criticism—have engaged in a prolific debate about globalization, yielding no consensus as to the defining terms of the discussion. Responses have ranged from utter dismissal of the phenomenon or its relevance as just a fad, to the extreme valorization of globalization as the organizing principle of an unprecedented new world order. The majority of such responses stress the uniqueness of globalization processes in terms of the pervasive *spatial* interconnectedness created by world economic systems, the technological revolution, or the creation of a global culture.[7] Other theories—less recognized as global—stress the *temporal* continuity and cumulative effects of globalization on local sociocultural structures, as they were constituted by colonial encounters and deployed by postcolonial displacements.[8] In addition, although most globalization theories agree at least on characterizing globalization broadly in terms of interconnectedness, few are the instances in which such interconnectedness is discussed across disciplinary boundaries—economic globalization is discussed as disconnected from cultural and political globalization, and so forth. This is not the place to critique extensively the literature on globalization or its lack of interdisciplinarity. Rather, I will proceed eclectically (following my anthropological views), drawing on both *spatial* and *temporal* approaches to globalization as they become relevant in addressing the current practices of *brujería*.

Following an inclusive characterization of globalization processes as the global flow of people, goods, and ideas through *time* and *space*, one can trace the effects of such processes since ancient times. It is especially true of the Caribbean that colonization and settlement (and, later, transatlantic slavery) produced major displacements of peoples, goods, and ideas that created, against all odds, the conditions for the establishment of new creole "local" cultures. Specifically, if globalization establishes a particular geopolitics and chronopolitics (the values of a particular place and period increasingly connected to other places and times), it also shapes and directs the constitution of knowledge by attributing meanings to people and things. Thus, local cultures, and in this case vernacular religions, would be shaped and transmitted not only through communal gatherings and face-to-face relations in the present, but also as a result of geographically unrelated groups and long-distance relations over long periods of time.[9] For example, anthropologist Eric Wolf's *Europe and the People without History* questions the classic anthropological evolutionist and area-studies assumptions that place those people without a written history (so-called primitive people) outside Western world history. Wolf demonstrates that such history is in fact the result of processes guided by intense trade relations that connected "primitive" people with Euro-American mercantilist centers of power. In this process and throughout these routes, the lives and cultures of allegedly isolated tribes and villages were structurally modified, their assumed "locality" or cultural "roots"—in anthropological terms—forever transformed.[10] Following this line of thought to the extreme, some globalization theories posit that capitalist expansion and the creation of a world market lead to the inevitable homogenization of cultures and the elimination of particular traditions—all of which resonate with the grim prognosis of *The Communist Manifesto* about the eventual disappearance of local traditions under the expansion of capitalism: "All that is solid melts into air and all that is holy is profaned."[11]

But globalization should not imply a total, all-encompassing homogenization of cultures. In some cases, epitomized in Benjamin Barber's *Jihad vs. Mc-World*, globalization might engender contradictions, not homogenization. He contends that, as a result of globalization, both "global theme parks"—cultural expressions connected by universal markets and technologies of communication—and the balkanization of nation-states (infused by parochial hatreds in which one ethnic group is pitched against the other) can operate simultaneously.[12] Another way to tackle the homogenization hypothesis critically is based on the premise that meaning is not intrinsic to objects but is attributed to them in the course of human thought and practice. One can then trace the "career" or "social life" of objects as they change their meanings over time and space, especially as a result of migration. As objects circulate in new contexts, they may thereby lose the meaning of their source society and acquire additional meanings.[13] This premise stands in sharp contrast to early theories of globalization that assumed that the circulation of goods over different spaces necessarily erases difference and creates a uniform culture. Daniel Miller shows that rather than eliminate differences between cultures, capitalist expansion might actually boost them, since particular consumption patterns already in place are what determine the degree and mode of acceptance of mass-produced and distributed commodities.[14] Indeed, as Featherstone, Lash, and Robertson argue, "the seemingly empty and universalist signs circulating in the world informational system can be recast into different configurations of meaning . . . and inform the (re)constitution and/or creation of individual and communal identities."[15]

Caribbean colonization processes provide excellent cases to test the career or social life of colonial policies, namely the emergent parochial practices that localized or "indigenized"[16] metropolitan colonial policies. Consider the implementation of Spanish colonial rule among its New World colonies and its involvement in the mercantilist world system. Although the policies were the same in Cuba and Puerto Rico, for example, on each island the results and the timing were slightly different. Depending on their particular ecology, demography, level of economic development, and geopolitical strategic status, the outcomes of the global monopolizing efforts of Spain resulted in a variety of indigenous solutions that in turn set up the conditions for their future trajectories. This conclusion may be successfully tested in assessing Caribbean colonial histories in light of Franklin Knight's suggestive argument about the joint effects of centrifugal and centripetal forces in the Caribbean. Drawing its societies into strong dependency relations with international markets on the one hand, these centrifugal forces propelled, on the other, a centripetal movement that forged strong local sentiments that provided the basis for crucial differences between the cultural and political agendas of metropolitans and creole elites.[17]

Often, however, local sentiments about freedom, independence, and progress, as well as about racism and discrimination, were direct responses to global ideologies imported to the colonies. Thus, in addition to economic forces—almost exclusively analyzed by theorists of globalization with the sheer exception of postcolonial theorists—the global flow of race ideologies, religious ideas, and ways of life that accompanied these economic forces were equally important in legitimating, and occasionally contesting, their implementation. Cultural politics were always part of colonization; indeed, as Frantz Fanon powerfully suggests in *The Wretched of the Earth*, the major weapon of the colonizers was the imposition of their image on the colonized people. This image embodied racist and classist ideologies that were translated into colonial policies of everyday life, and which shaped conceptions of the colonized self.[18]

Drawing on this premise and the enduring effects of colonialism on the self and our notions of identity, Stuart Hall writes that the "structure of identification is always constructed through ambivalence. Always constructed through splitting. Splitting between that which one is, and that which is the other."[19] This psychological differentiation breaks down in everyday life and institutional identifications, however, when the other reconstitutes and categorically defines who one is. Thus, in examining the vernacular religions of Puerto Rico, one should remember that Catholic colonial rule affected not only religious practices per se but also the categorization of families, social relationships, political attitudes, and, ultimately, personhood and citizenship—identifications that are still operative in many areas of social life.

Finally, considering globalization in line with world system theories only in dyadic core-periphery terms (as most globalization theories tend to do) misses the vital intra-Caribbean interconnections that have shaped Caribbean histories, in general, and Puerto Rico's history, in particular, since the onset of colonization. For example, a chain of critical local changes in Puerto Rico and elsewhere can be traced directly to the aftereffects of the 1804 Haitian Revolution. This view contrasts with a purely nationalist-bounded historiography tied exclusively to Puerto Rico's tortuous relations with Spain. Indeed, in addition to destabilizing the colonial order in Puerto Rico (as happened in the rest of the Caribbean), the Haitian Revolution indirectly worsened the living conditions of slaves and promoted a series of police edicts intended to control their every movement—as terrified slave owners feared the same fate as those in Haiti. It also created the economic conditions for the rise of Cuba as a major producer and exporter of sugar. All of Spain's overseas investments were naturally directed to Cuba, relegating Puerto Rico to a marginal position until the demand for its less-refined sugar increased in direct response to the American Civil War. Another instance of intra-Caribbean influences on Puerto Rico, one that has had a more direct import on its vernacular religion, was the result of mid-twentieth-century popular social turmoil in Santo Domingo, Haiti, and Castro's Cuba, which drove large numbers of its immigrants and exiles to move to neighboring Puerto Rico. These influxes, together with ongoing migration flows within the Caribbean and between the island and the U.S. mainland, have exponentially increased the transnational opportunities for ritual experimentation and learning within the practices of *brujería*.

If the particular history, culture, or religion of any one island in the Caribbean is, indeed, the composite result of a series of transnational processes over time, it is then critical to consider the global effects on the production of locality and the local construction of globality, or "glocality."[20] Further, the examination of Puerto Rican *brujería* as a form of "glocal" spirituality not only reveals its complex development in unprecedented ways but also affords the comparison with other Caribbean vernacular religions that have shared many of the same trajectories undertaken by Puerto Rico. *Brujería* practices—as other Caribbean vernacular religions—have been constituted in the interface between hegemonic colonial religious, state, and commercial powers, and the irreverent reactions of colonial Creoles.

HISTORICAL TRAJECTORIES OF GLOCAL SPIRITUALITY IN PUERTO RICO

The first glocal layer of *brujería* emerges in the interface of hegemonic Spanish Catholic colonial rule and intra-Caribbean demographic and religious turmoil, forging the creation of a maroon, creole society and culture. For four centuries the Catholic Church was the official religion of Puerto Rico. Conquistadores and missionaries imposed their religious beliefs, first upon the indigenous population and then on enslaved Africans. But evangelization, as in the French Catholic–ruled colonies, was partial and superficial among the majority of the creole population, especially among those living outside the walled cities. With the discovery of silver and gold in the southernmost colonies, the metropolitan economic and religious funding of Puerto Rico (and Cuba) diminished substantially, creating, among other things, a chronic scarcity of priests. This and the demographic isolation of most of its inhabitants contributed to the emergence of a maroon society that helped sustain and further develop, among other things, an antiecclesiastical form of medieval Catholicism (similar to its popular versions in Spain). Composed of homemade devotions and private miracles, it also incorporated indigenous and, later on, African religious practices. Recognizing the need for the creation of individual worship altars in light of the endemic lack of priests, and the isolation of the majority of the population living far away from churches and chapels, the church authorized and encouraged Catholic worship to be conducted in small country chapels (*ermitas*) by women devotees (*rezadoras*) with the help of *mantenedoras*—women in charge of guarding religious icons in their homes.[21] Much to the dismay of the church, creole home altars naturally mushroomed following these allowances, forever freeing devotees from the having to attend church services in order to achieve a spiritual relationship with God.

This appropriation of the sacred world by lay colonials was not seen with approving eyes by church authorities, of course, who endlessly tried to limit and control—unsuccessfully—such extraecclesiastical and irreverent appropriations of its functions. One such attempt was made when the church decided to stop posting *nóminas* (lists of saints believed to be the patrons of particular ailments and natural disasters). Under threats of heresy and excommunication, the church prohibited, for example, the manufacture and use of amulets; the practice of curing with *ensalmos* (magic spells); and the performance of *rogativas* (special prayers to prevent or diminish the effects of natural disasters)—unless such procedures were first sanctioned by church officials.[22] Slavery added yet another dimension to the creation of Puerto Rican glocal spirituality. As mentioned, strict restrictions on the times and modes of leisure allowed to slaves were established (as a consequence of the Haitian Revolution) by a series of edicts designed to prevent possible revolts and the flight of slaves, especially during festivals and rituals in which dancing and drumming were performed.[23] This first glocal layer of *brujería* (based on popular Catholicism) further developed through the centuries with added indigenous and African (ancestor and nature deities) forms of worship, and it became the true religion of poor and middle-class Puerto Ricans in rural and urban areas, who never ceased to define themselves as Catholic—vestiges of which we can observe even today.

By mid-nineteenth century, a second layer of glocal spirituality was added to the practices of *brujería*. This time it was the creole elite who adopted Kardecean Spiritism in their anti-Spanish, pro-independence fights, and fashioned new progressive national and civic identities (while still considering themselves Catholic) in opposition to the classist, metropolitan Catholic Church. This counterhegemonic move occurred throughout the short-lived liberal period of the first Spanish republic, during which the 1866 Decree of Freedom of Worship and the 1873 Abolition of Slavery were passed, and provided the stage for the further development of *brujería*. At this time, funding for Protestant missions, Masonic lodges, esoteric schools, and Spiritist centers added even more options for Puerto Rican vernacular religious experimentation.

The ideas of Scientific Spiritism as codified by Kardec had an immediate appeal among the Catholic *criollo* elite, especially his *The Gospel According to Spiritism* (1864), wherein he adapts the Gospel to the Spiritist beliefs in enlightened spirits and reincarnation. Interestingly, by the beginning of the twentieth century this book had begun to surpass the Bible in yearly sales: every family had a copy in its house right next to the Bible.[24] Spiritist centers had been holding *veladas* (spiritual night gatherings) since 1856, during which messages of enlightened spirits given by mediums were heard.[25] These *veladas* were soon perceived as a religious menace to the church and a political threat to the Spanish state, which imposed regulatory conditions on their gatherings.[26]

The popularity of Kardec's Spiritism marked a major shift in nineteenth-century Puerto Rican creole society (as in other Latin American and Caribbean societies) that continues into the present: namely, the transition from a clerical to a nonclerical, progressive relationship to the transcendental world. Writing in the 1990s and sharing the vision of previous Spiritist historians about the role of Spiritism in modern Puerto Rican society, Rodríguez Escudero succinctly characterized Spiritism as "a force that is called on to play an important role in the modern world and in our homeland."[27]

Scientific Spiritism can be described through a series of principles. There is a superior infinite intelligence (God) that finite men cannot completely comprehend; spiritual life is eternal and the soul immortal; all enlightened spirits (preeminently Christ) are projections of God and should be emulated; evocation of and communication with spirits are possible in certain circumstances (and everyone can develop these faculties); humans must live many material lives in order to evolve and reach perfection; the divine "law of cause and effect" makes us pay for our wrongdoing in subsequent reincarnations; through good deeds and charity toward our fellow humans, we can compensate for social debts (wrongdoings to fellow humans) acquired in previous existences; there is no hell or Satan, these being religious myths that contradict the essential goodness of God; and, finally, there are other inhabited worlds in the universe.[28] In the ensuing ethnographic sections, the relevance of these principles will be made clear as they become embodied in present-day *brujería* divination and healing rituals.

The third globalizing ideology to affect the practices of *brujería* can be best characterized as a "megarhetoric of developmental modernization"[29] in both economic and social terms. After the initial military government, following the U.S. invasion of Puerto Rico in 1898, the prospect of rationalizing and democratizing the state apparatus was welcomed around the early 1920s by a group of Puerto Rican intellectuals and professionals of disparate political affiliation, who began implementing such changes in various health, education, and economic programs—a process soon characterized as the "Americanization" of the Island.[30] Of course, after the U.S. invasion of the island and the final separation between church and state, Puerto Rican vernacular religions were freed from religious persecution and, until the late 1940s, freed as well from state prejudice. Under these conditions a popular form of Spiritism that included the veneration of Catholic saints, Indian and African spirits, and the practices of *curanderismo* (folk herbal healing) evolved, indeed flourished, alongside selected aspects of popular Catholic worship, including the rosary. Protestantism was also integrated in these popular forms of religiosity as a consequence of the "Americanization" process of the 1920s, when several Catholic families converted to Protestantism as a way to assert their progressive, modern aspirations.

By the time these aspirations became institutionalized in the medical and health systems in the years between the 1940s and the 1950s, *brujería* practices had begun to be persecuted for being perceived as atavisms, survivals of a preindustrial, nonscientific era, which the state apparatus was determined to erase from Puerto Rican society. *Brujos*, consequently, were vilified and persecuted as charlatans. Not coincidentally, this was the time that Operation Bootstrap (1948)—a U.S. government-sponsored program of industrialization by invitation—was launched. But in the early 1980s the negative public perception of *brujos* as charlatans changed dramatically when the discourse of heritage celebrated them as embodiments of Puerto Rican popular wisdom, by turning them, in effect, into cardboard tokens of the creole nation.[31]

The three glocal layers of *brujería* I have sketched so far have been suggested not only as instances of the glocal framework proposed in this essay, and the historic background for the ensuing ethnography of *brujería* in the present, but also as points of comparison with other vernacular religions in the Caribbean. The remainder of this essay traces in greater detail the latest glocal layer of *brujería*—guided, as mentioned earlier, by two different sets of apparently opposed global processes of expansion and essentialism, corresponding respectively to the forces of consumerism and heritage.

CONSUMERISM AND THE COMMODIFICATION OF FAITH

This latest phase for the development of *brujería* began right after the economic boom of the 1960s, when the U.S. ethos began to be incorporated in the healing and magic techniques of *brujería*. A laissez-faire orientation—in particular, the value embedded in free choice, both in economic and in cultural terms—helped not only to legitimate and make more visible those vernacular practices that had been hitherto marginalized, but also to inject them with new expansive options. The addition of an individualist ethos to the equation, plus the choices offered by consumerism, widened, albeit unwillingly, the space for vernacular religious choice and creativity.[32] These changes indeed took place, but not before *brujos* and their clients "punctuated, interrogated, and domesticated"[33] these new global forces to make them fit their spiritual ethos.

On a material level, Puerto Rico has opened up to an international market of Afro-Latin and Asian religious commodities—a process most palpable at *botánicas* (stores that sell religious paraphernalia, flowers, and medicinal and magical herbs). Responding to the idiom of consumerism, novelty has become a new tradition within *brujería*: "new and improved" ritual commodities—from magical potions and healing emulsions packaged in mass-produced bottles and aerosols, to an assortment of amulets, candles, magical perfumes, lotions, and figurines from all over the globe—are welcomed as signs of progress and improvement following the logic of capitalist expansion. For instance, on our way to a third *botánica* one morning, Haydée—the *bruja* I worked with in Puerto Rico for more than a year—said to me, "I always like to check out what's new here, . . . check out the latest novelty." In addition to icons of Catholic saints, we could find the Indio (a Native American warrior), the Madama (a powerful black woman), and Don Gregorio (a white Venezuelan medical doctor), as well as Japanese and Hindu deities, each with its own spiritual power. Clients could improve their "luck," for example, by buying an Ekeko, the Peruvian midget who is the spirit of wealth; Kwan Yin, the Buddhist goddess of fortune; or Ganesh, the elephant-headed Hindu deity of opulence.

A closer look at the forces of consumerism shows that they shape the expertise of *brujos* in more than one way. While *brujos* regularly go to *botánicas* to buy supplies, these shopping excursions provide another essential space for networking and gossiping about other *brujos* and *botánicas*. These excursions often end up becoming "spiritual duels," wherein *brujos* display their prowess by telling stories to each other and to *botánica* owners about difficult cases they have treated, or professional "symposiums" where valuable ritual information and practical advice are exchanged. After one such encounter and a divining session, for example, Eleggua (the *orisha* or deity at the top of the *santería* pantheon), the Congo (representing the *santería orisha* Changó), and the Monja (represented by the figure of a nun) were revealed as Haydée's new *protecciones* or spiritual shields. Following the advice of the spirits, she obviously added these new *protecciones* to her *altar* (an altar room used for consultations). Although Haydée said she was not planning to get initiated into *santería* (as some *espiritistas* do), she saw no conflict in adopting new *santería orishas* and their ritual paraphernalia because, within the ethos of *espiritismo* and *brujería*, the possibilities of encountering spiritual powers embodied in traditions and religions of all kinds are limitless.

This eclectic ethos has acquired a new significance with the current demographic changes in Puerto Rico. The intense intra-Caribbean circulation of ritual specialists—a free-flow migration of *espiritistas*, *santeros*, *brujos*, and New Age healers from Santo Domingo and Cuba—and the revolving-door migration of Puerto Ricans between the island and the mainland, have contributed visibly to the internal dynamism of Puerto Rican *brujería*, turning it more and more into a form of transnational vernacular religious practice. These encounters and the availability of ritual commodities from distant parts of the world yield incomparable opportunities for mutual learning and exchange, turning Puerto Rican *brujería* into a glocal vernacular religious practice. For example, there is an ongoing "cross-fertilization"[34] of healing practices when practitioners of Cuban *santería*, Dominican *vodou*, and Puerto Rican *brujería* meet at joint spiritual gatherings on the island or at initiation rituals anywhere between New York, Miami, Chicago, Haiti, or the Dominican Republic. These interactions have broadened the pool of saints, deities, and spirits, as well as the techniques that Puerto Rican *brujos* can draw upon, turning spiritual empowerment into a geographically boundless undertaking.

Territorial boundaries are also crossed by *brujos* through new technologies of communication, which they have rapidly incorporated, recognizing in them opportunities for extending their reach and influence. While *brujos* have always been able to fly themselves and their *trabajos* (magic works) spiritually to clients everywhere, nowadays they can also fly cleansing baths and amulets for protection against evil spirits via Federal Express. Long-distance consultations are given over the telephone, and cell-phones and beepers are worn all day long to provide the best service to clients. On one occasion Tonio, the famous *brujo* of Loíza (nearly ninety-four years old at the time of his death, in 1999), was sitting in his wheelchair watching television, as usual, when the telephone rang. Although Tonio had stopped working in his *altar* because of deteriorating health, he was able to advise a longtime client from New York about his work and marriage, and even gave him instructions on how to "activate" a *trabajo* that he promised to mail to him.

Global forces, both economic and demographic, originating elsewhere have been instrumental in reshaping the rituals of *brujería*, not by eliminating their unique trajectory but by highlighting them, not by reducing them to a standard practice—as some globalization theories had predicted—but by expanding the unique situatedness of *brujería* itself.

FAME AND TECHNOLOGICAL EXPANSION

In addition to actual spatial and ritual expansion, the proliferation of successful charismatic "electronic churches" has paved the way for an unprecedented acceptance and visibility of spiritual help in contemporary Puerto Rico. This has naturally boosted a local discourse of fame and celebrity around *brujos*, on which they shrewdly capitalize to advance their professionalization. Certain cable TV mediums or astrologers, such as Anita Casandra and Walter Mercado, who have achieved prominence among Latinos throughout the Americas, are looked upon as models of economic success. Emulating them, *brujos* have found several ways to assert their fame publicly, bragging about the number of clients they have, the number of hours or weeks clients need to wait and the distances they have to travel for a consultation, the socioeconomic status or fame of some of their clients, the complexity and elaboration of their altars, and the lavishness of the feasts given in honor of the saints. One often hears, in a tone at once complaining and proud, "La marquesina está llena!" (The waiting room is full!). In the presence of the rest of the clients, Haydée one day approached one of the women seated in her waiting room and artfully asked, "You are the one from North Carolina, aren't you? And of all the *brujos* on the Island, it is to *me* that you come—why?" Similarly, on various occasions Haydée, pointing to me, would ponder publicly (with only halfhearted modesty): "Why, of all the *brujos* in Puerto Rico, is she—a researcher—drawn to *me*?" We all knew that what she was saying through these rhetorical questions was that the spirits, supporting her enormously, drove me as well as her overseas clients to her in recognition of, and as a reward for, her prodigious *cuadro* or spiritual power.

As a sign of having been showered by the favor of spirits, the material prosperity of *brujos* also signals to clients that they have come to the right healer for help, since the same positive energies (*bendiciones* or blessings) of that healer will eventually be transmitted to them. It is therefore imperative that everything—from lavish clothes, well-equipped altars, new and bigger *santos* (figurines of the saints), and expensive gold-filled amulets, to generous communal feasts—indexes the financial and thus spiritual success of a healer. The fame of *brujos*, the number of people who follow them, and the richness of their environments simultaneously attest and increase their own blessings. This double meaning of being blessed constitutes the core of *brujería* in its present phase, defining it as a form of "spiritualized materialism."[35] The result of previous glocal layers of spirituality—created in the context of Catholic colonial rule, the import of Scientific Spiritism, and the Americanization of the island—*brujería* in its present form embodies the temporal thread of a series of "vernacular globalization"[36] processes.

SPIRITUAL ENTREPRENEURSHIP AND THE LOCAL
PUNCTUATION OF CONSUMERISM AND WELFARE CAPITALISM

Besides encouraging assertiveness and alertness in the material sphere, *brujos* redirect their clients toward a morally oriented attitude in pursuing these traits according to the Spiritist ethos encoded by Kardec. In line with the "law of cause and effect" and the notions of spiritual justice and reincarnation, the advice given by *brujos* can transform merely instrumental advantages into ones that are spiritually endowed—since every action in this world has an effect in the other, and every action affords an opportunity to improve our spiritual debts acquired in previous lives. *Brujos* thereby provide not only the "eyes and ears" for clients to find possible resources in bureaucratic organizations and capitalist enterprises, but also the "soul" or moral charter behind the demands and profits that can be made. Because *brujos* assume that some conflicts may originate in previous lives, they combine worldly and cosmic rulings, when solving transactions between offenders, victims, and, when relevant, state or private agencies. These rulings emerge during trance and contain ethical advice given by the spirits accompanied by practical ways to follow it. *Brujos* and the spirits understand the demands of a consumer society, but also remind their followers of the dangers of not following the spiritual laws of Spiritism; it is their way of punctuating the workings of consumerism and welfare capitalism.

The following is a good example of the ways in which *brujos* both attend to and control the forces of consumerism when it contradicts the ethos of Spiritism. Tonio, on one occasion, reprimanded Camilo, a lawyer protégé of his, for being narrow-minded and intolerant when he sued one of his clients for not paying all his fees. Tonio reminded him that although the penniless woman was in dire straits, she had paid him some of the money and then invited him for a wonderful meal. She cooked several of the very elaborate traditional Puerto Rican dishes eaten on Christmas day. "With that feast," Tonio said, "she paid you more than what she owed you in money." Had Camilo showed more generosity, Tonio concluded, the spirits would have provided him with more clients, and his earnings would have more than doubled. Cases such as this exemplify the labor of *brujos*, who act as spiritual brokers, attending to the complex relations between the state, businesses, individuals, and the spirits.

In the context of Puerto Rico's system of welfare capitalism, *brujos* are able to accumulate a form of spiritual capital (they call it *bendiciones*—i.e., blessings) in the course of their consultations with influential clients, which they can translate into material success for themselves and their other clients.

Depending on their relative fame, *brujos* are usually at the center of various social networks that might include members of the political, professional, and commercial elite. *Brujos* thus often find themselves at the crossroads of crucial channels of information. This pool of knowledge and connections, gathered during consultation and then exchanged in gossip with other *brujos*, comes in handy when informing their clients how to apply—on time and in the right manner—for federal help, a job, housing, social security benefits, and the like. *Brujos* also provide assistance in more direct ways, for example, by putting managers and directors in touch with potential employees. *Brujos* thereby become brokers between local and transnational corporations, redefining the locality and spirituality of their expertise to encompass state agencies and economic markets based on the island and elsewhere.

Knowledge and control over the transcendental world is now complemented with knowledge and control of market and civic forces. As a result, *brujos* have also become spiritual entrepreneurs, expanding their services to include those traditionally assigned not only to psychologists and social workers but also to officials of the labor, justice, and public health systems. For instance, after Hurricane Bertha hit the island in summer 1996, a subject that came up frequently in consultations was the Federal Emergency Management Agency (FEMA), which, among other things, deals with hurricane victims' complaints and demands. Federal funds allocated for these purposes were distributed according to the specifications and under the administration of the Puerto Rican government. Haydée, Basi, Tonio, and other *brujos* were well informed as to who was eligible to claim losses from FEMA and how, where, and when to file for them. Few knew that just by making a telephone call, a small but meaningful payment could be received without undergoing annoying appraisals. Because Haydée had an *ahijado* (spiritual protégé, literally, a "godson") whose sole job responsibility was answering hurricane-related emergency telephone calls for the government, she was fully aware of this pool of easily available money that had recently arrived; she directed her clients who had suffered the aftermath of the hurricane to make the best of it. Many were encouraged to make the first move by Haydée's saying, as she read the cards, "You'll cry when you receive this gift from FEMA. The money will help you take care of many things." In various areas, *brujos* help their clients take full advantage of the economic opportunities frequently opened up by Puerto Rico's ties with the United States; in doing so, they punctuate such assistance with the ethos of Spiritism. This is their silent way of intervention with the system.

Having delineated the expansionist impetus of *brujería*, I now consider the other source of change that had a formative if more indirect effect on *brujería*:

the production of heritage in Puerto Rico. As a local response to the worldwide interest in the production (and promotion) of essentialized ethnic identities in the public sphere, the production of heritage on the island actually freed *brujos* from previous accusations of charlatanism, ultimately raising the local cultural value of their hitherto denigrated spiritual practices.

HERITAGE AND THE IDEOLOGY OF MULTICULTURALISM

The expansion of *brujería* in ritual matters—promoted by the U.S. laissez-faire spiritual ethos, consumerism, and welfare capitalism—acquires an added significance in relation to the ethnic politics of Puerto Rican culture. The current worldwide ideology that informs the protection of minority rights and equality within nation-states has promoted—since roughly the last quarter of the twentieth century—the global production (and marketing) of essentialized ethnic identities. These global forces have been punctuated in Puerto Rico, catapulting the previously silenced Afro–Puerto Rican constituency into a greater public visibility and participation. During the 1950s, when the socioeconomic program of Operation Bootstrap was launched, a state-sponsored nationalist cultural project, Operation Serenity, was also launched. It was instrumental in forging a creole nation and identity that merged Taíno, African, and Spanish cultures. By 1980 this romanticized view of a creole nation was being contested by the pioneering work of Isabelo Zenón Cruz and others who, inspired by the accomplishments of the civil rights movement, disparaged the marginalization of Afro–Puerto Ricans and promoted a more historically conscious construction of Afro–Puerto Rican identity (and, by extension, of the nation as a whole).[37]

In this context, the rediscovery of the African heritage of Puerto Rico has taken center stage, and instead of vilifying African-based religious practices as obstacles to progress, this renewed nationalist program positively foregrounds Afro–Puerto Rican culture and its contribution to the formation of a creole nation. Pride has replaced the criticism of the 1940s and 1950s, when the same practices were framed as "superstitious" and "primitive"; African-based songs, prayers, and religious paraphernalia are now proudly consumed and exhibited in the public sphere. With the often uncritical efforts to rescue the "endangered" African traditions of Puerto Rico from extinction, this otherwise socially sensitive revitalization has ended up unintentionally essentializing them. Not playing into this cultural politics, yet protected by its public force, *brujos* are able to capitalize on this kind of cultural revitalization of Africanity, not only by freely drawing on African deities and rituals but also by being extolled in the media as repositories of popular wisdom. Some practitioners told me that with the recent change in attitudes, they can now, for instance, overtly call the Virgin of Charity "Ochún," the name of the African *orisha*, and likewise refer to Saint Barbara as "Changó," thus reversing the syncretic practices of colonial times. This trend follows similar developments elsewhere in the Caribbean and the rest of the Americas, which suggests that the re-Africanization of Puerto Rico is far from being an isolated local occurrence; rather, it appears to follow the previously mentioned ideological globalization of ethnicity—an issue that calls for further research.

Tracing globalization on purely economic grounds, therefore, tells only one part of the story, for it subjects the expansion of the West solely to the logic of capitalist expansion and the world market, which also implies—following the Marxist prognosis mentioned earlier—that economic expansion necessarily compromises or even endangers the national sovereignty and culture of peripheral nation-states. The other part of the story starts with ideological globalization; that is, the formation of modern nations is in itself the result—at least with regard to the communal spirit it should depend on and the modes of legal dominion it establishes—of the global expansion of the European nation-state model since the early nineteenth century. This model, critics of nationalism argue, had not only determined the conditions for the constitution of sovereign, spatially bound, nation-states and the international relations among them, but also their internal politics.[38] Within this orientation both the recent global attempts to promote democratization at the interstate level and multiculturalism at the intrastate level have acquired a local significance for Puerto Rico.

The case of Puerto Rico is a complex one on both counts. In a supposedly post-decolonization era, it is still on many levels a colony of the United States. Consider Puerto Rico as an "ethnonation"—following Grosfoguel, Negrón-Muntaner, and Georas[39]—that is, a nation without a sovereign state. Under this condition, the option of "cultural nationalism" allows for the existence of strong national sentiments without the prerequisite of achieving political sovereignty and a total break with the United States, which characterizes the ideology of "political nationalism."[40] Consider also the ideology of multiculturalism,[41] or the state's recognition of ethnic difference, which has replaced the discredited homogeneity image of the "melting pot" with that of the "salad" metaphor to best convey the idea of unity in diversity. The ensuing value placed on the politics of ethnic difference and hyphenated identities—for instance, African-American, Italian-American, and Chinese-American—reached the island by the 1980s and has influenced its local political culture ever since.

In the context of the unresolved political status of Puerto Rico vis-à-vis the United States of America, the ideology of multiculturalism fits well with the local politics of the ethnonation or cultural nationalism. It could serve—albeit for opposing agendas—simultaneously the political parties favoring independence, statehood (the integration of Puerto Rico as a U.S. state), and the current status quo or commonwealth. In this light, *brujería* not only could be annexed to a pluralist, cosmopolitan discourse of "alternative healing practices" but could also—for the purposes of establishing a "unique" ethno-national identity—be conveniently framed as a token of "our national heritage."

The power of heritage, Barbara Kirshenblatt-Gimblett notes, is that "[it] is a new mode of cultural production in the present that has recourse to the past" and, in this process, "adds value to existing assets that have either ceased to be viable . . . or that never were economically productive. . . . It does this by adding the value of pastness, exhibition, difference, and where possible, indigeneity."[42] As part of this process, African-based religious and musical elements have been rescued from oblivion since the 1980s by government and university organizations via sponsored public festivals, conferences, and events. For example, several biannual international symposiums on Afro-Caribbean religions were held at the University of Puerto Rico in the 1990s. Also, in the late 1980s the Centro de Estudios de la Realidad Puertorriqueña (CEREP) began publishing special issues on the forgotten African components of Puerto Rican culture and history. This concerted effort has been especially significant because, as many critics have suggested, the African "root" (one of the "three roots" of the Puerto Rican tripartite identity promoted since the mid-1950s that also includes Hispanic and Taíno identities) had been neglected compared with the other legacies. While some municipal and university organizations were promoting the African elements of Puerto Rican culture for educational purposes, commercial entrepreneurs pursued this trend on their own terms by "marketing heritage[43]—that is, marketing Puerto Rican African-inspired rituals and customs for tourist consumption.[44]

Similar processes may be identified in other parts of the Caribbean and Latin America, even though their effects have been more direct and extreme due to the hierarchical organization of some folk religions. For example, after centuries of having *brujería*-like persecution by the church and the state, Brazilian *candomblé* and Cuban *santería* have become tour destinations, their rituals often staged in the streets or religious houses and presented as tokens of "local color" for global consumption.[45] "The process of negating cultural practices," Kirshenblatt-Gimblett argues, "reverses itself once it has succeeded in archaizing the 'errors'; indeed, through a process of archaizing, which is a mode of cultural production, the repudiated is transvalued as heritage."[46] After having been under attack or condemned at various times in Brazilian and Cuban history, *candomblé* and *santería* have gone through a process of official folklorization and aestheticization that elevated them, respectively, to the pinnacles of Brazilian and Cuban "heritage."

Involving the media more than tourism, the effects of the folklorization and aestheticization of Puerto Rican *brujería* have been more indirect. Both in reporting and in constituting class-based, ideological attitudes about African-based religious practices, the role of journalism has been as prominent in this period as in the previous state building period of the 1940s and 1950s. The Puerto Rican intelligentsia have traditionally been involved in the publishing business; their influence on larger social issues has been and is still remarkable, for instance, in constituting a national imaginary. As intermediaries between global and state discourses of progress and development at the beginning of the twentieth century, and of multiculturalism more recently, they have shaped in great measure the ways people react to these global discourses not only by enabling practitioners to articulate their case in the media but also by presenting their practices in a favorable light. This change of attitude in depicting *brujería* and *brujos* in the public sphere as part of Puerto Rican heritage is having a remarkable impact on practitioners of vernacular religions, who are now aware of the part their practices play in the politics of the ethnonational culture of Puerto Rico.

CULTURAL NATIONALISM AND THE POPULAR WISDOM OF *BRUJOS*

Propelled by the ideology of cultural nationalism, the revalorization of the timeless or "folkloristic" aspects of indigenous Puerto Rican culture has rehabilitated *brujería* (called in the media by less controversial terms such as popular religion and *curanderismo* or folk healing) to fit a renewed nationalist agenda. Instead of vilifying folkloristic practices as obstacles to progress, this nationalist program—initiated by the Instituto de Cultura Puertorriqueña in the 1950s—has foregrounded Puerto Rico's own unique folkloristic *criollo* trajectory. Since the 1980s pride has replaced the criticism of the 1950s, when the same practices were framed, as mentioned earlier, by a development-inspired media as superstitious and as "survivals" of medieval beliefs. At that time newspapers, under the self-ascribed role of modern instruments of education, progress, and civility, set out to educate the masses. But since the 1980s the media's perception of their role in reporting on these folkloric practices has also changed drastically; and in striking contrast to the previous period, a number of newspapers became engaged in unraveling or uncovering hidden traditions. David Scott is right when he argues that cultural traditions "are not only authored; they are authorized."[47] The media became saviors not of rationality and civil society (as in the 1950s) but of "authentic" Puerto Ricanness. Saviors still, certainly, but of quite another kind: saviors of "endangered" Puerto Rican traditions.[48] In one of these newspaper articles, for instance, *santería* appears not as a dubious import from Cuba but as evidence of a continuous Afro–Puerto Rican tradition. Tracing its origins among slaves and maroons, author María J. Peña Signo refers historically to present-day Loíza as the "land of maroons," where a predominantly black population has maintained its African traditions under the guise of Catholic festivities, such as the feast of Santiago Apóstol. The strong impact of African influences on Puerto Rican culture is poetically described in this article through the trope of African drumming: "Blacks continued sounding their most precious musical instrument, at times hardly and at times just softly throbbing their hides to prevent waking up any suspicions among ambitious *conquistadores* that the African continent was indeed setting up its own banners in the new lands."[49]

This public revitalization of Afro–Puerto Rican identity enables those engaged in the strategic Africanization of Puerto Rico to identify with the struggle of other Afro-Caribbean societies and mainland African Americans, even as they assert their Puerto Ricanness. The reification of culture by nationalist discourses has enabled this revitalization; notably, a similar assumption about culture is shared by cultural anthropologists. The former argue that nations are cultural products that shape collective identities, and the latter that culture is a motivational force of human action.[50] Individuals have fleshed out these macroprocesses in personal, compelling ways. For example, suggesting the emergence of a new legitimate space for marginalized religious practices, a *santero* addressed the reincorporation or "revitalization" of African elements in Puerto Rican culture on the radio during an interview about *santería* in the summer of 1996. He said that there was no need for "syncretism" today. He was referring to the "defensive syncretism" of colonial times, when the worship of African deities had to be strategically camouflaged under the guise of devotional services to Catholic saints: no longer, for example, does the African orisha, Changó, owner of fire, love, and thunder, have to be worshiped through

Santa Bárbara, its Catholic face. He expressed this idea aptly and tersely: "To-day, Changó is Changó."

Concomitantly, in line with the ideology of the ethnonation, some *brujos* began to be featured since the late 1980s in newspapers as heroes, as unique voices of Puerto Ricanness, and as saviors of ancient Taíno and African tra-ditions. In this context, *brujos* were able to freely add and proudly show off "African"-based religious prayer songs (imported from Cuba or New York), and exhibit *santería* and *vodou* paraphernalia. Strategically thus appropriated, some key commercialized icons of *santería*, such as the seven powers and the beaded necklaces of the orishas, became creole symbols of an imagined, generalized notion of "African" ritual power (even without adopting the essential tenets of animal sacrifice and initiation rituals through which these symbols acquire their ritual power).

SPIRITUAL AND MATERIAL BLESSINGS: GLOCAL PROSPERITY AND SELF-IDENTITY

All in all, how is it that *brujería* has managed not only just to live but also to thrive under globalization, expanding in line within consumerism, while play-ing alongside the essentializing momentum of heritage? The idea of *bendi-ciones* is crucial. On the one hand, they reflect on the personal spiritual power of individuals, defined by the *cuadro* one has been born with or developed throughout one's life, and the battery of *protecciones* one is able to summon. On the other hand, *bendiciones* are signaled by the nature and number of com-modities one is able to consume, one's buying power, as well as by the public visibility and influence one is able to achieve. So, either as a potential force ready to be materialized or as an objectified reality that proves one's spiritual capital, *bendiciones* point to the ingrained desire to be economically and spiri-tually successful within *brujería* practices. Michael Taussig, addressing the si-multaneity of the materiality and ghostliness of modern fetishistic relations, suggests, "Fetishism elucidates a certain quality of ghostliness in objects in the modern world and an uncertain fluctuation between thinghood and spirit."[51] If both self and commodities become entangled in fetishist relations, one's personal power becomes materialized, and desired objects become spiritual-ized. Acquiring and at the same time confounding their assumed qualities, the need to perceive one's personal power as materialized in objects destabilizes both the self and the objects meant to embody it. *Brujería* thereby operates in a murky ground, articulating the desires and frustrations akin to high modernity and foregrounding the centrality of transnational forms of material consumption as proof, reflection, and anticipation of one's personal power.

The life-style choices made possible by consumerism under conditions of high modernity offer a more or less integral set of practices that an individual can embrace, "not only because such practices fulfill utilitarian needs, but because they give material form to a particular narrative of self-identity."[52] These narratives are complicated in Puerto Rico by both the ideology of multiculturalism and the modern-colonial relationship with the United States of America. The Comaroffs remind us that "[w]itches . . . embody all the contradictions of the experience of modernity itself, of its inescapable enticements, its self-consuming passions, its discriminatory tactics, its devastating social costs."[53] But for Puerto Rican *brujos*, the contradictions inherent in the production of heritage in a nation that is not sovereign must be added to these broader contradictions of modernity. While consumerism and fame allow for the expansion and eclecticism of *brujería* that are essential conditions for giving material form to desired narratives of self-identity—defined in no small measure by the idea of *bendiciones*—the concomitant discourse of the ethnonation limits what otherwise might appear as an open-ended set of choices offered by world markets.

Intimately associated with being blessed by the spirits, global consumerism fits rather well into morally grounded personal and civil local values following the Spiritist ethos, enriched now by a local politics inspired by the ideology of multiculturalism. The demand set up by the political status of Puerto Rico and its version of cultural nationalism has propelled a revitalization of religious practices previously deemed problematic. Through a conflation of spiritual and social responsibility to others, Puerto Rican *brujería* can now answer to a civic agenda; it can profit from the public-geared interest raised in its current practices as a result of the national quest for celebrating the heritage and popular wisdom of its ancestors. But it does so in keeping with its historically forged anti-institutional stance since colonial times. It is within this basic local attitude and predisposition that the recent incorporation of the bureaucratic gestures of welfare capitalism, religious commodities, and the discourse of celebrity within *brujería* need to be theorized.

Critics of the culture industry and consumerism tend to suggest that commercial forces taint the authenticity of culture and thereby the spiritual effectiveness of vernacular religions such as *brujería*. Coincidentally, those practitioners of organized Afro-Latin religions who fear the continuing contamination of their creole religions have voiced a similar concern. As a result, these groups have been engaging in recent years in "purging" Afro-Latin religions of Catholic elements that they claim have tainted the authenticity of their religious expressions, in particular with regard to authentic West African Yoruba components. Menéndez Vázquez termed this process in Cuban *santería* "yorubanization."[54] This is not a concern for practitioners of *brujería*. Indeed, recent Puerto Rican versions of spirituality have incorporated consumerism and heritage as politically situated responses to new criteria and opportunities for ritual effectiveness. This case resonates with Kelly and Kaplan, who have argued against classic assumptions of ritual fixity and for historically sensitive studies of ritual.[55] Defying extrareligious considerations of authenticity, Puerto Rican *brujería* shows that the values of consumerism, the welfare state, and heritage have been translated into ritual practices inspired by and responding to a Spiritist ethos. Only the ritual efficacy of improving and widening one's *bendiciones* is at stake.

Against assumptions held among outsiders, the social space in which *brujos* operate today is far from being situated on the margins of society, in the bush, or in communal settings. Surely its transmission does not depend solely on face-to-face interactions or on the existence of a preestablished local community. Individuality, technological innovation, extended services and choices, and the international circulation of ideas are some of the values directing both society and the practices of *brujería*. Indeed, the same principles that apply to any other enterprise also apply to *brujería*. Far from being a closed form that is centered in a locale or naturally ascribed to an ethnic group, *brujería* is an open form in constant change, its contours discontinuous and permeable. In addition to the direct effects of consumerism, technological expansion, and the discourse of celebrity, Puerto Rican *brujería* has developed a unique spirituality as a result of this and of previous glocal layers.

Evidently the economic influence of a free market and the transnational flow of ritual experts has had a remarkable impact on the practices of *brujería*, including the professionalization of *brujos*, their public fame, and the way clients choose who they consult. Although globalization theorists have emphasized the role of media, the global market, and communication technologies in shaping local cultures, they often point out as well their detrimental, unidirectional homogenizing influences. *Brujería* practices follow a definitely alternative script; they reflect the complex interplay of various global and local forces in non-unidirectional ways. On the one hand, the global circulation of "exotic" products and spiritual practices has destabilized any assumed fixity of *brujería* on ethnic grounds. And with this, any possible legitimation of *brujería* based on its folkloric, national character also has crumbled away. Yet, by the same token, the demands of constituting a Puerto Rican ethnonation have fostered the revitalization of an indigenous ethnonational spirit. This in turn has boosted the professionalization of *brujos*, even while they systematically have rejected any form of ethnic orthodoxy. While feeding into a boundless need for spiritual renewal and growth, imported "exotic" healing systems have been selectively added by individual *brujos*—now protected and encouraged by the national attention to folkloric forms of healing—with the aim of securing additional translocal spiritual power.

Indeed, not only are material and spiritual progress, as well as transnational expansion and ethnic revitalization, *not* mutually exclusive goals for practitioners of *brujería*; they are in fact intimately connected. Especially in a world guided by capitalist modes of production and the sensuous insatiable consumption of life-styles and self-images, *brujos* and their clients take advantage of the opportunities provided by multiculturalism and identity politics to openly expand their pantheon of spirits as well as their ritual expertise. Protected by the idiom of heritage, yet free of its constraints, *brujos* show that, far from being an endangered species, they are vital participants in the glocal forces of spirituality, consumerism, and heritage.

NOTES

An earlier version of this essay was presented at the 2003 American Folklore Society meeting in Chicago. I want to thank Amy Shuman for organizing the panel and suggesting an exciting problematic, and our discussant, Barbara Kirshenblatt-Gimblett, for her insightful and passionate comments. My appreciation also goes to Margaret Mills for providing the opportunity and encouragement to explore my thoughts on the connection between folklore and globalization, and to Roger Abrahams, whose work and conversation have been a constant source of inspiration. My thanks also go to Bernard F. Stehle for his finely honed editing suggestions.

1. *Brujería* is an emic or native term imported to the Spanish colonies at the time of conquest and in use ever since. Its closest translation in English is "witchcraft." To differentiate between the negative connotations of "witchcraft" and to capture the ways in which practitioners refer to *brujería*, the term "witch-healing" may offer a more accurate translation, yet reference to *brujería* honors the practitioners' defiant use of this loaded term as a form of empowerment. I conducted fieldwork and archival research in Puerto Rico from May 1995 until December 1996. The names of some places and people have been changed to protect their privacy. All the dialogue recorded in this essay was spoken in Spanish, and some of the textual sources are in Spanish as well. All translations are mine.

2. For excellent debates on the ways in which Puerto Rico defies classic definitions of "nation," see Duany, "Nation on the Move," 5–30; Duany, "Nation, Migration, Identity"; Duany, *The Puerto Rican Nation on the Move*; and Ramón Grosfoguel, "The Divorce of Nationalist Discourses from the Puerto Rican People: A Sociohistorical Perspective," in Negrón-Muntaner and Grosfoguel, *Puerto Rican Jam*, 57–76. Here I follow Duany's claim that Puerto Rico and its diaspora should be considered in assessing Puerto Rican identity and Grosfoguel's distinction between postcolonial and neocolonial states.

3. Sommer, "Puerto Rico a flote: Desde Hostos hasta hoy," 253–62. I wish to thank Teresita Martínez-Vergne for suggesting this excellent reference to me.

4. Grosfoguel, "The Divorce of Nationalist Discourses from the Puerto Rican People," 66–67.

5. Duany, "Nation, Migration, Identity," 6.

6. Grosfoguel, "The Divorce of Nationalist Discourses from the Puerto Rican People," 66–67.

7. Featherstone, *Global Culture*; Featherstone, Lash, and Robertson, *Global Modernities*; Hinkson, "Postmodernism and Structural Change," 82–101.

8. Bhabha, "DissemiNation"; Chambers, *Migrancy, Culture, Identity*; Clifford, "Diasporas," 302–38; Hall and du Gay, *Questions of Cultural Identity*.

9. Appadurai, "Disjuncture and Difference in the Global Cultural Economy," 1–24; Appadurai, *Modernity at Large*; Ferguson and Gupta, "Space, Identity, and the Politics of Difference," 3–120.

10. Wolf, *Europe and the People without History*, 34–39.

11. Marx and Engels, *The Communist Manifesto*, 12.

12. Barber, *Jihad vs. McWorld*.

13. Appadurai, *The Social Life of Things*; Errington, "Fragile Traditions and Contested Meanings," 49–59.

14. Miller, *Worlds Apart*.

15. Featherstone, Lash, and Robertson, *Global Modernities*, 2–3.

16. Appadurai, *Modernity at Large*, 89–113.

17. Knight, *The Caribbean*.

18. Fanon, *The Wretched of the Earth*.

19. Hall, "Old and New Identities, Old and New Ethnicities," 47–48.

20. Roland Robertson, "Glocalization: Time-Space and Homogeneity-Heterogeneity," in Featherstone, Lash, and Robertson, *Global Modernities*, 25–44.

21. Vidal, "Citizens Yet Strangers: The Puerto Rican Experience," 21, 213 n. 36.

22. Huerga, *Damián López de Haro*, 132.

23. Baralt, *Esclavos rebeldes*; Díaz Soler, *Historia de la esclavitud negra en Puerto Rico*, 175.

24. Arcadio Díaz-Quiñones, comments (Puerto Rican Studies Association, San Juan, Puerto Rico, 1996).

25. Cruz Monclova, *Historia de Puerto Rico, siglo XIX*, 643.

26. Ibid., 856–64; Yañez, *El espiritismo en Puerto Rico*, 19–20.

27. Rodríguez Escudero, *Historia del espiritismo en Puerto Rico*, 4.

28. Machuca, *¿Qué es el Espiritismo?*; Mesa Redonda Espírita de Puerto Rico, *¿Qué es el Espiritismo Científico?*; Rodríguez Escudero, *Historia del Espiritismo en Puerto Rico*; Santiago, "The Spiritistic Doctrine of Allan Kardec"; Yañez, *El Espiritismo en Puerto Rico*.

29. Appadurai, *Modernity at Large*, 10.

30. Silva Gotay, "Social History of the Churches in Puerto Rico, Preliminary Notes," 69.

31. Romberg, "From Charlatans to Saviors," 146–73.

32. This trend was facilitated by the rapid economic growth of the island between World War II and the 1970s, when annual personal income rocketed from $118 to $1,200. See Wagenheim and Jiménez de Wagenheim, *The Puerto Ricans*, 183–84.

33. Appadurai, *Modernity at Large*, 10.

34. Laguerre, *American Odyssey*.

35. Romberg, *Witchcraft and Welfare*.

36. Appadurai, *Modernity at Large*, 10.

37. Zenón Cruz, *Narciso descubre su trasero*.

38. Hall, "The Local and the Global: Globalization and Ethnicity," 19–39.

39. Grosfoguel, Negrón-Muntaner, and Georas, "Beyond Nationalist and Colonialist Discourses," 1–38.

40. Dávila, *Sponsored Identities*; Duany, *The Puerto Rican Nation on the Move*; Morris, *Puerto Rico*; Romberg, "The Pragmatics of Nationhood."

41. Taylor, *Multiculturalism*.

42. Kirshenblatt-Gimblett, *Destination Culture*, 149–50.

43. Domínguez, "The Marketing of Heritage," 546–55.

44. Romberg, "Performing a Postcolonial Colony?"

45. Ryle, "Miracles of the People," 40–50; Menéndez Vázquez, "¿Un Cake para Obatalá?!," 38–51.

46. Kirshenblatt-Gimblett, *Destination Culture*, 161.

47. D. Scott, "That Event, This Memory," 279.

48. Romberg, "From Charlatans to Saviors."

49. Peña Signo, "La santería es un culto ritualista," 6.

50. R. Foster, "Making National Cultures in the Global Ecumene," 235–60.

51. M. Taussig, "Maleficium: State Fetishism," 217.

52. Giddens, *Modernity and Self-Identity*, 81.

53. Comaroff and Comaroff, *Modernity and Its Malcontents*, xxix.

54. Menéndez Vázquez, "¿Un Cake para Obatalá?!"

55. Kelly and Kaplan, "History, Structure, and Ritual."

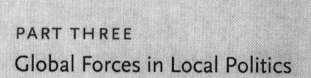

PART THREE

Global Forces in Local Politics

Small societies confront a series of internal and external political problems in an increasingly globalizing world. Valentina Peguero explores the increasingly important Caribbean-wide manifestation of women's grass-roots organizations that have contributed to the strengthening of democratic governments across the region, although democracy is neither a highly articulated goal nor a pre-requisite for the success of these movements. Caribbean female grass-roots organizations have formed strong networks linking local, national, regional, and international concerns in an effective mechanism of change and develop-ment. The specific foundational factors for female organizational militancy, she points out, vary considerably depending on time, place, and circumstances. Supported by local national and international organizations, Caribbean women have become active and influential agents of change in local societies although the overall success so far has been modest. Nevertheless, modern communica-tions have allowed grass-roots organizations to employ tactics and gain results that would have been impossible only a few years ago. In this respect, globaliza-tion has been an asset to small, isolated groups.

Race, color, ethnicity, and class have converged sharply throughout the course of Caribbean history, and perhaps nowhere more sharply than in the political life of Cuba. Aline Helg reviews the challenges during the twentieth century to come to grips with the domestic dimensions of these social issues while at the same time accommodating the indelible impact of North American hegemony.

8

Women's Grass-Roots Organizations in the Dominican Republic: Real and Imagined Female Figures

VALENTINA PEGUERO

Seeking change and empowerment, Caribbean women have formed vast networks of grass-roots organizations. The product of complex processes, the formation and growth of each organization respond to global developments and to the socioeconomic and political system of each individual nation.

Representative of the collaboration among women are the Federation of Cuban Women, the Federation of Dominican Women, the Guiana Women's Political and Economic Organization, the Jamaican Businesswomen's Association, the Popular Feminist Association of Women Workers of Puerto Rico, Solidarity among Haitian Women, and the National Women's Movement of Suriname. These organizations seek to reach their goals by articulating their demands at the local, regional, and national levels.

The conceptual meaning of *grass roots* is subject to multiple interpretations. For some scholars, policy makers, and other professionals, mobilizing resources, conducting political action, and obtaining direct representation and full community involvement are focal points of community-based organizations. Others perceive grass-roots groups as "aggressive" agents of social change.[1] Despite these differences, researchers and government officials concur that such organizations bring about community development, socioeconomic renewal, and political changes. In postdictatorship periods, for example, women's grass-roots organizations have become important agencies in the building of democratic societies.

Based on the premise that grass-roots organizations have become a vehicle for women's involvement in the global struggle for change and empowerment, this article, which studies in detail four cases of Dominican women's activism in the twentieth century, focuses on the resilience and determination of Caribbean women who have become models and leaders for other women to pursue their goals. This work also directs attention to the reality behind the symbols and myths of Caribbean women in art and textual references.

FORGED IMAGES, UNDERLYING REALITIES

Until the relatively recent emergence of fresh scholarship on women's issues, the role of Caribbean women in the nation-building process, public welfare, and progress in communities has languished in obscurity and misconceptions. Traditional textual references to Caribbean women portray a dichotomy. Literature on the topic projects images of either superabnegated mothers or sexy complacent mulattas. Since the nineteenth century, artistic expressions have reinforced such distortions. Thomas Stothard's *The Voyage of the Sable Venus from Angola to the West Indies* (1800), engraved by William Grainger, depicts an enslaved African woman's journey through the "middle passage." She has no chains; her face does not reflect pain or suffering. Obliterating the torment of this imagined woman, the artist presents her as an erotic and sensual creature, crossing the ocean in a ship embroidered with coral shells, ivory, and precious stones. Stothard's inspiration, according to Rosalie Smith McCrea, was a poem of the identical title by Isaac Teale, published in 1775.[2]

The canvas and the poem illustrate, in particular, the myths that surround women of African descent living in the Americas and, in general, reveal the twisted reality of women in the Caribbean. The travesty of female lives in the region took another turn in the twentieth century. Showing disconnections with the living conditions and sociopolitical realities of Caribbean societies, social studies conducted by researchers and policy makers in the 1950s and 1960s, as several scholars explain, helped create images of Caribbean women confined to the house and consumed by household chores, while their husbands were the main source of income. The discourse on domestic ideology overshadowed the reality that coexisting with the patriarchal family was a "vibrant living tradition of female economic autonomy, of female headed households."[3] The division of labor common in Caribbean households and, as Helen Safa points out, women's dual productive-reproductive role have encouraged this view of women as housewives and mothers, reinforcing the myth of the male breadwinner.[4] The fact is that in the Caribbean women provide approximately 35 percent of the household income. In the case of Barbados, for example, women head more than 40 percent of the households.[5] Caribbean women have tremendous economic responsibility and considerable economic independence.

In the fast-changing world of the twenty-first century, particularly as a result of industrialization and globalization of the economy, more Caribbean women participate in the labor force than do women in most parts of the Third World.[6] The myth of the male breadwinner persists, however, because, among other reasons, in the Caribbean as in many Western capitalist societies women usually receive lower wages and salaries than men with similar responsibilities. Far from being passive and dependent individuals, Caribbean women have contributed to national development in virtually every sector of society.

POLITICAL ACTIVISM OF DOMINICAN WOMEN'S ORGANIZATIONS

Caribbean women's militancy has a long history. In fact, the history of the Caribbean could not be properly analyzed without including the participation of women in the political process. Nonetheless, women's involvement in the political development of the region does not respond to a uniform agenda, and conflicts and internal divisions have surfaced among women's groups. But in general they share a common goal of promoting organizations that represent their sociopolitical views and gender concerns.

Based on the common understanding of globalization as "consciousness of the world as a whole," Caribbean women's move toward militancy is multidimensional. It encompasses economic, political, social justice, human rights, and environmental groups. The political activism of Dominican women acquired a nationalistic character and a global dimension during the struggle against U.S. occupation (1916–24). Peasant groups, particularly in the East, put together an effective resistance against the U.S. Marines, forcing them to fight for almost six years. When the guerrilla movement was at its height, a wave of nationalist discontent swept across the country, primarily in urban areas. Calling for resistance to imperialist domination, protesters organized a campaign of civil disobedience, demanded the immediate withdrawal of the occupation forces, and collected funds for an international propaganda campaign.

The Junta Patriótica de Damas (Patriotic League of Ladies), a grass-roots women's organization created on March 15, 1920, was important in this campaign. Under the leadership of Floripez Mieses, Abigail Mejía, Luisa Ozema

Pellerano, and Ercilia Pepín, thousands of women transformed themselves from housewives, workers, and professional women into "public agitators," as the U.S. military governor called the protesters. With a clear vision of the role they had to play in preserving the national sovereignty, women adopted a militant attitude, collected money to send delegates abroad to denounce the occupation, and gave speeches that galvanized audiences. Sharing the anti-intervention ideology, Haitian women also took to the streets to demand the end of U.S. occupation. (Haiti was occupied from 1915 to 1934.)

Dominican women used the flag as a symbol of their activism. Believing that the national ensign flying in front of the invaders would elevate the spirit of the people, the women distributed flags among the population, which were to be raised when Marines walked through the streets. Hundreds of women signed a letter prepared by Pepín that protested the occupation and sent it to the U.S. Senate Committee then studying the situation on the island.[7]

In San Pedro de Macorís in 1922, Petronila Gómez created the magazine *Fémina*, which was known as "the feminine voice" of the eastern region. It provided a literary and intellectual forum for women to demand their civic rights and to express their anti-imperialist sentiments. Renowned feminists such as Mejía and Rosa Smester echoed the anti-interventionist ideology by publishing, nationally and internationally, articles denouncing U.S. intervention and exalting nationalistic values. *El Album, Renacimiento, Noticias de Barcelona*, and other literary journals, as well as newspapers, expressed their political views.[8]

Invited by the military government to represent the Dominican Republic at the National American Woman's Suffrage Association in the United States in 1921, Pepín remained true to her principles and refused to attend. How was she going to accept the sponsorship of the government that had deprived her nation of its political independence? Pepín's attitude symbolized Dominican women's response to interventionism. Equally important, the Junta Patriótica de Damas provided the opportunity for Dominican women to actively participate in the struggle for national liberation. Their involvement in the nationalist struggle helped to invigorate Dominican resistance and reinforced the international support against the occupation.

The political mobilization of the Dominican people and worldwide protests compelled the United States to withdraw its forces by July 1924. After the U.S. troops left the country, women became further politicized on issues concerning gender and power. Considering ignorance as a tool of oppression (more women than men were illiterate), Delia Weber, Pepín, and other women founded Acción Cultural Feminista in 1928 to promote education as a means of liberation for all women. Focusing on the legal and political inequalities that deprived women of direct participation in national politics, female leaders also began a campaign to support women's right to vote.

Within the context of political globalization, which transcends nation-state borders and relates to regional identities of the "global civil society," the Junta Patriótica de Damas sympathized with Augusto César Sandino's struggle in Nicaragua (the United States occupied Nicaragua from 1912 to 1933, and Sandino fought against them and the U.S.-sponsored Nicaraguan National Guard from 1927 to 1933). Members of the organization, together with Pepín's students from the Colegio de Señoritas "México" ("Mexico" School for Girls), embroidered a replica of the Nicaraguan flag and sent it to Sandino on May 15, 1928. In a letter to Sandino, Pepín expressed that the ensign symbolized the national sovereignty of Nicaragua, the political and cultural connections that existed between the Nicaraguan and Dominican people, and the peace and liberty aspired by all the people of the Americas.

CARIBBEAN WOMEN'S ACTIVISM AGAINST POLITICAL OPPRESSION

Contemporary Caribbean history is intrinsically connected to women's political action and their networks of resistance against oppressive rulers. Within a global context, Caribbean women have played important roles in defying authoritarian governments and have led many protests against dictators. Analyzing the impact of political oppression on the family, researchers of Latin American and Caribbean women's movements have attached a gendered dimension to the active participation of women against dictatorial regimes.[9] But active participation is also women's conscious response to oppression in the domains of both politics and gender. Throughout the Caribbean region, political repressions have spurred women into collective action.

Representing women's determination to end oppression, women in Cuba organized the Association of United Cuban Women specifically to fight against Fulgencio Batista during his second term in office (1952–59). Playing an important tactical role, women held key positions in the urban underground movement and became part of the commandos. The Mariana Grajales combat platoon, an all-female unit, was out in front during the armed struggle in the Sierra Maestra. As recognized by Fidel Castro in his speech of January 1, 1959, women fought bravely and decisively to end Batista's government.

Women in Haiti formed blocks of resistance against the repressive regime of Francois Duvalier (1957–71) and his son Jean Claude Duvalier (1971–86). In *Walking on Fire: Haitian Women's Stories of Survival and Resistance*, Beverly Bell explains how solidarity was the key to women's resistance. The core activists in the movement adopted strategies to recruit supporters, and during the final years of the dictatorship a large proportion of women joined the opposition. To overthrow the regime, among other tactics, women used various subterfuges to disguise their resistance, including passing as Duvalierists to gain access to information that the opposition otherwise could not obtain.

In the Dominican Republic, women challenged the despotic regime of Rafael Trujillo (1930–61) and strongly influenced the fate of the dictator. Three sisters, Patria, Minerva, and María Teresa Mirabal, actively participated in the formation and development of the 14th of June Movement, the grass-roots organization that had perhaps the most profound impact on the political awakening of the Dominican generation of 1960. As one of the ideological founders of the organization, Minerva deserves particular attention.

MINERVA, FEMINIST AND REVOLUTIONARY

The strongest resistance against Trujillo developed during a crucial moment of Latin American politics: the triumph of Fidel Castro's revolution in Cuba in 1959. From the beginning, Castro, viewed as an example of what resistance and opposition could produce, attracted many who demanded changes and plotted revolutions in Latin America. The opposition against Trujillo, already strong, received an influx of professionals, government employees, and university students who joined in the struggle for freedom. Among them were Minerva and María Teresa and their husbands, Manuel (Manolo) Tavárez Justo and Leandro Guzmán Rodríguez, respectively. In time Patria, along with her husband, Pedro González, and their son, Nelson, became members of the underground resistance. As a result, the government punished the Mirabals and their relatives—prison and torture for the men; prison, torture, and death for the women.

The roots of Minerva's activism can be traced to her socioeconomic background and education. She, like her sisters, grew up in an upper-middle-class environment in the province of Salcedo and attended a Catholic girls school in La Vega, where she learned about Trujillo's reign of terror. Fathers, brothers, and other relatives of her classmates were victims of Trujillo's repressive methods.

Minerva's direct encounter with Trujillo took place in 1949, when Trujillo invited the Mirabal family to a gala and asked Minerva to dance with him. She showed no enthusiasm for the Jefe's preference, and the family left the party shortly after Trujillo danced with Minerva. The departure, considered an offense, landed Minerva and her father in prison for a short period. Afterward, Trujillo continued his harassment against the family and, in 1951, again incarcerated the father and put Minerva and her mother under house arrest. Minerva wanted to acquire a university education and ultimately became a law student in 1952. The academic environment reinforced her anti-Trujillista stance, as she was in contact with friends and members of the opposition. In addition, Minerva enhanced her political education by listening to forbidden radio broadcasts, particularly Castro's speeches. She memorized several paragraphs of Castro's famous oratorical piece, "History Will Absolve Me."

Because of her rejection of Trujillo's persona and his politics, when Minerva completed her university studies in 1957 the government denied her an academic title. Without a license to practice law, she turned her attention to revolutionary activities. Early in 1960, with her husband and hundreds of other Dominican men and women, she organized the resistance, which developed into the 14th of June Movement. The organization's name derived from the failed aerial invasion of June 14, 1959, when a group of Dominican rebels who had trained in Cuba and other Latin American countries landed in the Dominican Republic's northern mountains of Constanza. Confronted by the army, the group suffered a gruesome defeat.

Minerva challenged the members to emulate Castro's political and military strategy and proposed guerrilla warfare to eliminate Trujillo's regime. Within a global context, regarding revolution as the only way to change authoritarian rule, Minerva's plan responded to patterns of resistance and democratization that developed in the Caribbean, Latin America, and elsewhere in the 1960s.

WOMEN'S ACTIVISM AND THE 14TH OF JUNE MOVEMENT

Minerva's ideas took root in the minds of the organizers. When the 14th of June Movement was formally organized, it had the essential characteristics of a grass-roots organization aimed at conducting political action to benefit the masses. In terms of political participation, the organization increased membership by mobilizing people from every social stratum. To achieve its ultimate goals, the methods and the objectives of the organization were well defined. Anti-Trujillismo was the doctrine; guerrilla warfare was the method; and ending Trujillo's rule, as well as establishing a democratic government, was the goal.[10] To protect himself or herself from the dictator's rage, each member adopted a code name; Minerva was known as *Mariposa* or butterfly.

In January 1960 the underground brought together delegates from all the provinces. At this meeting only two women, Minerva and Dulce María Tejada Gómez, were present. The lack of female representation moved Minerva to recruit and to encourage other women to join the struggle. Many responded to the call, including her younger sister, María Teresa, and later her older sister, Patria.

María Teresa and Patria assumed visible roles: María Teresa became the secretary of the organization, and Patria offered her house for the rebels to meet and to store weapons and ammunition. María Teresa's underground name was *Mariposa #2*, and Patria, *Mariposa #3*. Gradually other women, many of them professional women—Tomasina Cabral, Miriam Morales, Asela Morel, Fe Violeta Ortega, and Josefina Padilla among them—joined the opposition.

A few months later, the Intelligence Military Service (SIM) found out about the movement's clandestine activities and launched a vicious persecution against the *catorcistas*, as the members of the political organization were known. Minerva and Manolo, María Teresa and Leandro, Patria's husband (Pedro), and 400 other men and women ended up in jail and were tortured, and many died. But the movement was unstoppable.

With time, it evolved into the most powerful grass-roots organization against Trujillo, attracting men and women, young and old, from all levels of society but primarily the middle and upper classes. Serving to strengthen the movement, in January 1960 the Catholic Church, which had supported Trujillo for three decades, issued a pastoral letter protesting the dictator's abuses.

In the meantime, Minerva's wide-ranging activism expanded, particularly the feminist aspect of her political agenda. Inside the prison, she began a cautious revolutionary indoctrination of nonpolitical women. Among other issues, she stressed the need for women to get an education and the influence women can exert in the political system. For her activism, the wardens punished Minerva. Tortured and humiliated, she refused to back down. One of her interrogators, recognizing her strength, said to other guards, "This woman, Minerva, is a man." She served as a model and inspiration for women's involvement in the struggle against Trujillo and in the global struggle against oppression. As the resistance movement grew, rumors that Trujillo wanted to kill Minerva spread among the opposition. Trujillo knew that Minerva was not only a revolutionary but also a charismatic leader. As described by Julia Alvarez in *In the Time of the Butterflies*, she became "the secret heroine" of the nation.

The dictator could not accept the idea that anyone opposed him. But women? That was intolerable. In Villa Tapia, on November 2, 1960, Trujillo expressed that his two biggest problems were the Catholic Church and the Mirabal sisters. On November 25, 1960, the Mirabal sisters paid for their activism with their lives. Trujillo's henchmen killed Minerva, Patria, and María Teresa, along with Rufino de la Cruz, the man driving their car, while they were returning home from visiting Manolo and Leandro, who were incarcerated in Puerto Plata (Patria's husband was jailed in the capital).

Afterward, a chain reaction of events gradually eroded the foundation of the dictatorship. Although the dictator had committed many political crimes, the killing of the Mirabal sisters trespassed the boundaries of the political realm. It touched a cultural nerve of society: family. These three women, mothers of young children, were also sisters and daughters, aunts and nieces. The crime produced national as well as international outrage. Members of the middle and upper classes, the United States, and other longtime supporters turned against the dictator. He was killed on May 30, 1961.

After their assassination, the sisters dominated popular images of women's resistance to violence and political oppression, and mobilized women, nationally and internationally, to participate. Globally, in terms of bringing to the forefront the violence suffered by women worldwide, the Mirabal sisters' actions had reached a range of women organizations.

During the First Latin American and Caribbean feminist conference that took place in Bogotá in July 1981, the Dominican delegation proposed to declare November 25 as a day for reflection and denunciation of all types of violence suffered by women in all parts of the world. On May 15, 1987, the International Women's Conference, meeting in Germany, declared November 25 as the International Day against Violence toward Women; and on December 17, 1999, the United Nations approved the petition. Thus, November 25 has acquired a historical and feminist dimension, and as expressed by Dedé, the surviving Mirabal sister, the legacy of Minerva, María Teresa, and Patria does not belong just to the Dominican people but to the world.[11]

Indeed, inspired by the three sisters, many organizations have developed all over the world, particularly in Latin America and the Caribbean. Every November 25, women remember the Mirabal sisters, reflecting and taking actions to stop violence against women. In June 1991, for example, a meeting of the Center for Women's Global Leadership (CWGL), with women representing twenty countries, called out for a global campaign of sixteen days of activism from November 25 to December 10, 1991, to end oppression and violence against all women. The time was chosen to commemorate the violent assassination of the Mirabal sisters. As reported by the organization in 2003, over the years the 16

Days network has multiplied and now includes participation from more than 800 organizations in over 90 countries. Women all over the globe, at local, regional, national, and international levels, join to observe the occasion.

The martyrdom of these three Dominican women has become also a subject in gender studies. In the Caribbean, Latin America, and the United States, schools and colleges include the Mirabals in their curriculum. Worldwide, the sisters are remembered in marches, protests, lectures, theater performances, and movies, and in numerous tributes and memorials dedicated to their courage and heroic actions.

INTERVENTION AND RESISTANCE: WOMEN'S MOBILIZATION

The legacy of the Mirabal sisters and the work of the *catorcistas* had other dimensions. The 14th of June Movement evolved into a leftist political party. It played an important role in the tumultuous events that followed the overthrow of Juan Bosch, the first elected president after Trujillo. He won the election in December 1962, pledging social and economic reforms. Businessmen, military leaders, and church leaders, as well as right-wing groups, opposed Bosch's government. These groups felt threatened by Bosch's social democratic agenda and accused him of being a communist. In addition, Bosch's lack of understanding of the Dominican reality after twenty-five years in exile led him to clash with friends and foes. On September 25, 1963, the opposition deposed Bosch and replaced him with a three-man civilian junta. The triumvirate disbanded the Congress, suspended civil liberties, and adopted other unpopular measures. Crystallizing Minerva's armed resistance method, in December a guerrilla movement, led by Tavárez, took to the mountains to fight against the triumvirate. Soon after, armed troops surrounded the rebels and forced them to surrender. Tavárez and other rebels died in the confrontation.

In the interim, democratic groups, revolutionary forces, and young military officers wanted a return to a constitutional government. Sharing these democratic principles and revolutionary fervor, and to prevent the installation of another dictatorship, female leaders built the Federation of Women, a coalition of women's organizations. The leaders of the organization called women to join efforts and to play a greater role in the political and civic life of the country. In response, showing how gender had shaped the content of women's political involvement, women voiced their disapproval to de facto government, flooded the streets to demand the restoration of a legitimate government, and asked all women to join the constitutionalist cause.[12]

On April 24, 1965, civil war broke out in Santo Domingo. Four days later, U.S. president Lyndon Johnson, claiming the need to protect American citizens, ordered 42,000 Marines to the Dominican Republic. Women from all political groups resisted this second intervention by the United States. Conscious of their important role in the struggle, women devised strategies and tactics that worked. Those residing in the area of resistance used their homes as headquarters or gathering places. Others became soldiers, nurses, and postal workers and served the revolution with conviction and dedication. Some assumed leading roles usually associated with men. Emma Tavárez stirred up the multitudes, shouting "Arms for the people!" Gladis Borrel, known as *La Coronela*, led a male brigade and encouraged women to join the commandos.

Artists and activists, such as Ada Balcácer, Elsa Núñez, and Souci de Pellarano, applied their painting skills to depict the impact of the invaders on people's lives and on the national landscape. In June 1965 at the Fine Arts Palace, the people had the opportunity to see the work of these and other female artists who used their talent to express their ideological stance. Joining the struggle, women writers organized the Cultural Front to express their anguish and patriotic sentiments in prose and poems. When the war ended by the middle of July 1965, women in great numbers joined the Federation of Women and the 14th of June Party.[13] In many ways, both groups endorsed Minerva's discourse of political liberation and struggle against oppression.

RURAL GRASS-ROOTS ORGANIZATIONS AND DOÑA TINGÓ

In addition to supporting political organizations, Caribbean women have been active in organizing rural, community-based groups. The initial efforts to develop this type of organization coincided with a critical period in the Dominican Republic. Human rights were being routinely violated. In addition, after Trujillo's death, the country faced innumerable political challenges and experienced a series of dramatic socioeconomic changes.

The agrarian reform, an attempt to distribute land to poor rural inhabitants, highlighted the problems of the post-Trujillo era. It was one of the most controversial projects of the Bosch administration. Initially his government distributed some of Trujillo's land to the peasants, an action that conservative groups labeled a communist-inspired threat to private property. (Previously, Joaquín Balaguer, who was Trujillo's last puppet president, confiscated the dictator's properties, and distributed sizable quantities of land to the peasants.) Bosch was ousted, and the agrarian reform created great expectations among the landless peasants. But their hopes were dashed; through political maneuvers and monetary paybacks to officials and officers, landowners and other land-grabbing people managed to acquire state land, impeding the implementation of the agrarian policy.

To discourage the peasants from cultivating the land, the "owners" de-stroyed the peasants' harvests, fenced their properties, and eventually evicted some peasants. The abuses, personal attacks, and ejection from the land that they had cultivated for generations drove the peasants to action. They formed community-based organizations, such as the Federation of Christian Agricul-tural Leagues (FEDELAC), to defend their right to work and own land. At the same time, rural women organized grass-roots groups called Club de Madres (Mothers' Club) in almost every province. Women who made handcrafted products, such as flower arrangements, pottery, and hand-sewn garments, were members in these clubs. A central goal of the club was to encourage rev-enue-generating activities. Operating within the informal internal marketing system, members sold their products to the inhabitants of their communities and the surrounding areas.

At first the clubs functioned locally without political affiliation or other con-nections. Gradually, the clubs evolved into regional federations and later, un-der the orientation of the Socialist Bloc, a coalition of leftist parties, moved into the well-structured National Confederation of Peasant Women (CONAMUCA).

Florinda Soriano, best known as Doña Tingó, an illiterate, religious peas-ant, a widow, and mother of ten children, joined both the Mothers' Club and FEDELAC. She exemplifies women's activism and a dedication to work for social justice. A woman of commanding character, firmness, and determination, Soriano became the symbolic mother of the peasants' resistance movement and the female figure of CONAMUCA.

Regular participation at the meetings and activities scheduled by the Moth-ers' Club and FEDELAC helped Doña Tingó develop her leadership skills. Listen-ing to others prepared her to deliver her message effectively. A woman who worked the land for forty years, Doña Tingó fitted well the picture of the Carib-bean woman agricultural worker. Working in the fields since she was a child, Doña Tingó did not receive a formal education, but she had a global vision: those who worked the land for years should own it. Eventually she emerged as a leader of the peasants' struggle to obtain land in the area of Hato Viejo, in the southern region of the country. She organized meetings for peasants to express their concerns and discuss actions to defend their rights.

Connecting the struggle with the cultural background of the peasants, Doña

Tingó resorted to songs called *décimas* to deliver her message. The lyrics expressed people's feelings and were used to vent frustrations and complaints, to reveal love, and, like oral history, to recount local or national events. The verses of the *décimas* provided the rural composers, men and women alike, with "universally understood rhythmic structure on which to base a wide range of commentary."[14] During the meetings, Doña Tingó encouraged peasants to action by challenging them with rhymes of which the land was the focal point. One of her preferred verses was:

Don't leave me alone
raise your voice
There is plenty of land
and it provides for everyone!

She regularly attended religious activities and sang psalms and spiritual songs in church with enthusiasm. On their way home from church, friends and neighbors joined Doña Tingó, singing *décimas* and other rhythms verbalizing the anger, rage, and the determination of the rural peasantry to confront those who oppressed them.

In an environment largely dominated by men, Doña Tingó's leadership was exceptional. As the rural inhabitants of Hato Viejo became more vocal, the landowners labeled Doña Tingó an instigator who was creating the conditions for an uprising of the rural masses. To deter her influence, the landowners harassed, jailed, and tried to bribe her, as well as other men and women from Hato Viejo, with no success. Following the theory of the "aggressive form of social change" of grass-roots groups, the peasants, under Doña Tingó's leadership, united their strengths and together brought Pablo Díaz, a landowner, to court, accusing him of illegal appropriation of their land.

The peasants' legal action would have been customary in a democratic system, but in the Dominican Republic of 1974, when the nation still was going through a period of transition to democracy, peasants were marginalized and exploited by the landowning class. Doña Tingó's actions infuriated Díaz, and he ordered one of his workers to kill her in November 1974. She was sixty years old.[15]

Doña Tingó died defending the right to 8,000 *tareas* (six Dominican *tareas* are approximately equal to one U.S. acre) that Díaz wanted to appropriate from the peasants, including her lands. After her death, Doña Tingó became "Mamá Tingó." She evolved from a woman peasant, to a woman leader, to a martyr. Symbolizing the peasants' resistance movement, her legacy became a tale of

bravery, compassion, and determination. Invoking Mamá Tingó, peasants organized marches demanding social justice and distribution of land. Balaguer,
who again was in power in 1974, declared the 8,000 *tareas* public land and
gave it to the peasants.

THE DOMINICAN WOMEN'S PEASANT MOVEMENT

By 1985 the peasants had formed a united front to demand their rights
through a powerful grass-roots organization, the Movement of Independent
Campesinos (MCI), with almost 80,000 members. In 1986 the first congress
of peasant women took place in Santo Domingo. More than 10,000 members
came from different regions of the country. Together they formed the Confederation of Peasant Women. Milagros Ricourt, who has researched CONAMUCA,
concludes that during the 1980s, the organization became one of the major
political forces demanding land and resources for the Dominican peasantry.
As an organization oriented "toward the promotion and advancement of peasant women," CONAMUCA was instrumental in some cases in offering women
the opportunity to take control of their community.[16]

The group mobilized thousands of women nationwide to demand justice,
to exert pressure to obtain land for its members, and to demand freedom for
prisoners jailed during land occupations. These women were taking actions
similar to those of men, but the nature of their protest was different and the
challenge to the patriarchal environment was highly unusual.

The women protested also against disadvantages associated with interdependence and financial globalization, such as the restrictions imposed by
the International Monetary Fund (IMF) agreement. The accord, signed by
President Salvador Jorge Blanco in April 1985, devalued the peso against the
dollar by almost 30 percent, reduced the buying power of the poor, and caused
considerable disruption in the domestic financial systems. To make matters
worse, the government imposed several austerity measures that led to popular
uprisings. During the demonstrations, CONAMUCA showed its strength with
massive participation of its members in protests organized in the southern
cities and in the capital.

Social protests provided a forum in which peasant women voiced their views
and engaged in political action; they became major political forces, as they
demanded better living conditions, land, and resources for the improvement
of their communities. CONAMUCA's data from 1987 indicate that women were
"in a better position, with 82.7 percent of the households owning land, with

an average of seven hectares each."[17] The percentage, to some extent, may be attributable to the resistance ideology laid out by Doña Tingó, encouraging female peasants to defy abuses, to fight for their rights, and to insist on the betterment of their communities.

Regrettably, affected by increased poverty in rural communities, the membership of CONAMUCA declined from 10,000 in 1986 to about 4,000 by the first decade of 2000. This reduction may be related to the intertwined connection between migration and globalization. Under economic pressure, thousands of women migrated nationally and internationally. Within the country, many moved from rural to urban areas where they could find jobs in the industrial sector, particularly in workshops and factories developed by the free-trade zones in Santo Domingo, Santiago, Puerto Plata, La Romana, and other provinces. Other women followed the trend of transnational migration and moved to Puerto Rico, Spain, the United States, Venezuela, and other countries.

In addition, the fragmentation of leftist parties and the weakness of labor unions were also forces that had a negative impact on CONAMUCA's strength. However, despite the reduction of its membership, the activism of the rural women, a fresh form of feminist action, helped change Dominican society as they pushed legislation to distribute land for all peasants and took a stand against domestic violence and gender inequalities.

DEVELOPMENT AND WOMEN'S EMPOWERMENT

Researchers have addressed the women's movement in the Caribbean, as well as in Latin America, in terms of gender, politics, race, and economic development. Within the financial context, since the majority of the people in the Caribbean are poor, economics has played a key role in women's mobilization. Across the region, different women's groups have emerged to empower their female members. As some scholars have postulated, many of these groups have a distinctive feminist focus, that is, mobilizing women and public opinion to meet practical and strategic gender interests and to incorporate women into development.[18]

Putting into practice the "practical and strategic gender interests" theory, Dominican female leaders are organizing grass-roots groups to help poor women to obtain bank credit. Under the leadership of Mercedes Canalda and a group of socially conscious citizens, composed of nine women and three men, the Dominican Association for Women Development (ADOPEM) was founded on July 14, 1982. Canalda conceived the idea while attending the opening of the

Women's World Banking organization in Cali, Colombia, in 1981. Recognizing the importance of women helping women, Canalda dedicated time and efforts to improve the lives of her female compatriots.

Within a holistic global approach aimed at encouraging the development of women and their families, ADOPEM offers financial assistance and guidance to women—primarily women who do not have access to the formal banking system—so that they can operate their own businesses. Leaders of the organization explain that most of the clientele are hardworking women without resources but with potential to become productive members of their communities.

The formation of ADOPEM had its roots also in the socioeconomic gulf that has deprived the poor of their fair share of the national income. The founders of the organization, most of them experienced bankers, economists, social workers, and other experts, knew well the social class disparity and the market inequality of the country, where the poorest half receives less than one-fifth of the GNP while the richest 10 percent has access to 40 percent of the national income. Such a discrepancy results from a combination of governmental apathy and a lack of resources, and from the wide fissure within society that allows a tiny minority to control the means of production and deprive the great majority of opportunities to share the wealth of the nation.

Because of the structure of the economic system and constraints of the financial sector, poor people have almost no means to obtain bank credit. Such restrictions are even more of an impediment for women because in addition to not having collateral to back their requests, in some instances commercial institutions discriminate against a household without a male figure as the head of the family.

Supporting women's advancement, one of ADOPEM's priorities is training women to manage their own finances. Since some members do not have a clear understanding of accounting, the first task is to teach them to separate capital from profits and to keep records of their investments. What appears to be a simple task is a complex and challenging endeavor: to teach these women to overcome educational and psychological barriers that have kept them on the margin of poverty.

The training center of the organization is responsible for the implementation of the instructional plan. It covers three main areas: management, to teach skills related to the operation and functioning of microfinancial enterprises; technical-vocational training, to provide training on financial and practical matters; and economic development, to integrate ADOPEM members into the formal sector of the economy (the last phase appears to respond to the global trend of economic interdependence). Applying an integrative vision, in coordination with other institutions, the organization has designed a diversity of programs to help women better manage not only their finances but also their lives.

Applying the concept of globalization as "consciousness of the world as a whole," these programs are designed to develop civic consciousness by instilling principles of good citizenship in the communities and by offering talks and workshops in areas of health, democracy, and importance of the environment, and other topics to empower women to have better lives and make their contribution to the well-being of society. In 2002 the training center instructed 3,000 women on topics ranging from basic mathematics to women's issues.

At the outset, its founders financially supported ADOPEM. But now, although it receives financial and management assistance from commercial, private, and nongovernmental organizations (NGOs), particularly Women's World Banking, the organization is almost self-supporting. As reported by the newsletter of the organization in September 2003, with productive investments ADOPEM managed a portfolio of U.S.$9.9 million in 2002.

With headquarters in Santo Domingo and a network of twelve regional branches, the group had a membership of 36,770 affiliates in 2002. Popularly known as El Banco de las Mujeres (The Women's Bank), ADOPEM promotes the social inclusion of poor women within the small-scale business sector. To facilitate such inclusion, the organization offers loans and services appropriate to its clientele. It is not a charitable or paternalistic organization. On the contrary, as an organization concerned with women's welfare, it is a catalytic women's enterprise.

With the motto "Money Always within Your Reach," entrepreneurial women may obtain loans from two programs. One type of loan is in the solidarity groups category, which offers loans to women living on the margin of poverty who have common goals and the willingness to work collectively. These groups function as an association of three to five women and operate small-scale businesses to repay the loan. Members who perform well and want to maximize their investments can apply for a micro-micro loan, which is essentially an incentive loan to motivate women to move up financially. The second type of loan falls into the category of individual credits. These funds are designed to provide individual loans to microentrepreneurial women. In addition, within the category of "nonproductive activities" (personal matters) credits are also accessible to the members of ADOPEM.[19]

At first the organization served only women, but after twenty years, in order to integrate the organization within the global perspective, ADOPEM started to offer financial and management services to men also. Some women were unhappy about the inclusion of men and expressed their concern with the potential for male dominance over the organization. But women are still the majority of ADOPEM's clients. In 2002, of 36,770 persons who benefited from ADOPEM's projects, 86 percent were women. Many were notable contributors to the informal and formal Dominican economy. Based on its performance, ADOPEM is considered by Women's World Banking as one of the leaders of Latin American and the Caribbean microfinancial sector.

In 2001 the organization received the Inter-American Development Bank's Award for Excellence in Microfinance. The success stories of many women sustain this reputation. Describing client case studies, the Women's World Banking newsletter of May 2003 charts the road to success of several women, who with the assistance of ADOPEM have opened new businesses, expanded existing ones, or started a new business venture. The case of Florentina Angeles Reyes demonstrates how grass-roots organizations have contributed to help women to pursue their goals by empowering them with financial—albeit limited—resources.

Reyes, a mother of three children, is a forty-three-year-old woman who lives with her seventy-one-year-old husband, a retired carpenter, in a neighborhood outside Santo Domingo. Wanting to earn her own money, Reyes began her business enterprise by selling a popular sweet bread called *arepas* at the construction site where her husband used to work. Then she ventured into several income-generating activities, including preparing lunches at home and delivering them to a nearby factory at noontime. The lunch business did not do well, but Reyes moved on. She borrowed money from ADOPEM and, together with her husband and an associate, began building rooms to rent. The rental endeavor began in 1997, and six years later the total value of her property was worth RD$2,000,000 (about u.s.$90,000).[20] Within the context of the Dominican real-estate market and the economic situation of poor people, Reyes's business operations reflect the important role played by the Banco de las Mujeres, as well as other organizations, in helping women develop their potential.

Focusing on women's resourcefulness, particularly on the experience of women who are engaged in the retail business of making and selling clothes, the director of ADOPEM explained to me that the organization helped a seamstress with designing skills to place her merchandise at first in the local market and eventually in foreign markets, in cooperation with an NGO from Italy. Now, the woman owns her own prosperous fashion shop, has an expensive house in a nice neighborhood, and her children go to private schools.

Certainly ADOPEM has not solved the fundamental problem of its clientele, which is entrenched poverty, but the organization gives women a sense of direction and financial support, as well as an opportunity for empowerment.

Equally important, by supporting revenue-generating programs for women, ADOPEM represents a break with the past in the history of Dominican women. Indeed, the functioning of the organization is a fundamental change in thought and action. By offering financial resources to poor women with no collateral, the organization directly challenges gendered power relations, as it frees many low-income women from male-dominated financial systems. In this sense, the Banco de la Mujeres links female urban dwellers to the global women's liberation movement. As an organization designing customized strategies and training programs to meet the needs of its members, the Banco also shows that in places where official policy and resources left women outside the mainstream of society, community-based organizations have assumed the role of leading female citizens to take charge of their lives through collective action and direct participation. Thus, grass-roots organizations in the Caribbean, such as ADOPEM, have been centripetal forces for communal development and the empowerment of women.

A visit to the Banco de la Mujeres offered this author the opportunity to visually grasp the impact of the organization on Dominican women. Familiar with the customary bank clientele, I was deeply impressed by the overwhelming presence of poor women in lines waiting to receive a loan, talking with female officers, or presenting some documentation for the bank to handle. During my visit I saw only four men: a security officer, a messenger, and two male visitors. The dynamics of the ADOPEM left a lasting impression on me. From a gender perspective, it shows that women's engagement in grass-roots activism is a way to defy social exclusion and to integrate women into national development.

NATIONAL DEVELOPMENT AND GRASS-ROOTS ORGANIZATIONS

In the Caribbean, as elsewhere in the world, women are underrepresented in high-level appointed and elected positions. Since the beginning of the nation-building process, Caribbean women leaders have worked to put an end to gender discrimination by forming organizations to empower women with equal rights. Measuring empowerment in terms of increased political participation, female Caribbean leaders pioneered the way for the women's movement that developed in the 1920s, 1930s, and 1940s, which helped women resist legal

marginalization. Women supported by women's coalitions have achieved political empowerment in municipalities and the legislature. In Puerto Rico, for
example, women obtained the right to vote in 1932, and since then many of
them have become mayors and congresswomen. In the mayoral race of the
town of Guayama, in 1952, women who were involved in the town's economic
and political development organized coalitions of women and supported the
candidacy of Obdulia Velázquez de Lorenzo, who won the election.[21]

Before the granting of universal suffrage in Jamaica in 1944, few women
became representatives in local and central governments. But after independence in 1962, in the British Caribbean in general, as they challenged their
governments to implement policies to recognize women's leadership, women
obtained positions as legislators in both houses and a few became cabinet
members. Similarly, in the French and Spanish Caribbean women have had
similar experiences, receiving appointments or entering electoral races after
they pressured the male-dominated system to stop political marginalization of
women.

Some have gone beyond having a voice in the legislature and have gained
executive power. Eugenia Charles, cofounder of the Dominica Freedom Party,
became the prime minister of Dominica in 1980 and the first female head of
the state in the English-speaking Caribbean. Similarly, Ertha Pascal-Trouillot, a
prominent lawyer and Haiti's first woman president, led a provisional government from March 1990 to February 1991. In Puerto Rico, the candidate of the
Partido Popular Democrático (Popular Democratic Party), Sila María Calderón,
won the governorship in 2000. In the Dominican Republic, Milagros Ortiz
Bosh, a well-known feminist and respected leader of the Partido Revoluciona-
rio Dominicano (Dominican Revolutionary Party), was elected vice president
in 2000 and was a candidate for the presidential election of 2004. Despite
these advancements, Caribbean women still await and struggle for a fair and
balanced recognition of their contribution to society.

CONCLUSION

In the global context of the twenty-first century, the struggle and the achievements of the Caribbean women's movement are stories in the making. Despite
myriad problems, Caribbean women have organized networks of political resistance, organized social protest, designed projects to achieve financial independence, and created associations to promote female solidarity. Now they are
an important, recognized part of history. The action, dedication, and sacrifices

of Caribbean women such as the Mirabal sisters and Soriano have acquired an iconic proportion. Promoting greater individual freedoms and justice, the cities of Atlanta and Salcedo, for example, created a sister city program connecting Martin Luther King's global vision of nonviolence to the Mirabals' struggle for political liberation.

Reflecting the effect of global linkages, grass-roots organizations have been instrumental in helping Caribbean women move from the periphery to the center of political action and to participate actively in economic advancement and in the formulation of policies that embrace women's issues. These undertakings, largely unrecognized, challenge the conventional assumption about the powerlessness of Caribbean women, confirm their strength, and demonstrate the struggle of women to have their voices heard and their actions validated.

Under the leadership of women in the Dominican Republic, for example, four grass-roots organizations—the Junta Patriótica de Damas, the 14th of June Movement, CONAMUCA, and ADOPEM—have shaped women's lives by carving out a gender space within the political spectrum and within the economy. These achievements also show the role played by Caribbean women's involvement in the global struggle for change and empowerment.

NOTES

Thanks to the University Personnel Development Committee (UPDC) from the University of Wisconsin–Stevens Point for providing financial support to research materials in the Dominican Republic. I would also like to express my appreciation to Gineida Castillo and William Lawlor for their assistance.
   1. See Couto, "Community Coalitions and Grassroots Policies of Empowerment."
   2. Smith McCrea, "The Voyage of the Sable Venus."
   3. Momsen, "Development and Gender Division of Labour," 232.
   4. Safa, The Myth of the Male Breadwinner, 37–38. See also Barrow, "Small Farm Food Production and Gender in Barbados," 181–187.
   5. Freeman, "Reinventing Higglering across Transnational Zones," 80.
   6. Momsen, "Development and Gender Division of Labour," 232.
   7. Peguero, "Mujeres dominicanas en la trinchera política," 308–9.
   8. For more information, see Alcántara, Mujeres dominicanas, 57–68.
   9. Schild, "Recasting 'Popular' Movements," 59–80.
  10. For Minerva's political activities, see Aquino García, Tres heroínas y un tirano, 107–16. See also Galván, Minerva Mirabal, 245–339.
  11. See Dedé's statement in El País, November 25, 2002, 11.

12. Cordero, *Mujeres de abril*, 21–50. Two scholars, Gineida Castillo and Magali Pineda, also provided information about the Federación de Mujeres Dominicanas.

13. Alcántara, *Mujeres dominicanas*, 109–19.

14. Pacini Hernández, *Bachata*, 10.

15. Some references on Soriano were compiled by Emilio Jácquez and were extracted from *Almanaque Escuela Radio Santa María* and from interviews conducted by the Department of Organization of Radio Santa María, Dominican Republic.

16. Ricourt, "From Mamá Tingó to Globalization," 10.

17. Cited in ibid., 9.

18. Deere, *In the Shadows of the Sun*, 106.

19. Most of the information on ADOPEM came from several annual reports, newsletters, and other printed materials obtained at the organization; from interviews with the director of ADOPEM, Dr. Mercedes Canalda, and with the executive director, Lic. Mercedes Canalda de Beras Goico, Santo Domingo, May 26, 2003; and from an interview with Dinorah Polanco de Sang, one of the founders of the organization, May 27, 2003.

20. *Women's World Banking's Newsletter*, May 2003.

21. Gallart, "Political Empowerment of Puerto Rican Women," 227–52.

9

Race and Politics in Cuba

ALINE HELG

Since the sugar boom and massive import of African slaves in the nineteenth century, people of African descent have represented between one-third and one-half of Cuba's population. Although far from being an overwhelming majority as in neighboring Jamaica and Haiti, throughout the past two centuries Cuba's blacks and mulattoes have struggled to be accepted as a full and equal component of their nation by the white elites. Obviously, since the 1860s no statesman or intellectual has advocated blacks' massive deportation to Africa. But the political elites have continuously sought to limit the rise of prominent Afro-Cuban leaders and to prevent the formation of Afro-Cuban autonomous political movements. Similarly, white elites have tried to discourage Afro-Cubans from joining diasporic organizations uniting peoples of African descent in the Americas. To this end, governments and political parties in power have resorted to a wide range of strategies, ranging from tokenism (the appointment of very few mulattoes or blacks to highly visible positions), selective integration into white-dominated organizations, and acceptance of limited elements of African-derived cultures into the mainstream, to the marginalization, repression, and physical elimination of Afro-Cuban dissenters. Central to these strategies has been the thesis, stated by pre- and post-1959 authorities alike, that the Cuban nation has achieved racial equality—to which the racism prevalent in the United States is generally opposed as the antithesis. In addition, in times of deep change, such as the decades after independence in 1902 and after the 1959 revolution, during which Afro-Cubans could have pushed for more than formal equality, the new authorities have curbed their autonomous action in the name of the national unity necessary to face the threat (often real) of a U.S. intervention and adopted paternalistic policies transforming them into passive recipients of state generosity. In the long term, these strategies have enabled Cuban authorities to place the blame for Afro-Cubans' continuing lower social position on themselves: if most of them are still poor despite legal equality and paternalism, it is allegedly due to their lesser capacities.

Still largely in effect today, Cuba's claim of racial equality persistently places Afro-Cubans in front of an insoluble dilemma. If they subscribe to the myth, they have to also conform to negative views of peoples of African descent and to comply with white superiority and absorption into white-dominated organizations. If they oppose the myth, they are accused of antiwhite racism and a lack of patriotism. In fact, the myth transforms any attempt by Cubans of African descent to assert their racial pride along with their nationalism into a threat to the unity of the nation, and any Afro-Cuban autonomous political challenge into a threat to impose a black dictatorship. Once identified, such threats justify all levels of government repression—including, in 1912, the racist massacre of between 2,000 and 6,000 Afro-Cubans—as a means to save Cuba. But government policies perceived as threatening the racial order can also be labeled as conducive to black dictatorship by white opponents. In the 1950s Fulgencio Batista's challengers did not hesitate to mix the red and the black scares to mobilize white Cubans against him. Whites from various political horizons did the same in 1960 to prevent Fidel Castro from directly tackling racism. Moreover, in a nation in which politics has been the principal arena of social negotiation and a major avenue of power and wealth, Afro-Cubans' continuing inability to effect an autonomous representation has repeatedly prevented them from obtaining change on their own terms.

Prosperity, the fear of a revolution along Haitian lines, and the presence of a large military garrison explain, among other reasons, why Cuba remained a slave economy and a Spanish colony until the late nineteenth century. Only in 1868, after the victory of the Union in the U.S. Civil War led to the abolition of slavery in the South, did a substantial number of Cubans rise up in arms against Spain. The first two anticolonial wars eventually did bring about the abolition of slavery in 1886, but not the island's independence or legal equality for Afro-Cubans, despite the fact that most of them had never been slaves or had gained freedom long before 1886. Thus, in 1895 blacks and mulattoes were among the first ones and the most numerous to join the Liberation Army to renew the fight against Spain. Indeed, although Afro-Cubans made up about 32 percent of a total population of a little more than 1 million according to official censuses, they represented between 50 and 75 percent of the combatants in the Liberation Army.

Black overrepresentation in the Liberation Army produced high expectations among Afro-Cuban soldiers and officers regarding their position in independent Cuba. At the same time, it created divisions within the leadership of Cuba Libre that contributed to the frustration of the revolution initiated in 1895. Two deaths were fatal in this process: that of the intellectual José Martí right at the beginning of the war and, eighteen months later, that of military general Antonio Maceo. Martí was one of the few white leaders with antiracist convictions as well as the architect of the balance between the mostly white Cuban exile community and the darker and poorer Cuban insurgents. Maceo, a mulatto veteran of all wars of independence, was the unquestionable leader of Afro-Cubans and lower-class Cubans, an autodidact and an extraordinary military strategist who by early 1896 had managed to carry the revolution from the east to the western end of Cuba. Rather than praising Maceo's victory, the white civilians in the Cuban Provisional Government maneuvered against him, alleging that he aimed at establishing a black dictatorship in Cuba. After Maceo's death in late 1896, white separatists in exile began to lobby in favor of a U.S. intervention in the war, which took place in 1898.

Although assisted by the Cuban Liberation Army, the United States claimed unilateral victory against Spain and occupied Cuba (as well as Puerto Rico and the Philippines) from 1898 to 1902. At a time when Jim Crow ruled the U.S. South, North American occupants viewed all Cubans, including those they named "so-called whites," as an inferior people whom they needed to prepare for "civilization" and self-government. No doubt the Cuba that the U.S. military found in 1898 was in a shambles and needed thorough programs of investment, public works, sanitation, and education. By promoting such programs (financed by Cuban moneys), the U.S. military facilitated Cuba's recovery. However, many U.S. policies openly discriminated against Afro-Cubans and penalized them. Moreover, the U.S. administration deliberately excluded Afro-Cubans in several areas at a crucial moment of Cuban history, just when the latter could have claimed positions in the government and the security forces on the basis of their leading role in the War for Independence. Still, these policies were effective because they drew on already existing patterns of racial discrimination and on overall Cuban white elite endorsement.

Predictably, in May 1902, the first independent government of Tomás Estrada Palma, a longtime U.S. resident and naturalized citizen, did not signify a rupture with the U.S. occupation. In addition, the Platt Amendment—which stipulated the right of the United States to intervene in Cuba in order to defend life, property, and liberty—limited Cuban sovereignty. Afro-Cubans were further marginalized by selective public employment and the subsidized immigration of over half a million Spaniards (mostly young men) between 1902 and 1925 aimed at whitening the island's population. Besides, a campaign to repress traditions of African origin was launched as a means of denigrating all Afro-Cubans. The mainstream press and white intellectuals, such as Fernando Ortiz, stereotyped African-derived religions as *brujería* (harmful witchcraft) and their followers as *brujos* (witches). At the same time, no antidiscrimination or welfare programs were promoted, on the grounds that the new constitution had established the equality of all Cubans. Nevertheless, in recognition of the decisive Afro-Cuban role in the wars for independence and before most other nations in the hemisphere with a substantial population of African descent, Cuba adopted universal male suffrage in 1902. With an electorate then divided between two parties, the Liberal and the Conservative, Afro-Cubans, who according to a U.S.-sponsored census counted for one-third of the voters, had a real chance at changing politics if they organized their own party.

The ruling elite attempted to prevent such an Afro-Cuban challenge with a rhetoric of liberalism and equality that concealed discriminatory policies. They gave visibility to a few Liberal and Conservative mulattoes, such as journalists Martín Morúa Delgado and Juan Gualberto Gómez, in order to channel the Afro-Cuban vote behind them. However, many Afro-Cubans began to show public discontent with the social status quo. Some war veterans organized in the short-lived Committee of the Veterans of Color (1902) to demand a fair share in public jobs; other Afro-Cubans joined the few racially inclusive labor unions; still others entered the dominant parties, especially the Liberal Party, to promote change. Many also strove to advance socially by learning to read and write. A handful of black intellectuals challenged the dominant racist ideology and denounced racism in their own newspapers. Most notable among them was Rafael Serra, a former tobacco worker who had spent the last war for independence mobilizing Cuban exiles in New York and returned to Cuba to found *El Nuevo Criollo* (1904–5).[1]

Other Afro-Cubans, mostly among the poor, continued to practice discreet forms of nonconformity with elite culture, notably the worshiping of African derived-religions such as *santería* and *palo monte* or belonging to the secret Abakuá Society. Having almost no political space in which to express their world vision, these men and women did so in their homes and neighborhoods and in some *sociedades de color* (Afro-Cuban recreational societies) and *cabildos de nación* (mutual aid associations originally sponsored by Spanish colonialism that perpetuated specific African heritages). To them, as to many people of African descent in other former slave societies in the Americas, attachment to a reconstructed African culture was not only a symbolic retreat against a racist society but also a dissident subculture that permitted collective self-affirmation.[2]

The revolution of August 1906, in which the Liberals protested fraud in the reelection of Conservative Estrada Palma, gave Afro-Cubans an opportunity to express their frustration publicly by participating en masse in the Liberal army. The Liberals, led by General José Miguel Gómez, promised that they would favor Afro-Cubans once in power. When the revolution prompted the second U.S. occupation of 1906–9, Afro-Cubans immediately lobbied for sociopolitical recognition, racial equality, and a share in government. From various parts of the island, they issued manifestos claiming that their massive participation in the independence struggle had proved their commitment to the republic, which, in return, owed them justice.

This mobilization culminated in the successful creation of the Independent Party of Color (PIC) in 1908, under the leadership of the war veterans Evaristo Estenoz and Pedro Ivonnet. By 1910, one year after the election of Liberal José Miguel Gómez as Cuba's second president, the party already counted between 10,000 and 20,000 members. It had achieved nationwide membership, linking the countryside to the cities and including day laborers, peasants, workers, artisans, and a few middle-class individuals mobilized by its message of black racial pride and its virulent condemnation of white racism. In addition, the party represented blacks as well as mulattoes and thus clearly demonstrated a racial consciousness of peoples of full or partial African ancestry.

Despite its name, the PIC was not separatist but sought the integration of Afro-Cubans in society and their participation in government. Its program addressed only a few issues directly related to race: it demanded an end to racial discrimination, equal access for Afro-Cubans to positions in public service and the diplomatic corps, and an end to the ban on "nonwhite" immigration. Most of the other demands aimed at improving the conditions of the popular classes regardless of race: compulsory free education from eight to fourteen years; free technical, secondary, and university education; state control of private schools; abolition of the death penalty; reform of the judicial and penitentiary systems; the eight-hour workday; priority for Cubans in employment; and the distribution of national lands to Cubans.

The content of the party's newspaper, *Previsión*, shows how difficult it was for the *independientes* to demand real racial equality in a hegemonic ideological context that denigrated peoples of African descent and concurrently promoted the myth of Cuban racial equality. For example, *Previsión* stigmatized African dance and drumming as "barbarisms of bygone days." It urged blacks to study

♦

and work hard and campaigned for the legal marriage of Afro-Cuban couples, without demanding new rights for women. Simultaneously, in line with the racial pride then expressed by some blacks in the United States, Haiti, and the British Caribbean, *Previsión* refuted white supremacy and claimed that all races were equal. It stressed the importance of Africa in human development. It wanted Afro-Cubans to be recognized as a full component of Cuban nationality. Afro-Cubans should be allowed to be proud to be both black and Cuban, they insisted.

Refuting the myth of Cuban racial equality, the PIC repeatedly resorted to the symbolism of slavery and colonialism to show continuities in postindependence whites' attitudes toward blacks. The party mobilized its constituency by publicizing cases of Afro-Cubans being turned down for jobs, denied service in restaurants and barbershops, and unfairly arrested or sentenced. Making a clear link to the U.S. South, it labeled these incidents as "moral lynchings" and argued that Cuban racism was particularly ugly because it was based on fear of blacks and was thus hidden. This characteristic implied permanent white control of blacks designed to prevent Afro-Cubans from thinking and acting on their own. At any sign of Afro-Cuban autonomous initiative, terrified whites and servile blacks brandished the specter of the Haitian Revolution. The party summoned Afro-Cubans to ignore them and to oppose racism—even, if necessary, with violence. Not surprisingly, the formation of a black party and its advocacy of violent opposition to racism were not approved by all Afro-Cubans. Several leaders, notably among Liberals and Conservatives, publicly opposed such strategies, which threatened their own patronage and which, they feared, would prompt white repression and increase racism.

Indeed, with its growing membership, the ensuing possibility of its electoral success, and its demand that Afro-Cubans have a proportional share in public jobs, the PIC had begun to represent a challenge to Cuba's white-dominated social structure. With public employment being one of the few avenues of social mobility in Cuba, the party's electoral gains would have considerably changed the makeup of the Cuban Congress, where blacks were represented well below their proportion in the electorate, creating new networks of patronage and increasing Afro-Cuban access to public employment, which in the long term would have affected socioracial hierarchies.

The white elite understood the *independientes'* threat and responded accordingly. In 1910 the leaders and dozens of followers of the PIC were arrested and prosecuted for allegedly conspiring to impose a black dictatorship in Cuba. The party was outlawed despite the fact that the trial against its members ended with a verdict of not guilty. To this end, the Cuban Congress defied the constitutional right to freedom of thought and association and passed an amendment conveniently proposed by Morúa, the only Afro-Cuban senator and a close ally of President Gómez. The Morúa amendment astutely banned the PIC on grounds that, by representing only blacks' interests, it discriminated against whites and violated the equality between Cubans guaranteed by the constitution.

When in 1912 leaders and supporters of the PIC organized an armed protest in the province of Oriente to obtain the relegalization of their party, the Cuban government misrepresented their protest as an Afro-Cuban "race war" that would transform Cuba into another Haiti. President Gómez sent the army and zealous white volunteers under the orders of the reputedly intransigent General José de Monteagudo to exterminate the protesters. The United States sent some Marines to protect U.S. sugar mills and anchored three battleships near Oriente as a "preventive policy." As the unprepared and poorly armed *independientes* chose to hide rather than to confront the massive forces sent against them, the Cuban army and the volunteer posses killed not only Estenoz and Ivonnet and hundreds of their followers but also scores of Afro-Cuban peasants—men, women, and children who were slaughtered simply because of their skin color.

That in 1912 the Cuban government chose to annihilate the challenge of the PIC by the racist massacre of between 2,000 and 6,000 Afro-Cubans reveals a fundamental ideological contradiction between liberal democratic principles positing the equality of all individuals and "scientific" racism. It shows that, in Cuba—as in other postslavery societies such as Jamaica during the 1865 Morant Bay Rebellion—equality and freedom were malleable concepts that whites in power could redefine at will through legal reform in order to repress any threats to the socioracial hierarchy. If apparently democratic legislation failed to silence black protest, racist massacre followed. Indeed, the slaughter of 1912 had a long-lasting impact on Afro-Cubans who afterward did not attempt to massively organize en masse independently from white-controlled parties.

Still, the killings of 1912 did not fully exorcize whites' fear of blacks. The black male *brujo* and the threat of Cuba's becoming another Haiti continued for years to haunt the imagination of many whites. Moreover, as before, in each instance of racial tension, Afro-Cubans were racialized, and their acceptance of white repression of blacks was tested. The *brujo* scare mobilized whites well into the 1930s. Alleged *brujos* continued to be arrested for practicing *santería*. Stories of blacks' kidnapping white children to use their blood and entrails in magic were still widely circulated. In 1919, in particular, a real *brujo* craze seized the island. The discovery, in late June, of the body of a little white girl presumably killed and eaten by black *brujos* in Matanzas prompted yet another upsurge of racism. In Matanzas, although the *brujos'* confession had probably been extorted under torture, mob violence erupted, and the police killed all the defendants. Shortly after, in Regla, a black Jamaican man was arrested in a store for giving candy to a white girl, allegedly planning to kidnap her for the purposes of *brujería*. A furious mob took the Jamaican from jail and tied him to the tail of a horse, dragging him through Regla's streets until the man died. Several Havana newspapers' headlines exultantly praised the people of Regla for their lynching ability. One of them went as far as to describe the lynching as a "step forward that we take toward civilization."[3]

Indeed, in 1919 the application to Cuba of the Judge Lynch law against black male *brujos* became the subject of a national debate, showing once again that the question of racial equality and Cuba's inferiority complex toward the United States had not been resolved. Several mainstream newspapers incited their readers to follow the example of U.S. southerners and to lynch *brujos*. Others, however, recommended the death penalty with no appeal but opposed lynching on the grounds that it was unfitting for modern civilization. Another argument against lynching was that, supposedly unlike U.S. southern blacks, blacks in Cuba were humble, easy to govern, and not inclined to rape white women, and thus should be dealt with by regular courts. As for anthropologist Fernando Ortiz, he opposed both lynching and the death penalty and held that both lynchers and *brujos* were "typical figures of African social life" who had no place in modern Cuba. As a congressman, he presented a bill "against antisocial superstitions" targeting traditional healing, *santería*, *brujería*, and cannibalism. A majority in the House, however, thought the current penal code applicable to crimes motivated by *brujería* and rejected his bill. Nevertheless, rumors of alleged *brujos'* attempting to kidnap white children continued to spread across the island for years, each time provoking a wave of arrests and antiblack violence that the press avidly reported.

The specter of a black revolution along Haitian lines was raised again at the few post-1912 attempts by Afro-Cubans to organize politically. In 1915, for example, renewed accusations of antiwhite racism were launched when some Afro-Cubans proposed to federate the *sociedades de color;* the press warned that black representatives from the Liberal and Conservative parties were about to form a group. Yet not only did Afro-Cuban congressmen never create a caucus, but the Morúa amendment banning parties along racial lines remained in force, and Afro-Cubans never formed another black party. As bitterly noted by the young Afro-Cuban journalist José Armando Plá, by the late 1910s black Cubans carried less political weight than in 1898, because fewer had been elected and because they now had no organization representing their own interests. He singled out two causes for this failure. First, Afro-Cubans had forgotten their "black identity" during the wars for independence, when they had to fuse their own future (slaves' freedom and racial equality) with the nation's future (independence). Second, since the advent of the republic, black politicians had been lured away from representing their people by mainstream political parties' pretense of making no racial distinctions.[4]

Afro-Cubans' inability to reorganize politically after 1912 resulted also from the widening gap between leaders and majority. Since independence, they had increasingly split along class and cultural lines. Although the census of 1919 shows that most Afro-Cubans remained employed in the same low-paid sectors of labor as in 1899 and 1907 (agriculture, unskilled work, domestic service, construction, and the tobacco industry), a few Afro-Cubans had succeeded in entering the upper middle class. By 1919, for example, there were 38 blacks among 1,578 lawyers, and 85 blacks among 1,771 medical doctors; for the first time, a few Afro-Cubans were registered as bankers and brokers. In the lower middle class as well, blacks were better represented as employees in retail trade, banking, transportation, and clerical work than in 1907—though still in marginal proportions. They had also made some gains in the public service, being 10 percent of the 11,004 government officials and employees (in fact, the same percentage as native white women) and 25 percent of the 16,638 policemen and enlisted soldiers, when their official proportion in the total population of 2,889,004 was 28 percent (a clear undercount). Constituting only one-half of the 89,656 women registered with a gainful occupation, Afro-Cuban women's share in female employment had continued to decline to the benefit of native whites, but their participation in the skilled jobs of teachers, nurses, and government employees was higher than in 1907. At the same time, in a society in which literacy had become more essential, differences between Afro-Cubans who could read and write (53 percent of those over ten years of age as compared with 62 percent among white Cubans) and those who were illiterate gained importance.[5]

As a result, in their endeavor to be accepted by white society, upper-middle-class Afro-Cubans often manifested their dissociation from the bulk of the *raza de color* (race of color). This attitude was especially common in the younger generation of professionals and intellectuals who had not experienced camaraderie with lower-class blacks in the Liberation Army and had not had expectations raised during the War for Independence only to be frustrated after 1898. These men founded in 1917 the elitist Club Atenas with the purpose of showing what differentiated them from most blacks: economic success, established patriarchal families, Western culture, and Cuban rather than black identity. One important effect of this lack of racial consciousness was the unwillingness of young black intellectuals to act collectively for the *raza de color*. They cared about the general advancement of Afro-Cubans only insofar as it could improve their own image and status in society. In fact, most of them subscribed to the myth of Cuban racial equality. Moreover, the new Afro-Cuban elite had internalized the concept of equality based on "merits" contained in the myth to such an extent that it viewed the difficulties of lower-class blacks as a direct consequence of their lack of education, morals, and hard work. With the inculcation of culture and bourgeois values in the Afro-Cuban popular classes, they thought, Cuba's "black problem" would be solved. Few of them recalled that in reality many current Afro-Cuban difficulties had been produced by continuing racism and discriminatory policies after abolition and independence.

Afro-Cuban middle-class conformity with the status quo also resulted from the election of General Gerardo Machado to the presidency of the republic in 1924. A populist Liberal, Machado embraced racial tokenism and appointed some members of this black middle class to government positions. He also courted Afro-Cuban *sociedades*, mostly the select Club Atenas, by giving them funding, which they greeted by supporting him and denying the existence of racial discrimination in Cuba.

The gap separating middle-class Afro-Cubans from those in the lower classes was also complicated by U.S. sugar companies' increasing reliance on Afro-Caribbean contract labor for the harvest after 1912: by 1930 an estimated 300,000 Haitians and British West Indians had migrated to Cuba, though most of them temporarily. These migrants brought with them languages, cultures, religions, levels of education, and experiences that often contrasted with those among Afro-Cubans. Symptomatic of these differences was the fate of the Jamaican Marcus Garvey's Universal Negro Improvement Association (UNIA) in Cuba. Although by the time of Garvey's 1921 visit to Havana, the UNIA counted fifty chapters on the island, these were mostly mutual aid societies for Jamaicans and Barbadians, as the UNIA's ideology of international black unity conflicted with many Afro-Cubans' attachment to both *cubanidad* (Cubanness) and blackness.[6]

In fact, after the 1912 slaughter, many lower-class Afro-Cubans realized that without a committed leadership able to unite them across class and region, it was individually and collectively safer to turn to active participation in white-led popular movements. In 1923 many joined the newly founded National Association of Veterans and Patriots, whose platform proposed the end of state corruption, an independent judiciary, women's suffrage, and priority to Cubans over foreigners in employment. Shortly after, some Afro-Cubans became members of the racially inclusive Communist Party of Cuba (PCC) and of the National Workers' Confederation of Cuba (CNOC) created in 1925. Both organizations were repeatedly repressed by the Rural Guard, obeying orders from President Machado. Yet, in the 1920s those who became the scapegoats for many Cuban problems were low-paid Afro-Caribbean sugar workers from U.S.-occupied Haiti and from Jamaica, who suffered much discrimination and violence. Antiblack racism persisted but had temporarily changed targets.

Nevertheless, racism against Afro-Cubans resurfaced rapidly. After Machado secured a second presidential term in 1928 by manipulating the traditional parties, opponents to his reelection founded new organizations against him. Among these, some key associations, such as the Directorate of University Students and the violent secret association ABC, were almost entirely formed by middle-class and elite white Cubans. These groups deliberately turned a blind eye to black workers' mobilization against the dictatorship and began to link Machado to the select Club Atenas, and by extension to all Afro-Cubans. Although ties of patronage did exist between this club and the increasingly unpopular President Machado, the use of racist accusations against Atenas by the ABC and others showed the white elite's continuing reluctance at seeing any Afro-Cuban political participation in the republic. Even more, some white supremacists created blatantly racist organizations, such as the Cuban Ku Klux Klan (a recognized chapter of the U.S. KKK) and the White National League.[7]

The 1930s to the 1950s witnessed growing political complexity, volatility, and violence, making any sweeping interpretation of this period impossible. The Great Depression dramatically increased the number of unemployed, not only in the sugar industry but also in tobacco production, public works, and state bureaucracy. Calls for the *cubanización* of the economy and attacks against Afro-Caribbean immigrants multiplied. In response, the PCC and the CNOC began to organize the key proletarian sector of the sugar industry. They advocated workers' cross-racial and cross-national unity and defended Afro-Caribbean immigrants. Simultaneously, in 1932 the PCC, following Josef Stalin's endorsement of national self-determination (only outside of the Soviet Union), initiated a campaign for the self-determination of the *franja negra* (black fringe) of Oriente, similar to the demand made by U.S. Communists for areas in the U.S. South populated by a majority of African Americans. The Cuban Communists argued that in southern Oriente, where whites were a minority, Afro-Cubans formed "a nation" and had the right to decide their future, including the creation of a separate state if they so desired. Although the party continued to advocate such self-determination until 1935, few Afro-Cubans from Oriente supported it as it clashed with their Cuban patriotism. Communist attempts at organizing sugar workers were more successful but very slow.[8]

As the second presidency of Machado turned violent and dictatorial, in the summer of 1933 disparate movements and strikes converged to prompt his downfall, which the United States could not prevent. The brief and complex revolution of 1933 that followed was simultaneously nationalistic, xenophobic, and racist, not only against Afro-Caribbean immigrants but against Afro-Cubans as well. On the one hand, in the turmoil of 1933 Cuban nationalism peaked, leading to the adoption of a law stipulating that 50 percent of the workers of any companies be Cuban, without reference to racial parity. Such law had been virulently denounced by the Communists as the means to divide workers. And, indeed, Afro-Cubans strongly supported the 50 percent law, which they considered a secure way to eliminate competition from Spanish and Afro-Caribbean immigrants.

Yet, as nationalist as it was, the revolution of 1933 also revived racism against Afro-Cubans, because many whites associated the dictatorship with Afro-Cubans, regardless of the fact that only a small portion of the latter had supported Machado. The ABC turned openly white supremacist; a new Ku Klux Klan Kubano was founded and, together with the already existing racist organizations, attacked blacks. The offices of the Club Atenas and of other middle-class *sociedades de color* in Havana and elsewhere were firebombed. The bureau of an anti-Machado and anti-ABC organization comprising mostly Afro-Cubans was also assaulted. In 1934, in a traditionally segregated public park in Trinidad, a white attacked an Afro-Cuban for entering the park's white section. A white riot followed in which several Afro-Cuban businesses were looted and one black man was lynched. In addition, throughout the island, Haitian and British West Indian workers were the targets of white violence. The government brutally deported thousands of Afro-Antillean workers, almost all of them Haitians due to the intervention of the British Foreign Office on behalf of Jamaicans and other British Caribbean colonials.[9]

Adding to the complexity of the 1933 revolution, at the same time as ABC and other groups endorsed racism, some white elite ideologues advocated national unity in the face of U.S. imperialism and the recognition of the Afro-Cuban contribution to the nation. White and black Cuban intellectuals, poets, and artists, influenced by the new interest in African art taking place in Paris and elsewhere, started to look for the African roots of *cubanidad*. None is more representative of this transformation than Fernando Ortiz, who abandoned his deterministic cultural racism of the 1900s to become a founder of the movement of *afrocubanismo* and the editor of the journal *Estudios Afrocubanos* (1937–46). While some white artists simply added African motives to their compositions, the black poet Nicolás Guillén protested racism, praised blackness, and longed for Cuba to become, culturally and racially, a mulatto nation. Afro-Cuban popular music born under slavery, such as the *rumba*, was stylized and purged of its most African and lower-class patterns to be commercialized and incorporated into mainstream culture. Nevertheless, this selective incorporation of reconstructed elements of black culture did not translate into a full embrace of Afro-Cubans as equals. Nor did it go unchallenged by several white Cubans who claimed, much like their peers in the Dominican Republic of anti-Haitian General Rafael Trujillo, that Cuban culture was only influenced by Europeans and Indians.[10]

After 1933 Sergeant Fulgencio Batista imposed himself as a strong man who installed and overthrew various presidents until he was himself elected on a populist platform in 1940. Afro-Cubans and the workers' movement began to organize against the ascending Right. In 1938 Cuba's *sociedades de color* joined in the National Federation of Black Societies in order to fight racism. That same year, the PCC was legalized, and in 1939 the pro-Communist CNOC reorganized itself into the Confederation of Workers of Cuba (CTC). In 1940 the redrafting of the Cuban constitution of 1901 allowed these Afro-Cuban and leftist organizations finally to open a debate on the issues of racial discrimination in the public sphere, employment, education, land ownership, certain labor unions, recreation and sports, and the practice of justice.

Interestingly, this new mobilization of Afro-Cuban mainstream politicians in favor of equality was a direct response to the violence and marginalization they personally experienced in the 1930s. It was also an attempt for them to regain their constituencies, who were being attracted by the Communists. Since its foundation in 1925, the PCC had been the champion of racial equality and had made antidiscrimination one its most vocal demands. Predictably, it had been able to rally a substantial black and mulatto membership. Unlike other parties, in the late 1930s the PCC showed its egalitarianism by sending three Afro-Cubans (out of six delegates) to the constituent convention. Because only five out of sixty-seven delegates to the convention were Afro-Cuban, it became obvious that other parties had few or no black or mulatto representatives. Moreover, these parties had no interest in tackling racism beyond a simple mention of race, together with sex, color, and class, among the categories under which the new constitution granted legal protection from discrimination. Due to black, labor, and Communist pressure, one article gave an active role to the Ministry of Labor in preventing racial discrimination in employment, but it did not follow the Communist proposition of proportional job allocation according to race. Furthermore, no legislation was passed afterward to guarantee the application of the egalitarian principles contained in the 1940 constitution.

Still, in 1940 the PCC contributed to Batista's election. At the same time, the party reached its highest pre-1959 electoral score, with 10 representatives elected to the 162-member lower house. Among them, several were Afro-Cubans, such as labor leaders Lázaro Peña and Jesús Menéndez and party intellectual Blas Roca. Surprising at first sight, the alliance between the Communists and Batista was understandable in the context of national fronts created then to fight fascism. In addition, Batista was of modest origin, often labeled a mulatto by elite opponents. His 1940 electoral platform was progressive, pro-labor, and included an agrarian reform and a literacy campaign. The Communists knew that they could gain representatives only through labor support and alliances with other political forces. By 1942 two Communists, among them Carlos Rafael Rodríguez (one of post-1959 Cuba's leading economists), had entered Batista's cabinet. Yet, with the rise of Cold War policies ordered from Washington, the opposition to Batista began to mix astutely the red and the black scares, and Batista opted to distance himself from his allies in the PCC (now renamed Socialist Popular Party) and, ultimately, to persecute them.

Despite the promises of the new constitution, the condition of Afro-Cubans did not improve in the 1940s and the 1950s. In contrast to the *machadato* (Machado's 1925–33 rule) and Batista's early government, the presidencies of Ramón Grau San Martín (1944–48) and Carlos Prío Socarrás (1948–52), both leaders of the Auténtico Party, appointed very few blacks or mulattoes to senior government positions. Progressively purged from its Communist leadership, the CTC gradually came under Auténtico control. This transition was often violent: for example, in 1948 Menéndez, who headed the sugar workers, was murdered. Just as the repressed Communists moved closer to the Federation of Black Societies to pursue their antiracist struggle, the federation too began to embrace a Cold War rhetoric; it expelled its Communist associates and became dependent on Auténtico patronage.

More generally, racial discrimination against Afro-Cubans in the public sphere continued unrestrained. Some incidents gave Cuba's exclusion of blacks an international dimension, in particular when in Havana the Hotel Nacional denied entrance to the African American artist Josephine Baker and the cabaret Tropicana did the same to African American tourists. In fact, after the 1933 "sergeants' revolt" led by Batista, one of the few existing avenues of social advancement for Afro-Cubans was the security forces. Unlike in other sectors, in the army, the rural guard, and the police Afro-Cubans were now represented proportionally to their demographic weight. Even at the rank of officer, although still underrepresented, they became more numerous and visible.

This very sectarian advance did not deter some Afro-Cuban intellectuals, disillusioned with cross-racial activism, from turning to black self-help. Prominent among them was the lawyer Juan René Betancourt, who advocated black cooperativism and businesses to overcome economic marginalization. For that purpose, he created the National Organization of Economic Rehabilitation. However, Betancourt's organization had limited success because only a tiny minority of Afro-Cubans owned independent businesses; the majority belonged to the working class or was unemployed.

In 1952 Batista staged a military coup that encountered only short-lived resistance. His dictatorship either tamed into obedience or repressed into silence the sectors that previously had been the most active in pushing for antidiscrimination. The CTC now under Auténtico leadership closely backed Batista. The National Federation of Black Societies oscillated between failed attempts to pressure the dictator into promulgating effective antidiscrimination laws and dependency on his subsidies. Given their earlier support to Batista, the Communists were unable to build a viable alliance against him. More tragically, Batista's dubious whiteness, the token support of his regime to a few well-known Afro-Cubans (the elderly veteran Generoso Campos Marquetti or the lawyer Miguel Angel Céspedes), and the fair representation of blacks and mulattoes in the armed forces revived the false accusations of an alliance between dictatorship and Afro-Cubans forged by the white middle-class opposition during the *machadato*.[11]

The alleged support of blacks for Batista's rule was strengthened by the fact that visible opposition to the dictatorship came first from the Partido Ortodoxo (founded in 1947 by former Auténticos to protest their leaders' corruption) and university students, two middle-class groups in which, for socioeconomic reasons, Afro-Cubans were a minority. Furthermore, the early followers of Fidel Castro and his July 26 Movement appeared to be mostly young, white, and middle-class. Without entering into the details of their ascension to power beginning in 1953, what contributed to the view that the anti-Batista movement was white and middle-class was not so much that it included no Afro-Cubans and workers, but the fact that no organization traditionally representing these two groups joined it. Most notably, the PCC openly rallied the anti-Batista struggle only in mid-1958. Also influential in this view is the fact that until 1959 the rebels showed no interest in redressing racial injustices: neither Castro's famous self-defense speech after the failed attack on the Moncada barracks in 1953 nor any major program platform in the following years mentioned the issue of racism in Cuba.

Immediately after the insurgents' victory in January 1959, Betancourt brought the racial question to the forefront, with two articles urging the revolutionary government to tackle the socioeconomic roots of racial inequality. He criticized past policies of tokenism but noted the absence of Afro-Cubans in the new civil leadership. Moreover, Betancourt reiterated the belief that Afro-Cubans needed to form a unified movement to promote change on their own terms. In March 1959 Fidel Castro addressed the issue by listing "racial discrimination at work centers" as one of the battles the government would fight—together with unemployment, poverty, and the high cost of living. He proposed to end racial discrimination by campaigning against public demonstrations of racism, by improving public education, and by building racially inclusive recreational centers. Whereas Castro's speech gave hope to many Afro-Cubans, it also prompted protest among white sectors, including some of the revolutionaries, outraged by the perspective of racial integration in entertainment, which they stereotyped as the forced dancing of white women with black men. Three days later, anxious not to divide Cubans' broad support to his movement, Castro publicly renounced any intention to fight racism in the private sphere and warned Afro-Cubans to be patient and avoid any disrespect of whites. Although condemning racism, he stressed that the solution was not antidiscrimination laws (then still advocated by the PCC) but color-blind hiring policies and gradual integration into racially inclusive schools.

Yet the revolutionary government took measures to eliminate the most obvious forms of racial segregation in public spaces. First, in May 1959, the beaches became open to all, but the private clubs to which they were attached remained free to exclude blacks and the poor from their facilities. Second, the public parks were desegregated, generally through redesign. Then, one year later, the government took the major step of nationalizing all private clubs—including the most select black societies, such as the Club Atenas. Regarding racial discrimination in hiring policies, in early 1960 the authorities decided that all new employees would be hired by the Ministry of Labor. This allowed the government to hire Afro-Cubans in significant numbers discretely, without having to promulgate antiracist legislation, which would antagonize all-white unions, such as those of railway and electricity workers. Similarly, the government tackled discrimination in housing by lowering rents and relocating the residents of predominantly black slums to new projects. The same goal was pursued in education by nationalizing all private schools—a bastion of white privilege—in July 1961 and by launching a nationwide literacy campaign that benefited Afro-Cubans disproportionately.

Undoubtedly, the fact that by the end of 1962, some 200,000 disaffected Cubans, most of them upper- and middle-class whites, had chosen exile in the United States of America speeded up racial integration as men and women abandoned jobs and homes. Yet Castro's government also had decided to avoid a national debate on racism and to direct the process of integration paternalistically by enacting social policies destined to benefit Afro-Cubans. The revolution was to be the generous benefactor, and Afro-Cubans, its grateful beneficiaries. In addition, the leadership focused on mass organizations, either already existing ones, such as the Federation of University Students and the CTC, or newly created ones, such as the Committees of Defense of the Revolution, the Federation of Cuban Women, and the National Association of Small Agriculturalists, to promote racial integration indirectly while bringing all Cubans under revolutionary control. Whereas the Federation of Cuban Women responded to the special needs of women, no mass organization was founded to target racism. Nevertheless, as early as February 1962 the authorities officially claimed that racial and sexual discrimination had been eradicated in Cuba.[12]

Of course, this was not the opinion of some Afro-Cubans who had expected that the government would focus not only on desegregation in the public sphere but on the deep cultural roots of racism. Betancourt left Cuba after the dissolution of the Federation of Black Societies, which he had hoped to head and transform into an autonomous organization for Afro-Cuban advancement. In a provocative book influenced by the movements of Négritude and anticolonialism, black intellectual Walterio Carbonell urged the Cuban Revolution to distance itself from the Western tradition and to acknowledge that its true starting point was the slave rebels and the maroons. As a result, Cuban revolutionary culture should be recentered around Africa and its descendants, Carbonell demanded. In response, his book was seized, and he spent about a year incarcerated without trial. From abroad, another black Cuban, Carlos Moore, argued that the Cuban Revolution was controlled by the white national bourgeoisie. Although he acknowledged that since 1959 overt racial discrimination had disappeared, he claimed that fewer Afro-Cubans participated in government now than before and that nothing was done to recognize Afro-Cuban contribution to Cuba's demography and history.[13]

These criticisms aside, the early cultural policies of the revolution sought to emphasize some specific African components of *cubanidad*. Often under the initiative of Afro-Cuban writers and artists, the National Theater of Cuba and the National Folkloric Ensemble organized shows of African-derived rituals and musics. Yet, simultaneously, the authorities stigmatized *santería*, *palo monte*, and, more aggressively, the secret Abakuá societies as primitive and superstitious expressions that did not belong to socialism.[14] In the mid-1960s, *santería* initiation rites were forbidden; reauthorized in 1971, they were submitted to many restrictions, notably the prohibition of minors' presence. As a result, well-entrenched stereotypes denigrating Afro-Cuban religions as witchcraft gained a new force, and the practice of these religions went underground.

In the 1960s, in fact, as the government claimed to have eradicated racism in Cuba, it made of this alleged victory a tool in its growing conflict with the United States of America. To be true, since the beginning of the Cold War, the exclusion of most African Americans from suffrage and the violent segregation exercised against them in the U.S. South annihilated any U.S. pretense to being a genuine democracy. Cuban revolutionaries were quick to use their successful integrationist policies to court African Americans. Already during a visit to the United Nations in October 1960, Fidel Castro moved the Cuban delegation to a hotel in Harlem to protest mistreatment in white Manhattan and to show his empathy with African Americans. Although not supportive of the accommodationism pursued by Martin Luther King (despite its similarities with Castro's approach), Cuban media kept their audiences well informed of all the advances and setbacks of the civil right movement. Radical African Americans advocating armed revolution found more enthusiastic support. Facing mounting repression in the United States of America, several, such as Robert F. Williams and Black Panther Eldridge Cleaver, escaped to Cuba, where at first they received a warm welcome. Quite likely, the Castro government decided to support the cause of African Americans also as a means of convincing Afro-Cubans that racism had disappeared from their own nation. Yet, once in Cuba, African Americans' beliefs in black pride and autonomy rapidly clashed with the paternalistic and integrationist views of the Cuban authorities. The government began to fear their possible proselytism among the Afro-Cuban youth at a time when Black Power was also gaining ground in Jamaica and other Caribbean islands. By the late 1960s several radical African Americans had left Cuba disenchanted.[15]

In the 1960s the Cuban government also became involved in African wars of decolonization. Although until the fall of 1965, Cuban military actions in Algeria and Zaire remained secret, from 1966 to 1976 Cuba's military commitment in Congo, Guinea-Bissau, and Angola began to be reported by the Cuban media. After the Cuban forces' victories in Angola against the South

Africans fighting on the side of UNITA (an Angolan anticolonial guerrilla movement turned anticommunist and covertly supported by Washington), the government redefined its African involvement as a struggle against apartheid and
indirectly against the racist United States of America. In doing so, it pursued
two goals. First, in the international realm the government aimed at gaining
support among the newly independent Third World nations now represented
at the United Nations as a safeguard against the continuing U.S. threat. Second, inside Cuba it projected the image of a nation freed of its remnants of
racism and ready to liberate the oppressed blacks of colonial Africa. Only after
1975, notably when it supported Ethiopia against Somalia in 1978, did Cuba
appear to abandon its anticolonial and antiapartheid struggle to align its African policy closely to that of the Soviet Union.[16]

Nevertheless, if the revolutionary authorities managed to avoid a national
debate on racism during the first two decades following 1959, one event seriously tarnished Cuba's image of a racial paradise: the Mariel boatlift in summer 1980, which began on the day 10,800 Cubans rushed to the unguarded
grounds of the Peruvian embassy to seek refuge and exile. In a surprising
response, the government declared anyone who wished to leave the island free
to go. A total of 125,000 men and women chose to go to Florida on small boats
provided by the Cuban exile community, despite officially promoted aggressive
demonstrations against them. For the first time since 1959, this wave of exiles
reflected the demography of the island and included substantial proportions
of Afro-Cubans and poor Cubans in general. The government added some
petty criminals to the exiles and claimed that those leaving were the scum of
the population. Such was also the perception of the white middle- and upper-
class Cuban exiles settled in Florida, who received this multicolored wave with
resentment. Although the Cuban authorities used the latter to boost images
of Miami exiles as racist capitalists, they could not hide anymore the fact that
many blacks and workers were discontented with the revolution.

Still, inside Cuba the issue of racial discrimination did not resurface in the
public debate until 1986, when both Castro and the PCC acknowledged that,
in reality, racism and sexism had not disappeared from Cuban society and
that more blacks, mulattoes, and women were needed in higher positions.
Indeed, in the Central Committee of the party (one of the country's top institutions, even if its real power is marginal) as well as in managerial positions,
Afro-Cubans were well below their official proportion of 34 percent of Cuba's
population.[17] Simultaneously, the leadership acknowledged that social policies
indirectly aimed at promoting the poor, women, and people of African descent
had reduced broad inequalities in education, employment, health, and hous-

ing, but had not eliminated the culture and behavior conducive to both white racism and black marginalization. White Cubans continued to have a dispro-portionately high share in the top institutions of the nation and the most pres-tigious and powerful positions, whereas Afro-Cubans were still overrepresent-ed in lower-status jobs, deteriorated housing, poverty-caused diseases, and the prison population. Even more troubling, according to studies by Cuban and foreign social scientists, pre-1959 negative stereotypes of Afro-Cubans held strong in the media, as the national television, for example, limited the roles played by black actors to slaves, *santería* practitioners, or the poor. Stereotypes also influenced state security, as those targeted by the penal code's provision of "social dangerousness," a provision allowing for the internment of individuals who have not committed a crime but display behaviors defined as precriminal, were predominantly black and mulatto.[18]

Whatever equalizing solutions the leadership envisioned at that time is un-known, because the political and economic realities of the Special Period fol-lowing the collapse of the Soviet Union in 1991 signified a watershed in Cuba's social policies. With Soviet subsidies vanishing and Cuba's isolation increas-ing, the gross domestic product fell by 40 percent between 1989 and 1993. Real salaries plummeted; food, medicine, and transportation became scarce. Socioeconomic differences increased dramatically. As much as Afro-Cubans, for being largely lower-class, had benefited from the social policies of the early revolution, so much were they adversely affected by the abrupt reduction of these policies in the 1990s.

In addition, since 1993 the government has introduced market-oriented measures aimed at stimulating the economy that further widen the socioracial divide. Most effective in re-creating inequalities has been the legalization of the dollar, without which increasingly fewer goods and services can be pur-chased. Yet the three principal ways of legally acquiring dollars further mar-ginalize Afro-Cubans and privilege white Cubans. First, family remittances from exiles, who are overwhelmingly white, go to their white relatives in Cuba, boosting their purchasing power. Second, the Cuban dollar economy—mostly the tourist industry, some joint ventures, and foreign businesses operating in Cuba—tends to hire disproportionately more white Cubans than Afro-Cubans. Third, the newly authorized self-employed businesses, ranging from bed-and-breakfasts to twelve-chair restaurants (*paladares*), souvenir production for the tourist industry, repair shops, and beauty parlors, also privilege whites over Afro-Cubans, because such businesses cannot be successful without a stable outside access to dollars—generally coming from exiles' remittances.

Of course, as salaries and pensions in the Cuban *peso* (national currency) economy are insufficient for survival, people with no legal access to dollars tend to turn to the informal sector and to illegal or immoral strategies, such as the black market, *jineterismo* (female or male prostitution available to tourists), or simply stealing state property. Although the few existing studies on the subject show that white Cuban men and women also resort to these strategies, because of enduring racial stereotypes illegal activities are perceived as being conducted mostly by Afro-Cubans.[19]

Besides, in these times of state neglect and uncertainty about the future, increasing numbers of Cubans, regardless of race, gender, and class, have turned to the practice of *santería* and other African-derived religions to give meaning to their lives. Although in blatant contradiction with Marxism-Leninism, these beliefs are now tolerated by the government.

The acceleration of racial inequalities under the Special Period have left today's attentive Afro-Cubans, like their ancestors after 1902, in front of an insoluble dilemma. If they denounce the resurgence of racism, they face possible repression. If they remain silent, they sanction the widening of the racial divide. Thus, several Afro-Cuban writers, artists, directors, and performers have begun prudently to express concerns about Cuba's growing racial inequality and renewed racism. None has taken the risk of actually organizing or proposing solutions. But among Afro-Cuban historians, social scientists, and film makers, several have decided to break the official silence over the program of the PIC and the ensuing massacre of thousands of Afro-Cubans by the army in 1912.[20] Anthropologists have focused on the study of continuing racial stereotyping among Cubans. And among the generation of Afro-Cubans born in the 1970s and early 1980s, who have spent much of their lives in particularly difficult economic conditions, some, such as the groups Orishas (*santería* deities), Obsesión, Anónimo Consejo (anonymous advice), and Amenaza (threat), have used rap and hip hop to protest discrimination and to advocate a new black pride.

As Afro-Cubans enter the twenty-first century with the socioeconomic benefits of the socialist revolution in shambles, they will need more than these daring but unorganized voices to prevent the socioracial gap from increasing. In the 100 years that followed independence in 1902, legal equality, pre-1959 tokenism, and post-1959 paternalism have not eradicated racism and old stereotypes, which have repeatedly resurfaced in times of crisis. Moreover, Afro-Cubans only attempt to organize autonomously—the PIC—ended in a massacre. Since the PCC has gained political hegemony and absolute power in 1961, it has ceased to fight for racial equality, as it did from 1925 to 1959. At the same time, if the first thirty years of the revolution did bring Afro-Cubans more equal access in crucial areas such as education and employment, the current resurgence of socioracial marginalization shows the vulnerability of these state-engineered transformations. For sure, recently globalization has allowed African-derived cultures and a few Afro-Cuban individuals to gain international recognition, but these are small symbolic victories against a backdrop of growing socioeconomic precariousness, which challenges Cuba's alleged racial harmony. Although no Afro-Cuban is suggesting the formation of an autonomous organization, the fact that now, after decades of silence, the PIC is being publicly debated demonstrate that, as in other Caribbean islands with a substantial population of African origin, political representation is not an obsolete issue.

NOTES

1. On racial policies and Afro-Cuban mobilization until the early 1920s, see Helg, *Our Rightful Share*. See also Fernández Robaina, *El negro en Cuba, 1902–1958*.
2. Murphy, *Santería: African Spirits in America*.
3. *El Día* (Havana), June 29, 1919. See also, for example, the popular *El Mundo* (Havana) during 1919.
4. See José Armando Plá's articles in the Afro-Cuban newspaper *La Antocha* (Havana) published between August and September 1918.
5. Cuba, Bureau of the Census, *Census of the Republic of Cuba, 1919*.
6. McLeod, "Garveyism in Cuba, 1920–1940," 132–68.
7. On developments in the 1920s and 1930s, see Fuente, *A Nation for All*, 91–95.
8. Serviat, *El problema negro en Cuba*, 116–22; Carr, "Identity, Class, and Nation," 83–116.
9. McLeod, "Undesirable Aliens," 599–623.
10. Moore, *Nationalizing Blackness*.
11. On the years 1935 to 1959, see Fuente, *A Nation for All*, 210–55; Castillo Bueno and Rubiera Castillo, *Reyita*.
12. This is also the thesis of the first book on the topic published in Cuba since 1959, Serviat, *El problema negro en Cuba*.
13. Carbonell, *Crítica*; More [Moore], "Le peuple noir a-t-il sa place dans la révolution cubaine?," 177–230.
14. For a fascinating insight into the revolution's struggle to eradicate Abakuá "behavior," see the posthumous film *De cierta manera* (1974) by Afro-Cuban director Sara Gómez.
15. For example, Clytus, *Black Man in Red Cuba*.
16. Gleijeses, *Conflicting Missions*.

17. The census of 1981 was the first one since 1953 to ask Cubans to give their race: 66 percent declared to be white; 22 percent, mestizo (mixed African ancestry); and 12 percent, black. However, many Cuban and non-Cuban observers estimate that Afro-Cubans make up 50 or 62 percent of the population. See "The Black Americas, 1492–1992," NACLA Report on the Americas 25.4 (February 1992): 19.

18. For a summary of these studies, see Fernandez, "The Color of Love," 110–12; Evenson, Law and Society in Contemporary Cuba, 156–58.

19. Fuente, A Nation for All, 317–21; Fusco, "Hustling for Dollars: Jineterismo in Cuba."

20. See Gloria Rolando's film, Raices de mi corazón (Cuba, 2000), and Castro Fernández, La masacre de los independientes de color en 1912.

PART FOUR
Global Markets for Local Products

It is probably no exaggeration to assert that since 1492 the Caribbean has always provided products for a global market. Despite the early complaint of Christopher Columbus that the Caribbean was a region "poor in everything," his sailors quickly took a liking to tobacco, and the admiral concluded his first report, written off the Azores in March 1493, in an extremely wistful way:

> In conclusion, to speak only of the results of this very hasty voyage, their Highnesses can see that I will give them as much gold as they require, if they will render me some very slight assistance; also I will give them all the spices and cotton they want, and as for mastic, which has so far only been found in Greece and the island of Chios and which the Genoese authorities have sold at their own price, I will bring back as large a cargo as their highnesses may command. I will also bring them back as much aloes as they ask and as many slaves, who will be taken from the idolaters. I believe also that I have found rhubarb and cinnamon and there will be countless other things in addition, which the people I have left there will discover. [Columbus, *Four Voyages*, 122–23.]

While cotton featured for a short while in Caribbean trade, the region would later make its name producing prodigious quantities of tobacco, coffee, and that product long familiar to the Iberian Europeans, sugar, from the imported sugarcane plant. By the middle of the twentieth century agricultural products were no longer major contributors to the gross domestic product of the region. Nevertheless, the region remains closely intertwined in various dimensions of global commercial interchange—and not merely as a recipient of foreign commodities, technologies, and services.

Jorge Giovannetti examines the historical, political, and identity discourses of Jamaican reggae during its formative years in the 1960s and 1970s and identifies the central elements behind its local, regional, and global appeal. He also questions whether the music is more successful than the messages of Jamaican history that constitute an indelible component of reggae. Nevertheless, reggae music has definitely been one of the most successful local products that have entered the global marketplace in modern times, overshadowing important trademarks such as Appleton Estate rums, Tia Maria coffee liqueur, Pick-a-peppa sauce, Red Stripe beer, and Ting beverage. Indeed, Jamaican reggae music has been widely appropriated within as well as outside the region, finding highly sympathetic audiences across Europe, Asia, and the wider Americas.

Rum has played an extraordinarily important role in the history of the Americas, and most recently it has entered the global marketing mix of transnational beverages. Anthony Maingot examines the history of this premier Caribbean product and discusses the unpredictable and surprising ways the rum market has been affected by events and circumstances not only within but also from outside the region. Unlike wine production that is significantly affected by geography, soil type, climate, and manufacturing technique, rum requires a simple distillation process, and the quality derives from blending skills and aging in white oak casks. Rum, therefore, can easily be—and indeed is presently—produced in many countries that cannot grow quantities of sugarcane. That is a challenge both for the industry as a whole as well as the regional Caribbean producers. While rum will probably continue to be produced in the Caribbean, the interesting question will remain whether such a product will be distinctively Caribbean—or if that specificity matters at all. In other words, does Caribbean rum even have to be produced in the Caribbean? Anthony Maingot masterfully navigates the surprising developments in the modern marketing of Caribbean rums and insightfully discusses the unpredictable future as the beverage goes global.

10

My music will go on forever.
Maybe it's fool say that, but
when me know facts me can say
facts. My music go on forever.
—BOB MARLEY, June 1975

Jamaican Reggae and the Articulation of Social and Historical Consciousness in Musical Discourse

JORGE L. GIOVANNETTI

INTRODUCTION

It was reported that in Tiananmen Square in 1989 protesters carried a banner that read "Get up, stand up for your rights," using the Wailers' song to air their discontent.[1] Far from there, in 1990, South Africa's reggae singer Lucky Dube appealed for the unity of Rastas, Europeans, Indians, and Japanese in his song "Together as One" (1988), during a concert in Johannesburg. Across the Atlantic, in northeast Brazil, the city of Salvador da Bahia has had its own Praça do Reggae since 1998 where reggae fans congregate every week. More recently, in the Caribbean island of Dominica, at a meeting of the United Workers Party in the summer of 2003 a speaker reacted critically to the prime minister's budget speech telling his audience that the one "who feels it, knows it," thus echoing the Wailers' song of that title. Given the indefinite nature of the term "forever" and the world events I have encapsulated here, one wonders if "wherever" would have been a more accurate forecast in the quotation that opens this essay. It is evident then, not only that reggae music is a phenomenon of worldwide appeal and an active item of global popular culture, but that the lyrics of the music are an important source for social consciousness in the wider Caribbean and the world.

Reggae certainly has very profound local roots in Jamaica, but it is a music with an unprecedented global appeal and no longer, as it has been argued, "a music which could only be created by a Jamaican in Jamaica for Jamaicans."[2] The impact of this music in popular tastes and cultural practices is unquestionable, either as a commodity marketed through the mass media or as a medium for the diffusion of the ideology and ethos of the Rasta movement. Reggae music has avid listeners in disparate places across world regions, and one could argue that most residents of major world cities surely come across some reggae-related symbol daily—and not necessarily because they go into a record shop. Through this music, millions of people around the world have come to know something about Jamaican history and society and have adopted the common wisdom that reggae music has "conscious lyrics." Yet, one could still ask, How does reggae music represent Jamaican history and society? What are these lyrics conscious of? And how aware are global listeners of their meaning and sociohistorical significance?

The noted literary and cultural critic Edward Said has written, "[T]he study of music can be more, and not less, interesting if we situate music as taking place, so to speak, in a social and cultural setting."[3] Thus, it is the purpose of this article to analyze reggae music in its original Jamaican context looking into the specific ways in which the music relates to the social and cultural history of the country where it emerged. I approach Jamaican popular music in its association with history (and historiography) in a dual perspective. First, reggae is seen as a historical narrative of the events that were taking place as the genre was emerging in the 1960s and 1970s. The lyrics of the music became, as it were, a testimony of the events and transitions of its own time and place. Second, I analyze reggae music as counterhistory, as a way of telling (and rescuing) a story of the Jamaican people "from below" in the specific sociohistorical context of colonialism and racism, concentrating on the slavery and postemancipation eras. It is my argument that we can consider reggae as a popular representation of the past, one that assumes a counternarrative to colonial and Western historical accounts and, in the process, rethinks the country's history as part of its national formation. The essay looks into some of reggae's central elements and foundational characteristics during its early days and development in the 1970s and 1980s, seeking to illuminate our understanding of the reasons for the global fascination with, and appeal of, this music and its culture. In other words, aside from the evident influences of the media, the market, and the music industry, I attempt to seek an explanation to reggae's worldwide popularity in its origins.

THE LIFE AND TIMES OF REGGAE MUSIC

Music and dance have been central to Afro-Jamaicans since the days of slavery, and reggae music—as all popular Jamaican or Caribbean music—is indeed heir to the way in which slaves used music to "escape" their sufferings and to enjoy their time out of the labor regime of the plantations. But reggae's more specific roots are to be found in Afro-Jamaican religious musical traditions and in the Afro–North American musical styles and genres that were adapted from the United States of America during the early decades of the twentieth century. Rhythm and blues and jazz were important for the development of Jamaican popular music, along with Afro–Latin American musical forms such as *rumba*, and the impact of indigenous musical styles like *mento, kumina*, revival, and *nyabinghi. Mento* is Jamaican folk music, similar to calypso, where string in-struments such as the guitar and the banjo play an important role. *Kumina,* revival, and *nyabinghi*, on the other hand, are all Afro-Jamaican and related to the religious movements or manifestations carrying the same name, all of them characterized by the use of drums. The *nyabinghi* in particular is related to Rastafarian meetings or "grounations." This combination of diverse influ-ences responded partly to the high mobility of Jamaican laborers who were exposed to other cultures in the U.S. South and Hispanic America (particularly Panama and Cuba, where the 1920s and 1930s were peak years for the devel-opment of Afro-Cuban music). While scholars have debated the degree of in-fluence of each of these different musical traditions, most have acknowledged the presence of each of these ingredients, which are evident to anyone who has listened carefully to early recordings of Jamaican popular music. Indeed, dif-ferent groups mixed all these influences in their musical productions; jazzlike winds are easily identifiable in the 1960s and coexist with the Afro-Caribbean drumming of songs such as the Folkes Brothers' "Oh Carolina" (1961) and Toots and the Maytals' "Bam, Bam" (1966).

The sound systems were another important feature in the development of Jamaican popular music. The electronic ensemble of a record player and one or two speakers emerged around the 1940s and 1950s as mobile infrastruc-tures used to play the music in public to people without ready access to other means of listening to the latest musical recordings. As the sound systems phe-nomenon grew, the dancehall culture of Jamaica expanded geographically as the owners of the sound systems performed in Kingston and the rural areas, and people organized and gathered for dancing venues. These venues became the local setting for the "clash" or competition between different sound sys-tems and also one of the most important ways for people to hear new music. While rhythm and blues and jazz were commonly played by the sound sys-tems, calypso and *mento* also found their space in the dancehalls.[4]

The sociohistorical setting for the mixture and cross-fertilization of these mu-sical ingredients was a changing and complex one. After the world economic depression in the 1930s, Jamaica experienced important economic and political transitions. The labor struggles of those years shook the colonial system and cleared the path toward national independence, which was obtained much later, in 1962. Also, the island's population underwent significant mobility in many directions; while migrants were returning from the English-speaking enclaves in Hispanic America, others arrived from their military service in the British West Indies Regiment, and yet others were leaving the country for Britain in search of new opportunities. Also, much of the population was moving from the countryside to the flourishing capital, Kingston. In the early 1940s, the population of the capital increased 80 percent, and by 1960 the city had 25 percent of the total population of the island.[5] Most of the rural migrants that searched for a better life as urban workers in the capital ended up on the margins of society, living in the ghettos of Kingston and becoming part of a growing urban proletariat, much of it underemployed or unemployed.

The ghettos had also become the refuge of many Rastas. Rastafari had originated in the 1930s and grew as a religious and social movement during the 1940s and 1950s under the leadership of messianic preachers such as Leonard Howell, Joseph Hibbert, Archival Dunkley, and Robert Hinds. This movement was nourished by the racial Pan-African ideas of earlier Jamaicans and adopted Jamaicans such as Robert Love, Alexander Bedward, and Marcus Garvey, as well as religious traditions such as Pentecostalism and Kumina. Its central beliefs became the divinity of the Ethiopian emperor Haile Selassie I (crowned in 1930), the perception of Jamaica as Babylon (a place of captivity and perdition), and the idealization of Africa as Zion or the "promised land" to which black Jamaicans had to be repatriated. While some leaders of the movement were in the public eye in the early years of its development, Rastafari acquired more visibility in the sixties and seventies. In 1960 the government commissioned three faculty members of the University of the West Indies (M. G. Smith, Roy Augier, and Rex Nettleford) to investigate the movement, its organization and aims, and to write a report that was published that same year as *The Rastafari Movement in Kingston, Jamaica*. At that time Rastafari's political activism increased (partly through the influence of the Guyanese historian and activist Walter Rodney), and some politicians appropriated their symbols for their political campaigns. Especially during the 1970s, the musical Bandwagon of the People's National Party and the debate between Michael Manley and Edward Seaga around the "Rod of Correction" (a stick said to be a gift from Selassie to Manley) were parts of this symbolism.[6]

The years leading to Jamaica's political independence were also full of social and economic contradictions. While there was significant economic growth based on foreign investment in mining (the bauxite industry), manufacture, and tourism, there was also increasing social inequality. In 1944 constitutional changes relieved the metropolis of some of the administrative political control of the island, and two leading political parties emerged to govern the British colony: the Jamaican Labour Party (JLP) and the People's National Party (PNP). Their leaders, Alexander Bustamante and Norman W. Manley respectively, led the country to independence in 1962. The cultural and musical landscape echoed Jamaican sociopolitical transitions as many local composers and performers sought to create—or to accelerate the creation of—a popular music that was originally Jamaican. The result was what came to be known as *ska*, a very danceable genre that combined the influences of rhythm and blues and *mento*, creating something unlike anything played before in the Jamaican soundscape. This music was highly popular in the early 1960s, and some of its most prominent performers were Byron Lee and the Dragonaires, the Skatelites, Toots Hibbert and the Maytals, and the Wailers. Virtually emerging at the same time as Jamaica gained its independence, *ska* songs such as Derrick Morgan's "Forward March" (1962) reflected the optimism of the time, encouraging people to have "fun" and "dance" because "we are independent." Morgan's song also called upon people to have "joy" and "praise" both "Alexander" Bustamante and "Mr. Manley."

During the second half of the 1960s, musical tastes changed toward a slower tempo with a style that was named *rocksteady*. In this new musical variant, wind instruments were less present than in *ska*, and the bass had a more prominent role. Also, the lyrics of the music became more explicit about social realities in the country. Both the slower rhythm and the more explicit social content of the music would be present in the style known as reggae, which emerged around 1967 or 1968. Reggae followed the 4/4 musical time with a downbeat emphasis in 2 and 4 rather than in 1 and 3. The bass acquired yet a more important role than in *ska* and *rocksteady*, by carrying the rhythm (a function usually resting in the drums). Reggae distinguished itself from its predecessors by its strong and critical social commentary, which responded to the social realities of the late 1960s and the repression under JLP leadership. The political tensions were epitomized in the social unrest that erupted when the government did not allow the university lecturer Walter Rodney to reenter the country.[7] Musically, social tensions were immortalized in the Ethiopian's "Everything Crash" (1968):

Look deh now, everything crash!
Firemen strike, watermen strike

Telephone company too

Down to the policeman too!

The song not only referred to the social tensions that had been accumulating for years but also portrayed the inevitable fate in the things to come: "Every day carry bucket to the well, one day the bottom must drop out!"

During the 1970s reggae became more popular and established itself as the definitive musical trademark for Jamaica, both nationally and internationally. Many of the songs' lyrics responded to social and political circumstances, particularly during the elections of 1972 when the leader of the PNP, Michael Manley, capitalized on the use of reggae artists in his political campaign. Delroy Wilson's "Better Must Come" (1971) became the slogan for the PNP and a cry for change in the conditions of life under JLP government. Indeed, Manley's promise of "change" and his musical Bandwagon—joined by Wilson, Max Romeo, the Wailers, and other musicians—were of great importance for the victory of the PNP in the 1972 elections. But his move toward "Democratic Socialism" two years later would serve as a catalyst for one of the most tense and violent political atmospheres in Jamaican history. The politico-ideological shift of the PNP was recorded in music when Max Romeo released his hit "Socialism Is Love" in 1974.

While some of Manley's socioeconomic policies gained him the support of the working classes and marginal groups, others—such as the nationalization of the bauxite industry and the introduction of property taxes—caused discomfort among some of the middle and upper classes that had supported him in 1972. Moreover, Manley's left-oriented rhetoric after 1974 was not exactly what the foreign investors in the country, some of the elites, or the United States of America wanted to hear.[8] Later, the country would enter into a period of "economic emergency,"[9] caused by a combination of the general economic crisis of the decade as well as by the PNP's economic policies and the flight of capital due to the apprehension on the party's political stance. Bitter political rivalry between the two leading parties and their supporters increased. This political divide was evident in the urban arena, as particular areas developed into garrison constituencies responding to either the JLP or the PNP. In the late 1970s, the United States' Central Intelligence Agency (CIA) was blamed for the crisis and political instability in Jamaica. Most of the events related to those tense years of the mid- and late 1970s were reported in the musical narratives of reggae—as happens with many other Caribbean music as calypso and *merengue*.

Marley's "Rat Race" of 1976 is one of the most representative songs of this period. The song mentioned how the "political violence fill ya city" and warned: "Don't involve Rasta in your say, say; Rasta don't work for no CIA." The lines that followed spoke of "collective security" and could not have been more pertinent to the time in which the song hit the airwaves; they reflected not only the government's use of police and military forces to confront the political warfare in Kingston but also the recruitment of civilians in policing activities through what was known as the "Home Guard."[10] The political state of affairs in the country during the late 1970s is also exposed in "Tribal War" by Third World in 1977 and echoed in Max Romeo's "War ina Babylon" (1976): "War ina Babylon, Tribal War ina Babylon." In this song, Romeo locates himself as a Rasta living on the outskirts of the city and offers what could easily be a photograph of Kingston's reality in those years: "I-man satta in the mountain top, watching Babylon burning red, red hot."

The scale of political violence in the late 1970s triggered efforts to accomplish peace among the different sectors. While Manley and Seaga signed a peace agreement in 1976, the people in the ghettos searched for peace in their own way through a truce between the different garrison constituencies in 1978,[11] and that same year reggae musicians performed in the One Love Peace Concert. Some songs from those years referred to the peace efforts in various ways, yet Peter Tosh's "Equal Rights" (1977) is perhaps the song that better illustrates the process from a critical perspective:

Everybody is crying out for peace
I'll say, none is crying out for justice
'till men get equal rights and justice

As the 1980 elections approached and the political violence and economic crisis persisted, a number of songs continued to comment on the situation. Released in 1979, "Armagideon Time" deals with both the social inequalities felt by the popular classes and the economic limitations endured by them.

A lot of people won't get no supper tonight
A lot of people going to suffer tonight
Cause the battle is getting harder
And this I-ration is Armagideon

The song notes several problems including the lack of "supper" for "a lot of people," an issue that was discussed the year before at a summit on world hunger in Jamaica.[12]

As is evident from the limited sample of reggae songs here, most of them were "in tune" with the society from which they emerged. By stressing this link between music and society, I am trying to highlight how music can be approached as a valuable source that sheds light into a particular time period or as a historical narrative and representation of that specific time. Reggae songs in the 1960s and 1970s provide not only a chronicle of the events and transformations that were taking place in Jamaica, but a particular perception of them written and performed for future generations. Reggae music served also as a popular representation of Jamaican colonial history opening a window to the deeds, events, and figures important for the Afro-Jamaican heritage.

"DO YOU REMEMBER THE DAYS OF SLAVERY?": COLONIAL HISTORY IN JAMAICAN REGGAE

Due to its association with the Rastafarian movement and the Jamaican underclasses, reggae music became representative of the worldview of Afro-Jamaicans. As such, the historical narrative in reggae songs has often portrayed dominant elements of the Rasta philosophy such as the perception of Jamaica as Babylon, Africa as Zion, and Jamaicans as "Israelites" that have to get back to the "promised land." The lyrics of many reggae songs thus came to rescue a history that inevitably linked black Jamaicans with Africa, the place from which their ancestors had been brought as slaves. Therefore, the slavery era and its subsequent history became central themes in reggae's historical discourse.

In reggae, Africa is basically represented as a point of origin for Afro-Jamaicans and as the promised land, where a physical or spiritual return must lead. The demand of Rastafarians for repatriation and their critical position toward Jamaica was framed in the memories of slavery, the slave trade, and the nature of the oppression lived under that system. Jacob Miller's "80,000 Careless Ethiopians" (1974) offers a random figure for those "careless Ethiopians" who were exiled in "Babylon" (Jamaica) and need to go back to "Mount Zion" (Africa): "80,000 careless Ethiopians, shall go down in Babylon." Bob Marley's cry to "set the captive free" and for a "movement of Jah people" to the "fathers' land" in the song "Exodus" (1977) also echoes metaphorically the (continuing) condition of Jamaicans as captives in a world of "downpression" and "transgression." In a constant dialogue between the past and the present, the "slave" and slavery itself (and, by default, freedom) became images widely used by reggae singers in their compositions. Slavery operated as a metaphor for the discrimination and marginalization of the 1960s and 1970s—a metaphor that was grounded on, or in continuity with, the realities of Jamaica's colonial past.

In "The Harder They Come" (1972), Jimmy Cliff stated that he "rather be a free man in my grave, than living as a puppet or a slave," a line that recalls that some slaves committed suicide as a way to "escape" their bondage.[13] Moreover, in the context of struggle and perseverance of Cliff's song, the line is yet more pertinent if we remember the executions of the slave rebels in the aftermath of the 1831 Baptist War. Most of them remained "courageous and confident" when they faced death as their punishment for struggling for freedom.[14] Other songs, such as Sugar Minnott's "River Jordan" (1979) advocates for the return to Africa—"home"—establishing the link of Afro-Jamaican people with the land of their forefathers, a connection that is established through the continuity of the experience of slavery: "So long we've been down in slavery; where, and now we just got to be free, yes, we want to be free." The song goes further to specify harsh realities of slavery: "So long we've been bound in shackles and chains."

Marley's "Slave Driver" (1973) and "Redemption Song" (1980) also revive the memories of slavery. The latter not only refers to the much needed emancipation from "mental slavery" but also recalls the very first stage of the ordeal of the slaves by referring to the "old pirates" who dealt with the slaves by selling them (or "I") to the "merchant ships." In "Slave Driver," Marley's impersonation notes: "I remember on the slave ship, how they brutalize our very souls." He provides a material representation of bondage by stating how, instead of freedom, the slaves remained "hold to the chain of poverty." The next step in the slave traffic is remembered by the group Third World in "Human Marketplace" (1977), a song that opens a window on one of the key experiences of African slaves in their transatlantic voyage.

Why is this buying and selling still going on?
In this . . . Human Marketplace
In this . . . Human Marketplace

The song repeats the same lines about "buying" and "selling" in a "human marketplace," recalling the descriptions that students of the slave trade and slavery have provided us about this inhuman process.[15]

Several songs make passing references to such ideas and practices of slavery. But it is Burning Spear, one of the leading starts of roots reggae, who has been most explicit in his denunciation of slavery regarding as "his task to brush history against the grain," to appropriate Walter Benjamin's phrase.[16] Spear does this in "Slavery Days" (1975) by going beyond brief mentions, describing the specifics of slave labor in Jamaica (and the Caribbean, for that matter), and telling the "half of the story" that needs to be remembered:

Do you remember the days of slavery? (Chorus; repeat in
   call and response)
And how they beat us (Chorus)
And how they worked us so hard (Repeat chorus)
And how they used us (Repeat chorus)
'Till they refuse us (Repeat chorus)

Not only does Spear remind us about the conditions of work in the plantations, but he also speaks about the collective suffering of that experience: "My
brother feels it . . . Included my sister too." The chorus continues: "Some of
us survived / Showed them God we are still alive." Through "Survival," Spear's
historical-musical discourse links his narrative of slavery with his personal
identification (as a black person) and sense of belonging and lineage with
those who experienced slavery. It is in the previous lines that Spear assumes
Benjamin's principle, through a critique of a certain view of Jamaican history
that cannot (or does not want to) remember the "days of slavery." Spear therefore encourages and begs his listeners to try to remember that history—his
story.

Other details of slavery are explained in the song "Moses Children" (1977),
where Bunny Wailer uses the metaphor of the children of Moses, the people
of Israel, to represent the slaves brought to the Americas through the Middle
Passage for a life under slavery.

Trial and crosses are always before me
Thorns and prickles in-a my way, my way
With the task-master always behind me
waiting for a chance
To take my life away

In this song, the singer urges the slave, embodied in the phrase "Moses Children," to express the reason for his suffering, the reason for his crying. In an
obvious reference to the labor conditions and the punishments under slavery,
the slave describes a situation in which he is haunted by "thorns and prickles"
and the "task-master" who tries to take his life. This particular slave "ignores"
why he is experiencing this suffering and attributes it to be in a situation
"where things don't seem to belong." The Caribbean, Sidney W. Mintz has
emphasized, was composed of people "from different places and who were not
in their own culture,"[17] and this is clearly evident in this slave's sense of unbelonging. "The slaves were uprooted, detribalised, de-named, [and] de-
humanised" when brought to the Americas, noted the Jamaican statesman

Michael Manley, adding that any discussion of "blues, calypso, or reggae" should begin at that point.[18] "Moses Children" and the cultural displacement of Wailer's suffering character clearly illustrate this.

Other parts of the song recreate the difficulties of the labor conditions and the ever-present reality of death. The dilemma of the slave is one between following his mind (perhaps escape or rebel) or "going astray."

My burdens sweating like a slave
to live another day
My burdens, If I didn't follow my mind
I would be gone astray

As the song continues, the slave further expresses his awareness of his unequal life conditions where he does not have resources (silver or gold). In another line the slave tells us that he works "like the weak who's got to feed the strong," recognizing the social structure and relations behind his situation of inequality vis-à-vis free persons.

Silver, silver, silver, and gold
have I none, have I none

. . . .

Working round the clock and obeying the gong
like the weak who's got to feed the strong

The song concludes with yet another reference to the realities of slavery in Jamaica when it mentions the slave driver.

Slave driver, dry bone crying in the wilderness
Slave driver, only muscle and
blood can stand the test

The slave drivers, who performed the will of the master in the cane fields, were selected not only for their physical qualities but also for their skills and knowledge of the plantation. The portrayal of the slave driver in Bunny Wailer's song resembles the description of the slave driver standing "with the long cart whip round his neck" while in charge of the slave gangs. Moreover, the complaints of the slave in the song, directed at the slave driver, also manifest the latter's intermediate position having both leadership within the slave community and the authority and power emerging from the master's trust in him for his duty. The authority of the slave drivers allowed them to inflict severe punishments on other slaves, which becomes evident when Wailer's slave states that the "task-master" can "take my life away."[19]

Wailer's link between the slave driver and his "burdens," "crying," and "pain" cannot be more accurate, if one looks at contemporary descriptions of life on the plantations. Henry Whiteley, a European who traveled to Jamaica to work in a plantation, witnessed the suffering of the slaves at the hand of the slave drivers in the final years of slavery in 1832. He wrote about how a driver flogged a slave "causing blood to spring at every stroke," a "spectacle" he described as "revolting" and that left him "horror-struck," trembling, and "sick," while the victim of the driver cried: "Lord! Lord! Lord!" Another first-hand account of the years of slavery, that of James Williams as an apprentice after 1834, is also revealing of the "pain" alluded by Wailer's song: "[T]hey give me the fifteen lashes; the flogging was quite severe, and cut my back badly." Williams's reference to the "handcuff[s]" and the "collar and chain" in his narrative is something also rescued in the songs that refer to the use of "chains" and "shackles."[20]

In 1838, little more than a year after the appearance of Williams's narrative, slavery officially ended in Jamaica. But the suffering of Afro-Jamaicans did not conclude with the collapse of that institution; racial, social, and economic marginalization and discrimination against black people continued unabated. The struggle of blacks also continued, and reggae's historical discourse goes beyond the era of slavery to document the continuing efforts of Jamaicans to achieve racial and social equality. Some examples of how reggae documents the years of postemancipation are to be found in the songs by Third World, Burning Spear, and the Mighty Diamonds. While Burning Spear looks at peasant life in Jamaica in "Man in the Hills" (1976), Third World takes us back to the Morant Bay Rebellion of 1865 in the song "1865: 96 Degrees in the Shade" (1977). Spear's "Marcus Garvey" (1975) and Mighty Diamonds' "Them Never Love Poor Marcus" (1976) remind listeners about one of Jamaica's leading historical figures, the Pan-African leader and founder of the Universal Negro Improvement Association (UNIA), Marcus Garvey.

One of the features of postemancipation Jamaica was that many ex-slaves moved completely or partially off the plantations to live as peasants cultivating their own crops. Whether as maroons or through the "flight from the estates" right after the end of slavery, the "hills" remained as a socioeconomic (and indeed political) alternative for Afro-Jamaicans during and after slavery (and even during the twentieth century as Rastas left for the fringes of urban Kingston). "Man in the Hills" by Burning Spear evokes that life in the "hills":

And if think we should live up in the Hills
Live up in the Hills do you

My brother go, go to the river
To carry the water, the water

It is precisely the natural environment, resources, and topography (hills, river) that are described by Spear that served the Jamaican maroons as a source of refuge from plantation slavery. In this respect, Mavis C. Campbell reminds us that Jamaica, "with its mountainous terrain, interspersed with countless hills, valleys, and rivers, with its deep ravines and its awesome cockpits with their narrow defiles and innumerable caves, is peculiarly suited for these [maroon] establishments."[21] Such an environment was also useful for peasants who did not want to remain attached to the sugar estates and preferred life through a subsistence economy.

Nineteenth-century peasants from the village of Stony Gut in the hills around Morant Bay in eastern Jamaica are at the center of Third World's "1865: 96 Degrees in the Shade." Late nineteenth-century Jamaica experienced economic hardships caused by the effects of the Civil War in the United States, epidemics, droughts, floods, and a fall in the price of sugar, in combination with deficient British colonial policies (ranging from problems in the education system to taxing and labor issues).[22] Most of the burden of these changes fell on the black Jamaican peasants, as it became evident in the report of the Baptist minister Edward Underhill after visiting the island in 1859. Underhill's opinions became public through a letter he wrote later in 1865 describing the conditions of the black population in Jamaica. Peasants started to organize and discuss their economic hardships and to complain not only to the local government but also to the very center of the British Empire, writing directly to the queen. Colonial Governor Edward John Eyre had recognized Jamaica's economic problems, yet "maintained that laziness was the major problem of the blacks."[23] The response from the queen to the peasants became known as the "Queen's Advice," which—like Eyre's position—relieved the government from any responsibility, arguing that the "prosperity of the laboring classes" depended "upon their working for wages" in the plantations and for the planters "when their labor is wanted, and for so long as it is wanted."[24] Such a position, coming from the other side of the Atlantic, ignored the realities of the country and, worse still, provided legitimacy to the unwanted ties of the black working classes and peasants to the planters and the plantations. The "Queen's Advice" only served as a catalyst to the actions of the people in St. Thomas in the East, where Paul Bogle, a native Baptist deacon, led Afro-Jamaicans to the Morant Bay Rebellion—a definitive turning point in Jamaica's colonial history.[25] Such an important event is remembered by Third World:

Said it was 96 degrees in the Shade
ten thousand soldiers on parade
Taking I and I to meet a big fat one
send from overseas

The song takes on the position of the black peasants to start an explicit and metaphorical narrative of the events leading to the rebellion of 1865. It makes a direct reference to the queen and her representatives in Jamaica. The narrative recognizes the location of colonial power where the "Queen's Advice" was produced ("overseas") and the representatives of that power ("the Queen employ"). Participants in the Morant Bay Rebellion addressed the sources of power and its symbols in Jamaica, as was evident from the way the protesters targeted the police station, the militia, the vestry, and the Court House—all symbols of colonial oppression. But the colonial government acted with its superior human and material resources ("ten thousand soldiers on parade") to crush the rebellion. Governor Eyre did not hesitate to mobilize the island's military troops in an act of cruel and excessive repression. The song tells us:

You caught me on the loose
fighting to be free
Now you show me a noose
on the cotton tree
Entertainment for you, martyrdom for me

The persecution becomes evident in the song ("You caught me on the loose fighting to be free"), as well as the context ("cotton tree") and the methods of retribution implemented by Eyre's military ("noose"). The memory of Morant Bay has been present not only in Third World's music but also in Kumina ceremonies in Jamaica: "Among those who remembered Eyre and the execution of Bogle, Gordon, and others, the hangings at 'Morant Bay cotton tree,' and the violence of the Maroon allies of the government are the descendants of the Central Africans of the Plantain Garden River district. At Kumina ceremonies they still sing of those who, on Governor Eyre's order, were killed and terrorized."[26] Along with the actual victims to Eyre's repression involving the cotton tree, one only has to consider the mystical and spiritual qualities attributed to it to realize that their spirit would remain alive in its branches. The reference to the cotton tree may also be alluding to Governor Eyre's mobilization of troops for the repression in Morant Bay in 1865. What is known now in Kingston as Half-Way-Tree was the location for an old cotton tree that served as the resting place for British military troops on their way to Spanish Town. The tree survived there until the late nineteenth century.[27]

Third World's song also exemplifies the vicious extremes of government repression when it says "entertainment for you, martyrdom for me." Accounts by professional historians have described how the punishments under martial law in Morant Bay were out of proportion, literally turning into entertainment for military officials and martyrdom for the prisoners. Gordon Ramsay, who put the martial law in practice in Morant Bay, is said to have forced prisoners to form a line to witness the executions. Moreover, under Ramsay's direction, the troops abused and punished people without any reason, having neither a previous trial nor incriminating evidence. And as we see in the lines below, "1865" refers to yet more specific aspects of the rebellion when it says "some may burn," which can either be a reference to the actual burning of the Court House, or to the fact that the military troops burned the houses of the people.[28]

> Some may suffer and some may burn
> but I know that one day my people will learn
> As sure as the sun shines, way up in the sky
> today I stand here a victim the truth is I'll never die

The song concludes in a prophetic mode and, echoing Jimmy Cliff's "The Harder They Come," reminds that those who were victims then in 1865 will "never die" and won't be forgotten. Indeed, the Morant Bay Rebellion remains one of Jamaica's most significant historical events and its martyrs have been immortalized. Paul Bogle and his alleged accomplice in the House of Assembly, George William Gordon, are now national heroes of Jamaica, and there is a memorial tombstone and a statue of Bogle in the town of Morant Bay.

Other historical figures are also present in reggae's historical accounts. "Recall Some Great Men" (1990) by Burning Spear tells us to "recall Paul Bogle, recall Marcus Garvey." This latter Pan-African leader is also the subject of Spear's "Marcus Garvey" and the Mighty Diamonds' "Them Never Love Poor Marcus." These reggae songs refer to Garvey's Jamaican times either before his departure from Jamaica to New York in 1916 or after his return to his native land when deported from the United States in 1927. In "Them Never Love Poor Marcus," the interpreters claim that Garvey was never well loved in Jamaica:

> Them never love him, oh no
> Them never love, them never love
> Them never love poor Marcus
> [till] they betray him

Behind this argument are the many problems found by Garvey himself in developing his organization in Jamaica where the colonial regime became an obstacle, and some black and colored Jamaicans found his ideas suspect.[29] The song, which came out in 1976, serves as a testimony to its own times, the late 1970s, when Garvey's importance to Jamaica was being ignored and the press questioned: "Isn't there a place for Marcus Garvey?"[30] The lyrics condemn to the "fire" those who never loved Garvey by equating them to the mythical figure of Bag-A-Wire, a traitor to the cause.

> Men like Bag-A-Wire should burn in fire
> The betrayer of Marcus Garvey

Jamaican social scientist Barry Chevannes has written about Bag-A-Wire, who was condemned to wander the streets of Kingston dressed in rags.[31] Besides the Mighty Diamonds, Burning Spear also reminds us of the myth of Bag-A-Wire in his song "Marcus Garvey."

> Where is Bag-A-Wire
> Is no where around
> He can't be found
> Friends betrayer
> Who gave away Marcus Garvey

Both of these songs clearly claim Garvey's central place in Jamaican history. At the same time, the reference to the betrayer of Garvey is a critique of those who set obstacles to the development of the Garvey movement in Jamaica. These obstacles, along with the fertile ground found by Garvey in the United States of America, set the context for his ultimate move to New York, where his organization gained international success and prestige (as well as detractors).

Garvey's second stage in Jamaica came after he was convicted for mail fraud (1923) and then released and deported from the United States (1927). Once back in Jamaica, Garvey did not hesitate to enter the political processes on the island by founding the People's Political Party, only to end up in prison again for his activities. However, Garvey's political program at this time is pertinent here as it was intended for the benefit of the working classes and marginal groups of Jamaica.[32] Thus, in one way or another, Garvey hangs on to the objectives promoted by the UNIA from its very beginning. It is then not surprising that in "Marcus Garvey" Spear refers at the same time to the way Garvey's words have "come to pass" and the material claims of those in need:

> Marcus Garvey words come to pass
> Marcus Garvey words come to pass

Can't get no food to eat

Can't get no money to spend

In calling attention to Garveyism's global dimensions, Charles V. Carnegie has recently noted that the monument and second grave of the UNIA's leader in Kingston has remained neglected (except on special occasions). Reggae music then rescues a figure that has been an "object of periodic gaze" even when grounded in "an emotionally textured collective past."[33] Its rescue in the Jamaican context of the 1970s and after was also indicative of the aspects, characters, and symbols of Jamaican history that the popular classes—through reggae—understood were representative and important for the country in the early years of the new nation.

THE LOCAL AND GLOBAL TRANSACTIONS OF REGGAE MUSIC

As it has been illustrated here, reggae served as a historical narrative of its own time. Its lyrics in the postindependence years chronicled events such as Jamaica's independence, the tensions of the late 1960s, the political trajectory of the PNP (through its slogans and ideological shifts), the political warfare of the late 1970s, the alleged U.S. interventionism (through the CIA), and the different views on obtaining social peace in the country. At the same time, reggae music operated as a popular representation of the Jamaican past. It produced a narrative of slavery, the postemancipation years, and black Jamaican heritage that reinforced Afro-Jamaican social and historical consciousness in the context of national formation in the postindependence years. Along with the Rastafari and the Black Power movement of those years (and, indeed, the movement for civil rights in the United States and elsewhere), reggae music was telling Afro-Jamaicans, "[T]his is part of your history, a part that needs to be remembered and which people have to be proud of."

Caribbean historians have used the surviving records of colonial and national governments in the archives, the written voices of people with access to print media, or the scholarly historical accounts by historians published by academic presses or in peer-reviewed journals. I would not dispute the disciplinary and methodological logic behind that. Yet, it is also true that outside of the scholars who do research on the music itself (that is, those who select music as the central aspect of their studies), few contemporary historians have analyzed Caribbean music as records of popular memory and as historical narratives that can be used in similar ways as—or together with—the printed sources, the dusty documents, and recorded interviews.[34] Barry W. Higman's

Writing West Indian Histories acknowledged the limited audience of professional historians and their written products and recognized both the greater
outreach of "amateur" historians and the existence of other forms of historical
representation.[35] But while reggae lyrics are charged with historical narratives,
they found no space in Higman's remarkable work. And despite their role as
a type of amateur historian, reggae singers are rarely considered as legitimate
producers of popular histories. Considering that the audiences of reggae music
are much larger than those of professional historians and that both music and
history writing are "cultural activities," one should reassess the importance of
the history contained in the lyrics of reggae and its historical narratives.

Despite the lack of recognition as a popular representation of the past,
reggae's function in the development of social and historical consciousness
has transcended the local context that I have highlighted here. Global com-
mercialization and delocalization of Jamaican music have had its impact in the
social and political role of the music in that the pertinence of the lyrics to world
audiences in disparate places around the world may be irrelevant (or simply
different).[36] The meaning and significance of the music is further resignified
by the mass media and cultural intermediaries in a complex process that includes the music industry and markets, composers and musicians. As a result,
reggae music is in many instances just another commercial item reproduced
by the music and popular culture industry and detached from "its presence in
time and space, its unique existence at the place where it happens to be," to use
the words of Walter Benjamin.[37]

But by the same token, through the globalization of reggae, the social message of the music has become yet more international, and, perhaps, its historical narrative has become more global. Reggae music has been central in the
diffusion of Rastafarian ideals and beliefs around the world,[38] and numerous
peoples of African descent (in Africa itself and its American and European
diasporas) have embraced reggae as both a music for sociopolitical protest
and as a recourse for the assertion of identity grounded in the memory of a
common experience of bondage, persistent discrimination, and oppression.
The important position of slavery and the slave trade in reggae's historical discourse, as it has been shown here, was not only important for the musicians
(and audiences) to assert their identity, but has also served to establish a black
Atlantic bridge with the African and African diaspora communities that have
welcomed reggae as their collective voice. African reggae artist Lucky Dube
in "Slave" (1987) uses the metaphor of slavery to refer to the problem of alcoholism ("liquor slave") but improvises to expose the position of black people

in South Africa: "I am a slave, in my own country." Princess Erika, a female singer born in Paris of African descent and influenced by Rasta culture, also recalls slavery in her song "Tant Qu'il y Aura" (As Long as There Is, 1999) by referring to the liberation of the "souls chained by the savages" and using as an example the figure of Harriet Tubman, the female African American slave who freed herself and then helped others to do the same during the times of slavery. The image of slavery also comes out in Brazilian reggae. In "História do Brasil" (2004), one of Bahia's leading interpreters, Edson Gomes, sings about coming from "certain place, forced to work," and in "500 Anos" (2001) he adds the racial aspect specifying how blacks have been "working for the whites" for 500 years. Back to the Caribbean, the Puerto Rican reggae group Cultura Profética has used its song "Advertencia" (Warning, 1998) to remember how the Spaniards "brought Africans to our island," "taking them from their beloved land" to an "unknown" place (again, the sense of unbelonging), "forcing them to work," "extirpating [them of] their life." Historian James Walvin noted that "there is something uniquely terrible about the oceanic slave trade which linked together Europe, Africa and the Americas"[39] for three centuries, and it should be no surprise then that in times of accelerated globalization something uniquely musical in reggae has brought together these world regions again.

The international appeal of reggae goes beyond how this music has embraced the black Atlantic historical experience, to the reaction on more pressing national and international political issues. And while the music industry increased the internationalization of Jamaican music and musicians during the 1970s, many of the social and political issues addressed in the lyrics transcended Jamaican national boundaries since the very moment in which the songs were penned down. During reggae's heyday in Jamaica, the lyrics of Peter Tosh's "African" (1977) and "No Nuclear War" (1985) referred respectively to African diasporas around the world without caring "where you come from" or minding "nationality" and to the dangers of nuclear warfare in the midst of the Cold War. Bob Marley's awareness of global issues is evident in a number of songs, from "War" (1976) to "Zimbabwe" (1979). As reggae has spread throughout the Caribbean and the world, the message coming from Caribbean localities continues to refer to issues of global concerns. In Dominica, female reggae artist Nelly Stharre cries for "Peace in the Middle East" (1999) and calls the "Leaders of the World" (2003) to act with regard to issues such as world hunger and deforestation (global warming), which cannot be tackled with "war and ammunition." Such messages, and many others, reassert reggae's sociopolitical role despite the influences of cultural intermediaries involved in musical production and distribution in today's communication age. But singers and performers still have to negotiate their repertoire, pleasing producers and audiences alike in a world where radical sociopolitical content may or may not be relevant. Such relevance will determine whether historically grounded statements on political and social identity will be downplayed by the media and market influences or will impact people's sense of social and historical consciousness in a meaningful way.

NOTES

In the preparation of this essay, the author is grateful to the editors of the volume and to Jorge Duany for their comments and editorial recommendations. Thanks also to Kevin A. Yelvington, who took time from his busy schedule for a last-minute consultancy on calypso, and to Givanni Ildefonso, who kindly introduced me to Princess Erika at the appropriate time. As always, I recognize the hard work of Manuel Martínez and his staff at the Office of International Inter-Library Loans of the University of Puerto Rico for providing first-quality service and efficient support for my scholarly work. The Department of Sociology and Anthropology and the Faculty of Social Sciences provided a release from my teaching responsibilities that enabled me to work on this essay.

1. "Marley's Lyrics Find a Place in Student Protest," *Star*, May 18, 1989, Newspaper Clippings Collection, Bob Marley Museum, Kingston, Jamaica.

2. Chang and Chen, *Reggae Routes*, 95.

3. Said, *Musical Elaborations*, xii.

4. On the sound systems, see S. Davis, "Taking Drums, Sound Systems, and Reggae," 33–34, and Stolzoff, *Wake the Town and Tell the People*, 41–48.

5. Roberts, *The Population of Jamaica*, 152–54; Clarke, *Kingston, Jamaica*, 78.

6. On reggae and politics, see Giovannetti, *Sonidos de condena*. Waters, *Race, Class and Political Symbols*, offers a more detailed analysis of the uses of reggae and Rasta symbols by Jamaican political parties.

7. R. Lewis, *Walter Rodney: 1968 Revisited*, 7–56; R. Lewis, *Walter Rodney's Intellectual and Political Thought*, especially chaps. 4 and 7.

8. See Manley, *Jamaica: Struggle in the Periphery*, 87–89; Davies and Witter, "The Development of the Jamaican Economy since Independence"; W. Bell and Baldrich, "Elites, Economic Ideologies and Democracy in Jamaica," 172–73.

9. "Economic Emergency," *Jamaica Daily News*, January 20, 1977, 1, 3.

10. García Muñiz, "Defence Policy and Planning in the Caribbean," 119.

11. "Vote Today: Leaders Sign Peace Pledge," *Jamaica Daily News*, December 15,

1976, 1; "Peace Comes to West Kingston: TRUCE!," *Jamaica Daily News*, January 11, 1978, 1.

12. "World Battle against Hunger," *Jamaica Daily Times*, June 15, 1978, 6.

13. On suicide among the slaves, more common among male and field slaves, see Patterson, *Sociology of Slavery*, 264–65; Higman, *Slave Populations in the British Caribbean, 1807–1834*, 339–47.

14. Turner, *Slaves and Missionaries*, 162.

15. See Tannenbaum, *Slave and Citizen*, 28; Patterson, *Sociology of Slavery*, 150.

16. Benjamin, "Theses on the Philosophy of History," 248.

17. Mintz, "Enduring Substances, Trying Theories," 295 (emphasis in the original).

18. Manley, "Reggae, the Revolutionary Impulse," 11.

19. My discussion on the slave driver is informed by the works of Patterson, *Sociology of Slavery*, 62, and Curtin, *Two Jamaicas*, 19–21. The quotation in the text is in Curtin's book (pp. 19–21), which in turn cites from the work of T. Roughley, *The Jamaica Planter's Guide* (London: n.p., 1823).

20. See Whiteley, *Excessive Cruelty to Slaves*, 3, and Williams, *A Narrative of Events*.

21. Campbell, *The Maroons of Jamaica, 1655–1796*, 10.

22. Holt, *The Problem of Freedom*, 215–309.

23. Sherlock and Bennett, *The Story of the Jamaican People*, 254.

24. As quoted in Lord Olivier, *The Myth of Governor Eyre*, 145. Also quoted in a slightly different way in Sherlock and Bennett, *Story of the Jamaican People*, 257.

25. For the most complete historical account of the Morant Bay Rebellion, see Heuman, *"The Killing Time."* See also Holt, *The Problem of Freedom*, 263–309.

26. Schuler, *"Alas, Alas, Kongo,"* 107.

27. See Rashford, "The Cotton Tree and the Spiritual Realm in Jamaica," 49–57.

28. See Heuman, *"Killing Time,"* 119 (on the burning) and 135–43 (on Ramsay's action). Heuman's account of the repression under martial law describes Ramsay as a mentally unbalanced person capable of the worst atrocities.

29. T. Martin, *Race First*, 7. For more details on the problems confronted by Garvey in Jamaica, see Brown, *Color, Class, and Politics in Jamaica*, 124–26.

30. See "Isn't There a Place for Marcus Garvey?," *Jamaica Daily News*, May 22, 1978, 22.

31. See Chevannes, "Garvey Myths among the Jamaican People," 128, and Chevannes, *Rastafari: Roots and Ideology*, 107.

32. See R. Lewis and Bryan, *Marcus Garvey*, 209–30, and T. Martin, "Garvey and the Beginning of Mass-Based Party Politics in Jamaica," 122.

33. Carnegie, *Postnationalism Prefigured*, 173–75.

34. See also, with regard to calypso music, the work of Rohlehr, *Calypso and Society in Pre-Independence Trinidad*, 288–319, and Yelvington, "The War in Ethiopia and Trinidad, 1935–1936," 218–19, 221–22.

35. Higman, *Writing West Indian Histories*.

36. See, for instance, Bilby, "The Impact of Reggae in the United States," 17–22; Finke, "Bibles, Blond Locks: The New Rastafarians," 1, 8–9; and Giovannetti, "Popular Music and Culture in Puerto Rico," 81–98.
37. Walter Benjamin, "The Work of Art," 214.
38. Savishinsky, "Transnational Popular Culture," 259–81.
39. Walvin, *The Slave Trade*, xi.

11

Rum, Revolution, and Globalization:
Past, Present, and Future of a Caribbean Product

ANTHONY P. MAINGOT

FIRST DISTILLATES IN THE AMERICAS

Particular countries go to great lengths to establish proprietary rights to certain spirits. Americans quite properly lay claim to bourbon and rye, the Scotch and Irish to whisky, the French to champagne and Cognac, the Japanese to sake, the Russians to vodka. Genever is very definitely Dutch while the Brazilians have declared *cachaça* (a form of rum-based alcohol) as exclusively theirs. Mexico, quite secure in its intellectual rights to the name tequila and taking advantage of the popularity of that spirit, has now prohibited the bulk export of that liquor, preferring to benefit materially and symbolically from its export in bottles and marketing by specific region of origin.

No such geographical claim can be made for sugarcane and its product, rum. The origins are too diverse. It is known that sugarcane, *saccharum offici-rum* or *officinarum*, grew in China and India thousands of years ago. Indeed, rum historians Hugh Barty-King and Anton Massel believe that it was first developed in New Guinea and spread from there to the Philippines and other parts of the Pacific Ocean and China Sea.[1]

There is little debate over the fact that it was the invading Moors who introduced cane into Spain. The Spanish word *azúcar* is derived from the Arabic *sukkar*. The route to the New World is described by Antonio Herrera y Tordesillas as going from Valencia to Granada in Spain to the Canary Islands.[2] Columbus brought it with him to the New World. It was first planted and processed in Hispaniola and spread from there to all the tropical and subtropical parts of the Spanish and Portuguese empires.

It is also established that under Spanish colonial rule the extract from the cane never developed beyond the most primitive of products. According to Venezuelan historian, José A. Luis Rodríguez, it was not until the early 1700s that a basic distillate called *aguardiente* was produced for local consumption.[3] Already in 1714 a Royal Cédula prohibited the distilling of this cane spirit—in the Americas and the Philippines—on the ground that it was "pernicious" to public health. This prohibition would remain in force until 1796 when the Spanish Crown finally allowed the free production and trading of *aguardiente* in Mexico and other Spanish territories.[4] Whatever the effects of the royal policy, it is doubtful that it was this royal prohibition against *aguardiente* alone that stunted the development of a palatable product in the Spanish colonies.

Three additional reasons merit consideration. First, the general monopoly over all trade with the colonies. This included, of course, protecting the Spanish sugarcane industries in Cataluña, Andalusia, and the Canary Islands as well as its wine industry. Again, colonials were known to *acatar pero no cumplir* (to obey but not carry out royal mandates), so laws would not be enough to stop the development of a serious rum industry. The second reason is much more relevant: the fact that the local demand was met through widespread smuggling of foreign rum. A French-Trinidadian, Dauxion-Lavaysse, describes a plantation in the town of Cariaco (Cumana) that had sugar and "a distillery for rum." In 1807 the governor, Manuel de Cagigal, endeavored to prevent the distillation of rum under the false pretense that it would injure the trade in brandies with Spain; but the true reason was that the rum trade, one of the English smuggling branches, brought large profits to his excellency.[5]

This brings us to the third element explaining the undeveloped nature of the Latin American rum industry right into the twentieth century: aesthetics. Given royal prohibitions, supplies by foreign smugglers, and the lack of Spanish distilling equipment, the product called *aguardiente* was barely palatable and, thus, hardly attractive to the local elites. The well-known 1735 account of Spanish engineers Jorge Juan and Antonio de Ulloa was typical. They describe the heat and social confusion in the Colombian coastal city of Cartagena, noting that all classes had to take a break at 11:00 A.M. called *hazer [sic] las once*. The difference was that what they called "persons of distinction" drank brandy, and "lower classes and negroes" drank a local product: "extracted from the juice of the sugar cane, and thence called *Agoa ardente de canna*, or cane brandy."[6]

As we shall see, this association of rum with the working classes and with the discomforts of the Tropics was not limited to the Spanish territories. Even one as charmed by the Caribbean, and Martinique in particular, as Lafcadio

Hearn (1850–1904) called attention to a climate and environment that, he said, invariably created a lethargy that "totally mastered habit and purpose": the blood is "thinned," the northern tint of health changes to a "dead brown." His dismal portrayal was very typical. "You have to learn," he wrote, "that intellectual pursuits can be persisted in only at risk of life; that in this part of the world there is nothing to do but to plant cane and cocoa, and make rum . . . and eat, drink, sleep, perspire."[7]

This association of rum (or *aguardiente*) with unbearable (to the European) heat and with the toiling classes would long operate against the aesthetic enhancement and prestige of the product. Additionally, no enhancement was possible as long as the product remained as described in the *Observador Caraqueño* of February 11, 1824: "[T]hat liquor called *aguardiente de caña* and vulgarly 'rum' when color is added, . . . is of terrible quality, pestilent of smell, and the local method used in distilling it puts it out of any competition with the rum from the English and Danish colonies or even that of Havana." The writer argued that it would be beneficial if the Venezuelan Congress would recommend the distilling techniques practiced in the English colonies.[8]

There is no evidence that in Hispanic America the status of both local rum and *aguardiente* changed much before the last quarter of the nineteenth century. Rodríguez Luis documents that Venezuelans did not begin using more modern distilling equipment until the 1880s or begin aging their rums until 1954. *Ron* was eventually differentiated from *aguardiente* in that it had been aged for a minimum of two years by law. "Up to then what we call rum," writes Luis Rodríguez, "was an *aguardiente* colored with caramel without any aging."[9] Not even Cuba produced palatable rum until the second half of the nineteenth century. Manuel Moreno Fraginals tells us that, while Cuban plantations exported molasses to North America, their distillates could not be exported because "[their rum] had the very unpleasant taste and smell of must."[10] According to Moreno, not until the mid-nineteenth century was palatable rum produced on the island.[11] Roland Ely, who largely ignores the distillation of *aguardiente* or rum in his massive tome on the Cuban sugar plantation, relates how "some" plantations distilled *aguardiente* for consumption by the blacks and for cleaning material "instead of soap and water" for the owners.[12] Similarly, José Chez Checo describes a Dominican distilling industry languishing in backwardness, unable to compete with imported rum (invariably indicated as Jamaican), often described as "the milk of the blacks." Late nineteenth-century contacts with Cuban manufacturers and government insistence that they participate in international competitions eventually turned the quality of Dominican rum around.[13]

This underdevelopment was also evident in the major Puerto Rican sugar estate "Mercedita," property of the Serrallés family, which in the twentieth century would market the very respectable "Ron Don Q." During the nineteenth century the estate kept no records of the amounts of rum distilled. In 1900 the estate sold a mere 9,000 pesos worth of rum.[14] Monopolistic royal policies and isolation from global trade and competition had kept the distillates from the Hispanic Caribbean in an underdeveloped state compared with the industry in the non-Hispanic Caribbean.

RUM AND THE BRITISH EMPIRE

While Spanish Americans appeared incapable of producing an attractive distillate from sugarcane, the exact opposite was true in the British islands right next door. In a world of monopolistic barriers that removed any incentives to produce exportable rum, the British declared rum to be a "nonenumerated" commodity, that is, one that could be freely traded. No less a mind than Adam Smith took note of this in his celebration of "liberalized" trade.[15] Thus, from the very beginning, West Indian rum has been a part of global trade, and it is not far fetched to attribute its quality to the need to meet external demands in quantity and quality.

Another interesting fact of rum is that it did not take long to start up a business. Note the case of Trinidad, a Spanish colony that up to 1797 exported no rum. It was conquered that year by Britain, and in 1808 Trinidad was a major source of the rum smuggled into Venezuela. The reality was that within ten years of the British conquest, Trinidad had 214 plantations exporting 460,000 gallons of rum and 100,000 gallons of *syrop* (molasses).[16]

While it is quite evident that distilling from sugarcane juice has been around for a very long time in various parts of the world, there is "no doubt," as Julie Arkell asserts, that the birthplace of the rum industry as we know it was the Caribbean islands and specifically the British islands.[17] In those islands rum stopped being a "byproduct" of the sugar plantation to become a major part of local hospitality and international trade.

Barbados is a good place to start the story of free trade and "good" (i.e., palatable) rum. Having settled the island of Barbados in 1627 and learned from the Dutch who settled in northeast Brazil how to plant its flat, sun-washed land with cane, the English did what others had done before: boil the cane juice until it produced two derivatives, raw brown sugar (*muscovado*) and molasses, its liquid by-product. Again, like others had done previously, they derived a distillate from the latter. That was as far as the similarities with past practice went. What the British in Barbados gave the world was a savory spirit properly called "Barbados waters."

At a time when others were dumping molasses into the rivers or used it as cattle feed,[18] Barbadians were making a much more profitable and enjoyable use of it. One gallon of molasses allowed the production of 1 gallon of rum, and a hundred weight of raw sugar was enough to produce 7.5 gallons of rum. So the plantation produced sugar, molasses, and rum, all of which had assured buyers. As its fame spread in navigation and Metropolitan circles, the liquid became known as "comfortable water." Rum's appeal went beyond pleasure and into health concerns when it was discovered that replacing the poisonous lead pipes on the pot stills with copper ones, plus adding more water and lime to the mix, gave rum all sorts of medicinal values. Getting rid of scurvy and combating the grippe were certainly two worthy and recommendable reasons for bending the elbow. Quality and quantity were improved when the pot stills were given ceramic boiling pans with a bulbous head heated by fire and copper tubing surrounded by water to condense the escaping vapor. The distillate normally contained 85 to 95 percent alcohol and was then diluted with water. It is clear that by the early eighteenth century the bugs had been worked out of the distilling process and a quality product was available. It has remained that way. Barty-King and Massel accurately note that "[r]um is one of the purest spirits, especially when fermented with a pure saccharomyces yeast culture, from pure cane juice and distilled by a skilled distiller. None of the poisonous methanol will be present and higher alcohol, ester and volatile acid fractions can be strictly controlled."[19]

No one should believe, however, that rum was consumed mainly for health reasons. Perish the thought! Simple, straightforward pleasure and an exuberant sense of hospitality explained the prodigious consumption of this pure spirit. In fact, the Barbadian, and present day West Indian, reputation as "groggists"[20] had very early origins. Not only were they extravagant in their consumption; they expected their guests to keep up with them. As one anonymous seventeenth-century explorer put it, the planter was "a German for his drinking and a Welchman for his welcome . . . he takes it ill if you pass by his door and not taste of [his] liquor."[21]

It appears that by the first quarter of the eighteenth century rum had acquired what Barty-King and Massel call "a certain respectability."[22] The planters certainly consumed considerable amounts of it. Note the words of a somewhat rum-shy governor of the Leeward Islands who, in the late eighteenth century, was in plain awe at the Barbadian appetite for rum: "The planters [of Barbados] think the best way to make their strangers welcome is to murther them with drinking; the tenth part of that strong liquor which will scarce warme the blood of our West Indians, who have bodies like Egyptian mummy's [*sic*], must certainly despatch a new-comer to the other world."[23]

But it was naval warfare and global trade that really gave the English and the Caribbean a head start in the manufacturing of decent rum. New myths about naval warfare were born when the British navy decided to do what the pirates were already doing: giving a "grog" or "tot" of rum twice a day to its sailors, even as the officers continued to drink port, sherry, or brandy. The navy, not wanting to show preferences, bought its rum in Barbados, British Guiana, and Jamaica (and later, Trinidad), put the blend into oak casks known as *rumbar-ricoes*, and sent it to sea as naval rum. In 1770 the ration of rum in the British navy was 22.8 gallons (86.11 liters) per year. The ration for British soldiers during the American Revolutionary War was 15.2 gallons and in the Caribbean, 22.75 gallons. Even George Washington, who as a young man had spent four months in 1751 in Barbados, provided his Continental army with a rum ration. Not surprisingly, given the tradition-bound nature of the Brits, it became a firm custom and a successful one indeed. "Splice the Main Brace!" was the call for a double tot of rum. The rum grog took on a heroic reputation when Admiral Nelson defeated Napoleon's fleet at the crucial battle of Trafalgar. That victory of the rum-drinking swabbies made it patently clear that rum, not claret or brandy, was the fighting man's drink. Of course, it was important that the grog be strong enough to "make a rabbit bite a bulldog" as the saying went.

By the mid-eighteenth century, rum was no longer just on the West Indian plantation or British ships but had joined the other established spirits as an essential—though perhaps not the most select—item in a gentleman's "wine cellar." For instance, an inventory of Thomas Jefferson's wine cellar in 1769 contained the following bottles: 15 of Madeira, 4 of "common" Lisbon wine, 54 of cider, and 83 of rum. Unfortunately there is no indication as to the origin of the rum, but one can surmise that it came from Antigua in the West Indies or from one of the many distilleries operating in Massachusetts. According to Pares, while Massachusetts's refineries provided most of the rum for consumers south of the Mason-Dixon Line, this was hardly the first choice of those who could afford something of higher quality. The latter was clearly the double-distilled West Indian rum, and of these, Jamaican was thought the best. However, because the English, Scottish, and Irish shared in the predilection for Jamaican rum, continentals turned to Barbadian, Grenadian, and St. Christopher rum. On the other hand, says Pares, the Virginian palate had a distinct preference for Antiguan rum.[24] And they drank prodigious amounts of it.

John J. McCusker, notes that while drinking among the men of the continental colonies might not have been up to West Indian standards, they were a hearty breed just the same. "John Adams' much overworked quote about molasses being the well-spring of the American Revolution," McCusker tells us, "takes on added meaning when we appreciate just what was at the bottom of that well. New Englanders did not float in a sea of rum—they drank it!"[25]

As table 1 shows, Virginians and Philadelphians were hardly behind the New Englanders in their consumption of West Indian rum; they reexported mighty little of the rum they imported. Clearly, there had to be both the occasions and the locations for the consumption of so much rum. And so there were. According to McCullough, there were as many as thirty bookshops "and twice the number of taverns and coffee houses" in the Philadelphia of Constitution-writing days. The "City Tavern," he says, was the great gathering place for members of Congress. Indeed, it was there that John Adams met George Washington.[26]

Keep in mind that in 1770 the total free population of the continental colonies was 1.7 million and that four-fifths of these were women and children. That year the small male population drank 7,517,000 gallons of rum—3.6 million of which was West Indian. In 1770 the average white inhabitant of the continental colonies drank 4.2 gallons of rum each year. Northern whites drank somewhat more rum than southern, 4.6 gallons each, as opposed to 4 gallons per person. By comparison, that same year the consumption in England and Wales of all distilled spirits, foreign and domestic, averaged 0.6 gallons per person. All this is, by 1970 standards, phenomenal. In 1770, the colonists drank in one year almost as much rum as modern Americans drink with a population nearly 100 times larger. But whites were not the only ones drinking rum. The historical record shows that slaves also enjoyed the pleasures of rum. As table 2 demonstrates, slaves used rum as a libation as well as for cooking. Table 3 illustrates the fact that rum continues to be used in cooking. But, here again, rum has none of the prestige of wine or sherry in fashionable cooking for the simple reason that while the former and latter quickly evaporate, the rum flavor does linger in anything cooked with it.

It is true, as Pares documents, that there were repeated attempts to curtail what the General Court of Connecticut in 1654 called the "many mischiefs" caused by "the great quantities of rhum that are imported into this colony and here consumed." But on most occasions that combination of public demand and state financial needs meant the inevitable "decline of morality into fiscality."[27] All of which explains the proliferation of distilleries in the thirteen North American colonies. In 1770 there were 18 sugar refineries but 118 distilleries,

TABLE 1. West Indian Rum Imported into, Reexported from, and
Retained in the Continental Colonies, 1770

| | IMPORTED | | | REEXPORTED | | | |
| | Overseas | Coast-wise | Total | Overseas | Coast-wise | Total | Total Retained |
Colony							
New Hampshire	85	2	87	32	0	32	75
Massachusetts	275	22	297	46	0	46	241
Rhode Island	211	5	215	2	104	106	109
Connecticut	458	15	473	0	139	139	334
New York	402	167	569	2	23	26	544
New Jersey	4	10	14	0	0	0	14
Pennsylvania	1,006	51	1,057	16	96	112	945
Maryland	281	54	335	0	2	2	333
Virginia	624	25	649	1	13	14	635
North Carolina	86	9	96	0	3	3	92
South Carolina	267	12	279	29	24	29	250
Georgia	61	8	69	3	3	3	65
New England	1,048	44	1,092	108	215	323	768
Total	3,780	380	4,160	133	380	513	3,647

Source: McCusker, *Rum and the American Revolution*, 1:400.

distributed as follows: Massachusetts, 51 (36 in Boston), which produced 2
million gallons per year or 43.2 percent of the total; Rhode Island had 20 (16
in Newport); Connecticut, 5; New Hampshire, 3; the rest were in New York,
Pennsylvania, and South Carolina.[28]

It is important to clarify the fact that there is no scholarly agreement on
rum consumption's contribution to public drunkenness in North America.
W. J. Rorabaugh maintains that the "high tide" of cheap rum brought with it
a new style of drinking: drunken clients spilling out of the "grog shops" and
into public spaces. He argues that rum was increasingly associated with "thiev-
ery, lechery and brutality."[29] Similar warnings were sent from the islands. In
1840 one Joseph John Gurney, a Baptist missionary, wrote his friend Henry
Clay, advising that "[t]he new rum of the West Indies is a tempting but most
unhealthy liquor and it has doubtless caused an unnumbered multitude of
untimely deaths."[30] Other scholars do not speak of any widespread alcoholism
or public drunkenness. In fact, McCusker is adamant that in North America

TABLE 2. Slave Uses for Rum

Tuesday August 12th 1766. This day the following slaves took a pleasant ride out to Portsmouth as follows

Viz

    Boston Vose
    Lingo Stephens and Phylis Lyndon
    Nepton Sipson and Wife
    Prince Thurston
    Caesar Lyndon and Sarah Searing

Necessaries bot for ye Support of Nature are as follows

Viz

To a pigg to roast	8	10	0
To so much paid for house room	7	4	0
To Wine	3	12	0
To Bread	1	8	0
To Rum	2	10	0
To Green Corn 70 Limes for Punch 20	4	10	0
To Sugar	2	4	0
To Butter	1	0	0
To Tea 40 Coffee 15	2	1	0
To 1 pint rum for killing Pigg	0	10	0
	33	13	0

Source: Bartlett, *From Slave to Citizen*, 13.

the outdoor life and work plus the harsh climate combined to cause a caloric expenditure that dictated a high-energy diet. And "rum helped to meet that demand."[31] Bear in mind also that the heavy rums generated by the pot stills at the time, along with their full flavor and aroma, were loaded with 147 calories per ounce, compared with the 83 in whiskey. That was twice the calories of a similar amount of molasses, also heavily consumed. Between their rum and the molasses (used in brown bread, baked beans, gingerbread, and pies and for the general "glazing" of meats and vegetables), these American colonials certainly had a sugar-rich diet. In the Caribbean, the explanation of the heavy drinking (or, should we say, excuse) was the need to counteract the intense heat and humidity. In the final analysis, whether in the islands or on the mainland, who could blame the serious groggist if he picked up the West Indian planter's belief that, "If you drink, you die. If you don't drink, you die. So, drink!"

TABLE 3. Recipe for Orange Flavor Pork Roast

4 lb. pork loin, boned and rolled

1 tbsp. rum

salt and pepper to taste

5 tbsp. water

1 tbsp. flour

1 tbsp. butter

2 tbsp. fat from roast

2//3 c. fresh orange juice

pinch of cayenne pepper

1 tbsp. guava (or red currant jelly)

4 tsp. grated orange rind

Preheat oven to 375°F. Season pork loin with salt and pepper to taste. Bake for one hour 10 minutes. Glaze with 1/4 c. of orange sauce and bake for an additional 20 minutes or until cooked thoroughly.

Orange Sauce: Mix flour and water until you have a smooth paste. Add the butter and fat, stirring constantly. Season with salt and pepper and cayenne. Add the orange juice and most of the rind. Simmer over low heat for five to eight minutes, stirring constantly. Add guava (or red currant) and rum.

Serve sprinkled with the remaining rind and garnish with orange slices if desired (serves 6–8).

Source: Ayala, *The Rum Experience*, 206.

Alas, rum would not always reign supreme. The economic "law of substitution" in alcoholic beverages tells us that over the long run people will switch to beverages that offer the highest alcoholic content per unit of cost. And, as such, in the nineteenth century changes in distilling technology and economies of scale provided the southern producers of bourbon and rye with advantages over rum. According to Rorabaugh, the annual American per capita consumption of distilled spirits (i.e., rum, whiskey, gin, brandy) hit its peak in the 1820s at more than 5 gallons. After that it went into a sharp and prolonged decline reaching its lowest point (1.2 gallons) in the 1940s. In the 1970s consumption stabilized at 1.8 gallons per capita. Rum imports stood at 1.2 gallons per capita in 1790, rising to 1.5 gallons in 1805, after which rum imports declined steadily, reaching 0.2 gallons per capita in 1850. During that same period the imports of coffee went from 1.0 pounds to 5.6 pounds per capita. Tea imports remained steady at 0.8 pounds per capita. The ready availability of coffee certainly affected rum sales. The switch also took place in Britain. In the early 1950s the average annual per person consumption of rum in the United Kingdom was 0.4 gallons, still a bit more than the Americans, who by 1968 drank one-tenth as much, or 0.04 gallons. Quite a drop from the 4.2 gallons their forefathers drank in 1770.

But rum had already played its seminal part in the industrialization of the thirteen colonies. And this "comfort water" had done some significant comforting indeed, as McCusker tells us. First there was the economic dimension. The distilling of rum in the continental colonies created a manufacturing industry second only to the shipping complex as an employer of local capital, managerial talent, and labor. Steadily in demand, rum and molasses served the colonial economy almost as a currency. The trade in rum helped the continental colonies to be, in the words of one disgruntled British West Indian sugar planter, "what the Southern [Colonies, the West Indies,] are falsely said to be, very rich." And, of course, there was the sheer pleasure of it all: "Rum by any name pleased the palates of men. As punch it softened the harshness of a Caribbean summer. As grog it made shipboard life more bearable for the sailor. As straight rum it took the edge off the cold environment of the continental farmer or lumberjack and warmed and nourished the Grand Banks fisherman. There can be little argument that rum helped in the conquest of North America."[32]

So, in the final analysis it did not matter that Winston Churchill once felt compelled to describe the Royal Navy as a sad trilogy of "rum, sodomy and the lash!" Rum—albeit in smaller amounts—was here to stay. For one, it continued to be a steady comfort to British blue-jackets until 1970 when new shipboard electronics required more brains than brawn. The U.S. armed forces had succumbed to prohibitionist pressures even earlier: in 1901 the army forbade the sale of alcohol on its posts, and in 1914 the navy stopped the ration of rum and banned all liquor from its ships. Interestingly enough, the Indian army did not abolish the ration of rum until political independence and the admission of abstemious Muslims to its national ranks.

It is ironic that the North American preference for rum began to decline just as there was a major technological revolution in its distilling. While the pot still continued and continues to be used, in 1830 an Irish coppersmith called Aeneas Coffey patented the "continuous" or "column" still. It was composed of two rectangular columns made of Kauri pine with copper plates between each section. This Coffey still allowed the distiller to separate the various vapor fractions thus enabling the manufacture, from similar raw materials, of light-, medium-, or strong-flavored rums. These continuous stills are now standard equipment everywhere even though, as is to be expected, they have been considerably improved by the addition of stainless steel, new air-cooled condensers, and modern carbon filters.

Aside from the changing patterns of consumption and preference, in the twentieth century, rum also had to confront what can only be called revolutionary challenges. One, Prohibition, was moralistic, the other, the Cuban Revolution, was socialistic. As we shall see, rum overcame both.

RUM AND U.S. PROHIBITION

Despite its long association with the growth and development of the American colonies, rum's status as a prestige drink had not been fully achieved. No matter how much of it the elite consumed, it was still identified with the *hoi polloi*. During the early years of the twentieth century, the *hoi polloi* referred to the new Irish and Mediterranean immigrants. As America drifted toward the intolerant years of Prohibition (1920–33), rum truly became the "Devil" or "Demon" spirit and was associated with what nativist Prohibitionists called "Rum, Rebellion, and Romanism." Prohibition was supported by Republicans and southern Democrats from rural America. It was the latter who repeatedly attempted to impose their rural asceticism on the growing immigrant populations of urban America. This is why nativism and prohibition went hand-in-hand. As Seymour Martin Lipset has noted, "To the ascetic small-town Protestants, these cities represented drunkenness, immorality, political corruption and cosmopolitanism."[33] Not surprisingly, one of the driving fears behind the prohibitionist Anti-Saloon League's push for the Eighteenth Amendment was their anticipation that the reapportionment of congressional seats due in 1920 would bring "forty new wet Congressmen" from "the great wet centers with their rapidly increasing population."[34] Be that as it may, the fact is that Prohibition represented the first revolutionary attempt to dispatch "demon rum" to the netherworld.

In order to understand the full dimensions of Prohibition, it might be useful to cite the words of the Eighteenth Amendment to the United States Constitution as adopted in 1919:

SECTION 1. Prohibition of Intoxicating Liquors
After one year from the ratification of this article the manufacture, sale, or transportation of intoxicating liquors within, the importation thereof into,

or the exportation thereof from the United States and all territory subject
to the jurisdiction thereof for beverage purposes is hereby prohibited.

SECTION 2. Enforcement
The Congress and the several States shall have concurrent power to
enforce this article by appropriate legislation.

This blanket legal prohibition lasted until 1933 when it was repealed by the
Twenty-first Amendment though individual states could, and did, continue
to "prohibit," that is, remain "dry." Fortunately for rum producers and rum
aficionados alike, as in the past, economic consideration would trump ascetic
morality in American society. As Lipset puts it, "Depression provided the death
blow for prohibition; repeal was regarded as a measure that would help spur
business and increase employment."[35] Left unsaid was the fact that it was
Prohibition that spawned the explosion in organized crime in the United
States—organizations that are alive and well to this day.

In the Caribbean, the impact of Prohibition varied with the distance between
the producer and the American market. Distant producers such as British
Guiana and the eastern Caribbean, including Trinidad, did not fare well. Closer
islands such as Cuba and the Dominican Republic, and the "bridges" such
as the Bahamas and British Honduras (now Belize) benefited. Geographical
proximity to the United States allowed smugglers, known as "rum runners,"
to smuggle not only rum but to benefit from the even larger trade in Scotch.
The fact is that "rum runners" carried more Scotch than rum. Prohibition in
the United States not only brought that British industry out of the depression it
was in in 1920 but made it boom. Imports of Scotch into the Bahamas (a British territory) went from 25,000 gallons in 1920 to nearly 6 million in 1930. In
fact, the "Cutty Sark" brand was specifically developed for this illegal but wildly
popular trade.[36] One can only surmise that there was little romantic glamour
and mileage to be gained from calling the smugglers "Scotch runners."

In all this, Cuba was particularly fortunate because it also picked up most of
the tourist trade. Alec Waugh recorded the different impact of abstention on
the tourist trade in the Caribbean and warned quite accurately that "a West Indian island that did not offer its visitors the opportunity of resisting the midday
heat with the cool, mellow and fragrant sustenance of a rum punch, stood little
chance of attracting tourist trade."[37] Given its size and general wealth, a large
assortment of American businessmen, engineers, soldiers, gangsters, and famous writers all began to turn Havana into a lively entertainment center and
with that came the drinking and promotion of new exotic rum-based cocktails
such as the daiquiri, the "mojito," and the "Cuba Libre."

Puerto Rico's fate was dramatically different from Cuba's. It was not merely the regulations about aging and packaging imposed on Puerto Rico, from which the Cubans were exempt; it was a matter of rum against self-rule. Given the ongoing struggle to expand the areas of self-government under U.S. colonial rule, that process was held hostage by the forces of Prohibition. The implications, says Arturo Morales Carrión, were clear: "[I]f Puerto Rico wanted a larger dose of self-government, the price was to do away with rum-drinking. Rum and home rule could not go together." What a strange irony, noted Morales Carrión, that now suddenly "[r]um . . . was the enemy of Caucasian constitutionalism!"[38]

The irony went deeper in its convoluted logic: Puerto Ricans, who up to then had never been given the privilege of a referendum on their political status, were suddenly summoned to a plebiscite on rum in 1917. The ballot showed a choice between a rum bottle and a coconut. Since both home rule and even U.S. citizenship were perceived to hang in the balance, the people voted to expel rum from the island. Predictably, people of means had their rum and Scotch smuggled in from Jamaica and Cuba, the poor had only their now homemade *cañita*. Morales Carrión explained the cultural peculiarity of what Gordon K. Lewis (protesting the American censoring of "suggestive" rum ads on the island) called "the vagaries of the American puritan conscience"[39] as follows: "The rum revenues were lost, but not the taste for rum or whisky. Prohibition became more than a social farce; it became a cultural aberration. It also left its imprint on local folklore. When someone had been fooled, it used to be said that he had been given coconut milk!"[40] One of the manufacturers who gave up distilling was the Edmundo B. Fernández firm that had been producing Ron del Barrilito since 1880.

Once Prohibition was lifted, it was the Puerto Rican rum manufacturers who were best positioned to enter the U.S. market. Not without ferocious competition from the Cuban and American rum distillers who, according to the last American governor in Puerto Rico, Rexford Tugwell (1941–46), had powerful lobbies in Washington.[41] This explains why the Serrallés family, who owned a major sugar estate in the south of the island and whose pot still began making "Ron Don Q" in 1865, objected to the entry of the Cuban Bacardís into Puerto Rico. A legal battle royal ensued and was litigated all the way to the U.S. Supreme Court, where, in 1936, the Bacardís won the right to operate a distillery on the island. The Cubans were now permanently in Puerto Rico and better, in the U.S. market, duty free. All this just before World War II when German U-boats, German territorial conquests, and shortages of shipping space made it impossible for Americans to import European liquors.

Then came the Roosevelt-Churchill exchange of forty-four U.S. destroyers for fourteen British bases in the Caribbean, sending thousands of GI's to the rum-producing islands. It was a profitable exchange all around. Anyone old enough to remember the Andrews Sisters singing a Trinidad calypso called "Rum and Coca Cola" will know that neither law nor religion could stop rum from becoming the Yankee's wartime "comfort water." This habit was brought back to the mainland, just in time to take advantage of the postwar tourist boom in Miami and Havana, which helped create a great rum industry in Cuba. However, the dark clouds of the second revolution were on the horizon for these Cuban rum families.

RUM AND THE CUBAN REVOLUTION

Cubans, despite having fought two brutal wars against Spain, still love their *madre patria*. So, when a Spanish authority on stocking a bar said, "the best rum, the rum of Cuba!"[42] Cubans relished the supreme compliment. To Cubans, rum is a matter of national pride, not of ideology. A scholar of the exiled Bacardí family writes unabashedly that Cuba early on produced "a more refined rum" than any of its Caribbean neighbors.[43] Similar pride—and similar absence of nuance about taste—is expressed by an expert who stayed with the revolution. "In truth," says this revolutionary, "there has never been nor could there ever have been at any time in history, or in any other country, a rum equal to ours. Not even close."[44] And, in an evident moment of exuberance, he exclaims, "Cuba: your virile rum bathes you." Cubans, and all Caribbean rum boosters should always keep in mind the Spanish saying, "There is no accounting for taste!"

Clearly, the association of rum with tropical eroticism is not exclusively Cuban. But Cuba had the artists and poets who could laud their product like few others in the region. Listen to the celebrated Afro-Cuban poet, Nicolás Guillén: "I am going to drink you in one gulp . . . like a glass of rum."[45] Given this passion for their national drink, one can fully understand the hurt of Cuba's historical and original rum-producing families upon having their estates confiscated by the Cuban revolutionary government in September 1960. Insult is certainly added to injury when a new revolutionary manager of the oldest major distillery (Bacardí, established in 1862) is quoted as saying that the Bacardís lost all knowledge of making good rum when they left Cuba, because they lost the aging facilities and the people, the best rum production men. The people with the experience, he says, didn't leave Cuba. "Rum production," according to this Cuban, "is associated with our nationality. We kept the talent, and we reorganized the rum production under the direction of the people. It was easy to take over rum production after these people left the country." He did tell the truth when he admitted that rum production was not a secret.[46] What he failed to mention was that marketing, if not precisely a secret, was a very definite skill. This, the Bacardí family took with them.

It was, of course, impossible for that Cuban rum-making family to know just how prescient its decision to diversify out of Cuba and into Mexico and Puerto Rico in the 1930s had been. In 1960, when Fidel Castro expropriated their distillery in Santiago de Cuba, they already had the world's single largest distillery in Cataño, Puerto Rico, and 450 active members of this rum-making dynasty were ready to make this business the most successful Latin American multinational corporation ever.

Crucial to Bacardí's survival and expansion has been the legal war over the Bacardí brand name. When revolutionary Cuba began to ship rum distilled in the confiscated factories under the label "Compañía Ron Bacardí Nacionalizada," the company's lawyers made sure they entered not a single port. That particular label is now one for the history books.

Proving that not even revolutionary governments can escape the impact of globalization, in 1993 the Cuban government entered into a joint venture with the French giant, Pernod-Ricard. Taking advantage of the fact that the Cuban government had registered the brand name Havana Club in the United States of America in 1976, the Cuban-French enterprise was in business. There is, of course, a story, both commercial and human, behind Havana Club. The label originally belonged to the José Arechabala family in Cuba, which sold rum under that label from 1930 until its property was confiscated in 1960. Unfortunately for them, and as distinct from the Bacardís, they let their U.S. registration expire. Cuba picked it up. In 1996 the Bacardí Company "purchased" (word is in dispute) the brand name from the exiled Arechabalas and attempted to market it. Now it was the Cuban government, with French and European Union support, that sued Bacardí for trademark infringement. The World Trade Organization finally judged that the United States of America could establish its own trademark rules at home. Havana Club cannot be sold in the United States of America.

Over the years in exile, the Bacardís have not been idle; they have energetically joined in the worldwide trend toward diversification and merging. This is what had been occurring in Trinidad. In 1973, Angostura Ltd. (Royal Oak) of Trinidad bought out Fernández Distillers Ltd. (of Vat 19 fame), and then sold a 40 percent interest in the company to Bacardí. The idea was to modernize and augment Angostura's distilling capacity and increase its exports. The sale did both without any negative effects on quality for the simple reason that Angostura's pride in its products (which includes famously Angostura Bitters) dovetailed nicely with Bacardí's historical insistence on uniform quality control. Bacardí's establishment in the Bahamas is equipped and geared toward maintaining quality throughout its worldwide distilleries. As Bacardí acquisitions went, the Trinidad deal was rather small. The big step came in 1993 when Bacardí acquired the Italian company Martini-Rossi for U.S.$1.4 billion. They also bought their way into the lucrative markets for tequila (Cazadores, Camino Real), Scotch (Dewar), gin (Bombay), brandy, liqueurs, beer, and aperitifs. By 2004 Bacardí rums were the top-selling brand in the United States. This appeared not to be enough; further diversification was to come since it was an industry-wide tenet that a bigger mix of liquors was crucial for competing in the global market. The one liquor missing in the Bacardí portfolio was vodka, a spirit that was growing by 25 percent annually compared with rum's annual growth of 5 percent. This explains why Bacardí paid a reported $2 billion for the French vodka Grey Goose, which controlled half the market for high-end vodka.[47]

Again, as another way of confronting the increased globalization of the liquor industry, the Bacardí-Martini Corporation is registered in Bermuda, a major international tax haven. By the end of the twentieth century, the company had 170 brands earning revenues of $3 billion, 6,000 employees working in Puerto Rico (where it was the largest corporate taxpayer), the Bahamas, and India. An opening of the China market for rum makes their India distillery a key player. It exported both bottled and bulk rum. Clearly, Bacardí has shown that it can survive and prosper in the new global arena of mergers and super companies, a world of aggressive competitiveness. Since it is no longer merely a niche company, the next logical step will be to go public in some form.

No one should believe that what Calvo Ospina calls the "rum war" between Cuba and the Bacardís is over. The success of the Cuban-Pernod Havana Club and its importance to the booming Cuban tourist industry guarantee that it is not over. Demonstrating the importance of rum to its all-important tourist industry, Cuba has now built a "rum museum" to promote Havana Club, and it is said to have been visited by some 150,000 tourists in 2003. Although Havana Club has only 1 percent of the market, compared with Bacardí's 25 percent, its sales are growing faster than the exiled brand. With important markets in Spain and Germany, it is growing 9 percent a year. In 2003 it sold 2 million cases; Bacardí sold 36 million. It has also been earning awards, which, as we shall note, may or may not say much. In many ways this "rum war" is a harbinger of the thousands of claims and counterclaims that might make any future transition in Cuba a most turbulent process. All these cases illustrate what Calvo Ospina calls the "famous conundrum," which he poses as an evident rhetorical question: "Who is the father? The man who sired the child only to desert it or the man who reared it?"[48] It will all depend on how the courts define "desertion." If a state confiscates a child, has the parent deserted it? According to *Forbes Magazine*, March 1, 2004, Pernod splits a $40 million a year profit with Cuba. While this makes it the fourth biggest national product contributor of hard currency after mining, tobacco, and fishing, it is a drop in the bucket compared with the $3.3 billion earned by Bacardí in 2003.

In the final analysis, therefore, it is evident that what the Cuban confiscations of 1960 did was to delay the marketing of good Cuban rums by four decades while stimulating the expansion and diversification of the Bacardí Company. As the colonists of North America and the planters of the West Indies understood centuries ago, rum represents both fixed and liquid assets, and the latter can be highly mobile. Today, the outsourcing of molasses makes virtually every aspect of the industry, including the "fixed" ones, mobile. As we shall see, what globalization has done is to elevate further the importance of marketing and diversification, which, more often than not, involves taking on a big foreign partner. This is as true for the Cubans as it is for the rest of the Caribbean.

GLOBALIZATION AND THE MODERN RUM INDUSTRY

Although it is a bit fatuous to argue over which is the oldest rum in the Caribbean, no one would argue with the statement that Barbados's Mount Gay is among the oldest in continuous production. The claim is that it goes back to 1660 and certainly the company has written records going back to 1703. It is also a fact that it is among the few major types of rum owned by a nonwhite family, at least since the Wards bought it in 1918. Again, few in the insular Caribbean would dispute the claim that Mount Gay and Barbados are virtually synonymous. All of which explains why the Ward family's decision in 1980 to sell a 60 percent share of the company to its American distributors, Foremost-McKesson Inc., was considered of sufficient national concern as to warrant a mention in the island's Parliament. A touching tribute to a grand family and its great product, to be sure. But selling Mount Gay was hardly a revolutionary or unique act. Since time immemorial, rum manufacturers in the non-Hispanic Caribbean have searched for better deals, from local governments and/or private parties or from foreign interests. What modern globalization has done is accelerate the process, encouraged by the trend toward regional markets, each with their own regulations and terms of trade. Whether it is the European Union, NAFTA, or the future Free Trade Area of the Americas, the trend toward relocation, consolidation, and product diversification will continue apace. In addition, quickly shifting taste preferences will accelerate what is called the "carrousel" strategy: shifting brands and types of spirit according to public preferences. All, of course, made from the same cane juice or molasses.

Four cases illustrate this trend of globalization.[49] J. G. B. Siegert and Sons Ltd. of Trinidad has been producing Angostura Bitters, a secret formula of herbs added to 80 proof rum, since 1840. In 1949 it began producing rum as Trinidad Distillers Ltd. In 1960 the Siegert family sold the company to the Trinidad government that turned right around and sold it back to the family. The rationale was that Angostura Bitters was part of the "national patrimony" and should not be sold to foreigners. Despite that, in 1972, the Siegerts sold a 40 percent share to the Bacardís. The company then bought out one of the oldest manufacturers on the island, J. B. Fernández Distillers, whose brands—VAT 19 ("the spirit of Trinidad"), White Star (the "star" of the rum shop), and Black Label—were known to every GI based on the island in World War II and to every carnival celebrant since. Neither Angostura Bitters nor any of these brands are regarded as any less national because of the part foreign ownership.

The other case study shows globalization in all its complexity and, some would say, all its sleight-of-handedness. In late October 1981 the late Puerto Rican historian and fellow "groggist" Angel Calderón Cruz and I went to the town of Arecibo looking for the "new" Myers distillery. The *San Juan Star* of October 18, 1981, had related how Seagram, which had bought the venerable Jamaican dark rum Myers in early 1950, had also just bought the Puerto Rico Distillers of Arecibo and its well-known rum for export only, Ron Rico. Beginning in 1981, Seagram began to export a "made in Puerto Rico" light rum under the label, "World Famous Myers's Rum." It was, said its advertising, a notch above the other Puerto Rican rums.

Well, we did find the distillery and it was hardly new. It was producing the new Myers light rum in the same stainless steel continuous columns with the same rectification plates and aged in the same barrels that had always, and continued to, produce Ron Rico. Both followed Puerto Rican regulations as to aging (two years minimum) and other aspects of production. What was the difference, we asked the plant manager. That, said the employee predictably, was a "company secret." Not so secret was that that single distillery in Arecibo also produced the following rums for local consumption: Granado, Palo Viejo, and Ron Llave. Also produced were the following gins: Calvert's (gin and vodka), Wolfschmidt, Nikolai, and Crown Russe. As if that were not enough from one plant, they also produced Cinzano red vermouth, Bourget liquors, and 4 million gallons of 190 proof neutral spirits for the pharmaceutical industry, for cocktail mixes, and for export to Norway for aquavit. The versatility of cane alcohol had found its maximum expression at the Arecibo plant!

Not surprisingly, Seagram soon had to drop its claim that it was producing a Puerto Rican rum of "Jamaican quality." One of the distillers complaining the loudest about the Seagram strategies was Serrallés. Two years later the Serrallés stopped complaining, and the family sold its business to Seagram. Puerto Rico now had only two distillers, Bacardí in Cataño and Seagram in Arecibo. The process did not end there, however. Seagram went on the market and, after a ferocious bidding war, the giant U.K. spirits merchant, Diageo PLC, outbid Bacardí giving Diageo all the rums made in Puerto Rico except for Bacardí. Diageo made two immediate changes: it stopped marketing Myers Puerto Rico and began shipping Ron Rico in bulk to the United States, where it was bottled and marketed by Jim Beam Brands.

Another good example of globalization is what we might call the "Allied" and "Domecq" story. In 1987, Allied-Lyons of the United Kingdom bought Hiram Walker and Company. With that purchase came the 30 percent stake in the Spanish firm Pedro Domecq that Hiram Walker owned. In 1994 Allied-Lyons convinced the conservative, 500-member-strong Pedro Domecq family to sell for U.S.$1.1 billion. Allied Domecq had every conceivable spirit among its stock, except rum. That was changed in 2002 through a deal with Diageo. As part of a U.S.$845 million deal to acquire Diageo's best-selling rum, Malibu, Allied Domecq (which also owns French champagne brands G. H. Mumm and Perrier-Jouet) also acquired the California sparkling-wine producer, Mumm Cuvée Napa. Part of the purpose was to give worldwide unity to the Mumm trademark.[50] The interesting thing is that Malibu (a flavored rum) is produced in Barbados by West India Rum distillery that also produces the excellent Cockspur as well as exporting bulk rum. Malibu sold 30 million bottles in 2002, much of it in France. As the stories of Mount Gay and Malibu demonstrate, globalization trends had reached Barbados in a big way. The upshot of all this globalization is that today rums are a major part of the liquor portfolios of the four top worldwide makers and distributors of distilled spirits. They are, in descending order by million of nine-liter cases sold in 2003, Diageo (92), Pernod-Ricard (54), Allied Domecq (48), Bacardí (36).[51]

The same process is occurring everywhere in the Caribbean. Take the case of what the island locals like to call the *capitale mondiale de rhum*, Martinique. On that island there is a pride so pronounced that one of its brands has advertised as follows for the past 100 years:

Le meilleur Rhum du Monde est le Rhum des Antilles.
Le meilleur Rhum des Antilles es le Rhum de la Martinique.
Le meilleur Rhum de la Martinique est Le Rhum Clement.
(The best rum of the world is the rum of the Antilles.
The best rum of the Antilles is the rum from Martinique.
The best rum from Martinique is Clement rum.)

Rhum Clement is now owned by the Rothschilds. The Rothschilds also own "CSR"—Cane Spirit Rothschild—in St. Kitts. Although the CSR label does not mention the word rum, preferring to call it a "new cane spirit," it is in fact a white rum sold as a high-end spirit, beautifully bottled and boxed.

Few of the other rums in Martinique can chastise Clement over this foreign ownership, however. Notice how globalization has transformed the ownership of many of the formerly family-owned rums:

Group La Martiniquaise: Dillon and Depaz
Societe-Cointreau: St. James and Balley
Marie Brizard: La Mauny
Delices d'Outre Mer: Neisson
Martini and Rossi: Duquesne and Trois Rivieres

Martinique exports 65 percent of its production to France and only 5 percent elsewhere. The remaining 30 percent is consumed locally, 90 percent of it as white rum. Anyone seeking out a family-owned rum on the island should go to that which the islanders call the *Doyen des rhumiers martiniquais*, André Dormoy's brands La Favorite and Courville, which enjoy the greatest local sales.[52]

Our fourth and final case will illustrate the impact of globalization. While shopping recently at an Albertson Super Market liquor store in Florida, I came across an 80 proof, light amber rum called Ron Vicaro. The label said it was "Barbados Rum," and that it was "traditionally distilled using a time-tested recipe." It also claimed to be "charcoal filtered." This would describe a Barbados rum. I was surprised first of all that this Barbados rum had a Spanish name. I was further perplexed when the store manager informed me that it is an exclusive Albertson label distributed by Fleetwood Distilling Products of Mira Loma, California. All a search on both Google and Arhnet threw out under Fleetwood was that it was a "home brewing, wine making and distilling operation." I later discovered that Albertson also carried a brand called simply Imported Rum, said to be from the Virgin Islands, also distilled in Loma Linda by a Leveque Corporation. Additionally, I discovered that Whaler rum is also "prepared and bottled" in Loma Linda. My question is: is Loma Linda, California, becoming some sort of new center of the globalized rum trade? Despite the fact that none of these rums was particularly memorable, I am sure that, given the strategies of "shelf location" and modest price, they probably will be money-makers for Albertson.

What do these "Barbados" and "Virgin Islands" rums, distributed from California as an exclusive brand of one food chain, tell us about the impact of globalization on the rum scene? Three points about the impact of globalization.

Point 1: Despite the fact that world sugar production and consumption grew by 57 percent and 63 percent respectively over the past eighteen years, table 4 shows how that production has shifted geographically. The Caribbean, where the industrial production of sugar began, is fading fast: from 11 percent of production and 29 percent of world exports in 1984–85 to 3 percent and 7 percent respectively in 2002–3. The decline is across the board but led most poignantly by Cuba. Figure 1 tells the dramatic story of the decline of Cuba and the rise of the new "star" of the Southern Hemisphere on the world cane sugar market, Brazil. During a recent trip to Martinique, I noticed that the packaged sugar on the tables at cafés was Brazilian. Brazil's production of sugar has increased by 144 percent since 1984–85. In Central America, it is Guatemala that is increasing its production and export of raw sugar and, as we will see, distilling and exporting top-quality rums.

A key question is, with every island in the Caribbean promoting "its" rum, but with dramatically declining sugarcane production, where is the raw material coming from? To tour Barbados, for example, is to visit golf courses where sugar grass once swayed in the breeze as far as the eye could see. In 1970 there were seventeen sugar and molasses factories operating; by 2004 there were only two. Barbados's foremost authority on the industry predicts that by 2005 there will be only one.[53] Even now Barbados is importing molasses for its expanding rum industry. There is one sugar factory left in Trinidad, and the one in St. Kitts will soon stop grinding cane. In Martinique subsidized bananas and pineapples grow where cane once did. And so it goes throughout the region, including Puerto Rico, which receives special mention shortly. Understand that with the exceptions of those in Brazil, Cuba, Australia, Guyana, Guatemala, Jamaica, the Dominican Republic, and a few others, most distillers have to import their molasses.

Can you call a Virgin Island rum made from Australian, Brazilian, or Do-

TABLE 4. World Exports of Raw Sugar

	1984–85	1989–90	1994–95	1999–2000	2002–3
North America	82	170	—	83	80
Caribbean	8,372	7,845	3,208	3,978	2,975
Central America	740	935	1,345	1,747	1,798
South America	4,350	1,738	2,644	8,500	11,003
Western Europe	33	—	—	2	2
Eastern Europe	288	—	8	46	20
Africa	2,172	2,103	1,575	2,409	2,725
Asia and Oceania	5,894	5,668	8,676	7,027	7,056
Middle East	470	—	—	—	—
Total	22,401	18,459	17,456	23,792	25,659

Source: U.S. Department of Agriculture at <www.usda.gov/htp/sugar>.

minican molasses "Virgin Island" rum? Yes, if the aging in casks and the blending is done in the Virgin Islands, no if the rum is imported in fiberglass containers and then merely bottled and labeled locally. For instance, in Carriacou (Grenada Grenadines) there is a strong rum islanders and sailors swear by, Jack Iron. The only thing Carriacou about it is the label. It is Trinidad white rum, 90 to 170 proof. I personally witnessed the same marketing sleight-of-hand in two major Grenadian "distilleries," which delicacy constrains me from mentioning. The point is that there is such a thing as Puerto Rican rum even though the island has gone from having 392,000 acres under sugar in 1952 to growing not one stalk of sugarcane four decades later. So where do the distilleries owned by Diageo and Bacardí, together the world's largest producers of aged rums, get their molasses? From the Central La Romana in the Dominican Republic.[54] La Romana even supplies the justly famous Ron del Barrilito (Two and Three Stars) since it receives its distillate from the Bacardí plant. The crucial thing is that the aging and blending of the 12,000 cases Fernández produces each year is done on its own premises and according to its own historical formula. The latter makes it a Puerto Rican rum.[55] The La Romana story contains another historical irony: that supplier of the raw materials of so many Caribbean rums is now owned by the Fanjul family, whose sugar estates were also confiscated in Cuba in 1960. The family migrated to Florida where its estates account for half the sugar produced in that state in 2002.

Point 2. It is an ages-old piece of wisdom that one of the best ways to insure

FIGURE 1. Sugar Exports from Brazil and Cuba, 1984–1985 to 2002–2003

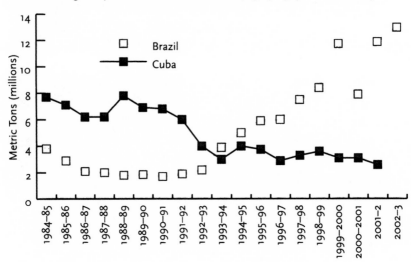

Source: U.S. Department of Agriculture at <www.usda.gov/htp/sugar>.

that the spirits have not been diluted or otherwise adulterated (such as "aging" with white oak chips rather than in casks) is to bottle, cork, and seal it at the source, that is, at the original distillery. The French labels with the claims of *Mise en Bouteille au Domaine* or *Appellation d'Origine Contrôlée* are assurances of that. What controls are there when spirits are bulk-shipped across the globe for distribution by agencies with no history in the rum business, as it has been known for hundreds of years? Bacardí maintains this control, but is this a universal practice? The following case illustrates the fact that strange things can occur around bulk shipping. On June 17, 1985, the *Jamaican Gleaner* carried the following headline: "Rum Shipment Sabotaged. Thousands of Gallons Replaced by Sea Water." It was thought not to be the first time this occurred. One can only wonder who received the diluted rum at the other end and hope that it received no "distinction" at some *concourse*.

Point 3. Finally, Caribbean people better come to grips with the consequences of globalization on the rum industry. They should keep four things in mind. First, sugarcane—as distinct from grapes—varies very little by type, soils, and climate as far as the making of molasses is concerned. Second, every distiller has access to the continuous still. Third, fermentation is hardly a secret process anymore. Fourth, since rum does not age in the bottle, aging in white oak casks is essential and everyone can buy these—the white oak "staves," "joints" and "heads," and the metal "hoops" for the making of "tight casks"—from Jack Daniels or Jim Beam or from Canada.[56] In short, there are really only two very key aspects of rum making: the aging in the white oak casks (preferably charred) and the blending of the rums. Without these casks for aging the spirit, there is no drinkable rum. A standard for aging is: white rum, one year; dark rum, three years; and anything over six years can qualify as an *añejo* or "aged" rum. The next step is the blending of rum of different ages, a process that provides the uniformity as well as the right to claim certain numbers of years of aging. This author had a rare glimpse into an island distillery's stock, which revealed 7,895 casks of under-three-year-old rum, which were valued at U.S.$3,000 per cask, but the eight casks of twenty-five-year-old rum were on the books at U.S.$125,000 each. It is in the blending of these rums that the art still lies.

These skills are no longer a Caribbean monopoly. There is a whole new generation of distinguished rums coming from long-established (but, until recently, hardly outstanding) distilleries in Venezuela, Colombia, Nicaragua, Panama, Guatemala, and even Australia. With the World Trade Organization demanding from the United States of America duty-free admission of all products and the European Union promising to drop all protective duties in the next few years, the Caribbean will be facing stiff competition from these rums as well as rums from the likes of the Philippines and Brazil. Make no mistake, the Brazilian sugarcane-derived *cachaça*, which the Puerto Rican rum lobby had successfully kept out of the U.S. rum market as a non-rum, is now taking full advantage of the situation: the Brazilian government has declared *cachaça* a generic name, and the success of its cocktail, the *caipirinha*, promises a bright future for that cane distillate. It could easily be renamed "rum" should a shift in demand take place.[57] After all, Brazil, which also produces and markets rum, had 650 sugar factories working as early as 1713, producing 3 million gallons of rum. Today Brazil is a major producer of molasses for the world's distilleries as well as for the over 500 brands of *cachaça* proudly displayed at its Museo da Cachaça in Rio de Janeiro. Not surprisingly, the world's largest producers and marketers of rum, Bacardí and Diageo (Seagram), are already in Brazil and poised to export moderately priced products to the U.S. and European markets.

CONCLUSION

With or without Cuba, the challenge facing the Caribbean is to develop a marketing strategy that highlights the quality and distinction of many of its rums. There are two aspects to this task. First, there is the aesthetic challenge:

moving away from the old stereotype of "rum and sweat," of elevating its prestige among the world's spirits. While the vast majority of Caribbean rum sales will continue to be of white rum, there is no reason why we cannot develop what the French describe as a capacity to *deguster sa liquor*—to sip and relish the rum. The Spanish call it *catar*: to examine, to taste with discrimination. As wonderful as the traditional Caribbean rum shop is for *bonhomie* and *camaraderie*, this is not where that product uplifting can take place.[58]

Unfortunately the effort to raise the prestige level of rum is not at all helped by the bewildering world of claims and outright public relations fluff. Take the recent case of Venezuelan claims. As noted, that country was very late (1954) in attempting to regulate for quality. Today Venezuela has created and patented a "Venezuelan Rum of Origin" label and its Alcohols Chamber supervises for quality. Brands such as Cacique and Pampero, owned by Diageo and representing 96 percent of Venezuelan rum exports, are making a big push for exports and thus for quality. The privately owned Santa Teresa rums are making similar efforts. Whatever their ultimate success in a crowded global rum market, the bragging has already started. Mexico, says the president of Santa Teresa, has its tequila, Cuba has its tobacco, Colombia has its coffee, and "Venezuela has three great products: oil, the most beautiful women in the world and the best rum in the world."[59]

Such claims are not unusual and illustrate the fact that the battle for distinction and recognition has reached truly confusing heights. Every country with a label is in the business and seeking recognition. In September 2003, the wire services carried the story that at the "Rum Festival Awards" in Canada, Guatemala's Zacapa Centenario 25 Years Old won "Best in the World." This is certainly a superb rum, and its increasing popularity in the United States of America and elsewhere is richly deserved. But, that same month, *Consumer* magazine declared Guyana's El Dorado 15 Years Old "World's Best." The Chicago Beverage Tasting Institute went even further, declaring it "The Best Spirit of 2001." But wait now (as West Indians say), the label of Virgin Island Cruzan Single Barrel Estate Rum (no age indicated) carries the claim "World's Best Rum 2000." This was awarded by the San Francisco World Spirit Competition. But the well-established London International Wine and Spirit Show awarded Australia's Beenleigh Rum the "World's Best." You have to have better than 20/20 vision to read the "1995" on the label. It is important because from 1998 to 2003 this London show awarded Guyana's El Dorado 15 Years Old the "Best Rum Worldwide" award. But not even this prestigious London "competition" helps the consumer make a choice. For seven out of the past ten years, it has judged El Dorado 12 Years Old "Best Spirit of the Caribbean." Isn't the "best of the world" inclusive of the Caribbean? Which El Dorado should I buy, 15 Years Old or the less expensive 12 Years Old?

There appears to be no end to *grand concours*: the Chicago Rum Tasting Institute, the Newfoundland Rum Festival, the New York "Rumfest USA," and the "Spirit of the Caribbean," held until recently in Saint Martin. Several questions have to be asked if these competitions are to be taken seriously and so contribute to standards and quality. First, who is competing? How do these "Best in the World" winners, for instance, compare with Trinidad's Angostura 1824, a 12-year-old, or Nicaragua's Ron Centenario Flor de Caña, a 21-year-old, or the equally old Appleton Anniversary (of which only 6,000 bottles were put on sale), or, from the French *rhum agricole* or *taffia* side, Barbancourt Reserve du Domaine, aged for 15 years in Limousin vats, or, indeed, the 33-year-old Martinican La Favorite (also a Gold Medal winner somewhere), as mellow and silky smooth as any distilled spirit on the market? Second, are the rums available for competition taken off the shelf or provided by the distiller? And, third, there is the matter of price: do you have to pay the considerable amounts these "anniversary" rums cost to enjoy a rum of extraordinary color, bouquet, and flavor? Absolutely not. Puerto Rico's Ron del Barrilito Three Stars is proof that you don't have to go bankrupt. The medals represented on its label (from competitions in Charleston and Buffalo) were certainly well earned. It is still family-owned and still the Puerto Rican connoisseur's choice.

So how is a discriminating Caribbean rum *catador* not only to decide what to believe and buy but how to promote his region's best? First, decide how you intend to use your rum. If mixed with colas, no need to pay a fortune, and it matters little if the rum is white or amber. If it's dark, a "Demerara-type," the molasses will make your mixed drink extra sweet and extra heavy on the calories. If, on the other hand, you like your rum neat or on the rocks or mixed with a little water or club soda, age does make an enormous difference. But, here again, beware of the new highfalutin and, in many cases, unreal language being used to describe a rum. A rum connoisseur is certainly entitled to provide nuanced descriptions of different rums, as do Luis Ayala and Julie Arkell in their useful books. But careful with the advertising hype. First thing to do is to read up on the history of the product. This will direct you to rums that have resisted the wear and tear of time and, especially, of globalization. Follow this by using your own palate and submit the rums to what is still the golden standard, which consists of four "tests":

1. Color. The longer in the cask, the more amber the spirit unless
   colored with caramel. This is a matter of taste. In Martinique, 90

percent of the rum consumed is white (*blanc*). This is the basis of the *ti ponche* or appetizer common to all Martinican tables.

2. Nose. The bouquet or aroma that you can detect right after a bottle has been opened or the rum poured in a glass. Aged rums should be served in a snifter like any brandy or Cognac.

3. Smoothness. Smoothness in the mouth and on the tongue. No harshness or raw alcohol-like flavors that burn rather than caress the palate.

4. Afterglow or finish. This is the aftertaste upon swallowing. If you have tested the "nose" and the "smoothness" appropriately, this afterglow should be a rewarding experience to all parts of the mouth and throat, thanking you for the smooth, silky, and glowingly warm feeling.

As the industry responds to globalization by consolidating in fewer and fewer hands, there is a real need for those who know the history of rum to demand quality and refinement in the product and not just in the advertising and promoting of it. While it is and always will be a part of a mass industry called tourism, there is no need for discerning individuals to lose their sense of discrimination and good taste.

NOTES

1. Barty-King and Massel, *Rum, Yesterday and Today*, 6.
2. Antonio Herrera y Tordesillas cited in Luis Rodríguez, *Los paisajes geohistóricos cañeros*, 20.
3. Ibid., 86.
4. See Hernández Palomo, *El aguardiente de caña en México*, 113.
5. Dauxion-Lavaysse, *Description of Venezuela*, 110.
6. Juan and Ulloa, *A Voyage to South America*, 34.
7. Hearn, *Two Years in the French West Indies*, 307.
8. Luis Rodríguez, *Los paisajes geohistóricos cañeros*, 128–29.
9. Ibid., 138, 152.
10. Moreno Fraginals, *El ingenio*, 1:245.
11. Ibid., 3:154.
12. Ely, *Cuando reinaba su majestad*, 506.
13. Chez Checo, *El ron en la historia dominicana*, 1:195ff.
14. Ramos Mattei, *La hacienda azucarera*, 85.
15. Smith, *An Inquiry into the Nature and Causes of the Wealth of Nations*, 1:173–75.
16. Dauxion-Lavaysse, *Description of Venezuela*, 335.
17. Arkell, *Classic Rum*, 12.
18. Moreno Fraginals, *El ingenio*, 1:244.

19. Barty-King and Massel, *Rum, Yesterday and Today*, 70.

20. James Pack explains the origins of the word "grog." In 1731 Admiral Edward Vernon began mixing the half pint of rum ration with water, sugar, and lime. Because he wore a waterproof boat-cloak known as a "grog," he was given the name "Old Grogram." Grog became part of the English vocabulary. See Pack, *Nelson's Blood*, 21.

21. Cited in Harlow, *Colonizing Expeditions*, 44.

22. Barty-King and Massel, *Rum, Yesterday and Today*, 19.

23. McCusker, *Rum and the American Revolution*, 1:199, 219.

24. Pares, *A West-India Fortune*, 125.

25. McCusker, *Rum and the American Revolution*, 1:446.

26. McCullough, *John Adams*, 81.

27. Pares, *A West-India Fortune*, 10.

28. McCusker, *Rum and the American Revolution*, 1:434.

29. Rorabaugh, *The Alcoholic Republic*, 30.

30. Joseph John Gurney, "A Winter in the West Indies," cited in Waugh, *A Family of Islands*, 248–49.

31. McCusker, *Rum and the American Revolution*, 1:447–48.

32. Ibid., 477, 538.

33. Lipset, *The First New Nation*, 390.

34. Odegard, *Pressure Politics*, 173.

35. Lipset, *The First New Nation*, 392.

36. Ensign, *Intelligence in the Rum War at Sea*.

37. Waugh, *A Family of Islands*, 333.

38. Morales Carrión, *Puerto Rico: A Political and Cultural History*, 195.

39. G. Lewis, *Puerto Rico: Freedom and Power in the Caribbean*, 205.

40. Morales Carrión, *Puerto Rico: A Political and Cultural History*, 202.

41. Tugwell, *The Stricken Land: The Story of Puerto Rico*, especially 424.

42. Quoted in Campoamor, *El hijo alegre de la caña de azúcar*, 88.

43. P. Foster, *Family Spirits*, 8.

44. Campoamor, *El hijo alegre de la caña de azúcar*, 88.

45. Quoted in ibid., 80.

46. Quoted in P. Foster, *Family Spirits*, 254.

47. *Wall Street Journal*, June 18, 2004, B-5.

48. Calvo Ospina, *Bacardí, the Hidden War*, 85.

49. All the cases cited here are drawn from the author's three decades of field research on Caribbean rums.

50. *Wine Spectator*, May 15, 2002, 16.

51. Bank of America Securities cited in the *Wall Street Journal*, June 18, 2004, B-5.

52. Camard-Hayott and Laguarigue, *Martinique: Terre de rhum*.

53. Interview with The Honorable Keith Laurie, Bridgetown, Barbados, February 10, 2004.

54. Sincere thanks to Humberto García-Muñiz of the University of Puerto Rico for the many years of sharing his impressive knowledge of sugar estates in the region.

55. See Rivera Marrero, "Tradición artesanal en la elaboración de ron," 128.

56. For the fascinating history of the art of cooperage, see Hankerson, *The Cooperage Handbook*.

57. Cachaça is also called "aguardente de cana" in Brazil. Brazilians (like the French and Haitians) distill it straight from the cane juice, and the expensive ones are aged in oak casks. A six-year-old Anniversary "Ypioca" from the state of Ceará has the distinct "nose" of the cachaça but settles smoothly and finishes as splendidly as the best aged rum.

58. For a wonderful account of the crucial (but sadly vanishing) role played by the rum shop, see Laurie, *The Barbados Rum Shop*.

59. Ramírez, "Venezuelan Rums Aim to Be Toast of World's Tipplers," *Forbes*, May 31, 2004, 2.

Bibliography

Alcántara, Virgilio, ed. *Mujeres dominicanas: De la sombra a la luz*. Santo Domingo: Secretaría de la Mujer, 2000.

Allen, Ray, and Lois Wilcken, eds. *Island Sounds in the Global City: Caribbean Popular Music and Identity in New York*. New York: Institute for Studies in American Music, Brooklyn College, 1998.

Almanaque Escuela Radio Santa María. Dominican Republic.

AlterPresse. "BID/Haiti: Reprise de la cooperation." Port-au-Prince, July 3, 2003. <http://www.medialternatif.org/alterpresse/>.

Alvarez, Julia. *In the Time of the Butterflies*. New York: Plume, 1995.

Amnesty International. "Haiti: Chamblain and Joanis Overnight Trials Are an Insult to Justice." London, August 16, 2004. <www.amnesty.org>.

Appadurai, Arjun. *The Social Life of Things: Commodities in Cultural Perspective*. Cambridge: Cambridge University Press, 1986.

———. "Why Public Culture?" *Public Culture* 1.1 (1989): 5–9.

———. "Disjuncture and Difference in the Global Cultural Economy." *Public Culture* 2.2 (1990): 1–24.

———. *Modernity at Large: Cultural Dimensions of Globalization*. Minneapolis: University of Minnesota Press, 1996.

Aquino García, Miguel. *Tres heroínas y un tirano*. Santo Domingo: Corripio, 1996.

Arkell, Julie. *Classic Rum*. London: Prion, 1999.

Arrieta Vilá, Rubén. "De todo un poco." *El Nuevo Día*, March 12, 2001, 93.

Arthur, Charles. "Raising the States: Haiti between Mayhem and Decertification." *NACLA Report on the Americas* 35.1 (July–August 2001): 42–43.

Austerlitz, Paul. "From Transplant to Transnational Circuit: Merengue in New York." In *Island Sounds in the Global City: Caribbean Popular Music and Identity in New York*, ed. Ray Allen and Lois Wilcken, 44–60. Brooklyn: Institute for Studies in American Music, Brooklyn College, 1998.

Averill, Gage. "Moving the Big Apple: Tabou Combo's Diasporic Dreams." In *Island Sounds in the Global City: Caribbean Popular Music and Identity in New York*, ed.

Ray Allen and Lois Wilcken, 138–61. Brooklyn: Institute for Studies in American
Music, Brooklyn College, 1998.

Ayala, Luis K. *The Rum Experience: The Complete Rum Reference*. Round Rock, Tex.:
Rum Runner Press, 2001.

Bacchetta, Marc, and Bijit Bora. "Industrial Tariffs Liberalization and the Doha
Development Agenda." WTO (World Trade Organization), Development and
Economic Research Division, 2003. <www.wto.org>, accessed November 2004.

Balmaseda, Liz. "Grace, Talent, Heart: Female Boxer Represents Sports' Ideal."
Miami Herald, October 24, 1998, 1B.

Baralt, Guillermo A. *Esclavos rebeldes. Conspiraciones y sublevaciones de esclavos en
Puerto Rico 1795–1873*. Río Piedras, Puerto Rico: Ediciones Huracán, 1981.

Barber, Benjamin. *Jihad vs. McWorld*. New York: Times Books, 1995.

Barrow, Christine. "Small Farm Food Production and Gender in Barbados." In
Women and Change in the Caribbean: A Pan-American Perspective, ed. Janet
Momsen, 181–93. Kingston: Ian Randle Publishers, 1993.

Bartlett, Irving H. *From Slave to Citizen: The Story of the Negro in Rhode Island*.
Providence: Urban League, [1954] 1972.

Barty-King, Hugh, and Anton Massel. *Rum, Yesterday and Today*. London: Heinemann,
1983.

Bazin, Marc. "Government Comments (B): English Version." Republic of Haiti,
Ministry of Planning and External Cooperation, September 26, 2001. Attachment
2, World Bank, "Haiti: Country Assistance Evaluation," 65–77. Report No. 23637.
Washington, D.C.: World Bank, February 12, 2002.

Bell, Beverly. *Walking on Fire: Haitian Women's Stories of Survival and Resistance*.
Ithaca: Cornell University Press, 2001.

Bell, Wendell, and Juan José Baldrich. "Elites, Economic Ideologies and Democracy in
Jamaica." In *Political Elites and Social Change*, ed. Moshe M. Czudnowsky, 150–87.
DeKalb: Northern Illinois University Press, 1983.

Benjamin, Walter. "Theses on the Philosophy of History." In *Illuminations*, 245–55.
With an introduction by Hannah Arendt. Trans. Harry Zorn. London: Pimlico,
1999.

———. "The Work of Art in the Age of Mechanical Reproduction." In *Illuminations*,
211–44. With an introduction by Hannah Arendt. Trans. Harry Zorn. London:
Pimlico, 1999.

Bhabha, Homi K. "DissemiNation: Time, Narrative and the Margins of the Modern
Nation." In *Nation and Narration*, ed. Homi K. Bhabha. London: Routledge, 1990.

———. "Of Mimicry and Man: The Ambivalence of Colonial Discourse." In *The
Location of Culture*, ed. Homi Bhabha and Teresa Miller, 85–92. London:
Routledge, 1994.

Bilby, Kenneth. "The Impact of Reggae in the United States." *Popular Music and Society*
5.5 (1977): 17–22.

"The Black Americas, 1492–1992." *NACLA Report on the Americas* 25.4 (February
1992).

Bretton Woods Project. "IFC Decision Pending on Controversial Free Trade Zone."
    <www.brettonwoodsproject.org/article.shtml?cmd%5B126%5D=x-126–18671>,
    accessed November 2004.

Brooks, George E., Jr. *Yankee Traders, Old Coasters and African Middlemen*. Boston:
    Boston University Press, 1970.

Brown, Aggrey. *Color, Class, and Politics in Jamaica*. Somerset, N.J.: Transaction Books,
    1979.

Butwell, Ann, Kathy Ogle, and Scott Wright. *The Globalization of Hope: Central America,
    Mexico and the Caribbean in the New Millenium*. Washington, D.C.: Ecumenical
    Program on Central America and the Caribbean (EPICA), 1998.

Calvo Ospina, Hernando. *Bacardí, the Hidden War*. London: Pluto Press, 2002.

Camard-Hayott, Florette, and Jean-Luc de Laguarigue. *Martinique: Terre de Rhum*.
    Bordeaux: Traces, 1997.

Campbell, M. C. *The Maroons of Jamaica, 1655–1796: A History of Resistance,
    Collaboration and Betrayal*. Westport, Conn.: Greenwood Publishers, 1988.

Campoamor, Fernando G. *El hijo alegre de la caña de azúcar: Biografía del ron cubano*.
    Havana: Editorial Científico-Técnica, 1985.

Carbonell, Walterio. *Crítica. Cómo surgió la cultura nacional*. Havana: Editorial Yaka,
    1961.

Caribbean Report. "US Exports of Foodstuffs to the Caribbean." London: Latin
    American Newsletters, RC-03-03, April 1, 2003.

CARICOM. *Common External Tariff of the Common Market*. Bridgetown, Barbados,
    1993.

Carnegie, Charles V. *Postnationalism Prefigured: Caribbean Borderlands*. New
    Brunswick, N.J.: Rutgers University Press, 2002.

Carpentier, Alejo. *La música en Cuba*. Mexico: Fondo de Cultura Económica, 1946.

Carr, Barry. "Identity, Class, and Nation: Black Immigrant Workers, Cuban
    Communism, and the Sugar Insurgency, 1925–1934." *Hispanic American
    Historical Review* 78.1 (1998): 83–116.

Carrington, Ben. "Double Consciousness and the Black British Athlete." In *Black
    British Culture and Society: A Text Reader*, ed. Kwesi Owusu, 133–56. London:
    Routledge, 2000.

Castellanos, Jorge, and Isabel Castellanos. *Cultura afrocubana*. Vol. 4. Miami: Ediciones
    Universal, 1994.

Castells, Manuel. *The Rise of the Network Society*. Vol. 1: *The Information Age: Economy,
    Society and Culture*. Malden, Mass.: Blackwell Publishers, 1996.

Castillo Bueno, María de los Reyes. *Reyita, sencillamente: Testimonio de una negra
    cubana nonagenaria*. Ed. Daisy Rubiera Castillo. Havana: Instituto Cubano del
    Libro, Prolibros, 1997.

Castillo Bueno, María de los Reyes, and Daisy Rubiera Castillo. *Reyita: The Life of
    a Black Cuban Woman of the Twentieth Century*. Durham: Duke University Press,
    2000.

Castro, Max J., ed. *Free Markets, Open Societies, Closed Borders? Trends in International*

Migration and Immigration Policy in the Americas. Miami: North-South Center Press, 1999.

Castro Fernández, Silvio. *La masacre de los independientes de color en 1912*. Havana: Editorial de Ciencias Sociales, 2002.

Chambers, Iain. *Migrancy, Culture, Identity*. London: Routledge, 1994.

Chang, Kevin O'Brien, and Wayne Chen. *Reggae Routes: The Story of Jamaican Music*. Kingston: Ian Randle Publishers, 1998.

Chevannes, Barry. "Garvey Myths among the Jamaican People." In *Marcus Garvey: His Work and Impact*, ed. Rupert Lewis and Patrick Bryan, 123–31. Kingston: Institute of Social and Economic Studies, 1988.

———. *Rastafari: Roots and Ideology*. Syracuse, N.Y.: Syracuse University Press, 1994.

Chez Checo, José. *El ron en la historia dominicana*. Santo Domingo: Ediciones Centenario de Brugal, 1998.

Clarke, Colin G. *Kingston, Jamaica: Urban Development and Social Change, 1692–1962*. Berkeley: University of California Press, 1975.

Clifford, James. "Diasporas." *Cultural Anthropology* 9.3 (1994): 302–38.

Club Amor y Ciencia Arecibo, Puerto Rico. *Tesoros espirituales: Dictados de ultratumba obtenidos en Arecibo*. Arecibo, Puerto Rico: n.p., 1913.

Clytus, John. *Black Man in Red Cuba*. Miami: University of Miami Press, 1970.

Cohen, Robin. *Global Diasporas*. Seattle: University of Washington Press, 1997.

Colón Díaz, Proviana. "Puerto Rico Welcomes John Ruiz as a National Hero." *Puerto Rico Herald*, <www.puertorico-herald.org/issues/2001/vol5n12/Media1-en.shtml>, accessed October 2004.

Columbus, Christopher. *The Four Voyages of Columbus*. Ed. and trans. J. M. Cohen. Baltimore: Penguin Books, 1969.

Comaroff, Jean, and John Comaroff. "Ethnography and the Historical Imagination." In *Ethnography and the Historical Imagination*, ed. Jean Comaroff and John Comaroff, 3–48. Chicago: University of Chicago Press, 1993.

———, eds. *Modernity and Its Malcontents: Ritual and Power in Postcolonial Africa*. Chicago: University of Chicago Press, 1993.

Cordero, Margarita. *Mujeres de abril*. Santo Domingo: Ediciones Populares Feministas, 1985.

Correa Velázquez, Melissa. "John Ruiz: Me duele, lo conocí y creía que era más hombre." *El Vocero*, March 8, 2001.

Council on Hemispheric Affairs. "Travesty of Justice in Haiti."

Couto, Richard A. "Community Coalitions and Grassroots Policies of Empowerment." *Administration & Society* 30.5 (November 1998): 569–94.

Cronin, Mike. "Which Nation, Which Flag? Boxing and National Identities in Ireland." *International Review for the Sociology of Sport* 32.2 (1997): 131–56.

Cruz, Albert. "Trinidad Sr. vs. Ruiz Controversy Endless." *San Juan Star*, March 13, 2001, 67.

Cruz Monclova, Lidio. *Historia de Puerto Rico, siglo XIX*. Río Piedras, Puerto Rico: Editorial Universitaria, Universidad de Puerto Rico, 1957.

Cuba. Bureau of the Census. *Census of the Republic of Cuba, 1919.* Havana: Maza, Arroyo y Caso, 1920.

Curtin, Philip. *Two Jamaicas: The Role of Ideas in a Tropical Colony, 1830–1865.* Cambridge, Mass.: Harvard University Press, 1955.

Dauxion-Lavaysse, Jean F. *Statistical, Commercial and Political Description of Venezuela, Trinidad, Margarita, and Tobago.* Westport, Conn.: Greenwood Press, [1820] 1969.

Davies, Omar, and Michael Witter. "The Development of the Jamaican Economy since Independence." In *Jamaica in Independence: Essays on the Early Years,* ed. Rex Nettleford, 75–104. Kingston: Heinemann Caribbean, 1989.

Dávila, Arlene. *Sponsored Identities: Cultural Politics in Puerto Rico.* Philadelphia: Temple University Press, 1997.

Dávila Colón, Luis. "Irma y su milagroso caldo de gallina." In *Aprendiz de mago,* 124–25. San Juan: Forsa Editores, 2000.

———. "Entre las sogas y las pasarelas." *El Vocero,* May 16, 2001, 37.

Davis, N. D. "The Etymology of the Word Rum." *Journal of the Royal Agriculture and Commercial Society of British Guiana* 4 (1885): 76–81.

Davis, Stephen. "Taking Drums, Sound Systems, and Reggae." In *Reggae International,* ed. Stephen Davis and Peter Simon, 33–34. New York: Rogner and Bernhard, 1992.

Deere, Carmen Diana, coord. *In the Shadows of the Sun: Caribbean Development Alternatives.* Boulder: Westview Press, 1990.

Desch, Michael C., Jorge I. Domínguez, and Andrés Serbin, eds. *From Pirates to Drug Lords: The Post–Cold War Caribbean Security Environment.* Albany: State University of New York Press, 1998.

Díaz-Quiñones, Arcadio. Conference comments. Puerto Rican Studies Association, San Juan, 1996.

———. *El arte de bregar.* San Juan: Ediciones Callejón, 2000.

Díaz Soler, Luis M. *Historia de la esclavitud negra en Puerto Rico.* 4th ed. Río Piedras: Editorial Universitaria, Universidad de Puerto Rico, 1974.

Domínguez, Virginia R. "The Marketing of Heritage." *American Ethnologist* 13.3 (1988): 546–55.

Dorronsoro, Josune. *Pal Rosti: Una visión de América Latina (Cuba, Venezuela y México, 1857–58).* Caracas: Ediciones GAN, 1983.

Duany, Jorge. "Nation on the Move." *American Ethnologist* 27.1 (2000): 5–30.

———. "Nation, Migration, Identity: Rethinking Colonialism and Transnationalism Apropos the Case of Puerto Rico." Department of Sociology and Anthropology, Swarthmore College, 2001.

———. *The Puerto Rican Nation on the Move: Identities on the Island and in the United States.* Chapel Hill: University of North Carolina Press, 2002.

Dunn, Hopeton S. *Globalization, Communications and Caribbean Identity.* Kingston, Jamaica: Ian Randle, 1995.

Dupuy, Alex. *Haiti in the World Economy: Class, Race, and Underdevelopment since 1700.* Boulder: Westview Press, 1989.

———. *Haiti in the New World Order: The Limits of the Democratic Revolution.* Boulder: Westview Press, 1997.

————. "Haiti: Social Crisis and Population Displacement." United Nations High Commissioner for Refugees, Emergency and Security Service, WRITENET Paper Series No. 18/2001. Geneva: UNHCR, March 2002. <www.unhcr.ch/cgi-bin/texis/vtx/rsd?search=coi&source=WRITENET>.

————. "Who Is Afraid of Democracy in Haiti? A Critical Reflection." Haiti Papers, no. 7, 1–12. Washington, D.C.: Trinity College, June 2003.

Easterly, William. "The Lost Decade: Developing Countries' Stagnation in Spite of Policy Reform 1980–1998." *Journal of Economic Growth* 6 (June 2001): 135–57.

Easterly, William, Michael Kremer, Lant Pritchett, and Lawrence Summers. "Good Policy or Good Luck? Country Growth Performance and Temporary Shocks." *Journal of Monetary Economics* 32.3 (December 1993): 459–83.

ECLAC (Economic Commission for Latin America and the Caribbean). *Globalization and Development.* United Nations, ECLAC. General LC/G.2157 (SES.29/3), 2002.

————. *Intra-CDCC Trade and Investment.* LC/CAR/G.694, 2002.

————. *The Development of Services in the Caribbean.* LC/CAR/G.718, 2003.

————. *Caribbean Tourism, Trends, Policies and Impact, 1985–2002,* WP/2003/12, November 2003.

————. *Economic Survey of the Caribbean, 2003–2004,* September 13, 2004.

Economist Intelligence Unit. "Country Profile: Haiti, 2000–2001." London: Economist Intelligence Unit, 2000.

Edwards, Eric. "Rumble at Clemente: Hopkins Runs Gauntlet of Angry Fans." *San Juan Star,* July 12, 2001, 94.

Ely, Roland T. *Cuando reinaba su majestad el azúcar.* Buenos Aires: Editorial Sudamericana, 1963.

Ensign, Eric S. *Intelligence in the Rum War at Sea, 1920–1933.* Washington, D.C.: Joint Military Intelligence College, 2001.

Errington, Shelly. "Fragile Traditions and Contested Meanings." *Public Culture* 1.2 (1989): 49–59.

Evans, Peter. "The Eclipse of the State? Reflections on Stateness in the Era of Globalization." *World Politics* 50 (1997): 62–87.

Evenson, Debra. *Law and Society in Contemporary Cuba: Revolution in the Balance.* Boulder: Westview Press, 1994.

Fanon, Frantz. *The Wretched of the Earth.* Preface by Jean-Paul Sartre. Trans. Constance Farrington. New York: Grove Press, 1963.

Featherstone, Mike, ed. *Global Culture, Nationalism, Globalization and Modernity.* London: Sage, 1990.

Featherstone, Mike, Scott Lash, and Roland Robertson, eds. *Global Modernities.* London: Sage, 1995.

Ferguson, James, and Akhil Gupta. "Space, Identity, and the Politics of Difference." *Cultural Anthropology* 7.1 (1992): 3–120.

Fernandez, Nadine T. "The Color of Love: Young Interracial Couples in Cuba." *Latin American Perspectives* 23 (Winter 1996): 99–117.

Fernández Robaina, Tomás. *El negro en Cuba, 1902–1958. Apuntes para la historia de la lucha contra la discriminación racial.* Havana: Editorial de Ciencias Sociales, 1990.

Finke, Nikki. "Bibles, Blond Locks: The New Rastafarians." *Los Angeles Times*, March 15, 1987, sec. 6, 1, 8–9.

Flatley, Jonathan. "Warhol Gives Good Face: Publicity and the Politics of Prosopopoeia." In *Pop Out: Queering Warhol*, ed. Jennifer Doyle, Jonathan Flatley, and José Muñoz, 101–30. Durham: Duke University Press, 1996.

Fonseca, Marvin. "Trinidad Sr.: Commission Should Not Honor Ruiz." *San Juan Star*, March 9, 2001, 81.

Foster, Peter. *Family Spirits: The Bacardí Saga*. Toronto: McFarlane, Walter and Rose, 1990.

Foster, Robert J. "Making National Cultures in the Global Ecumene." *Annual Review of Anthropology* 20 (1991): 235–60.

Fouchet, Max-Pol. *Wifredo Lam*. Paris: Cercel d'art, 1989.

Freeman, Carla. "Reinventing Higglering across Transnational Zones: Barbadian Women Juggle the Triple Shift." In *Daughters of Caliban: Caribbean Women in the Twentieth Century*, ed. Consuelo López Springfield, 68–95. Bloomington: Indiana University Press, 1997.

Fuente, Alejandro de la. *A Nation for All: Race, Inequality, and Politics in Twentieth-Century Cuba*. Chapel Hill: University of North Carolina Press, 2001.

Fusco, Coco. "Hustling for Dollars: Jineterismo in Cuba." In *Global Sex Workers: Rights, Resistance, and Redefinition*, ed. Kamala Kempadoo and Jo Doezema, 151–66. New York: Routledge, 1998.

Gallart, Mary Frances. "Political Empowerment of Puerto Rican Women, 1952–1956." In *Puerto Rican Women History: New Perspectives*, ed. Félix Matos Rodríguez and Linda Delgado, 227–52. Armonk, N.Y.: M. E. Sharpe, 1998.

Galván, William. *Minerva Mirabal: Historia de una Heroína*. Santo Domingo: Taller, 1997.

García, Chu. "Una victoria a pulso de coragón." *El Nuevo Herald*, March 5, 2001, 6c.

García, Pepo. "Tranquilo el liderato estadista." *El Nuevo Día*, May 15, 2001, 30.

García Muñiz, Humberto. "Defence Policy and Planning in the Caribbean: The Case of Jamaica, 1962–88." In *Conflict, Peace and Development in the Caribbean*, ed. Jorge Rodríguez Beruff, J. Peter Figueroa, and J. Edward Greene, 110–45. London: Macmillan, 1991.

Giddens, Anthony. *Modernity and Self-Identity: Self and Society in the Late Modern Age*. Stanford: Stanford University Press, 1991.

Giovannetti, Jorge L. *Sonidos de condena: Sociabilidad, historia y política en la música reggae de Jamaica*. Mexico City: Siglo XXI, 2001.

———. "Popular Music and Culture in Puerto Rico: Jamaican and Rap Music as Cross-Cultural Symbols." In *Musical Migrations: Transnationalism and Cultural Hybridity in Latin/o America*, ed. Frances R. Aparicio and Cándida Jáquez, with María Elena Cepeda, 81–98. New York: Palgrave Macmillan, 2003.

Gleijeses, Piero. *Conflicting Missions: Havana, Washington, and Africa, 1959–1976*. Chapel Hill: University of North Carolina Press, 2001.

Griffith, Ivelaw L., ed. *The Political Economy of Drugs in the Caribbean*. New York: St. Martin's Press, 2000.

Griffith, Ivelaw L., and Betty N. Sedoc-Dahlberg, eds. *Democracy and Human Rights in the Caribbean.* Boulder: Westview Press, 1997.

Grosfoguel, Ramón, Frances Negrón-Muntaner, and Chloe Georas. "Beyond Nationalist and Colonialist Discourses: The Jaiba Politics of the Puerto Rican Ethno-Nation." In *Puerto Rican Jam: Essays on Culture and Politics,* ed. Frances Negrón-Muntaner and Ramón Grosfoguel, 1–38. Minneapolis: University of Minnesota Press, 1997.

Grunwald, Joseph, Leslie Delatour, and Karl Voltaire. "Offshore Assembly in Haiti." In *Haiti—Today and Tomorrow,* ed. Charles R. Foster and Albert Valdman, 231–52. Lanham, Md.: University Press of America, 1984.

Gupta, Akhil, and James Ferguson, eds. *Culture, Power, Place: Explorations in Critical Anthropology.* Durham: Duke University Press, 1997.

Gutmann, Matthew C., Félix V. Matos Rodríguez, Lynn Stephen, and Patricia Zavella, eds. *Perspective on Las Américas: A Reader in Culture, History, and Representation.* Oxford: Blackwell, 2003.

Gwynne, Robert N., and Cristobal Kay, eds. *Latin America Transformed: Globalization and Modernity.* Oxford: Oxford University Press, 1999.

Haiti (République d'Haiti). Ministère de la Planification et de la Coopération Externe. *Bilan Commun de Pays pour Haiti.* Port-au-Prince: République d'Haiti, n.d.

———. Ministère de la Planification et de la Coopération Externe. *Cadre de politique économique et programme d'investissement public.* Port-au-Prince: République d'Haiti, 1994.

Haiti en Marche. "Visite houleuse du PDG du FMI au Parlement." *Haiti en Marche,* May 29–June 4, 1996.

Hall, Stuart. "The Local and the Global: Globalization and Ethnicity." In *Culture, Globalization and the World System: Contemporary Conditions for the Representation of Identity,* ed. Anthony D. King, 19–39. Minneapolis: University of Minnesota Press, 1997.

———. "Old and New Identities, Old and New Ethnicities." In *Culture, Globalization and the World System: Contemporary Conditions for the Representation of Identity,* ed. Anthony D. King, 40–90. Minneapolis: University of Minnesota Press, 1997.

Hall, Stuart, and Paul du Gay, eds. *Questions of Cultural Identity.* London: Sage, 1996.

Hamilton, Edward. *Rums of the Eastern Caribbean.* Culebra, Puerto Rico: Tafia Publishing, 1995.

Hankerson, Fred Putnam. *The Cooperage Handbook.* New York: Chemical Publishing Co., 1947.

Harlow, V. T., ed. *Colonizing Expeditions to the West Indies and Guiana, 1623–67.* London: Hakluyt Society, 1925.

Hearn, Lafcadio. *Two Years in the French West Indies.* Oxford: Zigual Books, 2001.

Helg, Aline. *Our Rightful Share: The Afro-Cuban Struggle for Equality, 1886–1912.* Chapel Hill: University of North Carolina Press, 1995.

Hernández Palomo, José Jesús. *El aguardiente de caña en México, 1724–1810.* Seville: Escuela de Estudios Hispano-Americanos, 1974.

Heuman, Gad. *"The Killing Time": The Morant Bay Rebellion in Jamaica.* London: Macmillan Caribbean, 1994.

Higman, Barry W. *Slave Populations in the British Caribbean, 1807–1834*. Baltimore: Johns Hopkins University Press, 1984.

———. *Writing West Indian Histories*. London: Macmillan Caribbean, 1999.

Hillman, Richard S., and Thomas J. D'Agostino, eds. *Understanding the Contemporary Caribbean*. Boulder and Kingston: Lynne Rienner and Ian Randle, 2003.

Hinkson, John. "Postmodernism and Structural Change." *Public Culture* 2.2 (1990): 82–101.

Holt, Thomas C. *The Problem of Freedom: Race, Labor, and Politics in Jamaica, 1832–1938*. Baltimore: Johns Hopkins University Press, 1992.

Huerga, Álvaro, comp. *Damián López de Haro: Constituciones Sinodales de Puerto Rico 1645*. Ponce: Universidad Católica de Puerto Rico, 1989.

Institute for Justice and Democracy in Haiti. "Human Rights Violations in Haiti: February–May 2004." *Institute for Justice and Democracy in Haiti*, July 19, 2004.

———. "Human Rights Update." *Institute for Justice and Democracy in Haiti*, July 26, 2004.

Inter-American Development Bank. *Integration and Trade*. INTAL 15, vol. 5, September–December 2001.

International Monetary Fund. *Balance of Payments and CARICOM Trade in Services*. 2000.

———. "Haiti: Staff-Monitored Program." *IMF Country Report*, no. 03/260, August 2003.

James, Clara. "Haiti Free Trade Zone: Aristide's 'Different' Capitalism Is the Same Old Story." *Dollars and Sense*, November–December 2002.

James, C. L. R. *Beyond a Boundary*. Durham: Duke University Press, 1993.

James, Harold. *The End of Globalization: Lessons from the Great Depression*. Cambridge, Mass.: Harvard University Press, 2001.

Juan, Jorge, and Antonio de Ulloa. *A Voyage to South America*. John Adams translation. New York: Alfred A. Knopf, [1735] 1964.

Kelly, John D., and Martha Kaplan. "History, Structure, and Ritual." *Annual Review of Anthropology* 19 (1990): 119–50.

Kirshenblatt-Gimblett, Barbara. *Destination Culture: Tourism, Museums, and Heritage*. Berkeley: University of California Press, 1998.

Klak, Thomas, ed. *Globalization and Neoliberalism: The Caribbean Context*. Lanham, Md.: Rowman & Littlefield, 1998.

Knight, Franklin W. *Slave Society in Cuba during the Nineteenth Century*. Madison: University of Wisconsin Press, 1970.

———. *The Caribbean: The Genesis of a Fragmented Nationalism*. 2nd ed. New York: Oxford University Press, 1990.

Laguerre, Michel S. *American Odyssey: Haitians in New York City*. Ithaca: Cornell University Press, 1984.

Landaluze, Víctor Patricio. *Tipos y costumbres de la isla de Cuba*. Havana: Editor Miguel de Villa, 1881.

Laurie, Peter. *The Barbados Rum Shop*. Oxford: Macmillan Education, 2001.

Leroy, Eric. *Images du Rhum*. Martinique: Fondation Clement, 1996.

Levine, Robert M. *Cuba in the 1850s: Through the Lens of Charles DeForest Fredricks.*
    Tampa: University of South Florida Press, 1990.
Lewis, Gordon K. *Puerto Rico: Freedom and Power in the Caribbean.* New York:
    Harper & Row, 1963.
Lewis, Rupert. *Walter Rodney: 1968 Revisited.* Jamaica: Canoe Press, 1994.
———. *Walter Rodney's Intellectual and Political Thought.* Kingston: Press of the
    University of the West Indies, 1998.
Lewis, Rupert, and Patrick Bryan, eds. *Marcus Garvey: His Work and Impact.* Mona,
    Jamaica: University of the West Indies Press, 1988.
Lipset, Seymour Martin. *The First New Nation.* Garden City, N.Y.: Doubleday Anchor,
    1967.
López Nieves, Carlos. "Debate Olímpico." *El Nuevo Día,* August 19, 1993, 79.
Luis Rodríguez, José Angel. *Los paisajes geohistóricos cañeros en Venezuela.* Caracas:
    Academia Nacional de la Historia, 1986.
Machuca, Julio. *¿Qué es el Espiritismo?* Puerto Rico: Casa de las Almas, 1982.
Maingot, Anthony P. "Rum: A Review Essay." *New West India Guide* 60 (1986).
———. "From 'Devil Rum' to Universal Drink." *Caribbean Magazine* (Spring–
    Summer 2002).
Manley, Michael. *Jamaica: Struggle in the Periphery.* London: Third World Median &
    Writers and Readers Publisher, 1982.
———. "Reggae, the Revolutionary Impulse." In *Reggae International,* ed. Stephen
    Davis and Peter Simon, 11–13. New York: Rogner & Bernhard, 1982.
———. *The Poverty of Nations.* London: Pluto Press, 1991.
Manzano, Juan Francisco. *The Life and Poems of a Cuban Slave: Juan Francisco Manzano,*
    1797–1854. Ed. Edward J. Mullen. Hamden, Conn.: Archon Books, 1981.
Marquis, Christopher. "$1 Billion Is Pledged to Help Rebuild Haiti, Topping Request."
    New York Times, July 21, 2004.
Marrero, Leví. *Cuba: Economía y sociedad.* Vol. 2. Madrid: Editorial Playor, 1974.
———. *Cuba: Economía y sociedad.* Vol. 8. Madrid: Editorial Playor, 1980.
Martin, Randy, and Toby Miller. "Fielding Sport: A Preface to Politics." In *SportCult,*
    ed. Randy Martin and Toby Miller, 1–13. Minneapolis: University of Minnesota
    Press, 1999.
Martin, Tony. *Race First: The Ideological and Organizational Struggles of Marcus Garvey*
    and the Universal Negro Improvement Association. Westport, Conn.: Greenwood
    Press, 1976.
———. "Garvey and the Beginning of Mass-Based Party Politics in Jamaica." In
    The Pan-African Connection: From Slavery to Garvey and Beyond, ed. Tony Martin,
    111–31. Dover: Majority Press, 1983.
Marx, Karl, and Frederick Engels. *The Communist Manifesto.* New York: International
    Publishers, 1848.
Masters, Roy. "Breeding Cuba's Champs." August 27, 2004.
    <http://smh.com.au/olympics/articles/2004/08/26/1093518004990.html>.
McCullough, David. *John Adams.* New York: Simon & Schuster, 2001.

McCusker, John J. *Rum and the American Revolution: The Rum Trade and the Balance of Payments of the Thirteen Continental Colonies*. 2 vols. N.p., 1989.

———. "The Business of Distilling in the Old World and the New World during the Seventeenth and Eighteenth Centuries." In *The Early Modern Atlantic Economy*, ed. John C. McCusker and Kenneth Morgan, 186–226. Cambridge: Cambridge University Press, 2000.

McGowan, L. "Democracy Undermined, Economic Justice Denied: Structural Adjustment and the Aid Juggernaut in Haiti." Washington, D.C.: Development GAP, January 1997.

McLeod, Marc. "Garveyism in Cuba, 1920–1940." *Journal of Caribbean History* 30.1–2 (1996): 132–68.

———. "Undesirable Aliens: Race, Ethnicity, and Nationalism in the Comparison of Haitian and British West Indian Immigrant Workers in Cuba, 1912–1939." *Journal of Social History* 31.3 (Spring 1998): 599–623.

Meeks, Brian, and Folke Lindahl, eds. *New Caribbean Thought: A Reader*. Kingston: University of the West Indies Press, 2001.

Meiksins Woods, Ellen. "Capitalist Change and Generational Shifts." *Monthly Review* 50.5 (October 1998): 1–10.

Menéndez Vázquez, Lázara. "¿Un Cake para Obatalá?!" *Temas* 4 (1995): 38–51.

Merret, Christopher. "Sport and Nationalism in Post-Liberation South Africa in the 1990s: Transcendental Euphoria or Nation Building?" *Sport History Review* (2003): 33–59.

Mesa Redonda Espírita de Puerto Rico. *¿Qué es el Espiritismo Científico?* San Juan, Puerto Rico, 1969.

Mialhe, Federico. *Viaje pintoresco alrededor de la isla de Cuba*. Havana: Litografía de Luis Marquier, 1850.

Miller, Daniel. *Worlds Apart: Modernity through the Prism of the Local*. London: Routledge, 1995.

Miller, Toby. "Competing Allegories." In *SportCult*, ed. Randy Martin and Toby Miller, 14–38. Minneapolis: University of Minnesota, 1999.

"The Ministry of Rum." <www.ministryofrum.com>, accessed November 2004.

Mintz, Sidney W. *Sweetness and Power: The Place of Sugar in World History*. New York: Penguin Books, 1986.

———. "Enduring Substances, Trying Theories: The Caribbean Region as Oikoumenê." *Journal of the Royal Anthropology Institute*, n.s., 2.2 (June 1996): 289–311.

Momsen, Janet. "Development and Gender Division of Labour in the Rural Eastern Caribbean." In *Women and Change in the Caribbean: A Pan-American Perspective*, ed. Janet Momsen, 232–46. Kingston: Ian Randle Publishers, 1993.

Moore, Robin Dale. *Nationalizing Blackness: Afrocubanismo and Artistic Revolution in Havana, 1920–1940*. Pittsburgh: University of Pittsburgh Press, 1997.

Morales Carrión, Arturo. *Puerto Rico: A Political and Cultural History*. New York: Norton, 1983.

More [Moore], Carlos. "Le peuple noir a-t-il sa place dans la révolution cubaine?"
    Présence Africaine 52 (1964): 177–230.
Moreno, Aurelio. "Ruiz se suelta a hablar: Le lanza reto a Lewis." *Miami Herald*,
    March 5, 2001.
Moreno Fraginals, Manuel. *El ingenio: Complejo económico, social cubano del azúcar.*
    3 vols. Havana: Ciencias Sociales, 1978.
Morris, Nancy. *Puerto Rico: Culture, Politics, and Identity.* Westport, Conn.: Praeger,
    1995.
Moya Pons, Frank. "Dominican National Identity in Historical Perspective." *Punto 7
    Review* (1996): 23–25.
Murga, Vicente, and Álvaro Huerga, comp. *Episcopologio de Puerto Rico III. De Francisco
    de Cabrera a Francisco de Padilla (1611–1695).* Ponce, Puerto Rico: Universidad
    Católica de Puerto Rico, 1989.
———. *Episcopologio de Puerto Rico IV. De Pedro de la C. Urtiaga a Juan B. Zengotita
    (1706–1802).* Ponce, Puerto Rico: Universidad Católica de Puerto Rico, 1990.
Murphy, Joseph. *Santería: African Spirits in America.* Boston: Beacon Press, 1993.
Naim, Moises. "Fads and Fashion in Economic Reforms: Washington Consensus or
    Washington Confusion?" *Third World Quarterly* 21.3 (2000): 505–28.
Negrón-Muntaner, Frances. *Boricua Pop: Puerto Ricans and the Latinization of American
    Culture.* New York: New York University Press, 2004.
Negrón-Muntaner, Frances, and Ramón Grosfoguel, eds. *Puerto Rican Jam.*
    Minneapolis: University of Minnesota Press, 1997.
Newfield, Jack. "The Shame of Boxing." *Nation*, November 12, 2001.
Nuñez Meléndez, Esteban. *Plantas Medicinales de Puerto Rico. Folklore y Fundamentos
    Científicos.* Río Piedras, Puerto Rico: Editorial de la Universidad de Puerto Rico,
    1982.
Odegard, Peter. *Pressure Politics: The Story of the Anti-Saloon League.* New York:
    Columbia University Press, 1928.
Olivier, Lord. *The Myth of Governor Eyre.* London: Leonard & Virginia Woolf at the
    Hogarth Press, 1933.
Orozco, Manuel. "The Impact of Migration in the Caribbean and Central American
    Region." <www.focal.ca>.
Ortiz, Fernando. "Informe del doctor Fernando Ortiz, Presidente de la Sociedad
    de Estudios Afrocubanos, aprobado por la junta directiva de dicha sociedad,
    pronunciándose en favor de las comparsas populares habaneras." In *Las
    comparsas populares del carnaval habanero, cuestión resuelta*, ed. Antonio Beruff
    Mendieta. Havana: Molina y Cía., 1937.
Otero Garabís, Juan. *Nación y ritmo: "Descargas" desde el Caribe.* San Juan: Ediciones
    Callejón, 2000.
———. "Terroristas culturales: En 'guagua aérea' 'traigo la salsa.'" Unpublished
    manuscript, Harvard University.
Pacini Hernández, Deborah. *Bachata: A Social History of Dominican Popular Music.*
    Philadelphia: Temple University Press, 1995.

Pack, James. *Nelson's Blood: The Story of Naval Rum*. Annapolis, Md.: Naval Institute Press, 1982.

Padilla, Félix. "Salsa Music as a Cultural Expression of Latino Consciousness and Unity." *Hispanic Journal of Behavioral Sciences* 2.1 (1989): 28–45.

Paese, Gabrielle. "Commonwealth Gives Puerto Rico a Sports Identity." July 26, 2002. <www.puertorico-herald.org/issues/2002/vol6n30.PRSportsBeat>.

———. "Cast Your Vote: Is Félix Trinidad Sr. out of Line to Try to Stop the P.R. Boxing Commission from Giving John Ruiz Boxer of the Year Honors?" *Puerto Rico Herald*, <www.puertorico-herald.org/issues/2002/vol6n07/PRSportsBeat0607-en.shtml>, accessed October 2004.

———. "Trinidad Coming out of Retirement? Volleyball, Gold Notes." *Puerto Rico Herald*, December 26, 2003.

———. "Trinidad Wins WBA Middleweight Title." *San Juan Star*, May 13, 2001, 110.

Pares, Richard. *A West-India Fortune*. London: Longmans, Green, Archon Books, [1950] 1968.

———. *Yankees and Creoles: The Trade between North America and the West Indies before the American Revolution*. London: Archon Books, [1956] 1968.

Patterson, Orlando. *The Sociology of Slavery: An Analysis of the Origins, Development and Structure of Negro Slave Society in Jamaica*. London: Macgibbon & Kee, 1967.

———. "Ecumenical America: Global Culture and the American Cosmos." In *Multiculturalism in the United States*, ed. Peter Kivisto and Georgeanne Rundblat, 465–80. Thousand Oaks, Calif.: Pine Forge Press, 2000.

Paulvin, Jean Claude, ed. *Panorama de l'économie Haitienne*. Port-au-Prince: ECOSOF, 1997.

Peguero, Valentina. "Mujeres dominicanas en la trinchera política: La lucha de Minerva Mirabal." In *Historia de las mujeres en América Latina*, ed. Juan Andreo and Sara Beatriz Guardia, 307–22. Murcia, Spain: University of Murcia, 2002.

Peña Signo, María J. "La santería es un culto ritualista." *El Reportero*, July 24, 1982, 6.

Pérez, Jorge L. "'Explican' a Bernard Hopkins." *El Nuevo Día*, July 13, 2001, 143.

Pieterse, Jan Nederveen. "Globalization as Hybridization." In *Global Modernities*, ed. Mike Featherstone, Scott Lash, and Roland Robertson, 45–68. London: Sage, 1995.

Pope, Dudley. *The Buccaneer King*. New York: Dodd, Mead, 1977.

Portes, Alejandro. "Global Villagers: The Rise of Transnational Communities." In *Transnationalism from Below*, ed. Michael Peter Smith and Luis Eduardo Guarnizo, 74–77. New Brunswick, N.J.: Transaction, 1998.

Preeg, Ernest H. *Haiti and the CBI: A Time of Change and Opportunity*. Miami: Institute of Interamerican Studies, Graduate School of International Studies, University of Miami, 1985.

Prevost, Gary, and Carlos Oliva Campos, eds. *Neoliberalism and Neopanamericanism: The View from Latin America*. New York: Palgrave Macmillan, 2002.

Quintero Rivera, Angel. *Salsa, sabor y control: Sociología de la música tropical*. Mexico: Siglo XXI, 1998.

Ramírez. "Venezuelan Rums Aim to Be Toast of the World's Tipplers." *Forbes*, May 31, 2004, 2.

Ramos Mattei, Andrés. *La hacienda azucarera: Su crecimiento y crisis en Puerto Rico (siglo xix)*. San Juan: CEREP, 1981.

Rashford, John. "The Cotton Tree and the Spiritual Realm in Jamaica." *Jamaica Journal* 18.1 (February–April 1985): 49–57.

Regis, Humphrey A., ed. *Culture and Mass Communication in the Caribbean: Domination, Dialogue, Dispersion*. Gainesville: University Press of Florida, 2001.

Ribas, Fernando. "Soy un boxeador más completo." *El Nuevo Día*, October 1, 2001, 123.

Rich, Bruce. *Mortgaging the Earth: The World Bank, Environmental Impoverishment, and the Crisis of Development*. Boston: Beacon Press, 1994.

Richardson, Laurie. "Feeding Dependency, Starving Democracy: USAID Policies in Haiti." In a report from *Grassroots International*. Boston: Grassroots International, 1997.

Ricourt, Milagros. "From Mamá Tingó to Globalization: The Dominican Women Peasant Movement." *Women's Studies Review* (Spring 2000): 9–12.

Rivera, Raquel. "Para rapear en puertorriqueño: Discurso y política cultural." M.A. thesis, Centro de Estudios Avanzados de Puerto Rico y el Caribe, San Juan, Puerto Rico, 1996.

———. *New York Ricans from the Hip Hop Zone*. New York: Palgrave, 2003.

Rivera Marrero. "Tradición artisanal en la elaboración de ron." *El Nuevo Día*, July 30, 1995, 128.

Roberts, George W. *The Population of Jamaica: An Analysis of Its Structure and Growth*. With an introduction by Kingsley Davis. Cambridge: Cambridge University Press, 1957.

Rodríguez, Gregory. "Boxing and Masculinity: The History and (Her)story of Oscar de la Hoya." In *Latino/a Popular Culture*, ed. Michelle Habell-Pallán and Mary Romero, 252–68. New York: New York University Press, 2002.

Rodriguez, Sandra. "Boricua, aquí o allá." *El Nuevo Día*, March 10, 2001.

Rodríguez Escudero, Néstor A. *Historia del Espiritismo en Puerto Rico*. Quebradillas, Puerto Rico: n.p., 1991.

Rohlehr, Gordon. *Calypso and Society in Pre-Independence Trinidad*. Port of Spain: Gordon Rohlehr, 1990.

Roman, Gene. "Another False Choice." *Puerto Rico Herald*, March 28, 2001, 222. <puertorico-herald.org/issues/2001/vol5n13/FalseChoice-en.shtml>.

Romberg, Raquel. "The Pragmatics of Nationhood, Migration, Citizenship, Band Cultural Identity." Paper presented at the American Ethnological Society meeting, San Juan, 1996.

———. *Witchcraft and Welfare: Spiritual Capital and the Business of Magic in Modern Puerto Rico*. Austin: University of Texas Press, 2003.

———. "From Charlatans to Saviors: Espiritistas, Curanderos, and Brujos Inscribed in Discourses of Progress and Heritage." *Centro Journal* 15.2 (Fall 2003): 146–73.

———. "Performing a Postcolonial Colony? Locations and Dislocations of Puerto

Rican Folklore and Nationalism." Paper presented at the Latin American Studies Association meeting, Las Vegas, October 2004.

Rondón, César Miguel. *El libro de la salsa: Crónica de la música del Caribe urbano.* Caracas: Editorial Arte, 1980.

Rorabaugh, W. J. *The Alcoholic Republic: An American Tradition.* Oxford: Oxford University Press, 1979.

Ryle, John. "Miracles of the People: Attitudes to Catholicism in an Afro-Brazilian Religious Center in Salvador, Bahia." In *Essays in the Social Anthropology of Religion,* ed. Wendy James and Douglas H. Johnson, 40–50. New York: Liliar Barber Press, 1987.

Safa, Helen. *The Myth of the Male Breadwinner: Women and Industrialization in the Caribbean.* Boulder: Westview Press, 1995.

Said, Edward. *Musical Elaborations.* London: Vintage, 1992.

Salvucci, Linda K. "Supply, Demand, and the Making of a Market: Philadelphia and Havana at the Beginning of the Nineteenth Century." In *Atlantic Port Cities: Economy, Culture, and Society in the Atlantic World, 1650–1850,* ed. Franklin W. Knight and Peggy K. Liss, 40–57. Knoxville: University of Tennessee Press, 1991.

Sánchez, Luis Rafael. *La guagua aérea.* San Juan: Editorial Cultural, 1994.

Santiago, J. J. "The Spiritistic Doctrine of Allan Kardec: A Phenomenological Study." Ph.D. diss., Gregorian University, 1983.

Santiago Arce, Luis. "Abrazo sabaneño para el campeón." *El Nuevo Día,* March 6, 2001, 128.

———. "Siempre seré la misma persona." *El Nuevo Día,* July 21, 2002, 126.

Santori, Fufi. "De aquí . . . ¿o de allá?" *El Nuevo Día,* March 13, 2001, 129.

Savishinsky, Neil J. "Transnational Popular Culture and the Global Spread of the Jamaican Rastafarian Movement." *New West India Guide* 68.3–4 (1994): 259–81.

Schild, Verónica. "Recasting 'Popular' Movements: Gender and Learning in Neighborhood Organization in Chile." *Latin American Perspectives* 21.2 (2003): 59–80.

Schmitz, Gerald J. "Democratization and Demystification: Deconstructing 'Governance' as Development Paradigm." In *Debating Development Discourse: Institutional and Popular Perspectives,* ed. David B. Moore and Gerald J. Schmitz, 54–90. London and New York: Macmillan and St. Martin's, 1995.

Schuler, Monica. *"Alas, Alas, Kongo": A Social History of Indentured African Immigration into Jamaica, 1841–1865.* Baltimore: Johns Hopkins University Press, 1980.

Schwartz, Rosalie. *Pleasure Island: Tourism and Temptation in Cuba.* Lincoln: University of Nebraska Press, 1997.

Scott, David. "That Event, This Memory: Notes on the Anthropology of African Diasporas in the New World." *Diaspora* 1.3 (1991): 261–84.

Scott, James C. *Domination and the Arts of Resistance: Hidden Transcripts.* New Haven: Yale University Press, 1990.

Serviat, Pedro. *El problema negro en Cuba y su solución definitiva.* Havana: Editora Política, 1986.

Sheller, Mimi. *Consuming the Caribbean: From Arawaks to Zombies.* London: Routledge, 2003.

Shepherd, Verene. *Women in Caribbean History.* Kingston: Ian Randle Publishers, 1999.

Sherlock, Philip, and Hazel Bennett. *The Story of the Jamaican People.* Kingston: Ian Randle Publishers, 1998.

Silva Gotay, Samuel. "Social History of the Churches in Puerto Rico, Preliminary Notes." In *Towards a History of the Church in the Third World: Papers and Reports about the Issue of Periodization,* ed. Lucas Vischer. Geneva: Ecumenical Association of Third World Theologians, 1985.

Sims, Lowery Stokes. "Myth and Primitivism: The Work of Wilfredo Lam in the Context of the New York School and the School of Paris, 1942–1952." In *Wifredo Lam and His Contemporaries, 1938–1952,* ed. Giulio V. Blanc and Maria R. Balderrama, 71–90. New York: Studio Museum in Harlem, 1993.

Smith, Adam. *An Inquiry into the Nature and Causes of the Wealth of Nations.* London: Penguin, [1776] 1970.

Smith, M. G., Roy Augier, and Rex Nettleford. *The Rastafari Movement in Kingston.* Mona, Jamaica: Social and Economic Studies, 1960.

Smith McCrea, Rosalie. "*The Voyage of the Sable Venus*: Connoisseurship and the Trivializing of Slavery." Paper presented at the Society for Caribbean Studies conference, University of Warwick, July 1–3, 2002.

Soederberg, Susanne. "The Emperor's New Suit: The New International Financial Architecture as a Reinvention of the Washington Consensus." *Global Governance* 7 (2001): 453–67.

Sommer, Doris. "Puerto Rico a flote: Desde Hostos hasta hoy." *Op. Cit.* 9 (1997): 253–62.

Stallings, Barbara. "The New International Context of Development." In *Global Change, Regional Response: The New International Context of Development,* ed. Barbara Stallings, 349–87. New York: Cambridge University Press, 1995.

Stark, Jeffrey. *The Challenge of Change in Latin America and the Caribbean.* Miami: North-South Center Press, 2001.

Steady, Filomina Chioma, ed. *Black Women, Globalization, and Economic Justice: Studies from Africa and the African Diaspora.* Rochester, Vt.: Schenkman Books, 2002.

Stiglitz, Joseph. *Globalization and Its Discontents.* New York: Norton, 2002.

Stolzoff, Norman C. *Wake the Town and Tell the People: Dancehall Culture in Jamaica.* Durham: Duke University Press, 2000.

Stubbs, Jean. "Women and Cuban Smallholder Agriculture in Transition." In *Women and Change in the Caribbean: A Pan-American Perspective,* ed. Janet Momsen, 205–18. Kingston: Ian Randle Publishers, 1993.

Taft-Morales, Maureen. "Haiti: Issues for Congress." *CRS Issue Brief.* Washington, D.C.: Congressional Research Service, December 19, 2002.

Tannenbaum, Frank. *Slave and Citizen.* With an introduction by Franklin W. Knight. Boston: Beacon Press, [1946] 1992.

Taussig, Charles William. *Rum, Romance and Rebellion*. New York: 1928.

Taussig, Michael. "Maleficium: State Fetishism." In *Fetishism as Cultural Discourse*, ed. Emily Apter and William William Pietz, 217–47. Ithaca: Cornell University Press, 1993.

Taylor, Charles. *Multiculturalism: Examining the Politics of Recognition*. 2nd ed. Princeton: Princeton University Press, 1992.

Torres, Carlos, ed. *The Commuter Nation: Perspectives on Puerto Rican Migration*. Rio Pedras: Editorial de la Universidad de Puerto Rico, 1994.

Torres Rivera, Pablo. "Aplausos para John Ruiz." *El Nuevo Día*, March 11, 2001, 166.

Torres-Saillant, Silvio. *El retorno de las yolas: Ensayos sobre diáspora, democracia y domincanidad*. Santo Domingo: Ediciones Librería La Trinitaria, 1999.

Tugwell, Rexford G. *The Stricken Land: The Story of Puerto Rico*. New York: Doubleday, 1946.

Turner, Mary. *Slaves and Missionaries: The Disintegration of Jamaican Slave Society, 1787–1834*. Urbana: University of Illinois Press, 1982.

UNDP. *Human Development Report*, 1999.

———. *Human Development Report*, 2002.

———. *Making Global Trade Work for People*. London: Earthscan Publications, 2003.

UNESCO. *General History of the Caribbean*. 6 vols. London: UNESCO and Macmillan, 1997–2005.

U.S. Department of Agriculture. <www.usda.gov/htp/sugar>, accessed October 2004.

Vega Curry, Jaime. "Latente en la mente de Tito la posibilidad del retiro." *El Nuevo Día*, September 26, 2001, 156.

———. "Vuelve a salir el sol." *El Nuevo Día*, October 1, 2001, 124.

Vellinga, Menno, ed. *The Dialectics of Globalization: Regional Responses to World Economic Processes: Asia, Europe, and Latin America in Comparative Perspective*. Boulder: Westview Press, 2000.

Vidal, Jaime R. "Citizens Yet Strangers: The Puerto Rican Experience." In *Puerto Rican and Cuban Catholics in the U.S., 1900–1965*, ed. Jay P. Dolan and Jaime R. Vidal, 11–143. Notre Dame, Ind.: University of Notre Dame Press, 1994.

Villelabeitia, Ibon, and Joseph Guyler Delva. "Haiti to Integrate Rebels into Police Force." *Reuters*, March 23, 2004.

Volk, Alex. "Made in Haiti: Discontent with New Free Trade Zone." *Washington Report on the Hemisphere* 22.15 (August 2002): 3–5. Washington, D.C.: Council on Hemispheric Affairs.

Wagenheim, Karl, and Olga Jiménez de Wagenheim, eds. *The Puerto Ricans: A Documentary History*. Princeton: Markus Wiener, 1996.

Walvin, James. *The Slave Trade*. London: Sutton Publishing, 1999.

Waters, Anita. *Race, Class and Political Symbols: Rastafari and Reggae in Jamaican Politics*. New Brunswick, N.J.: Transaction Books, 1985.

Waugh, Alec. *A Family of Islands*. Garden City, N.Y.: Doubleday, 1964.

Whiteley, Henry. *Excessive Cruelty to Slaves: Three Months in Jamaica in 1832: Comprising a Residence of Seven Weeks on a Sugar Plantation*. London: J. Hatchard, 1833.

Williams, James. *A Narrative of Events, since the First of August, 1834, by James Williams, an Apprentice Labourer in Jamaica*. Ed. Diana Paton. Durham: Duke University Press, 2001.

Williamson, John. "What Washington Means by Policy Reform." In *Latin American Adjustment: How Much Has Happened?*, ed. John Williamson, 7–19. Washington, D.C.: Institute for International Economics, 1990.

Willoughby, Malcolm F. *Rum War at Sea*. Washington, D.C.: Government Printing Office, 1964.

Winters, L. Alan, et al. *Negotiating the Liberalization of the Temporary Movement of Natural Persons*. London: Commonwealth Secretariat, March 2002.

Wolf, Eric R. *Europe and the People without History*. Berkeley: University of California Press, 1982.

World Bank. *Current Economic Position and Prospects of Haiti*. Report No. 410-HA. Washington, D.C.: World Bank, April 1974.

———. *Current Economic Position and Prospects of Haiti*. Vol. 1: *Main Report*. Report No. 1243-HA. Washington, D.C.: World Bank, December 1976.

———. *Current Economic Position and Prospects of Haiti*. Vol. 1: *Main Report*. Report No. 2165-HA. Washington, D.C.: December 1978.

———. *Haiti: Policy Proposals for Growth*. Report No. 5601-HA. Washington, D.C.: World Bank, June 1985.

———. *Haiti: Public Expenditure Review*. Washington, D.C.: World Bank, January 1987.

———. *Economic Recovery in Haiti: Performance, Issues and Prospects*. Report No. 7469-HA. Washington, D.C.: World Bank, December 1988.

———. *Haiti: Restoration of Growth and Development*. Report No. 9523-HA. Washington, D.C.: World Bank, 1991.

———. *World Development Report: The Challenge of Development*. Washington, D.C.: 1991.

———. *Haiti: Country Assistance Strategy*. Report No. 15945-HA. Washington, D.C.: World Bank, August 1996.

———. *Haiti: The Challenge of Poverty Reduction*. Vol. 1. Report No. 17242-HA. Washington, D.C.: World Bank, August 1998.

———. *Reforming Public Institutions and Strengthening Governance*. Washington, D.C.: World Bank, 2000.

———. *Globalization, Growth, and Poverty: Building an Inclusive World Economy*. Washington, D.C.: World Bank, 2002.

———. *Haiti: Country Assistance Evaluation*. Report No. 23637. Washington, D.C.: World Bank, February 2002.

Yañez, Teresa Vda. de Otero. *El espiritismo en Puerto Rico*. San Juan, Puerto Rico: n.p., 1963.

Yelvington, Kevin A. "The War in Ethiopia and Trinidad, 1935–1936." In *The Colonial Caribbean in Transition: Essays on Postemancipation Social and Cultural History*, ed. Bridget Brereton and Kevin A. Yelvington, 189–225. Gainesville: University Press of Florida, 1999.

Zenón Cruz, Isabelo. *Narciso descubre su trasero. El negro en la cultura puertorriqueña*. Vol. 1. Humacao, Puerto Rico: Editorial Furidi, 1974.

Contributors

Antonio Benítez-Rojo (1931–2004) was the Thomas B. Walton, Jr. Memorial Professor at Amherst College. He held visiting positions at Harvard, Yale, Brown, Pittsburgh, Emory, Miami, UC-Irvine, UMass-Amherst, and Colegio de España (Salamanca, Spain) and was consulting editor of the New World Studies series (University Press of Virginia), as well as a member of the editorial/advisory boards of *Review: Latin American Literature and Arts*, *Hispanic Review*, *Amazonian Literary Review*, and *Caribe*. Several of his books have been translated into English: *The Repeating Island: The Caribbean and the Postmodern Perspective*, co-winner of the 1993 Modern Language Association Katherine Singer Kovacs Prize, for an outstanding book in the field of Latin American and Spanish literatures and cultures; *Sea of Lentils*, a novel, listed as a Notable Book of 1992 by the editors of the *New York Times Book Review*; and *The Magic Dog and Other Stories*, which includes "Heaven and Earth," a Pushcart Prize winner. *A View from the Mangrove*, his most recent collection of stories, was jointly published in 1998 by Faber and Faber and the University of Massachusetts Press. This work was nominated for the PEN/Book-of-the-Month Translation Prize. He recently published in Spain the novel *Mujer en traje de batalla*, a best seller. In Cuba, where he directed the Center for Caribbean Studies until 1980, Benítez-Rojo published four collections of short stories, two novels, and several critical editions. There he won the Casa de las Américas Prize and the Union of Cuban Artists and Writers Prize. Samples of his works have been translated into nine languages (English, French, German, Italian, Portuguese, Czech, Bulgarian, Hungarian, and Turkish) and have been included in more than fifty anthologies, among them *The Oxford Book of Latin American Short Stories*, *The Picador Book of Latin American Short Stories*, and *The Oxford Book of Caribbean Short Stories*. In the United States he has published in the *Massachusetts Review*, *New England Review* and *Bread Loaf Quarterly*, *Literary Review*, *Review: Latin American Literature and Arts*, *Bloomsbury Review*, *Callaloo*, *Conjunctions*, *MLN*, *Latin American Literary Review*, *Research in African Literatures*, *Review of Contemporary Criticism*, *Modern Languages Quarterly*, and *Caribbean Studies*, among other journals. Benítez-Rojo published numerous scholarly articles, most of them on Caribbean literature and culture. He has contributed to several major scholarly projects, such as *The Cambridge History of Latin American Literature*, *A History of Literature in the*

Caribbean, The Oxford Book of Latin American Essays, and *The Encyclopedia of Aesthetics* (Oxford University Press). In 1998 he edited *Literature of the Hispanic Caribbean to 1900,* a set of two CD-Roms for Primary Source Media.

Alex Dupuy received his Ph.D. in sociology from the State University of New York Binghamton University in 1981. He is professor of sociology at Wesleyan University in Middletown, Connecticut. His areas of specialization are the sociology of development, the Caribbean, and Haiti. Dupuy is the author of *Haiti in the World Economy: Class, Race, and Underdevelopment since 1700* (1989); *Haiti in the New World Order: The Limits of the Democratic Revolution* (1997); and numerous articles, the most recent of which is a report for the United Nations High Commissioner for Refugees, Emergency and Security Service, "Haiti: Social Crisis and Population Displacement."

Juan Flores is a professor in the Department of Black and Puerto Rican Studies at Hunter College (CUNY) and in the Sociology Program at the CUNY Graduate Center. In recent years he has also been visiting professor at Rutgers, Princeton, Columbia, New York University, and Harvard. From 1994 to 1997 he served as Director of the Center for Puerto Rican Studies at Hunter, and is currently Director of Hunter's Mellon Minority Fellowship Program. He received his B.A. from Queens College in 1965 and his Ph.D. from Yale University in 1970. His doctoral training and early teaching career were in the field of German literature and intellectual history. His research and teaching focus on social and cultural theory, popular culture, and ethnicity and race, especially Puerto Rican and Latino studies. He is the author of *Poetry in East Germany* (*Choice* magazine award), *The Insular Vision* (winner Casa de las Américas award), *Divided Borders: Essays on Puerto Rican Identity,* and *From Bomba to Hip-Hop: Puerto Rican Culture and Latino Identity.* He also is the translator of *Memoirs of Bernardo Vega* and of *Cortijo's Wake* by Edgardo Rodríguez Juliá, and coeditor of *On Edge: The Crisis of Latin American Culture.* His work has appeared in numerous journals and newspapers in the United States and Latin America, including *Daedalus, Journal of Ethnic Studies, Revista de Ciencias Sociales, Harvard Educational Review, Casa de las Américas,* and *Modern Language Quarterly.* He is coeditor of two book series, one on Cultural Studies of the Americas for the University of Minnesota Press, the other on Puerto Rican Studies for Temple University Press. He has served on editorial boards for several journals, including the *Americas Review, Black Renaissance, Social Text, Science and Society,* and *Latino Review of Books,* as well as on the boards of directors of the New York Council on the Humanities, the Recovering the Hispanic Literary Heritage Project, and the Latin Jazz Project of the Smithsonian Institution.

Jorge L. Giovannetti teaches in the Department of Sociology and Anthropology of the University of Puerto Rico, Río Piedras, where he is also affiliated with the Institute of Caribbean Studies. He is the author of *Sonidos de condena: Sociabilidad, historia, y política en la música reggae de Jamaica* (2001) and coeditor of a special issue of *Caribbean Studies* on Garveyism in the Hispanic Caribbean (2003). His research interests include popular culture and music, race, ethnicity, and migration in the Caribbean. He is currently working on a study of the experience of black Caribbean migrants in Cuba during the early twentieth century.

Aline Helg received her Ph.D. from the University of Geneva, Switzerland, in 1983 and taught for many years at the University of Texas at Austin. She is presently a member of the Department of History at the University of Geneva. She has published *Our Rightful Share: The Afro-Cuban Struggle for Equality, 1886–1912* (1995), which was also published in Spanish in Cuba in 2000 and has won the 1995 Wesley-Logan Prize from the American Historical Association, the 1997 Elsa Goveia Book Prize from the Association of Caribbean Historians, and the 1998 Gordon K. Lewis Memorial Award from the Caribbean Studies Association. From 1992 to 1995 she designed, organized, and directed a pioneer scholarly exchange program between the University of Texas at Austin and the University of Havana in Cuba, financed by the John D. and Catherine T. MacArthur Foundation, Program for Peace. In addition, she is the author of *Civiliser le peuple et former les elites: L'education en Colombie, 1918–1957* (1984) and its Spanish translation (1987, 2001) and of several articles on Cuba, Colombia, and race in the Americas. She has just published *Liberty and Equality: Free People of Color, White Elites, Slaves, and Indians in Caribbean Colombia, 1770–1835* (2004).

Franklin W. Knight is Leonard and Helen R. Stulman Professor of History at Johns Hopkins University, Baltimore, and President of The Historical Society (USA). He earned a Ph.D. from the University of Wisconsin in Madison in 1969 and joined the Johns Hopkins faculty in 1973. A past president of the Latin American Studies Association, Knight has held fellowships from the Social Science Research Council, the National Endowment for the Humanities, the Center for Advanced Study in the Behavioral Sciences, The Ford Foundation, and the National Humanities Center. He served as academic consultant to the television series *Columbus and the Age of Discovery*; *The Buried Mirror*; *Americas*; *Plagued: Invisible Armies*; *Crucible of Empire: The War of 1898*; and *The Crucible of the Millennium*. Knight's major publications include *Slave Society in Cuba during the Nineteenth Century* (1970); *The African Dimension of Latin American Societies* (1974); *The Caribbean: The Genesis of a Fragmented Nationalism* (1978; 2nd ed., rev. ed. 1990); *Africa and the Caribbean: Legacies of a Link*, coedited with Margaret Crahan (1979); *The Modern Caribbean*, coedited with Colin A. Palmer (1989); *Atlantic Port Cities: Economy, Culture and Society in the Atlantic World, 1650–1850*, coedited with Peggy K. Liss (1991); and *UNESCO General History of the Caribbean*, vol. 3: *The Slave Societies of the Caribbean* (1997). He cotranslated *Sugar and Railroads: A Cuban History, 1837–1959* by Oscar Zanetti and Alejandro García (1998) and edited a new translation by Andrew Hurley of Bartolomé de Las Casas, *An Account, Much Abbreviated, of the Destruction of the Indies* (2003). In addition, he has published more than 82 articles, chapters, and forewords, as well as more than 140 book reviews in professional journals.

Helen McBain works with the Trinidad office of the Economic Commission for Latin America and the Caribbean. She holds a Ph.D. in economics from the University of the West Indies and served for many years as the Deputy Director of the Institute for Social and Economic Research of the University of the West Indies in Kingston, Jamaica. Her numerous publications deal with banking and general economic performance in the English-speaking Caribbean.

Anthony P. Maingot is professor emeritus of sociology at Florida International University. He received his Ph.D. from Yale University. Before joining FIU in 1974 he taught at Yale University and the University of the West Indies in Trinidad and has been visiting professor at the Institute of Developing Economies, Tokyo, the Institute d'Etudes Politiques, Aix-en-Provence, and the Rand Corporation. A founding editor of *Hemisphere*, he is a member of the Board of Contributors of the *Miami Herald*, a member of the Board of Directors of Caribbean Affairs, and Senior Vice President of the Caribbean Resources Development Foundation (CARDEV). His publications include *The Military in Latin American Sociopolitical Evolution* (with Lyle McAlister and Robert Potash, 1970), *Caribbean Migration as a Structural Reality* (1983), *A Short History of the West Indies* (with John Parry and P. M. Sherlock) (1987), *Small Country Development and International Labor Flows: Experience in the Caribbean* (1990), *Trends in US Caribbean Relations* (1994), and *The United States and the Caribbean* (1994), as well as numerous articles in academic journals in several languages around the globe.

Teresita Martínez-Vergne is professor of history at Macalester College in St. Paul, Minnesota. She obtained her Ph.D. in Latin American history at the University of Texas at Austin in 1985, and taught for a few years each at Colgate University and the University of Puerto Rico at Río Piedras. She has received grants for research writing and travel from the National Humanities Center, Ford Foundation, American Philosophical Society, and Fulbright Foundation. She is the author of *Shaping the Discourse on Space: Charity and Its Wards in Nineteenth-Century San Juan, Puerto Rico* (1999), *Capitalism in Colonial Puerto Rico: Central San Vicente in the Late Nineteenth Century* (1992), and numerous articles. Her new book on the notions of citizenship in the early twentieth-century Dominican Republic will appear in 2005.

Frances Negrón-Muntaner is an award-winning film maker, writer, scholar, and cultural critic. She is the recipient of Ford, Truman, Scripps Howard, Rockefeller, and Pew fellowships. Negrón-Muntaner holds an M.A. in Visual Anthropology and Fine Arts from Temple University and a Ph.D. in Comparative Literature from Rutgers University. She is the editor of two books, *Shouting in a Whisper: Latino Poets in Philadelphia*, and *Puerto Rican Jam: Essays on Culture and Politics*. Her first collection of prose and poetry, *Anatomy of a Smile and Other Poems*, is forthcoming from Isla Negra Editores. Her upcoming two books are *Boricua Pop: Puerto Ricans and the Latinization of American Culture* (New York University Press) and *None of the Above: Puerto Rican Culture in the New Century* (Palgrave Press). Negrón-Muntaner also writes for the *San Juan Star* and the *Puerto Rico Herald* (online). She is the founder of Miami Light Project's Filmmakers Workshop (a program that seeks to promote independent film making in South Florida), a founding board member of NALIP, the National Association of Latino Independent Producers, and the fund raiser and organizer of a yearly gathering of scholars, artists, and policy makers on Puerto Rican affairs, the Puerto Rican Forum.

♦

Valentina Peguero is a professor of history at the University of Wisconsin–Stevens Point. She holds a Ph.D. in history from Columbia University. Her publications include *Peña y Reynoso y amantes de la Luz* (1985); *The Military and Society: From the Captains General to General Trujillo* (2003); *Visión general de la historia Dominicana* (1978), a widely used textbook in both the Dominican Republic and the United States; as well as several articles, including "Teaching the Haitian Revolution: Its Place in Western and Modern History," in *History Teacher* 32.1 (1998), and "United States Military Intervention in the Dominican Republic in 1965," in *The Sixties in America*, edited by Carl Singleton (1999).

Raquel Romberg received her Ph.D. in Folklore and Folklife from the University of Pennsylvania in 1998. After holding a Mellon postdoctoral fellowship at the Institute of Global Studies in Culture, Power, and History at Johns Hopkins University, she taught anthropology and folklore at Swarthmore College and the University of Pennsylvania. She is currently an assistant professor in anthropology at Temple University. Romberg is the author of *Witchcraft and Welfare: Spiritual Capital and the Business of Magic in Modern Puerto Rico* (2003). Her publications include "Whose Spirits Are They? The Political Economy of Syncretism and Authenticity," *Journal of Folklore Research* 35.1 (1998); "Saints in the Barrio: Shifting, Hybrid and Bicultural Practices in a Puerto Rican Community," *Multicultural Review* 5.2 (June 1996); and "From Charlatans to Saviors: *Espiritistas, Curanderos,* and *Brujos* Inscribed in the Discourses of Progress and Heritage," *Centro Journal* 15.2 (2003). Her new book, *Voices of Healing Spirits: The Poetics of Divination and Trance,* is expected shortly. Professor Romberg's research interests include religions of the African diaspora, globalization, performance, creolization, and historical anthropology, the ethnography of communication, culture, and power.

Index

CPSIA information can be obtained at www.ICGtesting.com
Printed in the USA
LVOW10s0803150116

470677LV00002B/118/P